PEAK TRUMP

THE UNDRAINABLE SWAMP
AND THE FANTASY OF MAGA

DAVID A.
STOCKMAN

© 2019

CONTRA CORNER PRESS

in conjunction with

Charles Street Research

To Isabelle, our 20 month-old granddaughter, who will unfortunately inherit the folly described herein.

TABLE OF CONTENTS

i

PROLOGUE

PROLOGUE

Peak Trump happened on September 20, 2018, when the S&P 500's giant bubble topped out at 2941. It has been downhill for the market ever since then; and with much more meltdown to go, it means that the Donald, too, is heading for a great big fall.

Indeed, we think the odds that he will be accorded the Dick Nixon Memorial Helicopter ride to Gonesville before the end of his term are, once again, not inconsiderable and are rising ineluctably.

That's because at the end of the day the Donald is not remotely the force of nature he's been made to seem by the Trump-obsessed media. To the contrary, he's actually a political flyweight, megalomaniacal incompetent and bile-ridden bully who stumbled into the Oval Office against all odds; and then lucked-out a second time by riding high on the final two-year crest of a deeply impaired and unsustainable economic recovery cycle and monumental stock market bubble.

So doing, however, the Donald committed the most egregious rookie mistake in the history of the American presidency. That is, he insouciantly embraced a financial bubble that was destined to crash and took ownership of a struggling, geriatric business cycle expansion that had "recession ahead" written all over its forehead.

Even on purely mechanical calendarized basis, Trump's embrace of the current economy was sheer folly. By January 2017, the weakest and most artificial business expansion in American history was already 90 months old. It thereby stood barely a year shy of the legendary 1960's "guns and butter" expansion (105 months), and it was also just 29 months from the all-time record expansion of the 1990s tech boom (119 months).

But unlike today, the late stages of the 1990s cycle had benefited from immense tailwinds which implied there was plenty of juice to keep the expansion going. For instance, Uncle Sam was running a 2% of GDP budget surplus by the year 2000, which obviated any upward pressure on interest rates or tendency for US Treasury borrowing to squeeze-out private investment.

Likewise, the Fed's balance sheet stood at only $500 billion versus $4.5 trillion at the recent peak. Accordingly, there was no urgent need back then to throw-on the monetary brakes, and, in fact, there still existed immense headroom to "stimulate" demand if needs be.

Overseas, the tailwinds were equally strong. The Red Ponzi was just then bursting out of the starting blocks and had not yet buried itself in debt, malinvestment and fevered speculation. Also at the turn of the century a newly energized single-currency Europe was fixing to (temporarily) borrow and spend like there was no tomorrow.

Notwithstanding these powerful tailwinds, of course, the hideously inflated dotcom and tech bubbles splattered during the course of 2000 and after, eventually sending the main street economy into recession in the spring of 2001.

Nor was that abrupt end to the longest business cycle expansion in history a one-off aberration. As we elaborate below, the 83% crash of the NASDAQ 100 during 2000-2002 (and lesser but still severe declines in the S&P 500 and Russell 2000 small cap index) marked a wholly new trigger sequence for recessions in the age of Fed-driven Bubble Finance.

To wit, recessions now originate in crashing Wall Street bubbles—not in the retrenchment of household and business credit on main street, as was historically the case.

Needless to say, by the lights of his own (correct) campaign rhetoric, Trump inherited a dotcom-scale financial bubble, but no macroeconomic tailwinds whatsoever. In fact, the main street economy was struggling in the midst of an aging, artificial recovery that had been kept alive after the September 2008 financial meltdown only by means of $10 trillion of public borrowing and a spree of Fed money printing and negative real interest rates that had no parallel in prior history or even a reference in any known economic textbook.

In that context, nobody with an ounce of economic comprehension or even in possession of a well-crafted "shovel-ready" economic recovery program would have dreamed that the wheezing, structurally incapacitated American economy of January 2017 could be successfully repaired on the short remaining cyclical runway available. The apt metaphor about the great distance required to reverse the direction of an aircraft carrier on the open seas hardly captured the extent of the challenge.

The Reagan Formula Ignored

In fact, under the far less daunting circumstances of January 1981, Ronald Reagan had long ago set the proper template: He never stopped blaming Jimmy Carter and the Democrats for the colossal mess he had inherited until after the ship of state had finally turned—with no inconsiderable help from Paul

Volcker—in a sustainably positive direction and he had been re-elected by a landslide in 1984.

Needless to say, unlike the Gipper, the Donald had no time left, no plan, no economic comprehension and no humility whatsoever. Within months of the inauguration, he pivoted from running against Obama's failed economy to celebrating an ostensible Trumpian boom that was nothing of the kind, and still isn't as we document below.

And that's why the Donald's fabulous two-year ride on the cresting phase of the greatest financial bubble ever inflated by rogue central bankers and reckless Wall Street momo chasers is coming to an abrupt end. The fact is, now that the support levels and safety ledges of the stock market's chart monkeys have all been taken out, its vulnerability to the next crash and the main street economy's exposure to the next recession is coming into sharp relief.

As to the latter, the history books will record that the Donald never saw it coming.

Owing to his impulsive, immense and incorrigible ego, he has remained utterly blind to the fact that the unemployment rate always falls below 4% during the final months of a long economic expansion cycle. So those monthly prints from the BLS weren't any kind of vindication at all of his Tax Cut/Fiscal Debauch or his Trade and Border Wars—or even his ballyhooed regulatory reforms, which mainly amounted to cancelling prospective Obama regulatory schemes in the energy and environment areas that had not yet even taken effect.

Indeed, taking credit for the falling headline U-3 rate at the tail-end of a business cycle is equivalent to claiming credit for the daily sunset. Likewise, a few random quarters of 3%+ economic growth had exactly nothing to do with MAGA.

No Trumpian Boom

Thus, the unemployment rate at month #90 of the aforementioned business expansions—the two longest ones in modern history— was 3.7% and 4.5%, respectively, compared to 4.8% when Trump took office.

Moreover, during the remaining months of the 1960s and 1990s expansions, the headline unemployment rate dipped slightly lower to 3.5% and 3.9%, respectively, but that's all she wrote. Both times the US economy succumbed to recession within months of hitting the U-3 lows.

Historically, therefore, sub-4% unemployment rates have actually been flashing red warnings signs of trouble just around the bend. And this time there was absolutely no reason to think otherwise and every reason to expect the worst.

Nevertheless, the Donald heedlessly and incessantly embraced the transient 3.7% unemployment rate as if it were all his doing—when it was actually a clanging warning bell to pull out the stops blaming the swamp creatures of the Imperial City for a Fake Boom that couldn't last.

As we indicated, nowadays under the Fed's baleful regime of deep financial repression and cowardly coddling of the stock market, recessions are triggered by imploding financial bubbles, not the traditional catalyst of main street credit and economic retrenchment.

For example, on the eve of the 2001 recession the annualized real GDP growth rate had exceeded *4.0%* for 16 successive quarters. Yet that didn't preclude an end to the business expansion shortly thereafter owing to the thundering collapse of the dotcom and tech bubbles.

Likewise, in the new world of central bank driven financialization, a few random quarters of 3.0%+ real GDP growth is nothing to write home about, either.

The failed Obama economy, in fact, had posted 11 quarters of greater than *3.0%* annualized real GDP growth. But they didn't last and owing to periodic reversals and stall-outs, they averaged into the weakest recovery cycle growth rate by far in prior history.

Indeed, by month #90 of the present so-called recovery the evidence of fundamental economic impairment was palpable. Donald Trump was inheriting an anemic US economy where real GDP was still only *13%* above its prior peak way back in Q4 2007. By contrast, at the same point in the 1990s recovery cycle real GDP was up by *37%* and had risen by *48%* by the like point of the 1960s cycle.

Beyond that, all the other post-war business cycles had already ended much earlier than month #90. As the blue line in the chart dramatically underscores, the US business cycle was living on borrowed time and faltering momentum the very hour that the Donald was sworn to office.

In the context of that astonishing shortfall from all prior cycles, the Donald had no silver bullet at all; just an overweening ego that could not resist taking credit for the residual momentum of what was actually an unsustainably imbalanced economy.

Even then, he embraced a great big economic nothingburger without a hint of awareness. The ballyhooed Trumpian boom, in fact, was never comprised of much more than talking point spin and statistical cherry-picking.

During the first seven quarters on the Donald's watch, real final sales (GDP less inventory swings) have actually grown at just *2.69%* per annum, and that's no material acceleration at all from Obama's final 11 quarters when the growth rate had been *2.53%*.

Indeed, if there was ever a measure of the Trumpian delusion, the above referenced *0.16%* of statistically meaningless incremental growth is surely it.

So loudly taking ownership of what candidate Trump had correctly called a "big, fat, ugly bubble" was not merely short-sighted and outright dumb; it was actually profoundly insulting to the left-behind voters of Flyover America who elected him.

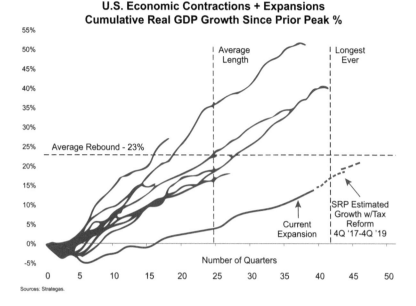

U.S. Economic Contractions + Expansions
Cumulative Real GDP Growth Since Prior Peak %

Flyover America Betrayed

After all, they were the victims of today's rotten regime of mountainous public and private debt, relentless Fed money pumping, hideous Wall Street windfalls to the 1% and the job and growth-destroying plunder of cash flows by the stock-option obsessed C-suites of corporate America.

The Donald wouldn't have gotten within a country mile of the Oval Office had it not been for the desperation of those left-behind voters in the rust belt precincts of western Pennsylvania, Ohio, Michigan, Wisconsin and Iowa where he squeaked through in the Electoral College.

To redeem his MAGA promises, therefore, Trump needed to attack the fundamental causes of a failed Main Street economy, and failed was the word for it.

Despite Wall Street's endless ballyhoo about tiny and often revised or reversible gains in the monthly in-coming data, the big picture trends told the true, dismal story. To wit:

- there has been zero growth in real median household

11

income since the year 2000;

- the US economy has generated virtually no new full-pay, full-time Breadwinner jobs for 18 years;

- the so-called "recovery" from the Great Recession which was so anemic that there still has been no net gain in manufacturing output since November 2007; and,

- most crucially, a gargantuan $800 billion trade deficit has consigned vast stretches of Flyover America to be off-shored, hollowed-out and left to flounder.

Needless to say, the common cause of main street's economic malaise wasn't a sudden failing of capitalism at home or an onslaught of imports, immigrants and nefarious trade machinations by governments aboard.

In fact, it was the handiwork of Imperial Washington and the self-serving consensus of its bipartisan ruling class in favor of permanent war, unchained welfare entitlements, fiscal incontinence, unsustainable debt-fueled household spending, rampant corporate financial engineering and Keynesian monetary repression and "wealth effects" central planning at the Fed.

So with the markets now retreating from the final, spasmodic swelling of the giant bubble he inherited, the question recurs as to whether the Donald has begun to fix anything at all or has even laid a glove on any of the fundamental causes of America's baleful economic predicament?

Trump's Mission Accomplished— Disruption, Not Remediation

As we shall demonstrate in the chapters which follow, the answer is not even a close call. He has done neither—and, in accordance with his real mission as the Great Disrupter, has actually made matters inestimably worse with his misbegotten Trade Wars, Border Wars, Fed-bashing and Fiscal Debauch.

Even his much welcome but furtive tilt toward a primitive

version of "America First" foreign policy has mostly been been stymied, smothered and sabotaged by the Deep State incumbents who continue to run the government. And that's been abetted in no small measure by the phalanx of failed generals and neocon interventionists that Trump has unaccountably installed in key offices.

On that score, in fact, the Donald has essentially deep-sixed his own parade. His promise to march from the far-flung follies of Empire First to a more modest and inward looking notion of America First has already been largely derailed at his own hand.

That's because the desperately needed pivot to fiscal and national security sanity was stopped cold by the Donald's mindless $100 billion per year boost of an already vastly excessive and waste-ridden national defense budget. And now that crucial pivot has been further blocked by a reckless economic and political war against Iran that will do exactly nothing to further the security and safety of the American homeland.

Moreover, by feeding the massive Warfare State budget, which already totals over $1 trillion per year when you add-in the cost of foreign operations, military and economic aid, homeland security and the due bills for past wars represented by interest on war bonds and Veterans benefits ($200 billion year year), Trump has precluded any possibility of fiscal discipline.

Here we are referring to the twin fiscal menace of the Warfare State and the Welfare State, and the iron law of their expansion. To wit, whenever the former is being ramped upwards at full tilt, the war hawk and neocon dominated GOP is put out of business on the fiscal retrenchment front, meaning there is no legislative coalition that can possibly arrest the drift of what amounts to a fiscal doomsday machine.

Moreover, in the current instance that iron law of fiscal expansion was never in doubt because the Donald himself took entitlements off the table by foolishly pledging to never touch the $2 trillion per year Social Security/Medicare monster that lies at the heart of the Federal budget.

Trump then added insult to injury via his unfunded $1.7 trillion tax cut and massive defense and domestic spending increases. All told, the result was a guaranteed $20 trillion explosion of the Federal debt over he coming decade.

Moreover, this Trumpian Fiscal Debauch could not have occurred at a worse time: To wit, it came at the tail end of the business cycle when fiscal retrenchment is supposed to occur and also at the point when the Fed had belatedly begun to extract itself from the impossible corner into which it had painted itself.

Notwithstanding the barbs from the Oval Office and the lame pleadings of the Wall Street brats who believe they are entitled to an endlessly rising stock market, the Fed has actually reached a point of desperation where replenishing its dry powder has become a matter of institutional self-preservation.

What we mean is that the Keynesian apparatchiks who inhabit the Eccles Building recognize their untrammeled power to dominate the entire financial system directly and the US economy indirectly is now at stake. That's because its open-ended remit depends upon the Fed's ability to function as a recession-fighting savior after economic downturns— even when such main street setbacks are invariably caused by its own misbegotten policies.

Accordingly, having dithered and delayed the process of normalization for years, it now must restore interest rates to a level which affords the FOMC something to "cut" in the next crisis; and it must likewise shrink its balance sheet substantially in order to recoup head room to "expand" once the next recession inevitably hits.

So regardless of whether the Fed "pauses" on the previously scheduled 2 or 3 interest rate increases in 2019, we believe it will continue to shrink its balance sheet at an unprecedented $600 billion annual rate. And that's where the Trumpian fantasy of MAGA will come a cropper.

Why The MAGA Fantasy Will Come A Cropper

The bond pits will need to absorb $1.2 trillion of new Federal borrowing and $600 billion of existing bonds being dumped by the Fed during the current fiscal year, and far, far larger amounts in the years thereafter and as far as the eye can see.

But that's not going to happen at a sub-3.00% yield on the ten-year Treasury. Not in a million years.

Stated differently, crunch time is coming to the casino and that's what is sure to bring the Donald down. The stock market is heading not only for another 50% correction (1500 on the S&P), but also toward a long L-shaped bottom rather than the quick V-shaped rebound which occurred after 2009.

That's because the Fed and other central banks are so far behind the curve that they have virtually no possibility of truly normalizing monetary conditions before the third and most unstable and unwarranted financial bubble of this century finally splatters all over the casino.

And that will surely transpire because the Fed foolishly pegged the money market rate to the zero bound for seven straight years (from December 2008 to December 2015). In fact, with only a handful of monthly exceptions, the Federal funds rate (blue bars) has been well below the annual inflation rate (red bars) for 108 months running.

That means money market rates have been negative in real terms for nearly a decade, yet negative carry costs are the mother's milk of speculation on Wall Street, and this time the Fed has fueled a full decade of exactly that. It's why the casino is chock-a-block with financial explosive devices (FEDs) from stem to stern.

Nine Years of Negative Real Interest Rates

So as these reckless and interconnected bets continue to unwind—sometimes violently so—the Fed and other central banks will be impotent to arrest the carnage.

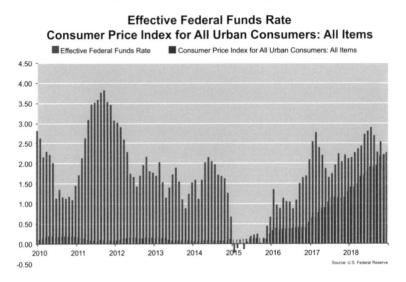

Effective Federal Funds Rate
Consumer Price Index for All Urban Consumers: All Items

In part, that's because the magnitude of bottled-up speculation in the financial system after seven years on the zero-bound and nearly nine years of negative real interest rates simply dwarfs the build-ups which previously occurred during the dotcom/tech bubble and the Greenspan housing and credit bubble. During those bubble expansions, the Fed had pegged the funds rate at a *far higher bottom* and then for only a few quarters, not nine years, as is evident in the chart below.

Worse still, before each of the two prior stock crash-triggered recessions, the Fed got the money market rate up and re-loaded for "cuts" well before the crash incepted. Thus, the Eccles Building ratcheted the funds rate to *6.50%* more than a year before the dotcom recession incepted in March 2001; and had ratcheted it up to *5.25 %* nearly two-years before the Lehman meltdown of September 2008.

Accordingly, it was able to goose Wall Street with a *550 basis point* reduction in the cost of carry trade speculation after the 2001 recession and cyclical bottom; and, likewise, to slash the Fed funds rate by *525 basis points* (down to zero) after the 2008 meltdown and recession.

To be sure, slashing the overnight money rates on Wall Street did exactly nothing for Flyover America's deeply indebted households, but it was a godsend to Wall Street speculators. It enabled the latter to fund their positions directly with nearly zero-cost repo or unsecured credit or indirectly through the implicit carry-trades available on the options market or at the bespoke trading desks of the Wall Street prime dealers.

What this meant, of course, is that the Fed deployed massive firepower on both occasions to artificially and hyper-aggressively force a robust reflation of asset prices in the casino. When combined with massive QE in 2008-2009, especially, the result was a drastic V-shaped rebound of the stock averages that erased entirely all of the losses and lessons imposed on speculators and leverage-based momentum traders by the Great Financial Crisis (GFC).

The GFC, in fact, was the most terribly "wasted" crisis in modern financial history: The capital and money markets were not disciplined or repaired, but quickly reverted to a full-on casino-style modus operandi.

And the fatally debt-encumbered main street economy was not really deleveraged one bit. Combined household and nonfinancial business debt today stands at $30.5 trillion compared to $24.3 trillion at the 2007 pre-crisis peak.

Self-evidently, with the Federal funds rate still encapsulated in the red circled "normalcy" range shown below, there will be no 525 basis points of rate slashing available to goose Wall Street into a pell mell reflation of financial asset prices this time around the barn. Instead, the casino will twist and turn at the bottom.

That's especially true because this time there is also drastically more bottled up inflation in financial asset prices than there was at the 2000 and 2007 tops. So the impending unwind of nearly a decade of rampant carry trade speculation will be unusually violent and deep; and, in the absence of Fed money market rate slashing capacity, also unusually long-lasting.

This stock market shock, in turn, will trigger another Wall Street-style recession in which desperate C-suites toss jobs, inventories and restructuring charges overboard with reckless abandon in a futile effort to appease the trading gods and rescue their evaporating stock options.

Once again, of course, Flyover America will bear the brunt of recession and that will elicit a renewed wave of dislocation, demoralization and sense of betrayal among the Trumpian base. Indeed, if the Donald had even remotely grasped the financial time-bombs he was inheriting, he would have attacked the Wall Street speculators from day #1, and aggressively house-cleaned the Fed as their culpable handmaid and enabler.

Needless to say, the Donald choose to puff-up his chest and thrust it directly into harms' way, instead. So when the heavy

Fed Funds Rate

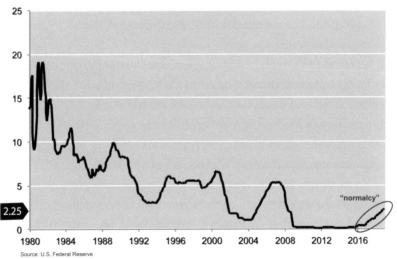

Source: U.S. Federal Reserve

18

shoe of a collapsing stock market and recessionary economy hits the pavement, it will be all over for his two year joy-ride.

Trump's 2016 electoral base was always fragile and reflective of a what amounted to a political Hail Mary by the disenfranchised millions who voted for him in the burned-out and left-behind counties and precincts of Flyover America.

But when the US economy lapses into another downturn and the MAGA myth is visibly rebuked and eviscerated, the Donald's patented immigrant bashing and Border and Trade War rhetoric won't cut it.

Donald Trump, like Richard Nixon before him, will find himself home alone in the Oval Office—with the hinterlands betrayed, the GOP defenders silenced and the Imperial City thirsting for the kill.

No Cigar For CNN

Nevertheless, let us be clear: It is the impending hammer of financial collapse and economic retreat that will be the Donald's undoing, not the long-running CNN/MSM political indictment. And it is the pending assault on the paychecks of the voters and the bank accounts of the Republican donors which will awaken the GOP pols from their one eye-open slumber and mobilize them to defenestrate the Donald.

That is not to say, of course, that the endless anti-Trump bloviation of the mainstream media's talking heads and their collaborators among the Washington establishment and the Dem pols has been for naught.

They were right, for instance, about Trump's temperamental unsuitability for the office, but that's a national blessing in disguise. The Donald has single-handedly discredited the Imperial Presidency like never before, and that's the sine qua non of wresting democratic governance from the clutches of the Deep State and its permanent Washington nomenklatura.

The same is true with respect to the charge that the Donald has alienated most of the outside world—friend and foe alike—and has thereby badly diminished America's global "leadership."

But, ironically, that will surely remain his lasting (and likely only) accomplishment.

What we mean is that the ruination of prosperity and liberty in America by Imperial Washington has no hope of surcease until the latter declares a war, occupation or intervention and no one shows up for the party.

That outcome, at least, the Donald has pretty much guaranteed.

Still, more than anything else, the Donald's fluke elevation to the Oval Office has finally caused the Deep State to come out of hiding and bare its fangs against American democracy itself.

So doing, it has awakened the sleepwalkers of the Foxified Right about the immense dangers of the Warfare State and the sweeping surveillance and police state apparatus that has been created in the service of the neocon's misbegotten war on terrorism and quest for Empire.

In a word, the terrifying capabilities, resources and (purported) credibility of the nation's $75 billion per year intelligence community were hijacked by top Obama officials led by then CIA Director, John Brennan, in furtherance of a plot to first forestall Trump's election, and then to re-litigate the outcome and eviscerate his Presidency after the voters had spoken.

No greater threat has ever been mounted against America's constitutional democracy than the plain as day collusion of Brennan, Rice, Comey, Clapper, Yates, McCabe, Rosenstein, Strzok, Page et. al. to thwart the will of the electorate.

That Deep State assault incepted in the utterly unjustified investigation of Russian influences on the Trump campaign during July 2016; became blatantly overt in the crude Comey/ Yates entrapment ploy against General Flynn on the eve of

Trump's inauguration; and then went full-on public, seizing the Justice Department's investigative and law enforcement machinery via the Mueller Special Counsel appointment in order to conduct an abusive, bare-knuckled witch-hunt against the president and any and all bystanders who could be used to discredit his incumbency.

Needless to say, the mainstream media is so caught up in the anti-Trump mania fomented by the Imperial City's ruling classes and partisan shills that the plain fact of the attempted coup by the Deep State has been completely muffled. Indeed, this very real homegrown case of election meddling by the intelligence and law enforcement agencies of the American state has been virtually covered in spray-paint by CNN and the rest of the MSM via the Russia/Trump collusion counter-narrative.

Yet the latter is so preposterous and threadbare as to virtually force the ultimate question. Namely, given the fact that Russia's GDP is just 7% of that of the US and that Washington's defense spending is 12X greater than the Kremlin's, how in the world can rationally-thinking adults view Russia as any threat whatsoever to the security and safety of the American homeland—-to say nothing of the implied existential threat embodied in the current anti-Kremlin fulminations?

The RussiaGate Hoax—A Form Of Washington Bereavement Ritual

There is a simple answer, of course, and it's not about the Kremlin's threat to national security or even the silly social media click-baiting efforts of a pint-sized St. Petersburg troll farm operated during the 2016 election by a second tier Russian oligarch and nationalist agitator. In fact, if Russia didn't exist, the Imperial City would have needed to revive Orwell's enemy states of Eurasia or Eastasia.

That's because the Dem party and the Washington

establishment have been so traumatized and rebuked by losing to a buffoon like Donald Trump that they have embraced a virtually fictionalized Russian meddling story to explain the November 2016 outcome. For them, RussiaGate has apparently become a form of bereavement ritual.

Indeed, without the implicit postulate that Trump could not have won the presidency without massive and decisive external intervention, the bare facts of the Russian meddling story fall on their own face.

In this context, there is also something slightly more. However he got there, candidate Trump—and to a lesser extent President Trump—never bought into the Imperial City's post-2012 anti-Putin narrative for the utterly rational reason that it's unwarranted.

The real Putin, as opposed to the Imperial City's cartoon caricature, is a completely sober and rational nationalist leader of the semi-impoverished, rump-state of Russia. The notion that he's an expansionist aggressor and mini-Hitler in the making is just the latest invention of Imperial Washington, which desperately needs a foreign enemy to justify its $1 trillion annual fleecing of America's taxpayers, current and unborn.

In this instance, the actual truth is more nearly the opposite. It was Washington's aggressive expansion of NATO to Russia's very borders and its financing and recognition of the Ukrainian nationalist/crypto-Nazi coup on the streets of Kiev in February 2014 which forced Putin to take defense actions.

Even then, it was limited to accommodating the overwhelming desire of the Russian-speaking population of Crimea to return to mother Russia, which it had been an integral part of for 171 years, rather than being ruled by the hostile political parties which seized power in Kiev.

The War Party's Phony Case Against Alleged Russian Aggression

The same was true of Putin's limited support for the Russian speaking populations of the Donbas (eastern Ukraine). It takes only a surface knowledge of the blood-soaked history of the region to understand why the Russian speakers there took up arms against Kiev after the 2014 nationalist/Nazi coup.

The 1930s Stalinization of the Donbas' iron, steel, coal, chemical, engineering and armaments sectors essentially moved reliable Russians into the factories and towns; and in the process liquidated or sent to Siberia Ukrainian nationalists and other political dissidents who didn't cotton to Uncle Joe's form of socialist dystopia.

Soon thereafter came the World War II battles which pitted Ukrainian collaborators with Hitler's Wehrmacht against the Russified locals. In the first instance, the former conducted a scorched earth march through the Donbas on the way to Stalingrad. Then, when the battle of Stalingrad was won, the Red Army retaliated in kind against the Ukrainian collaborators during its equally destructive march back through Ukraine on its way to Germany.

So exactly what dog did the American people have in that hunt?

Obviously, the safety and security of the homeland was not impacted a whit by an unnecessary re-opening of the Ukraine's bloody modern history. That's especially true since the current fight between Kiev and the Russian-speaking eastern provinces was owing to Washington's after-the-fact meddling in the country's 2010 election, which resulted in the deposing of its dully elected President by a Washington-funded street mob.

Besides, the Ukraine for centuries has been a Russian vassal and set of meandering borders looking for a country. In that context, Washington's ridiculous demand that Crimea be "returned" to Ukraine is downright laughable.

Crimea was never part of the Ukraine after it was purchased for good money from the Ottomans by Catherine the Great in 1783. The "return" in question amounts to Washington's insistence on enforcing the dead hand of the Soviet Presidium, which transferred Crimea to the Ukrainian Socialist Republic in 1954 as part of Khrushchev's consolidation of power after Stalin's death.

It may well be that the candidate Trump didn't know all the ins-and-outs of this history and Washington's phony demonization of Putin and Russia.

Then again, he wasn't house-trained by the War Party, either; and he had enough common sense to see that rapprochement with Russia was the #1 priority—if his inchoate desire to reorient US foreign policy to an America First standard was to gain any traction at all.

Yet that is also the very reason why the whole groundless Russia-collusion narrative got traction in the first place. To wit, the Imperial Washington groupthink was so invested in demonization of Putin and in the risible exaggeration of the Russian threat that Trump's rejection of the War Party line was taken as proof that the Russians had something on him.

Stated differently, the entire Mueller witch hunt rested on the blind proposition that the Kremlin had blackmail because there was purportedly no other possible basis for Trump's Russia friendly position or for even such minor common sense steps as removing from the GOP platform the neocon's idiotic proposal to supply the Kiev government with lethal arms.

Needless to say, Mueller's legal thugs have not found a sliver of evidence to support the collusion/blackmail predicate because Trump's pro-rapprochement position rested all along on common sense, not nefarious doings.

But what the whole Deep State coup has accomplished is something quite lethal for American democracy. To wit, it has opened-up a no-holds barred war between two dangerous statist factions in the Imperial City.

On the one hand, the anti-Trumpers have already seized the machinery of state to nullify the democratic process. Apart from the fact that candidate Trump defied the Imperial City's anti-Kremlin policy line, no honest custodian of the national intelligence machinery would have ever opened up the FBI investigation of the Trump campaign in July 2016 based on the ultra thin gruel available. And that's to say nothing of obtaining a FISA warrants to wiretap the campaign headquarters of the Republican candidate for president.

Those actions were massively beyond the pale. After all, the target of suspicion was Carter Page, a complete no count who was a mere campaign volunteer and had never even meet Donald Trump.

Likewise, the FISA warrant was based on the hideous, Clinton-paid-for Dossier and the drunken musings of Baby George Papadopoulos, who was an even more peripheral figure in the campaign than Carter Page.

In an honest democracy, Comey, Clapper or Brennan would have gone to candidate Trump and shared their concerns about the purported Russian connections of Page and Papadopoulos, which didn't amount to a hill of beans anyway. And it is absolutely certain that both of these no counts would have been unceremoniously booted from the 26th floor of Trump Tower— without or without a parachute.

The plain fact is, Trump didn't know them, didn't need them and had not said a single word during his campaign based on whatever they were doing, which was actually above board, anyway.

By the same token, from that screaming abuse of state power there metastasized the entire RussiaGate narrative, the despicable prosecution of General Flynn for doing his job and the launch of the Mueller witch-hunt designed to remove from the nation's highest office the Trumpian threat to the Deep State's rule.

Not surprisingly, the Donald has fought back in his patented street brawling style. But so doing, he has defaulted to policy positions which are no less statist than those of the anti-Trumpers.

To wit, his massive defense build-up, unhinged Border Wars and all-out Trade War assault on China are designed to mobilize and incense his red state political base, not solve any notable national problem as we document in the pages which follow.

At the end of the day, of course, it will be American capitalism, democratic governance and the prosperity and liberty of the people that will end up the worse for the wear.

Still, the Deep State coup has visibly failed, and soon the misguided Trumpian protectionist and statist economic agenda will be crushed by the collapse of the giant Wall Street financial bubble and the phony, debt-fueled recovery that was the source of the Donald's temporary sojourn in the Oval Office.

We have chosen to label this baleful state of affairs as Peak Trump, and in the chapters to follow we attempt to explain why it happened and where it goes from here.

On the latter score, we claim no clairvoyance about the future whatsoever. But what we do know is that Washington's Empire abroad and phony prosperity at home is terminally failing; and that whatever comes next won't be MAGA.

Not by a long shot.

PART 1

The Fed's Rotten Regime of Bubble Finance — Mortal Enemy of MAGA

CHAPTER 1

The Delusions Of MAGA

Earlier this year on tax filing day, Donald Trump took to some strident bragging — assuring America's long-oppressed taxpayers that happier times beckon. In fact, he insinuated that MAGA is not just a slogan. By his lights, apparently, we are already living the dream. To wit:

On this Tax Day, America is strong and roaring back. Paychecks are climbing. Tax rates are going down. Businesses are investing in our great country. And most important, the American people are winning.

We beg to differ. Profoundly.

The Donald is not leading America to the promised land. Instead, he's leading it to war abroad, fiscal and economic calamity at home and a crisis of governance that pales Watergate into insignificance.

To be sure, these baleful outcomes were baked into the cake when Trump took the oath 24 months ago, and there was never any rational reason to think he could reverse the tide.

As we argued at the time of casting our vote for the Donald, his historic role is to function as the Great Disrupter — tying the system in knots and causing the malefic Washington/Wall Street consensus to become irreparably fractured and thoroughly discredited.

But he can not possibly fix anything because he has no

agenda, no mandate and no capacity whatsoever to lead.

His domestic program boils down to crude protectionism, nasty xenophobia, epic fiscal profligacy and primitive Fed-bashing in behalf what amounts to negative real interest rates forever.

Likewise, his foreign policy is a function of who he talks to last among his worsening team of failed and fleeing generals and bloody-minded neocons. His recent official declaration of economic war on any nation in the world with the temerity to buy oil from Iran without a waiver or permission from Washington is a case in point.

And his notion of White House leadership consists, apparently, of early morning tweet-storms from the East Wing Residence; periodic outbursts of demagogic oratory to packed stadiums in Red State America; and, at midterm-election time, a brimstone and bile-ridden attack on a motley band of "invaders" who were hundreds of miles from the Texas border and posed absolutely no threat to America's security.

The Christmas Eve Tax Cuts — The Most Irresponsible Fiscal Policy Ever

The single thing that the mainstream media acknowledges as a "success" is the Christmas Eve tax cut of 2017, but that will soon prove to be the most counterproductive and irresponsible fiscal policy action in modern history. Or even ever.

After all, the Donald inherited a real bad boy — a built-in $700 billion deficit for the current fiscal year (FY 2019). But the King of Debt was nonplussed, electing to pile on $300 billion of tax cuts ($285 billion revenue loss plus interest) for next year alone.

Shortly thereafter, of course, he kept the government lights on by signing the Horribus appropriations bill last February. So doing, he traded $63 billion of higher domestic spending and more than $100 billion of unfinanced disaster relief for $80

THE DELUSIONS OF MAGA

billion of added defense money.

In all, the Trumpite/GOP has pushed the coming year's borrowing requirement toward $1.2 trillion. This means, in turn, that the bond pits will be flooded with $1.8 trillion of "homeless" treasury paper after accounting for $600 billion of existing debt the Fed will be dumping under its QT (quantitative tightening) program.

Here's the thing. No one has ever tried — or even contemplated — financing government paper amounting to $1.8 trillion or 8.8% of GDP at the tippy-top of a business cycle that will enter record old age (123 months) before FY 2019 is over.

Indeed, the very idea of it is pure madness. It will shatter the nation's entire Bubble Finance economy before it is done.

By way of historical comparison, the Federal deficit was $160 billion or 1.1% of GDP at the top of the last cycle (FY 2007) and the Fed was still buying the public debt, not dumping it.

In fact, it bought $30 billion of Treasury paper that year, meaning the net burden in the bond pits was $130 billion or just 0.9% of GDP.

So what looms just ahead is a flood of government paper into the bond pits which will be 10X bigger (relative to GDP) than was the case at the last cycle peak on the eve of the financial crisis.

Moreover, if you go back to the cyclical peak in FY 2000, the Federal budget had posted a $235 billion surplus and the Fed's balance sheet had purchased another $25 billion. So back then at the cyclical peak, Washington actually removed $260 billion of supply from the bond pits — a sum that amounted to 2.6% of GDP and obviously eased the burden on interest rates rather than massively pressuring them as at present.

Besides, the Chinese were still buying Treasury paper hand-over-fist during both of those prior peaks. By contrast, among the many wars the Donald has on his mind is a trade war with the Red Ponzi that has now gone Full Monty: The already implemented 10% tariff on $250 billion of Chinese goods will almost certainly escalate to a 25% tax on $530 billion of annual imports from China come March 2019.

Student Body Left — The Great Global Pivot To QT

On that score, we have no way of knowing whether the Donald's once and (likely) former dictator friend, Xi Jinping, will deliberately dump any of his $1.5 trillion hoard of US treasuries (when you count what is in nominee accounts in the Cayman Island, Belgium etc) as the next step of the trade war.

But it actually doesn't matter what the motivation or trade war strategy is in Beijing: The overwhelming odds are that China will need to sell, not buy or hold, US treasuries in the years ahead in order to counteract capital flight in the face of a rising dollar.

Indeed, as Mr. Xi wrestles with his $40 trillion debt bomb and the towers of speculation that have built up inside the Red Ponzi, he may well move to aggressively plug the remaining foreign exchange loopholes and fill China's jails with "enemies of the people."

But that will only further motivate the flight of capital to places where the Red Emperor cannot seize it. That is to say, as China's fleeing wealthy dump yuan to get away from their communist paradise, Mr. Xi will have to be selling his hoard of US Treasuries in order to keep his currency from imploding.

The same is true of the eurozone. The ECB will be out of the QE business by the end of 2018, and into a German-led sound money pivot to QT by the end of 2019 (a German is slated to succeed Draghi next year). Since the global sovereign bond markets are fungible and arbitraged, that shift too will reduce the central bank uptake of US Treasury bonds.

Indeed, the contrast between the ECB's balance sheet at the

last cycle peak in 2007 and the present is startling. Back then it was $1.5 trillion and had ample headroom above; today it has ballooned to $5.2 trillion and has nowhere to go except smaller.

In other words, the $1.8 trillion of homeless US treasury paper in the bond pits of Wall Street is not an aberration and it's not isolated. In fact, a tectonic shift is now underway in global financial markets which will soon turn the financing of America's soaring public (and private) debts into a veritable nightmare.

As we address in subsequent chapters, the Fed has belatedly shifted to interest rate normalization and balance sheet shrinkage in a desperate effort to restore its dry powder to combat the next financial crisis or recession.

But that will cause what amounts to a "student body left" swing among the entire convoy of Keynesian central bankers around the world who will need to shrink their own balance sheets commensurately. Otherwise they will see their exchange rates collapse against the dollar — a development which in many cases would fuel domestic inflation, capital flight and a funding crunch on upwards of $10 trillion of dollar denominated debt issued by foreign governments and companies.

What we are saying is that the King of Debt has no clue about the $21 trillion powder keg of public debt he inherited and how it was financed on the cheap owing to the monetary madness of the Fed and other central banks.

During the past 15 years, in fact, the central banks of the world have undertaken a collective money printing spree that has not even a remote historical precedent — with their balance sheets rising from $4 trillion to $25 trillion over that span.

Needless to say, every dollar of that $21 trillion expansion was plucked from thin air. That is, it consisted of central bank confected digital credits which were used to purchase trillions of government debt from dealers and investors, and to then sequester those bonds and other securities on the balance sheets of the central banks, as depicted in the graph below.

That did tip the supply/demand balance — and mightily so — in favor of far higher bond prices and lower yields than would have resulted had the soaring public debts of the US and other nations been financed honestly out of the limited pool of private savings.

But now the Powell Fed has launched an epochal pivot to QT — and properly so. The Fed's balance sheet alone is shrinking at a $600 billion annual rate as of October 2018. And in the next several years, the ECB, the People's Bank of China and most others will be forced to make the same pivot.

As is evident in the far right hand margin of the chart, the global central bank balance sheet has already begun to shrunk slightly — a trend reversal that will accelerate sharply during the next two to three years.

Since the global bond market is fully arbitraged, the implications are crystal clear: The world is heading into a monumental Yield Shock and a generational reversal of what

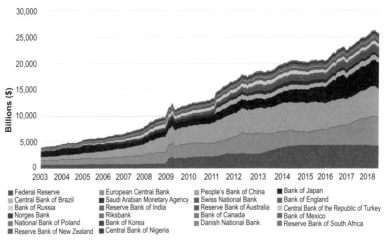

Balance Sheet Of Global Central Banks

As of May 31, 2018. Source: Haver Analytics

has been 35 years of falling interest rates.

So the question recurs: Could the Trumpite/GOP have picked a worse time to launch an unprecedented deficit eruption than in the 10th year of an aging business cycle expansion?

Not in a thousand years would be the sober answer, but some day the history books are likely to use far less antiseptic terms to describe the insensible folly now masquerading as Trump-O-Nomics.

And that get's us to the heart of the MAGA delusion. The Donald was sold a bill of goods about the efficacy of tax cuts by a motley combination of supply-side ideologues, GOP politicians pandering to their donor base and the K-street business lobbies.

Yet the presumption that this fiscally reckless tax cut amounts to some kind of economic growth elixir is the primary basis for the Donald's mistaken assumption that the US economy is now booming and fixing to surge even more.

Yield Shock — The Financial Rip Van Winkle Moment Ahead

We debunk the Trump Boom narrative thoroughly in chapter 3, but suffice it here to note that tax cuts are just plain not efficacious if they are deficit-financed and the resulting public debt is not monetized by the Fed or other central banks. That's because if the public debt isn't monetized (i.e., purchased) by the central bank, it "crowds out" private investment and the related economic activity (GDP).

But since the Fed is now actually demonetizing the debt (i. e., reducing its holdings), a growth-retarding spike in bond yields is sure to happen; and that is even more true at this ultra-late moment in the cycle.

Moreover, tax cuts are also not efficacious if they fund corporate financial engineering moves such as stock buybacks and M&A deals rather than investment in productive assets; or if on the individual side they are temporary and are delivered primarily through credits rather than marginal rate cuts.

Needless to say, all of the above negatives apply to the Christmas Eve tax cut bill in spades. We further debunk the GOP's phony claims that this taxpayer bonanza financed on Uncle Sam's credit card has anything at all to do with genuine supply side incentives in Part 2.

But suffice it here to note that the Yield Shock that lies dead ahead will slam all sectors of the US economy, not just Uncle Sam's finances. That's owing to an unanticipated surge in the carry cost of the massive debts which have been accumulated by business and households during the long years of the central bank bond-buying and deep interest rate repression depicted above.

Indeed, the Fed's pivot to QT is fixing to generate a financial Rip Van Winkle moment: After a 30-year slumber, the "crowding out" effect of government borrowing will be coming back with a vengeance, and for a reason which is as old as the law of supply and demand.

To wit, global central bank demand for debt securities peaked about a year ago at a rate of more than $2 trillion per annum, but has now dropped below the flat-line for the first time in modern history. So as QT spreads globally, the central bank component of demand for debt securities will not only drop out of the supply/demand equation, thereby pushing yields higher, but will actually leap-frog to the other side of the scale.

That is, the money printers that fueled that global bond bubble of the present era are about to become the bond-dumpers of tomorrow. They will be adding to the supply of bonds for sale rather than bidding for bonds to take out of circulation and sequester on their balance sheets. So doing, central banks will force meaningful yields back into the bond trading pits as the latter perform their job of discovering the yield that clears the market.

On crucial thing that this revived bond market price discovery process will expose — in the manner of Warren Buffett's metaphor about the plight of naked swimmers when the tide goes out — is the risible "savings glut" humbug promulgated by Ben Bernanke and other central bankers.

The latter never remotely happened. The "glut" actually consisted of the $21 trillion central bank balance sheets expansion shown above; it was the functional equivalent of "savings" in terms of its impact on the bond market supply/demand equation and therefore interest rates and the level and shape of the yield curve.

It's as if arsonists were running around a burning building with a can of kerosene screaming that there is a fuel glut. But now for reasons of institutional survival, as we develop below, they have jettisoned the kerosene and manned the water hoses.

Needless to say, you don't remove $21 trillion of supply from the global bond markets without leaving big-time dislocations and distortions in this massively hollowed out financial space — even beyond the evident and purposeful falsification of interest

World Market Capitalization

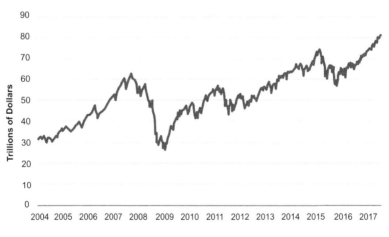

Source: Bloomberg

rates which ensued.

One monumental consequence, of course, was the massive global hunt for yield and risk-asset based returns in the equity markets. During the same 15-year period in which central bank balance sheets soared by $21 trillion, the market cap of the world's bourses erupted by $50 trillion per the graph above.

To be sure, some part of that gain was owing to genuine economic and profits growth, but a substantial portion was actually attributable to PE multiple expansion. That is to say, as the central banks systematically drove bond yields and cap rates lower with their big fat $21 trillion thumb on the scale, the reciprocal effect was to inflate PE multiples and other asset valuation yardsticks.

Our point here is not to begrudge the punters and gamblers who rode this $50 trillion equity market tsunami to fabulous riches over the last 18 years: It wasn't real, and the next stop on the bubble express is something like the 2007-2009 meltdown shown in the graph above when the global equity market cap plunged by nearly 60% from $60 trillion to $25 trillion.

The equivalent plunge this time would amount to $50 trillion, but a reprise of the V-shaped rebound which occurred after 2009 is now out of the question because the central banks have already shot their wad. The various forms and phases of QE — which were essentially a $21 trillion monetary fraud — were the work of a one-trick pony.

In fact, the reason the central banks are suddenly pivoting to QT under the leadership of the Fed is to hastily replenish their dry powder. But it's too late. They will destroy the Everything Bubble long before they get back to "normal" interest rates and balance sheets — even as they fear that after the next crash they will be impotent to reverse the carnage, and that the stimulus pony will then be taken out back and shot.

Nevertheless, one of the skeletons lurking inside the world's $80 trillion stock bubble is the economic corollary of delirious windfall gains on existing financial assets. To wit, on the margin wealth gains from financial asset inflation have supplanted real money savings from current income.

Step-Child Of Bubble Finance — A Savings Drought

If the aim of investors is a certain stock of wealth relative to current and prospective income, upwards of three decades of financial asset inflation have steadily dulled the incentive and need to save and forego current consumption.

For instance, even though by 2004, global equity markets had been inflating at a far more rapid pace than income growth for upwards of two decades, the $30 trillion of stock market capitalization at the time represented 68% of global GDP, which was about $44 trillion.

By contrast, the $80 trillion global equity capitalization at the peak a few months ago represented about 100% of current year worldwide GDP. So even though worldwide income back in 2004 was undoubtedly over-capitalized in the equity markets, it has now become egregiously so after the post-2008 print-a-thons.

Consequently, even if you give the benefit of the doubt to the implicit 2004 capitalization rate of 68%, global stock markets today would be worth about $55 trillion. You can characterize the $25 trillion excess at the recent bubble top, therefore, as the windfall to savers and investors owing to central bank financial repression.

To be sure, we doubt whether anything in the real world is clinically mechanical and quantitative to the nearest trillion. But we are quite confident that the fantastic central bank bond buying spree and resulting massive equity bubbles of the last several decades has driven the real money savings rate to rock bottom levels.

What this means is that the real money savings pool is inordinately shallow and that, therefore, Buffett's proverbial swimmers — governments, households and companies — which have been borrowing hand-over-fist owing to the negligible cost of carry, are going to be in for the mother of all Yield Shocks when they have to refinance their giant debt loads at steadily higher rates.

Indeed, there can be no doubt about the shallowness of the US pool of household savings and it is merely symptomatic of worldwide conditions. For instance, the legendary Japanese savers, who hived away upwards of 20% of income four decades ago, are currently saving at low single digit rates.

Likewise, based on the Commerce Department's current method of counting, the US household savings rate historically posted in the 10-15% range (it's a residual derivative after all spending has been subtracted from current income). But the savings rate then dropped into the 8-10% zone during the Reagan era, and has continued to trend lower ever since, tagging just 6.4% in Q3 2018.

That's thin gruel when the central banks are no longer sucking up trillions of bond supply annually. So, barring the

Downtrend In Personal Savings Rate Since 1971

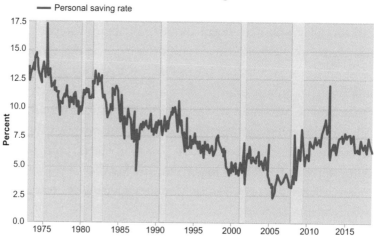

Source: U.S. Bureau of Economic Analysis

Shaded areas indicate U.S. recessions

onset of recession, the 10-year US Treasury yield will break through **4.0%** before the end of FY 2019 and continue to climb steadily higher from there — with 5.0% easily reachable during the years just ahead.

Indeed, it is hard to see any other outcome when the household savings rate in the US is still in the sub-basement of history and when the central banks are on the sidelines; and when, also, the inexorably rising dollar FX rate (due to escalating US yields) will make currency hedging prohibitively expensive for private foreign investors.

On of the insidious Wall Street lies of the present Bubble Finance era is that stocks are to be bought because interest rates are low. The unstated part of that proposition, however, is that they have been ordained by the financial gods to stay low forever, world without end.

But that was a Big Lie. And it's exactly why the main street economy is in big trouble — trouble that has been made immeasurably worse by the lunatic Trumpite/GOP fiscal debauch.

The historic fact is, all US borrowers — public and private — have been implicitly embracing the permanent low interest proposition. So doing, they have steadily and systematically driven the US economy's aggregate leverage ratio to unprecedented heights.

America's Rolling National LBO

As shown below, it amounts to a rolling national LBO. Back in 1970 when the US dollar was still anchored to a fixed weight of gold and to the Bretton Woods system of fixed exchange rates and worldwide financial discipline, the ratio of total public and private debt to national income was just under 1.5X; and, as it happened, that ratio had been virtually constant for the previous one-hundred years.

But especially after Alan Greenspan launched the modern

era of Keynesian central banking and massive money pumping in 1987, household, business, government and financial sector debt in the US has gone parabolic, rising from barely $10 trillion in 1987 to $53 trillion on the eve of the financial crisis in early 2008.

Since then, and notwithstanding all the ballyhoo about post-crisis deleveraging, credit market debt outstanding has continued to climb to just under $70 trillion (blue area), even as national income (GDP) has just reached the $20 trillion mark (orange area).

In this world of big numbers, however, there is a very simple way to cut to the chase. It cannot be denied that during the century between 1870 and 1970, when the US leverage ratio adhered tightly to the golden mean of leverage at around 1.5X income, the American economy grew and prospered like no other economy in recorded history until then.

So 48 years later we have a struggling economy carrying a debt burden equal to nearly 3.5X national income. Investment bankers would call that "two extra turns" of debt relative to the

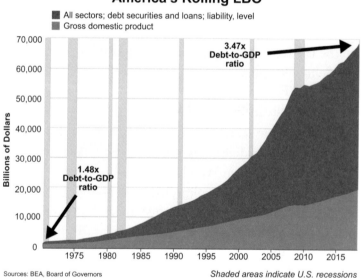

America's Rolling LBO

■ All sectors; debt securities and loans; liability, level
■ Gross domestic product

3.47x
Debt-to-GDP
ratio

1.48x
Debt-to-GDP
ratio

Sources: BEA, Board of Governors   *Shaded areas indicate U.S. recessions*

historic 1.5X leverage ratio.

In round terms, those two extra turns amount to $40 trillion!

That's the number that measures the incremental debt the American economy has taken on during the course of this multi-decade rolling LBO.

Having spent nearly two decades in the LBO business on Wall Street and learned some lessons about leverage the hard way, we can say with some considerable experience that low interest rates are a lethal financial drug. They function to obfuscate how dangerous excessive levels of debt actually are until it is too late to avoid the cash flow crunch from rising rates or an unexpected drop in current income.

Needless to say, both of those untoward places are where the Fed's epochal pivot to QT in conjunction with the soaring Treasury borrowing requirements is taking us. In effect, America is lugging a $40 trillion Debtberg and the ship of state is being captained by a 21st century Edward John Smith.

Captain Smith famously went down with the Titanic, but he at least knew what he hit. By contrast, our" best economy ever" President doesn't have a clue.

But he is going to be finding out right soon. Notwithstanding that the public debt has increased by nearly 140% since the eve of the financial crisis, rising from $9 trillion to $21 trillion, Federal interest expense has inched-up by only 35% owing to a steady decline during the past decade in the weighted average cost of the Federal debt.

In effect, that's the part of the Debtberg lurking below the water-line. Even if the Donald wanted to and could stop the growth of the public debt, interest expense will soar by $350 billion if rates rise to 4.0% on the benchmark 10-year note, and the rest of the yield curve follows.

Even then, there is another nasty surprise element to the interest normalization story. To wit, the Fed's QE bloated

Financial Repression: Soaring Federal Debt, Lagging Interest Expense

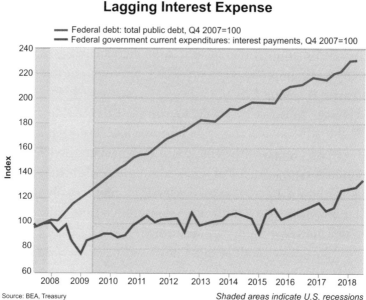

— Federal debt: total public debt, Q4 2007=100
— Federal government current expenditures: interest payments, Q4 2007=100

Source: BEA, Treasury

Shaded areas indicate U.S. recessions

balance sheet has been a fountain of fabulous paper profits because it was paying comparatively nothing on its liabilities while harvesting the interest payments from $4.5 trillion of treasury and GSE securities.

At the peak, its "profits" exceeded $100 billion per year, and under law it remitted these profits to the US Treasury where they functioned as a de facto offset to interest expense.

That is, in a puzzle palace routine that could only be invented in Washington, the Treasury paid the Fed interest on the bonds it had purchased with zero-cost fiat liabilities, and then turned around and sent most of the money back to the Treasury after taking a multi-billion slice off the top to fund its operating expenses, and to pay banks a pittance on their excess reserves deposited at the Fed.

But now this puzzle palace money shuffle is boomeranging. To force interest rates higher, the Fed's has had to raise its so-called IOER (interest on excess reserves) to just above its fed funds target (now 2.38%), thereby boosting its payments to the banks from single digit billions a few years back to $45 billion at present.

At the same time, its interest earnings are falling on it slowly shrinking portfolio, and it may also be forced to take reserves (which reduce income) to account for the mark-to-market losses, as well. In short, what peaked as a $117 billion Fed remittance offset to government interest expense has already dropped to $65 billion per year and will go far lower as the Yield Shock spreads through the global bond markets.

Of course, the Donald has no intention whatever of curtailing the now explosively growing Federal debt. He has embraced a hideously unnecessary $100 billion increase in national security spending and a drastically stepped up pace of military operations around the world that will drive it still higher.

At the same time, he's taken Social Security and Medicare off the table, does not have the inclination or votes to curtail Medicaid and the means-tested entitlements and has pumped $63 billion extra into the swamp of domestic appropriations in order to procure votes for his military lunacy.

And on top of all that and with the Federal tax take at just 16.6% of GDP — among the lowest non-recession levels since WWII — he now wants to cut middle class income taxes by another 10%, which would generate a further $200 billion per year in red ink.

The Debtberg Bites Back

In short, the Federal government's own Debtberg is fixing to bite back with soaring debt service costs. But as we detail in Part 2, the Trumpite/GOP now has the Federal budget on a path toward $20 trillion of new debt over the next decade, which will make the impending explosion of debt service costs all the more incendiary.

This means that the public debt that would exceed $40 trillion and 140% of GDP by 2028 if current trends are left unchecked.

Yet there is now no prospect whatsoever of stopping what amounts to a Fiscal Doomsday Machine because the Donald has retired the GOP from its fundamental job in American politics — the job of fighting for fiscal rectitude.

Of course, over the decades after Reagan the GOP had progressively abandoned that job, anyway. But the irony now is that the Great Disrupter has so thoroughly demolished the GOP's credibility and political will on the fiscal front that there is literally nothing left to stop the on-rushing deficit eruption from bringing an aging business expansion to its knees.

That especially because the now soaring borrowing requirements of the US Treasury are not the half of it. The unfolding Yield Shock will hammer the rest of the economy, too, including the $14.8 trillion of debt being carried by the business sector, the $15.3 trillion burden on households and the $20 trillion outstanding in the financial sector

Using the 10-year US Treasury Note (UST) as a proxy for the yield across all sectors, it is worth noting that during 2017 it averaged 2.30%, meaning that a rise to 4.0% would notionally lift debt service expense across the entire US economy by 170 basis points compared to last year (2017).

Since households, business, governments and financial institutions collectively owe $70 trillion, the incremental interest costs at the 4.0% benchmark UST yield would be nearly $1.2 trillion. And sooner or later, in fact, most interest rates would track the upward path of the UST benchmark. So what lies ahead is an annualized rise in the interest burden which is more than 4X the size of the Trump tax cut.

Yes, interest payments are circular: Someone gets interest payments from those who owe.

But that accounting identity will be of no consolation to

the bottom 80% of US households, which are already leveraged to the gills; or to most US business, which are already lugging $14.8 trillion of debt compared to just $6.2 trillion at the turn of the century.

As to the explosion of corporate and non-corporate business debt depicted in the next chart there is another crucial angle that we elaborate upon below. Namely, that the overwhelming share of the debt build-up since the year 2000 has funded financial engineering measures and the disgorgement of corporate cash and balance sheet capacity to Wall Street, not the acquisition of productive plant, equipment and technology assets to be deployed on main street.

That is to say, the aforementioned $14.8 trillion of business debt is now in place and will be generating ever rising interest expense. But the $15 trillion in stock buybacks, dubious M&A deals and excess dividends paid out by corporate America since 2006 will be adding precious little to future earnings and cash flows.

A fundamental reason why the heavy-handed financial

Massive Increase In Business Debt Since 2000

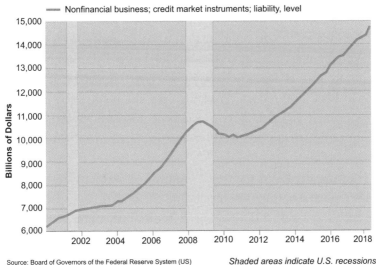

Nonfinancial business; credit market instruments; liability, level

Source: Board of Governors of the Federal Reserve System (US)   *Shaded areas indicate U.S. recessions*

repression policies of the central banks have been so counter-productive is that they have destroyed pricing signals among capital and money market borrowers. As business debt burdens marched steadily higher per the above chart, interest expense actually fell owing to the drastic reduction in yields forced into the fixed income markets by the central banks.

Thus, on the eve of the financial crisis in 2007, the corporate piece of nonfinancial business debt stood at $6.06 trillion. Interest payments on it during that year amounted to $605 billion, representing a 10.0% average rate.

By 2017 Q1, nonfinancial corporate debt had grown to *$8.7 trillion*. But annual interest expense had declined to just *$491 billion*, meaning that the average yield on corporate debt had been cut in half to just *5.6%*.

Needless to say, that 5.6% yield was exactly the wrong price signal because it was artificial and unsustainable.

But it is surely also the reason companies have mortgaged their balance sheets to buy back stock and fund dubious M&A deals. To wit, ultra cheap debt consistently made debt-financed acquisitions look accretive to earnings because the added interest expense on the acquired assets was so low; or made stock buybacks look accretive because the incremental interest was far outweighed by the decrements to the share count.

What we are saying is that the current ballyhooed record corporate profits actually have a glass jaw. Almost all of the gain in S&P 500 reported earnings per share since the pre-crisis peak at $85 per share in the June 2007 LTM period is owing to drastically reduced interest expense and shrunken share counts.

During the LTM (latest 12 months) period for September 2018, reported earnings — excluding the one-time impact of the tax cut — were $124 per share. Yet $30 per share of the $39 gain since June 2007 was due to lower after-tax interest expense and much of the balance reflected reduced share counts owing to buybacks, not organic profits growth.

Needless to say, the coming Yield Shock will shatter the aforementioned glass jaw. Given the same 170 basis point rise in the benchmark 10-year UST referenced above, the after-tax cost of debt would rise from $20 per share for the S&P 500 in 2017 to in excess of $50 per share.

Financial Repression: Soaring Business Debt, Lagging Interest Expense

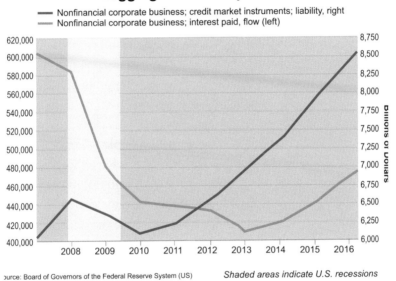

— Nonfinancial corporate business; credit market instruments; liability, right
— Nonfinancial corporate business; interest paid, flow (left)

Source: Board of Governors of the Federal Reserve System (US)   *Shaded areas indicate U.S. recessions*

In short, the coming Yield Shock will generate a fiscal bloodbath in Washington and drastically increased carry costs for main street businesses and households. The effect will be to make mincemeat of MAGA — if the Donald is still around to witness the carnage.

But the trouble ahead is not only due to the coming collision of debt-besotted public and private balance sheets with normalizing interest rates. The fact is, the US economy is exceedingly weak right now as it shuffles toward the longest expansion in history.

Contrary to the Donald's endless boasting and Wall

Street's rosy-colored glasses, there never was even a semblance of a Trump Boom and no acceleration at all from the tepid 2% growth economy Trump inherited in January 2017, as we demonstrate in chapter 2.

So even as it steams toward the Yield Shock ahead, the US economy is not coming from a position of strength.

CHAPTER 2

The Trump Boom — A Mirage
By Any Other Name

The Donald never had a snowball's chance in hell of Draining the Swamp — let alone making MAGA. So Flyover America is fast on its way to being betrayed yet again.

This should have been evident all along because from day one Trump lacked even a simulacrum of a program to rectify America's failing economy. And Trump-O-Nomics isn't a policy — it's a dog's breakfast of Trade War and Border War populism and about the worst combination of fiscal debauchery and monetary profligacy ever proposed.

The stock market boom that peaked in September 2018, therefore, wasn't even remotely the kind of well considered endorsement of Trump-O-Nomics that you can take to the bank.

To the contrary, it was just one last rip of Wall Street's army of gullible speculators and momentum chasing robo-machines. The latter have been rewarded by central bank liquidity injections, financial repression and price-keeping operations for so long that they could probably get bulled-up on a plan to harvest green cheese from the far side of the moon.

In fact, what we are dealing with on both main street and Wall Street is not responses to the Donald's policies and palaver at all, but simply residual momentum. Both the in-coming macro-data and the stock indices are essentially tracking the "last mile", so to speak, of the trends — business cycle expansion and rising bull market — which have been in motion for nearly a decade.

Needless to say, these post-crisis debt and bubble driven trends are anything but healthy and are clearly not sustainable. They inhabit a financial fantasy-land confected during a decade of the most reckless fiscal and monetary policies ever conceived.

So the very idea of boasting about the data prints of a badly impaired 115 month-old business expansion and a speculation driven 119 month-old bull market smacks of rank amateurism and stunning political naiveté. It's as if the Donald is joyfully carrying around a platter and inquiring about where exactly to place his head.

Too Late To Brag — The Cycle's 115 Months Old And Expiring

What we mean is that when you are at the top of the second longest business cycle in history, it is far past the time to be bragging about the current economy and the allegedly good data flashing in the rear-view mirror; and imperative, instead, to assess the headwinds coming at the windshield and their implications for steering the vehicle.

That's especially because the headwinds facing the current aging cycle are ferocious compared to what prevailed when the record 119 month run of the 1990s finally rolled over into recession in March 2001.

Back then, there were virtually no macroeconomic headwinds visible. The Federal budget was in surplus; the Fed had finished its tightening cycle at a 6.5% funds rate nine months earlier; Europe was busting out of the single-currency starting gates; and the Red Ponzi was just finding its export sea legs and had only $2 trillion of debt.

Today's circumstances are the opposite — with massive headwinds accumulating like never before. The US Treasury will be borrowing $1.2 trillion this year; the Fed is still at a 2.38% funds rate and way behind the curve; the European economies are again rolling over and global trade is slowing sharply; and the Red Ponzi sits precariously atop $40 trillion of debt and an economy drowning in wasteful malinvestment, hideously inflated real estate markets and inexorably slowing GDP growth.

With the cycle at 115 months of age, therefore, any of those headwinds could trigger a downturn. But in combination they make the odds of a US recession during the next 12-24 months overwhelming.

Historic Economic Recoveries Average 41 Months

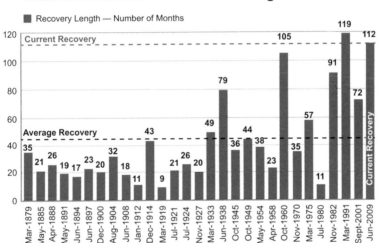

Needless to say, there is nothing strategic or even tactical about the Donald's foolish embrace of an aging stock market bubble and a wizened economic cycle. It's just a glandular lurch — the impulsive action of an incorrigible megalomaniac grasping for anything which can be portrayed as a personal "win", including even dodgy successes (like the U-3 unemployment rate) that are sure to implode at any moment in time.

In fact, the Trump Bump — which the Donald has

embraced with all fours — will prove to be the most lunatic stock market mania of modern times. As its implosion now gathers force, even the casino revilers will soon be shaking their heads in a grand consternated chorus of "what were we thinking?"

What kept the insane Trump Bump going as long as it did, of course, was nine-years of embedded mental muscle memory in the casino. The latter held that buying the dip always — but always — results in a profitable gain.

And that's especially so if you are a Wall Street insider speculating with the various forms of carry trade leverage available in the options market or from the bespoke trading

50 Occasions To Buy The Dip Since 2009

desks of Goldman and the other big gambling houses.

Indeed, if you survived the plunge between the Lehman bankruptcy in September 2008 and the March 2009 bottom, there were literally 50 buyable dips during the years of fabulous gains which followed. Getting rich had never been so easy.

The one-way market depicted in the graph above, of

course, was not on the level. It was the malefic handiwork of the Fed and its global convoy of fellow-traveling Keynesian central bankers. Its extended run in financial fantasyland finally extinguished every remnant of fear in the casino — until some time in early October when the last mullets standing presumably took the bait.

The Chart-Monkeys Will Go Screeching Out Of The Casino

Now comes the reckoning, and at the mechanical level its not all that complicated. When there are no dip-buyers left — why then the trading charts get eviscerated and the chart-monkeys go screeching out of the casino.

To wit, back on October 3rd when the S&P 500 re-tested its September 20 Trump Bump peak at nearly 2930, the index was safely above its alleged multiple layers of support; it had printed 2% above its 50-DMA, 6% above its 200-DMA and 11% above its 350-DMA (50 week).

Yet during the next 40 trading days to Christmas Eve, the index plunged nearly 600 points (20%), through its vaunted supports like a hot knife through butter. Every one of them was blown away including the 50-week average, which is considered the absolute Maginot Line by the chart monkeys.

And that was only a forewarning of the potential for a sickening free-fall which lies ahead. After all, when you finally reach a bubble's asymptote there is no one left up there in the nosebleed section of the casino except other sellers.

Nor in the present circumstance is accelerating economic growth and rising profits going to save the day. That's because the Donald's allegedly booming main street economy is no more real or sustainable than was the stock market's last rip.

The truth is, the main street economy went essentially nowhere during the radically lopsided post-crisis recovery referenced in Chapter 1. And, aside from short-run aberrations in the recent headline GDP numbers which resulted from the Trump's impending trade wars and tax cuts financed by Uncle Sam's credit card, it has not accelerated in the slightest.

For example, the chart below shows seasonally adjusted annualized rates of change for real final sales. The latter is a more stable and indicative figure than real GDP because it excludes highly volatile quarter-to-quarter changes in the rates of inventory stocking and destocking, which essentially wash-out to zero over any meaningful period of time.

You don't need a calculator to see that there is essentially no difference in the fluctuating quarter-to-quarter growth rates during the past seven quarters of the Trump economy compared to the quarters during the Obama presidency after the US economy had dug out from the Great Recession.

In fact, the average real final sales growth rate under Obama was 2.53% per annum and under Trump it's been 2.69%. We'd call that close enough during its final 11 quarters to the same thing for government work and also tepid on both accounts.

Moreover, the more salient point is that 90% of the gain depicted by each of the red bars below reflects not the fruits of White House policy machinations, but the workers, entrepreneurs and companies of capitalist America pushing the ball of economic activity forward yard-by-yard, quarter after quarter.

Indeed, the great scam of the present era is the bipartisan lie under which Washington policy makers take full credit for growth and jobs, as if the $20 trillion American economy would be one great big stagnant void without monetary and fiscal stimulus from Washington.

Bipartisan Tommyrot — Washington Doesn't Cause Economic Recovery Or Growth

That's tommyrot. As we demonstrate below, monetary stimulus after 2008 essentially never left the canyons of Wall Street. And fiscal deficits never really stimulate unless they are monetized by the Fed, but in today's world Fed bond-buying only fuels financial asset inflation, not main street activity.

In fact, the only contribution to growth attributable to either of these presidents is a negative one. That is, both Obama and Trump heavily mortgaged future taxpayers as they attempted to inject borrowed spending power into the short term GDP prints.

But that's nothing to boast about since these obligations will eventually take a far greater toll in debt service payments and reduced growth over the indefinite future.

In any event, there is no more comprehensive measure of current activity rates in America's $20 trillion economy than real final sales. And by that core metric the main street economy was essentially chopping slowly forward under Obama.

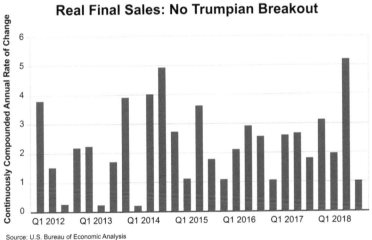

Real Final Sales: No Trumpian Breakout

Source: U.S. Bureau of Economic Analysis

Alas, that punctuated pace of slow advance has not accelerated one bit since the Donald moved into the Oval Office — including the mere 1.0% growth rate of the most recent quarter (Q3 2018).

As we indicated above, most of the Donald's boasting about the "greatest economy ever" amounts to claiming credit for the daily sunset. Thus, having entered office at the top of a labored but long running business expansion, which is now in month #115, Trump inherited 83% of the improvement in the unemployment rate shown below between the 10.0% recessionary peak posted in early 2010 and today's 3.7% rate.

To be sure, the U-3 unemployment rate is a pretty lousy statistic and misleading measure of labor market conditions for reasons we detail below. But notwithstanding its manifold defects, it is self-evident that the U-3 unemployment rate tracks the natural growth of American capitalism during a business cycle expansion, and that there has been no meaningful acceleration from the pre-existing downward trend since January 2017.

Technically speaking, in fact, during 2010-2016 the unemployment rate declined by 0.7% per month and during the first 22 months on the Donald's watch the decline has averaged 0.6% per month.

Likewise, on a non-farm payroll count basis, the jobs gains was 208,000 per month during Obama's last 22 months and 196,000 per month during the first 22 months on the Donald's watch.

Unless you have the GOP talking points, therefore, this chart will give you no hint as to when the Donald took over and turned around the failing Obama economy. That's because he actually didn't.

Accordingly, the chart below is not any kind of success marker at all; it's a clanging warning bell that unless the economic gods have abolished recessions, the likely future direction of the red line in the graph is up, and smartly so.

History Lesson: 3.7% Unemployment Always Marks The Cycle's End

As we indicated in the Prologue, there have been only two other business cycles in modern history that even breeched the 100 month duration marker. The first of these was the Kennedy-

U-3 Unemployment Rate:
No Trumpian Breakout From Trend

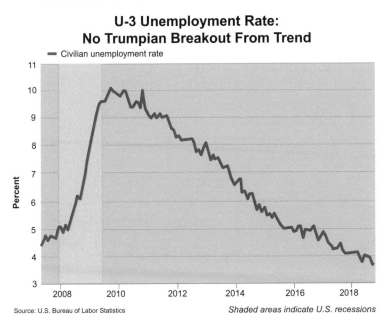

Source: U.S. Bureau of Labor Statistics   *Shaded areas indicate U.S. recessions*

Johnson "guns and butter" expansion of the 1960s, which lasted 105 months and is encompassed by the green area of the panel shown below.

But as also shown by the red line marking the U-3 unemployment rate, within barely a year of hitting 3.7%, the US economy had tumbled into recession.

In short, when the unemployment rate plunges below 4.0% there usually isn't much time left on the cyclical clock. So what's actually warranted is focus on the recessionary troubles ahead, not a boast about riding the unemployment rate to the final monthly bottom.

Indeed, this plain old business cycle fact of life has been thoroughly lost on the Donald, although you might think that his multiple brushes with bankruptcy, which occurred during economic downturns, might have at least sensitized him to that unassailable reality.

Still, the cyclical story has been the same over and over: Peak performance levels are reached repeatedly and downturns

U-3 Unemployment Rate During 1960s Expansion

■ Civilian unemployment rate

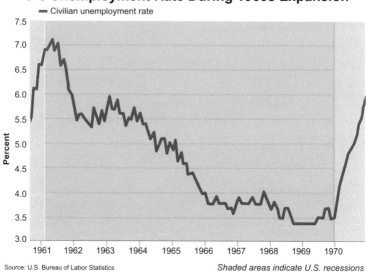

Source: U.S. Bureau of Labor Statistics   *Shaded areas indicate U.S. recessions*

always ensue.

Indeed, the other long (and record) expansion represented by the Greenspan Fed-fueled tech boom of the 1990s, which lasted 119 months, provides an even starker warning than the 1960s go-round.

That time the U-3 hit its low of 3.8% in April 2000, but what had been the genuine booming economy of the 1990s was in recession 11 months later. And we do mean booming: real GDP had grown at a 4.0% year-over-year rate for 16 straight quarters before April 2000.

Needless to say, the rearview mirror gazers of that era didn't see a recession coming, either. And for a reason that is absolutely on point at present.

To wit, the rolling stock market crash after March 2000 is what brought the main street economy down as the corporate C-suites began to throw employees, inventories and "impaired" assets overboard in an effort to propitiate the Wall Street trading gods.

The bursting of central bank fostered financial bubbles, in

fact, is the new catalyst for recession, meaning that charts like this one are lagging indicators waiting to be monkey-hammered by the next Wall Street crash.

If could not be more evident that once a long expansion is in motion, the BLS' primitive U-3 unemployment rate inexorably drops toward the lower right of the green panels displayed in these charts. That is, the red line (U-3 unemployment) essentially embodies cyclical gravity at work — propelled by the underlying forces of capitalist growth.

U-3 Unemployment Rate During 1990s Expansion

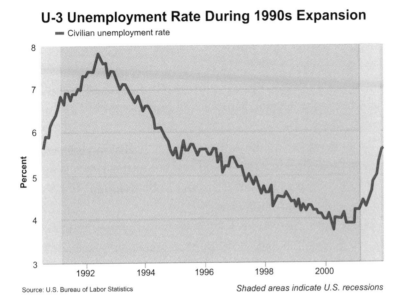

Source: U.S. Bureau of Labor Statistics   *Shaded areas indicate U.S. recessions*

Indeed, about the only thing different about the U-3 trend chart for 2010-2018 compared to those for the 1960s and the 1990s is that the putative "last mile" has not yet been recorded. That is to say, it will likely take only a few more months for the green space of expansion to give way to the next recession and a rapid upturn in today's ballyhooed 3.7% unemployment rate.

So the cyclically bottoming U-3 unemployment rate was in motion long before the Donald shuffled into the Oval Office and his relatively brief tenure to date has absolutely nothing to do with it. If anything, it is another bright red cap heralding that what comes next is, in fact, not MAGA!

Best Wage Gain In Years My Eye

The same kind of cyclical fortuity pertains to the Donald's boasting about workers finally getting a wage gain, as purportedly reflected in the most recent year-over-year gain of 2.8%.

In fact, the September 2018 nominal wage gain (red line) is about at the lowest it's been since the late 1960s; and in real terms, the story is even worse.

To wit, between 1955 and 2000, inflation-adjusted compensation per hour (purple line) grew at a *1.75%* annual rate — and that's the average across seven business cycles, including recession years.

By contrast, we are now at the top of the second longest business expansion in history, and real compensation was up just 0.1% over the past 12 months ending in September.. That's not even up — it's a rounding error.

That's right. Siting check-by-jowl with the no-change level, the purple line below shows that year-over-year real wage growth has now clocked in at virtually the weakest late cycle gain on record.

Actually, the Donald's boasting about what amounts to a cyclical gain in jobs is all the more ironic because during the campaign he trashed the very BLS numbers (and appropriately so) that he now brags about. At one point he even cited our own view that the only meaningful measure of unemployment is the share of total potential adult labor hours that are not employed in the monetized economy, which happened to be about 40%!

That's because otherwise you count apples, oranges and cumquats in the numerator when it comes to "employed" persons, and you have a denominator computed from arbitrary

Long-Term Trend In Nominal And
Real Worker Compensation

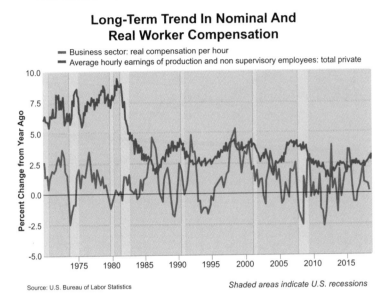

- Business sector: real compensation per hour
- Average hourly earnings of production and non supervisory employees: total private

Source: U.S. Bureau of Labor Statistics

Shaded areas indicate U.S. recessions

BLS definitions of who's in the "labor force" and who's not. For all practical purposes the resulting fraction called the U-3 unemployment rate is a close second cousin to meaningless statistical noise.

Indeed, it doesn't take even 10 minutes worth of investigation to show that the BLS' tightness gauge — the U-3 unemployment rate — is not even remotely all that.

As analyst Jeff Snider has cogently demonstrated, we are at *3.7%* unemployment only because the labor force participation rate as measured by the BLS has plunged.

In fact, at the same *3.7%* so-called full employment rate which pertained when the Maestro was riding high in the late 1990s, the labor force participation rate was north of *67%*, not today's *62.7%* (September).

And that means that the Donald's alleged lowest ever unemployment rate rests on the back of *16.6* million workers who have purportedly gone missing!

We don't think any workers have actually gone missing, of course, and believe instead that the actual unemployment rate

Two Labor Stories

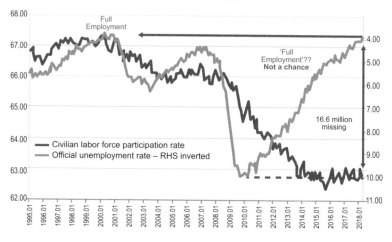

is upwards of **40%** when measured on an available hours basis, as demonstrated below. But suffice it to say here that there is a reason why Wall Street economists and Washington politicians alike insist on using the patently ridiculous and grossly erroneous numbers manufactured by the BLS data mills.

To wit, the BLS jobs data — and especially the U-3 unemployment rate — function as a convenient "help wanted" sign for government interventionists and stimulators. The implication is that the free market's pricing system for labor, goods and services doesn't work very well, and that the wise guiding hand of the state is needed to regulate an economic ether called "aggregate demand."

That is to say, the US economy resembles a giant economic bathtub, and the aim of government policy is to keep it filled exactly to the brim. That way, everybody's got a job, a good wage, a nice life, no (inflation) worries and perhaps is even rid of sniffles and hangnails, too!

So when the U-3 unemployment rate is at 11%, 8% or 5%, there is purportedly a large deficiency of demand, signaling that the state and its central banking branch need to pump more spending into the bathtub via fiscal or monetary stimulus.

Likewise, when U-3 reaches the alleged "full employment" rate at +/- 3.7% that's a signal the tub is close to full and that interest rates need to be raised in order to curtail credit expansion and spending, thereby insuring that an inflationary overflow does not upset the macroeconomic applecart.

Forget The FOMC: The Labor Pricing System And Say's Law Are The Best Route To True Full Employment

But here's the thing. The 12 members of the FOMC might as well be standing out on Independence Avenue waving their arms in order to keep marauding elephants from over-running the Eccles Building!

That's about how useful U-3 is as a measure of labor market or macroeconomic conditions; and it's also about as worthless as is the Fed's endless pegging of money market rates and massive intrusion in the bond markets in the misguided furtherance of capitalist prosperity.

The fact is, the potential labor supply from both domestic and off-shore sources is so limitless that the only thing needed to mobilize more employed hours is the pricing system, not the monetary politburo's (FOMC) machinations in the financial markets.

At a high enough wage rate, you will get housewives out of the kitchen, students off their duffs, more volunteers for over-time, and, if need be, more peasants out of the Chinese or Vietnamese rice paddies. In today's globally networked, traded and welfare-enabled world, there will never be a physical shortage of labor hours — just the right price to bring latent hours into monetized production.

Needless to say, the latent hours now sequestered in Federally subsidized basket-weaving classes or playing shuffle-board on early retirement or disability do raise market-clearing wage levels at the margin. But you can solve that problem by cutting welfare benefits, not giving the Fed a mandate to fiddle with interest rates and financial asset prices.

That latter only fosters increasingly destructive gambling, bubbles and malinvestments in the financial system, not higher production, employment and prosperity on main street.

Indeed, there is no need for central bankers at all when it comes to economic growth, jobs, incomes and prosperity. That's because Say's Law is as valid today as it has always been.

Work, effort, production and enterprise are what create both current income and future growth. Demand flows from supply and spending flows from income; capitalism doesn't need any U-3 obsessed central bankers to make it all happen.

Likewise, the labor pricing system in a $20 trillion economy has it hands down over the 12 PhDs, bankers and Washington apparatchiks who sit on the FOMC. If the market is heavy with latent labor hours, real wage rates will come down; and if it's light, real wage rates will rise sufficiently to attract the needed hours.

In fact, now that most of the monopoly industrial unions have been broken or defanged — even the old Keynesian saw about "sticky" wages is self-evidently inoperative. The truth is, there is nothing about the contemporary labor market that requires the helping hand of the Federal Reserve at all.

Moreover, there is no even theoretical possibility of runaway wage inflation of the type that industrial unions led by the UAW and Steelworkers were able to generate in the late 1960s. That because virtually every manner of goods produced in the US economy and a growing portion of services can now be supplied from off-shore, and often at far lower wage rates — even adjusted for productivity and transportation — than paid by domestic suppliers

So let us remind once again: The BLS data is built on the flawed notion that labor inputs can be accurately measured by a unit called a "job" and that an economic trend in motion tends to stay in motion.

To the contrary, in today's world labor is procured by the hour and by the gig — meaning that the "job" units counted in both the establishment and household surveys are a case of apples, oranges and cumquats. The household survey, for example, would count as equally "employed" a person holding

- a 10-hour per week gig with no benefits;
- a worker holding three part-time jobs adding to less than 36 hours per week with some benefits; and
- a 50-hour per week manufacturing job (with overtime) providing a cadillac style benefit package.

Beyond that, the underlying monthly surveys are tiny, primitive and utterly lacking in quality control among respondents. As a result, the statistical wizards at the BLS smooth it all over with ad hoc adjustments and guesstimates (e. g. the notorious birth-death model) and trend-cycle statistical models that essentially project into the current month the statistical trend line then underway.

In short, the monthly jobs report is not an accurate empirical snapshot of where the real world labor market actually is; it's a modeled projection of where the BLS bureaucrats and their Keynesian tutors think it should be.

And that's also why the BLS "jobs" confection is useless at turning points in the business cycle. During the 2008-2009 employment collapse, for instance, it initially over-reported the nonfarm payrolls by more than *500,000* jobs per month because it assumed the previous trend was still in motion — even as employers were throwing workers overboard with reckless abandon after the Lehman meltdown on Wall Street.

Aside from cyclical turning points (mostly triggered by the Fed itself), the larger context is this: The natural tendency of a capitalist economy is to expand if the working age population is growing and if the state does not excessively retard investment and productivity growth.

69

Non-Farm Payrolls 2008-09 Then and Now

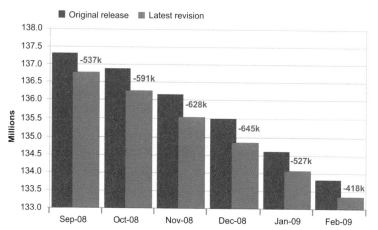

Those natural expansionary forces have been at work in tepid form since the recessionary correction of 2008-2010. It is capitalist momentum, not Washington stimulus, that accounts for the some 8.7 million jobs which were lost in the Great Recession and then "born again" during the recovery, as well as for the modest incremental net job gains that have been generated since breakeven was achieved in 2014.

Even on a headcount based employment metric, however, the peak-to-peak gain is nothing to write home about because the headwinds of debt and Bubble Finance have been so strong.

Thus, between November 2007 and September 2018, the US working age population expanded by 194,000 per month. Yet laboring under the yoke of Washington's oppressive economic policies, the BLS establishment jobs count rose by only 85,000 per month.

Needless to say, employing only 44% of the available labor force growth is not full-employment. But it does underscore why the current 3.7% unemployment rate is an artifact of the BLS puzzle palace, not proof of booming prosperity on main street.

In any event, what is ultimately important is the growth rate of actual labor units (hours) employed and the relationship of that to the available potential labor force — not simply the BLS "jobs" model. The latter basically floats on the back of the natural capitalist business cycle expansion and enables the monetary politburo in the Eccles Building to claim credit for what are really nothing more than statistical proxies.

The Labor Market Is Not Awesome — The Real Unemployment Rate Is 40%

We think there is a far more insightful and accurate way to look at labor utilization and to assess whether or not the glowing state of affair claimed by both the Fed and the White House has actually been achieved.

As we indicated above, back in the year 2000 (the last time U-3 hit 3.7%) what we consider to be the comprehensive unemployment rate was *34.6%*. Today it stands at **40.0%**.

Since the turn of the century, therefore, there has been enormous deterioration in the US economy's use of its potential labor supply. Yet as the Baby Boom rapidly ages and the Welfare State burden soars, that is a very bad thing.

Stated differently, the US has not utilized the last 9 years of so-called recovery to get back to true full employment — as implied by the BLS reports and the Donald's braggadocio about strongest ever labor market.

Instead, it has wasted a crucial decade in front of the Baby Boom retirement bow-wave, which is now coming down the pike at an accelerating rate. That is, we have essentially been peddling backwards with regard to deploying potential labor hours, thereby eroding rather than enhancing America's capacity for economic growth and rising real incomes.

Yet more labor hours deployed are absolutely essential to pay the taxes that will be needed to prevent the US Welfare/Warfare State from fiscally capsizing in the decades immediately ahead.

In this context, we measure the potential labor force as the

US population 20-69 years of age and assume that in theory every adult could work 2000 hours per year in the monetized labor market. (40 hours per week, 50 weeks per year).

That's not intended as some kind of moral imperative, of course. It's just a statistical benchmark that doesn't depend upon some bureaucrat's whim about who should be working (and therefore be in the BLS labor force count) and who is excused.

It also avoids the non-comparability over time problem — for instance when more spouses elect to work outside the home or twenty-somethings elect to become quasi-permanent students on the back of Uncle Sam's no-questions-asked student loans.

Indeed, the standard BLS statistics with respect to the official labor force and employment in the monetized economy are riddled with just these kinds of anomalies.

For example, the BLS counts three jobs for a two-earner $100,000 per year family which hires a full-time housekeeper, but just one job for the identical $100,000 family where one spouse works in the monetized economy, one-stays home and works in the non-monetized household sector and neither hires a third person to do the home chores.

The same logic applies to the 30-year-old still in graduate school living on Uncle Sam's student loans versus holding a job in the monetized economy; or the ex-office worker on disability who got a bad back and corporal tunnel bending over a typewriter; or the 60% of able-bodied recipients on foods stamps who are currently unemployed and not looking for work; or the millions of millennials in mom and pops basement who sell empty beer bottles on eBay a few hours per day.

Many factors drive whether potential labor hours get sequestered outside of the monetized economy in housework, studentdom, on the welfare rolls, in the black market drug trade or in mom's basement. But the interest rate on overnight fed funds is surely the least of them.

Nevertheless, under today's demographic and fiscal circumstances it is imperative that the comprehensive unemployment rate begins to drop, not rise as it has been for most of this century. That's the only way Uncle Sam can find the tax receipts needed to prevent a complete societal civil war a few years down the road.

But contrary to Wall Street's bullish ballyhoo and the Donald's boasting, it's not happening. In December 2000, there were 175.5 million adults aged 20-69 — meaning that the implied potential labor force amounted to 351 billion labor hour per annum. During that same month, the BLS measured 229.5 billion hours actually employed in the non-farm economy at an annual rate.

Accordingly, unemployment amounted to 121.5 billion hours or 34.6% of the potential available hours.

By contrast, the adult population 20-69 years of age is now 212.3 million and available hours total 424.6 billion per annum. Against that, the BLS most recent measure shows 255.6 billion hours actually employed — implying 169 billion unemployed labor hours and a 40.0% comprehensive unemployment rate.

Stated differently, between the two 3.7% anchor points on the U-3 unemployment during the last 18 years, the level of unemployed US labor has increased by nearly 48 billion hours per annum, and the rate has risen commensurately.

More important, potential labor grew by 73.6 billion hours or at 1.06% per annum during that period, while actually employed hours rose by only 26.1 billion and 0.59% per year.

And that's exactly the skunk in the woodpile — barely half the newly available labor hours are being put to work.

By contrast, during the 1981 to 2000 peak-to-peak periods, the potential labor force grew by 2.2% per annum, and labor hours actually utilized rose by nearly an identical 1.9% annualized rate. So back then, 86% of the labor hour growth got employed.

That is to say, in 1980 the Baby Boom was just beginning to flood the labor market and female participation rates in the monetized economy were rising rapidly; and that swelling wave of additional hours was put to work almost completely.

So with employed hours growing since 2000 at just 25% of the rate recorded during the prior two decades, we are actually at the opposite end of "the best labor market in a generation" and not even in the zip code of a labor shortage.

The reason for that is not hard to find. Fed policy has badly damaged the main street economy via its massive inflationary incentive for off-shoring of high value production and jobs while turning the C-suites of corporate America into predatory dens of financial engineering.

At the same time, Welfare State policy has further drained labor resources from the monetized economy with massive increases in food stamp, disability, Medicaid and other welfare programs and student loans and aid.

In the latter case, for example, there were about 30 billion potential labor hours per year sequestered in studentdom in 2000. That figure for hours kept outside of the monetized job market is now 40 billion.

Likewise, in the year 2000 about 13 billion potential labor hours were sequestered on the Social Security disability rolls, which figure has since grown to 21 billion missing labor hours.

Needless to say, if you want to fix the real labor market problem, remove the fiscal subsidies and incentives for keeping potential hours off the market.

But most importantly, abolish the FOMC. It's the reason the long-term main street growth is slouching toward the flatline and why the Donald's ersatz populism doesn't have a ghost of a chance of making MAGA.

The Q2 Boom That Wasn't And The Failed Economy That Remains

It's now pretty evident that the 4.2% GDP print for Q2 was actually a perverse and unsustainable feedback loop from the Donald's misbegotten Trade War and Fiscal Debauch.

That is, a lot of exports got pulled forward to beat the retaliatory tariffs and consumers spent up a storm on the back of Uncle Sam's credit card funded tax giveback.

Thus, real exports grew at an extraordinary 9.3% annual rate during Q2 and accounted for a full one-fourth(1.1 percentage points) of the ballyhooed 4.2% headline gain. A big piece of that export surge, however, was soybeans steaming into the Chinese ports and vast pig farms before Beijing's own retaliatory tariff took effect in July.

Sure enough, soybean exports have now plummeted and total real exports actually posted at a negative 3.5% growth rate in Q3. That is, the factor which put a "4" in the Q2 GDP report and got the GOP talking point writers conjuring up phony images of a return to the halcyon days of Ronald Reagan was nothing more than a Washington induced intra-quarter shuffle — and stupid one at that.

Likewise, personal consumption expenditures (PCE) rose by 3.8% and 4.0% per annum in Q2 and Q3, respectively. So doing, they contributed fully 2.8% and 2.9% of the headline GDP growth in those quarters.

But here's the curveball. During Q2, real PCE rose by $119 billion at annualized rates, but real disposable personal income was up by only $87 billion. Apparently, juiced up with their tax cuts or drinking the Donald's Cool-Aid or counting their stock market winnings, US households raised spending during the quarter by 37% more than their income gain.

And it wasn't an aberration. The PCE gain in Q3 was $127 billion on the back of just a $87 billion gain in real disposable income. So this time households raised their spending by 45% more than their income gain!

There is another word for this besides (self-evidently) unsustainable: Namely, robbing rainy day savings accounts in order to live high on the hog today. And in fact, the household savings rate plummeted from an already low 7.2% in Q1 to 6.8% in Q2 and 6.4% in Q3.

At the current level, household savings are back at rock-bottom — meaning virtually all of the alleged acceleration to the 3.5%-4.2% growth range during the last two quarters was owing to a one-time, unsustainable drawdown of household savings.

In fact, the Q1 savings rate of 7.2% was itself nothing to write home about, and compares to a 8.0%-10.9% average during the Reagan-Bush era and the 12%+ rates which prevailed during the US economic heyday prior to 1980.

Still, had the household savings rate remained at the 7.2% level of Q1, PCE growth would have been a far more modest 2.0% and 0.4% in Q2 and Q3, respectively. And that means, in turn, that without robbing the household piggy bank, the US

Source Of Recent Consumption Growth: Declining Savings Rate

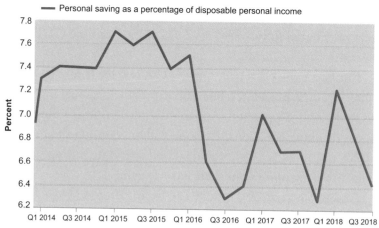

Source: U.S. Bureau of Economic Analysis

76

economy would have generated real GDP growth of just 2.8% in Q2 and only 1.0% in Q3.

And that's not a growth revival or Trumpian acceleration. Most certainly it's not MAGA.

But as they say on late night TV, there's more — and most especially a huge $113 billion favorable inventory swing between Q2 and Q3. In turn, that served to camoflauge some big time bad news in the composition of the 3.5% headline GDP growth rate for Q3.

Beneath The Noise — The US Economy Went Nowhere In Q3

As it happened, the Keynesians' favorite table in the GDP accounts — contributions to percent change in real gross domestic product — let the cat out of the bag. It shows that inventory stocking accounted for 2.07%, or nearly three-fifths, of the 3.5% headline gain during Q3, but that business CapEx contributed the tiny sum of 0.12%

Needless to say, there is no confusion about why the sudden surge of inventory investment happened — especially since new order rates have been cooling rapidly in recent months. To wit, this was not the free market at work based on honest economics; it's the footprint of the Donald's impending Trade War scarring the living bejesus out of domestic importers, retailers and supply chain managers.

So out of self-defense they have scrambled like crazy to get goods off the containerships and into the warehouse before they get hammered by the 25% Trump Tariff next March. So doing, they turned a punkish 1.0% growth quarter (based on final sales) into a 3.5% headline, (including inventory stocking), thereby providing another misguided excuse for the Donald to boast and for the Wall Street sell-side to call in the sheep for still another shearing.

By the same token, the other side of the business investment account — fixed plant, equipment and technology — went completely AWOL in Q3. That is, corporate America is having an all-time record $2.5 trillion financial engineering party this year — stock buybacks, M&A deals and dividends — but it only increased CapEx at a 0.8% annualized rate during the third quarter.

Consequently, the CapEx share of headline GDP growth amounted to a pitiful 3% of the third quarter gain.

Then again, the cost of the 21% corporate rate and 20% pass-through deduction for unincorporated businesses is $172 billion this year and $1.8 trillion over the next decade. So the Q3 rounding error gain in investment is obviously not much return — especially not when it's paid for with Uncle Sam's credit card rather than honest spending cuts.

Here's the bottom line: A kind of perverse feedback loop now appears to be operative. That is, bad trade and fiscal policy is generating short-term GDP pull forwards and unsustainable surges that are drastically ballooning the headline GDP growth number. In turn, these bloated headlines are then being used to justify the wrong-headed policies which caused them, and even argue for more, as in the Donald's pre-midterm shilling for a 10% middle class tax cut that would generate another $200 billion per year of red ink.

When you de-powder the pig, however, an altogether different — and more accurate — narrative emerges. To wit, if you take the export push and pull out of the numbers for Q2 and Q3, hold inventory investment at zero change in both quarters and keep the savings rate constant at 7.2%, the resulting GDP growth numbers are remarkably less awesome.

In Q2 we add back 1.2% to remove the inventory destocking and subtract 1.4% for the excess PCE growth from the savings drawdown and 1.1% for the one-time export surge. That results in a 2.9% growth rate for the second quarter.

Likewise, for Q3 we subtract 2.1% for the huge inventory

build-up and 2.5% for the share of PCE growth attributable
to the savings rate drawdown and add-back 0.45% to reverse
the negative impact of the soybean/export collapse. Alas, that
computes to a 0.7% GDP decline for the quarter.

That's right. It is entirely possible that the US economy is
already slouching into recession.

Still, our purpose in presenting these detailed adjustments
designed to remove the distorting effects of Trumpian policies
is not merely to quibble with the Donald's bothersome boasting
about the performance of what he has now taken to calling "my
economy."

The much bigger point is that there has been no favorable
step-change or acceleration of the main street economy since
November 2016; and that actually, the US economy has
continued to plug along a sub-par growth rut, even as it edges
deeper into cyclical old age.

As it happened, the average real GDP growth rate during
Obama's first term was only 1.5% per annum because the
first year and one-half was consumed by the Great Recession
and its immediate aftermath. Yet in the second term, the US
economy should have sprung back by leaps and bounds from its
recessionary ditch — and most especially owing to the alleged
massive fiscal and monetary stimulus that was brought to bear
on the ostensible recovery.

But there was no cigar. Between Q4 2012 and Q4 2016
real GDP grew at just 2.3% per annum. And then after seven
quarters under Trump, the adjusted gain per the above figures is,
well, 2.4% per annum!

The crucial point is that there has been no Trump driven
resurgence whatsoever of a weak, tired and aging business
expansion. So what is lurking under the covers of the now
bursting stock market euphoria is the same old failed economy
that the Donald inherited, but one which is now 115 months
old and fixing to be assaulted by what amounts to the crackpot

economics of a leveraged New York City real estate gambler.

In Part 2 we will examine why Trump's, trade, fiscal, monetary and border policies are antithetical to the restoration of traditional growth rates and the revival of prosperity in Flyover America. But since they do not reverse the long-standing trend of mainstream economic policy but only make it worse, it is first necessary to document the utter failure of these incumbent policies and debunk the claim of the Fed/Wall Street money axis that the American economy is emerged from the Great Recession in the pink of health.

CHAPTER 3

Peak Trump: Hapless Legatee Of The Financial Crisis That Never Ended

The history books will record that The Donald peaked on September 20, 2018. That's when the S&P 500 made an all-time high at 2940 and when the Donald went all-in embracing the most dangerous and unstable Everything Bubble in modern times.

And it was, ironically, also the 10th anniversary nearly to the date of the failed first TARP vote in the U. S. House of Representatives on September 29, 2008.

By a vote of 228-205 that day a majority of the House — led by two-thirds of the GOP — opted for honest capitalism in America; and to allow Wall Street speculators who had grown rich ridding a giant financial bubble fostered by the Fed to face their just deserts.

The 700-point, 7% Dow drop that day, in fact, was just the beginning of a long overdue financial purge. Excessive debt and rampant financial asset inflation had been building in the US economy since Tricky Dick Nixon deep-sixed the dollar's anchor to gold and the postwar Bretton Woods system of fixed exchange rates and international financial discipline in August 1971.

But the financial rot had dramatically intensified in the years after Black Monday of October 1987 when Alan Greenspan had panicked and rescued Wall Street from a bloodbath brought on by rampant speculation in a new invention called stock portfolio insurance.

He then went on to erect a crooked monetary regime based on "wealth effects." That encompassed stock market price-keeping operations (implied puts and coddling of trader sentiment), systematic suppression of interest rates and an inflationary quadrupling of the Fed's balance sheet from $200 billion to $800 billion during his 19-year tenure.

For want of a better term, this entire regime of Bubble Finance had come crashing down when its most egregious Wall Street practitioner, the venerable Lehman Brothers, shocked the world with its bankruptcy filing on September 15.

But there should have been no mystery: Lehman's $600 billion balance sheet was loaded with the toxic waste of its mortgage securitization mills, undistributed junk bond underwritings and far-flung speculations in leveraged real estate. Yet much of this illiquid and dodgy paper was being funded with super-cheap short-term money market instruments and repo that made for richly profitable spreads while funds were available, and an instant liquidity crisis when this "hot money" evaporated in the September panic.

Lehman Brothers: Poster Boy For Bubble Finance — Then And Still

Needless to say, Lehman Brothers was no outlier; it was the poster-boy for the financial casino which had risen up on Wall Street after 1987, where once had stood quasi-honest and reasonably disciplined and stable capital and money markets.

At the time of the TARP vote, in fact, Washington's rescue brigade was already aggressively on the move. The credit default swap gambling operation that sat atop AIG's fully solvent insurance subsidiaries had already been bailed-out with an $85 billion lifeline from the Fed; Morgan Stanley was totally insolvent and was being kept on life-support by upwards of

$100 billion of emergency liquidity injections from the New York Fed; and with the grim reaper breathing heavily on their necks, Goldman, Merrill Lynch and the Citigroup investment bank were negotiating for a lifeline, too.

Still, then and there loomed the financial Rubicon: Wall Street was desperate for a bailout and main street did not need one.

The overwhelming share of small and mid-sized main street banks and thrifts did not own much subprime, had ample FDIC insured and sticky depositor funds and were in no danger of failing or facing runs, despite the urban legends to the contrary which have grown up since.

And while main street households had been lured into the Greenspan bubble — it was not mainly for livelihood and jobs, but for a one-time spree of consumption spending that had been financed with cash-out mortgages or MEW (mortgage equity withdrawal). Greenspan and Bernanke had actually patted themselves on the back for inducing millions of American families to pawn their castles in order to get a loan for a trip to Disneyworld or to speculate in the stock market.

At the peak in 2006-2007, MEW amounted to about $600 billion per annum, which was equal to about 6% of PCE (personal consumption expenditure). That made the in-coming macro-data look better than the deteriorating fundamentals warranted, and even induced Bernanke to take victory laps crowing about the Fed's allegedly deft delivery of the Great Moderation during that period.

But when the subprime mortgage bubble finally burst, the MEW gravy train dried up and most of main street America got back to living within its means — not exactly a fatal state of affairs in any event.

To be sure, there were upwards of 18 million mortgage defaults over 2007-2017, but in the overwhelming share of cases, homeowners did not become homeless and without shelter; they just lost their small down payments, became renters and perhaps learned a hard lesson about the dangers of too much leverage.

As it happened, not only did main street not require a bailout — it didn't get much benefit from TARP and the Fed's massive money pumping operations, anyway, as we demonstrate below.

Instead, the bailout funds went overwhelmingly in the first instance to the rescue of the remaining Wall Street gambling houses — Morgan Stanley, Goldman Sachs and Citigroup directly; and Merrill Lynch, Wachovia and Washington Mutual through Washington DC arranged and lubricated shotgun mergers.

But more importantly, the Fed's utterly insane liquidity tsunami in the fall of 2008 took its balance sheet from $900 billion to $2.2 trillion in 94 days — a gain equal to 145% of the footings it had accumulated during the entire first 94 years of its existence!

Needless to say, that stopped the entire financial cleansing process cold. With virtually zero interest rates on the Fed's liquidity lines and essentially no credit questions asked, the gambling houses were shored up; and the way was paved for a massive, continuous nine-year reflation of what were already

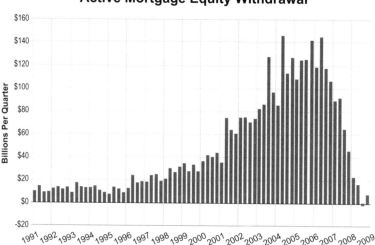

Active Mortgage Equity Withdrawal

Source: http://www.calculatedriskblog.com

vastly over-valued financial markets.

Bookends: The Wall Street Bailouts Of September 2008 And Peak Trump In September 2018

So what filled the bookends between the post-September 2008 doubling down on Bubble Finance and Peak Trump in September 2018 was a dramatic worsening of the condition which gave rise to the Great Financial Crisis in the first place.

To wit, the financial bubble on Wall Street got immensely bigger and more unstable, while the Fed's systematic economic damage to main street intensified enormously. The latter was owing to a further Fed-induced outbreak in the corporate C-suites of jobs and income killing financial engineering and off-shoring of production.

Stated differently, the Fed's lopsided reflation — Wall Street but not main street — in the period between the 10-year bookends was a gigantic mistake; it further bifurcated America's economic and financial life, and was so unsustainable that it was only a matter of time before the fantasy would be reversed.

Two statistics encapsulate the story. Between the pre-crisis peak in late 2007 and September 2018, the inflation adjusted NASDAQ 100 index rose by a whopping 200% while industrial production gained just 3%.

Self-evidently, 11 years of boom on Wall Street and stasis on main street could not stand as an economic matter, but there was something more: America's democratic machinery may have become enfeebled and side-lined by Imperial Washington's permanent ruling class, but the 2016 election proved that when things get far enough askew, the unwashed masses can still make themselves heard.

The fact is, Trump happened owing to the wrong road taken (bailouts) after September 29, 2008.

It gave the Fed 10 more years to hammer the main street economy with its spurious 2.00% inflation target, which sent more jobs and production off-shore, and to subsidize via financial engineering the strip-mining of corporate balance sheets and cash flows in order to pump dividends, stock buybacks and M&A deals back into the Wall Street casino.

This second and even greater round of Bubble Finance, of course, finally sowed a tidal wave of economic hurt and social resentment in the burned-out industrial districts of Flyover America. That's why Trump came out of nowhere, conquered the electoral college on the votes of former Rust Belt democrats and then sojourned briefly in the Oval Office,

But the crisis of September 2008 never really ended and certainly wasn't fixed; it was just swept under the rug by Washington's massive violations of the requisites of sound money, fiscal rectitude and free market financial discipline; and then doubled-down upon until the Everything Bubble reached its asymptote on September 20, 2018.

So now begins a retracement back to the interrupted financial purge of September 2008 and an even greater crisis that will end in ignominy for the Donald and in staggering political and economic setbacks for the nation.

Red Versus Blue State Economy — The Fetid Fruits Of Doubling Down

As we have indicated, the original post-Lehman meltdown was the capstone of decades of fiscal profligacy and egregious money-pumping by the Federal Reserve. These misbegotten policies had temporarily juiced current economic results, but so doing they had also deeply impaired and capriciously bifurcated the national economy and polity.

On the one hand, soaring household debts, relentless Fed fostered inflation of domestic costs, prices and wages and an addiction to destructive financial engineering in the corporate C-suites had deindustrialized much of the vast economic expanse of Flyover America.

These wrong-headed Washington policies had caused the off-shoring of massive amounts of America's productive base and generated enormous and chronic current account deficits. These deficits have been continuous since the late 1970s and have turned the US into the greatest debtor nation in history, owing the rest of the world more than $7.5 trillion at the end of 2017.

To be sure, Keynesian economists and the establishment commentariat say not to worry. These figures purportedly mean that that global investors love America and want to bring their capital here, even if the US economy is blatantly profligate!

We address the utter folly of that canard in much of what follows, but one economic truth cannot be denied.

To wit, the plunging bars in the chart above are a proxy for the devastating migration of much of America's productive industrial economy to off-shore venues; they measure the economic demise in those rust belt precincts of Flyover America which ultimately put Donald Trump in the White House.

At the same time, Washington's foray into statist destruction of sound money and fiscal rectitude has capriciously conferred

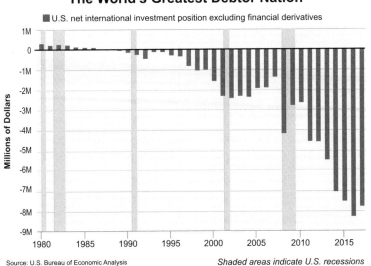

The World's Greatest Debtor Nation

U.S. net international investment position excluding financial derivatives

Source: U.S. Bureau of Economic Analysis   *Shaded areas indicate U.S. recessions*

financialized prosperity on selective pockets of American society scattered along the coasts and sprinkled among the hinterlands.

These economic precincts have prospered mightily — albeit unsustainably — from both the vast bloating of the financial sector and the relentless inflation of assets prices, as well as from the tax-and-debt fueled state enterprises of war, medical care and education.

As to the financialization, the chart below makes clear that since the 1970s — but especially after the Greenspan era of aggressive monetary expansion incepted in 1987 — household assets have been winning the race with income by a country mile.

Since 1970, for example, the market value of household assets has soared by 28.2X — from $4.3 trillion to a staggering $122.7 trillion as of Q2 2018. By contrast, personal income has risen by only 19.7X during the same period.

What that means, of course, is that each dollar of income has been associated with rising amounts of assets. In 1970, the household sector held $4.90 of assets for each dollar of personal income and by the time of Alan Greenspan's arrival at the Fed that figure had inched up to $5.20.

But after Greenspan figuratively discovered the printing press in the basement of the Eccles Building on October 19, 1987, when the market plunged by 22% in a single day, the contemporary asset bubble was off to the races. By the eve of the financial crisis in 2007 it had reached $6.80 and now stands at $7.05 of assets per dollar of household income.

Actually, the more accurate ratio currently is $8.35 of assets per dollar of personal income after you deduct transfer payments. And that's appropriate since most of America's heavily transfer payment dependent households have disproportionately lower asset holdings, if any at all.

In effect, the capitalization rate of household income has been soaring for three decades. Yet why should it?

If anything, it should be falling because the quality of

household income has been deteriorating badly. That's partially due to a much higher ratio of transfer payments to earned labor and capital income; and also due to the fact that the overall growth rate of earned income has been sinking steadily since the turn of the century, as we document below.

The truth of the matter is that this rising capitalization rate is phony and unsustainable. It reflects the artificial fruits of central bank money-pumping and systematic falsification of financial asset prices; it is the talisman of America's failed, bifurcated economy.

Had this $122 trillion household asset bubble been evenly distributed it would be bad enough: The long years of the financialization party would have been shared by all — as would have the deflationary hangover when the morning-after eventually came.

But the asset bubble has been far more perverse. As we demonstrate in what follows, it was purchased on the backs of Flyover America, but ended up in the hands of the bicoastal elites

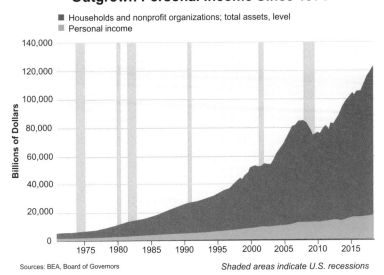

Household Assets Have Massively Outgrown Personal Income Since 1971

■ Households and nonprofit organizations; total assets, level
■ Personal income

Sources: BEA, Board of Governors   *Shaded areas indicate U.S. recessions*

and the top 1% which owns more than 40% of all financial assets.

As demonstrated in the chart below, on the eve of the Greenspan money-pumping era, the top 1% held about 34% of household net worth and the bottom 90% had about 32% — levels that had been steady for most of the post-war period.

But since then there has been a distributional trainwreck. By 2016 the bottom 90% share had plummeted to 21% — largely due to the crash of heavily leveraged (mortgaged) housing assets held by the middle class. At the same time, the top 1% share had soared to 40% — a level never before seen in American history, including in the far less complete and reliable data for 1929.

At that moment in time (2016), you could not find one mainstream economist or commentator in a thousand who was aware of the data below or who thought it mattered. But the people of Flyover America knew they had been cheated. Big time.

So they voted on November 8, 2016 with their hurts and their resentments.

More crucially, the bombastic outsider from Trump Tower came out on top against all odds during the wee hours of that historic election because he had discovered an unlikely route to

The Top 1% Continue to Covet the Wealth

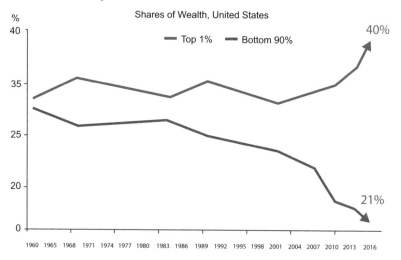

power almost by accident.

Namely, he had learned after demogoguing Mexicans and immigrants in the early days of his campaign that he could channel and mobilize Flyover America's economic hurts and social resentments by pounding relentlessly at the nefarious trade practices of foreign countries and the threat to personal security and jobs posed by an alleged flood of illegal immigrants pouring across the Mexican border.

Neither of these propositions were remotely true, of course, and they had nothing at all to do with fixing the economic mess fostered by the Imperial City's fiscal profligacy and monetary mayhem.

In fact, as well shall demonstrate in Part 2, the five pillars of the Donald's ersatz populism — Trade Wars, Fiscal Debauch, Low-Interest Folly, Immigrant Demonization and Military Spend-a-Thon — are guaranteed to bring the Era of Bubble Finance to a thundering crash.

But as we will also show, at least this time the 1% are rather certain to take the hardest pounding and to up-chuck much of their ill-gotten 40% share of the national wealth.

That's the part about which the Donald was utterly oblivious when he embraced from the Oval Office the very same "big, fat, ugly bubble" which he had denounced on the campaign trail.

Stated differently, the Bubble put him in the White House; its imminent implosion threatens to carry him out.

2008 Crisis Interrupted And Why It Matters

What matters at present is that the crisis of September 2008 never went away. It merely represented the first down-leg of financialization coming undone, and is now re-emerging in even more virulent and dangerous form.

Back when the crisis was interrupted and deferred for what became a full decade, it was essentially concentrated in the canyons of Wall Street owing to the blow-up of the securitization meth labs. In turn, these mishaps set off a contagion of falling prices for the dregs of the sliced and diced subprime mortgage pools and other dodgy assets held in investment bank inventories, of which Lehman held the most fetid collection.

These dubious assets had been accumulated during the housing and credit booms that the Fed had ignited after the dotcom crash. When soaring defaults on the underlying mortgages caused a sell-off of the securitized derivatives, the liquidation accelerated rapidly; and it was compounded by the Fed's folly of mechanically pegging and transparently telegraphing its money market interest rate targets.

As we have seen in the case of Lehman, this kind of absolute money market certainty had encouraged Wall Street to recklessly fund these risky, sticky, longer-term mortgage, real estate and junk bond assets with hideously mismatched liabilities. The latter consisted heavily of hot, short-term money market instruments (unsecured commercial paper and repo) that suddenly dried up in the summer of 2008, forcing dealers to dump even more toxic junk into the market.

Still, the fallout of the Wall Street crisis had initially penetrated Flyover America only obliquely — owing to the fact that the mortgage refi machine, which had been generating hundreds of billions of MEW-based middle class spending, suddenly shutdown.

Likewise, the predatory income production and housing activity generated in the mortgage broker boiler rooms, which peddled low-rate ARMS (adjustable rate mortgages) to economically marginal households, was also stopped cold. That was going to happen anyway, of course, because these marginal borrowers could not remotely hope to afford their subprime mortgages — once the ultra-low "teaser" rates reset and escalated sharply higher.

Both avenues of the housing boom came to a screeching halt when Wall Street melted-down, triggering what would otherwise have been a mild housing-focused downturn. But what transformed the so-called Great Recession into a rout on main street was the corporate C-suite response to plunging stock prices in the fall and winter of 2008-2009.

To wit, by then the Fed's cancerous regime of Bubble Finance had turned the C-suites of corporate America into options obsessed stock trading rooms and financial engineering joints. Almost instantly, a recession that was not even visible in the summer of 2008 to the Goldilocks worshipping economists of both Wall and Washington alike turned virulently south as depicted below.

But the crash of business inventories and employment shown in the chart happened not for the classic reason that main street interest rates were soaring and household and business credit got crunched, but because the C-suites were desperately attempting to propitiate the new trading gods of Wall Street.

The sacrifices they offered consisted of sweeping so-called "restructuring" plans that amounted to shit-canning payrolls, inventories, facilities and balance sheet assets with nearly reckless and frenzied abandon.

During the brief 11-month period after August 2008, more than *6 million* workers were tossed overboard and *$150 billion* of inventories or 10% of outstandings were hastily liquidated.

Even a superficial post-mortem of the data shows that the Great Recession was a drastic over-reaction based on the underlying economics. Demand did not fall by anything close what was implied by the C-suite initiated strum und drang.

Bernanke's Great Depression 2.0 Narrative — Unadulterated Hogwash

But it was a godsend to the Keynesian money-pumpers at the Fed who had actually caused the subprime crash and Wall Street meltdown in the first place. Instead of finding themselves impaled on the hot-seat of blame that they richly deserved, they swiftly turned the tables, morphing into putatively heroic economic firemen who saved the day.

Most especially, the C-suites' frenzied assault on their own employees and company operations permitted the phony Great Depression scholar and inflationista who had become Fed head, Professor Ben Bernanke, to run around Washington with his hair on fire.

So doing, he hysterically claimed that a reprise of the 1930s was at hand; and that extraordinary and heretofore unimaginable levels of monetary and fiscal intervention were needed to arrest a slide into Armegeddon. He later even boasted that he alone had summoned the courage to "print," and had brought the rest of the government along kicking and screaming.

Needless to say, the entire Bernanke-inspired narrative was unadulterated hogwash. The circumstances of 2008 were not remotely similar to those of 1930, most notably because back then America was a massive global creditor and exporter, which got monkey-hammered when the stock market and foreign subprime loan bubble of the day crashed in October 1929.

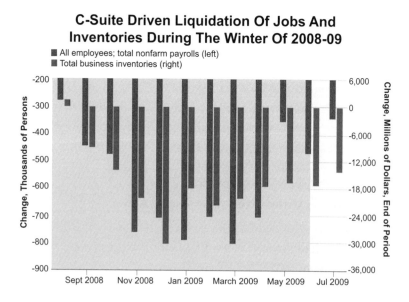

C-Suite Driven Liquidation Of Jobs And Inventories During The Winter Of 2008-09

■ All employees; total nonfarm payrolls (left)
■ Total business inventories (right)

Source: U.S. Bureau of Labor Statistics, U.S. Bureau of the Census   *Shaded areas indicate U.S. recessions*

That caused foreign demand for what had been booming US exports to crater by 80% — along with a sudden, violent plunge in CapEx for what had been urgently needed expansion of domestic plant and equipment during the Roaring Twenties. These twin blows, in turn, had necessitated a genuine old-fashioned liquidation of excess inventories, fixed capital, labor and unsustainable bank credits.

In contrast, by 2008 America was already a giant global debtor and importer. Washington was also a prodigious dispenser of Welfare State income and safety nets, the principal financier of what had become massive domestic health care and education cartels and a fount of money for the nation's obscenely bloated war machine.

Accordingly, there was not a snowball's chance in the hot place that demand and domestic economic activity would have meaningfully declined: Massive spending for war, health care, education, retiree transfer payments, means-tested safety nets and much more, none of which existed in 1930, would have proceeded apace.

With these robust Welfare State and Warfare State shock absorbers in place, there was not even a remote risk that any modest main street adjustment to the overdue meltdown on Wall Street would have become a self-fueling depressionary spiral.

Bernanke's scary Great Depression 2.0 warnings, in fact, were really about a Fake Depression.

That's especially because the structure of the America's import-dependent and state spending-bloated economy in 2008 was upside-down from that of 1930: The Hoovervilles this time actually sprung-up amidst the time-immemorial poverty of the Chinese countryside.

That happened in the fall and winter of 2008-2009 when global trade swooned and upwards of 100 million suddenly redundant migrant workers were sent from the closed-down export factories in eastern China back to the interior rice paddies.

But the pettifogging professor at the helm of the US central bank did not wait even a few weeks for the smoke in the canyons of Wall Street to clear after Lehman went down; and for it to become obvious that the real recession was destined to happen in China, not the already burned-out precincts of Rust Belt America.

So the Fed doubled-down into a frenzy of liquidity pumping that amounts to the financial policy crime of the century. As summarized below on September 3, 2008 the balance sheet of the Fed was $905 billion and it had taken 94 years to get there from the day the Fed opened for business in 1914.

Yet by early December after an insane frenzy of liquidity pumping the Fed's balance sheet stood at $2.213 trillion.

So in just 94 days a no count academic scribbler — who ended up on the Fed by accident because the political hatchet men around George W. Bush didn't trust Easy Al Greenspan to be easy enough (imagine that!) if electioneering so required

Bernanke's Balance Sheet Explosion

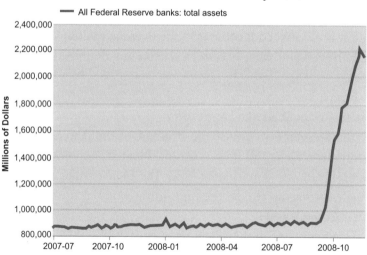

Source: Board of Governors of the Federal Reserve System (US)

— increased the Fed's balance sheet of plucked-from-thin-air liabilities by 145% more than all his predecessors had done during the first 94 years of the Fed's existence.

And then, after the fact, this mountebank had the nerve to make the aforementioned boast. Actually, in printing Fake Money with reckless abandon, Bernanke had displayed something unusual — but it wasn't courage!

Bernanke's monetary crime was all the more breathtaking because it was utterly uncalled for. He and the former Dartmouth line-backer, Hank Paulson, who may or may not have worn a helmet during his playing days and who had been sent to Washington by Goldman Sachs to occupy the Secretary of Treasury's office, had single-handedly panicked Capitol Hill into resuscitating the TARP bailout after it had been courageously voted down by the House back-benchers.

In turn, the reckless act of enacting a blank check $700 billion Wall Street bailout in early October 2008 further fueled the panic in the C-suites. Instantly, the Washington-generated Great Recession was off to the races.

Yet save for the TARP induced wave of fear, the C-suite panic would have calmed down. And save for the insane flood of liquidity depicted above, the last remaining gambling houses on Wall Street — Merrill Lynch, Goldman Sachs, Morgan Stanley and the Citigroup holding company — would have met their maker in the Chapter 11 courts, enabling the meltdown in the canyons of Wall Street to burn-out in due course with little spill-over to the main street economy and Flyover America.

How The Wall Street Bailouts Decimated Flyover America

As it happened, of course, the worst of both worlds transpired. The Washington TARP and money pumping panic both made the Great Recession deeper and more painful than it need have been and also arrested in its tracks the liquidation of the Fed fueled financial bubbles that had been gestating on Wall Street for more than three decades.

As we have indicated, the egregious reflation of the Fed-fostered financial bubbles permitted the stealth destruction of American capitalism to have an extended lease on life. That is, the Wall Street casino became red hot with reckless speculation and radical mis-pricing of stocks, bonds, derivatives and other financial assets confected by the same toxic waste labs which had brought on the mortgage securitization fiasco.

So doing, it sucked the C-suites into even more systemic strip-mining of corporate cash flows, payrolls, investment accounts and debt capacities in the service of financial engineering. That is, flushing cash back into Wall Street to goose their stock prices and pad the value of their stock options.

Consequently, upwards of $15 trillion of stock-buybacks, M&A deals and excess dividends since 2006 have pumped a tsunami of cash into the Wall Street gambling pits. These flows, needless to say, did fuel the greatest risk asset bubble ever — even as it atrophied the vitality and growth capacity of the main street economy.

The Fed's eight year money-pumping spree after the 2008 meltdown also caused a good crisis to go to utter waste. In the immediate aftermath of the crisis, the C-suites had temporarily sobered up, sharply reducing financial engineering outlays for stock buybacks, M&A deals and dividends to a range of $500-700 billion per annum.

But year after year of cheap debt and Fed price-keeping operations undergirding a relentlessly rising stock market caused prudence to be thrown to the winds. Financial engineering outlays came roaring back, and during 2018 are expected to hit an off-the-charts $2.5 trillion.

Stated differently, had Washington allowed Wall Street to undergo the bleeding cure it desperately needed in September 2008, the Everything Bubble might not have happened; and the

Record Financial Engineering

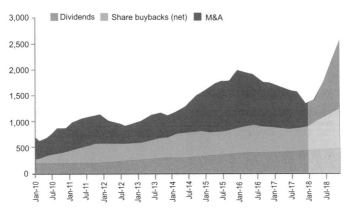

Source: CompuStat, FactSet, Bloomberg, Dealogic, UBS

condign justice of a Trumpified White House might not have materialized.

There would have been at least an opportunity for the politicians on both ends of Pennsylvania Avenue to discover that Keynesian monetary central planning was an unmitigated evil; and that the Fed's massive seizure of financial power after it was untethered from the Bretton Woods gold standard by Nixon in 1971 needed to be thoroughly rescinded.

Under a shackled Fed, it is at least possible that it's lunatic pursuit of domestic inflation at no less than 2.00% per annum — when deflation was called for by the competitive realities of the global economy — might have been abandoned.

In turn, that might have encouraged the C-suites to get back to the business of building strong, growing and fiercely competitive business operations, rather than functioning as financial engineering joints devoted to the enrichment of top executives.

But it was not to be. As we have indicated, the crippling economic impairment and bifurcation of the US economy not only continued to gather force after the Lehman meltdown — it was actually intensified dramatically by the post-crisis spree of central bank money-pumping and sweeping financial asset price falsification.

Donald Trump — Ben Bernanke's Gift To America

So this proposition bears repeating: The Fed's reckless money-pumping is what put the final economic kibosh on Flyover America and thereby fostered the freakish election result of 2016. The Donald is well and truly Ben Bernanke's gift to America.

With a few exceptions, the red areas of the electoral map below, representing the counties that the Donald won in 2016, are victims of the great deindustrialization wave that Washington fostered after 1971.

The economic hurt in these burned-out districts is attributable to the massive off-shoring of production and jobs. That occurred with malice aforethought after Greenspan thoroughly institutionalized Keynesian monetary central planning at the Fed in October 1987; and most especially after Bernanke took it off the deep-end in response to the 2008 Wall Street meltdown.

Likewise, the blue counties are overwhelmingly the beneficiaries of financialization, the casino-fueled asset inflations and the tech and social media bubbles. They also thrive on the prodigious dispensations of America's vast Welfare State and the enormous defense, health care and education cartels which are fed from the coffers of Imperial Washington.

In this context, the Donald's endless outbursts of economic illiteracy actually match the chart above. He never had a clue as to the central banking origins of the hurt and resentment he encountered in Flyover America. Nor did he ever proffer even a vague semblance of the policy measures that would be needed to rectify the damage and actually generate something which approximates MAGA.

Instead, the Donald simply promulgated a Fake Diagnosis

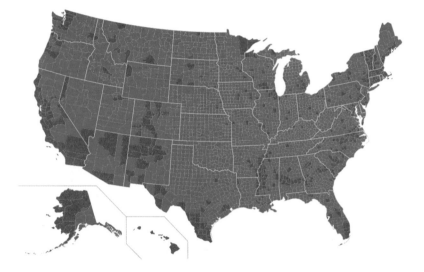

and peddled it far and wide to the masses of Flyover America's red counties.

Namely, that the cause of main street's economic decline was nefarious foreigners. By the Donald's telling, it was illegal immigrants flowing across the Mexican border and ill-paid Chinamen working in the Red Ponzi's teeming export factors which have destroyed the American Dream and have stolen their once and former prosperity.

So his solution boils down to Trade Wars and Border Wars — the very thing which could turn Bernanke's failed Bubble Finance into a Trumpian catastrophe.

No part of the Donald's diagnosis or solution is remotely true, of course. Flyover America's prosperity was not destroyed by threats which arose from outside its borders; the whole baleful decline was fostered within the Imperial City itself.

That is, in the Warfare State complex, the bloated Welfare State, the domestic pork barrel network, the racketeering shops on K-Street, and, most especially, the Federal Reserve/Wall Street money axis.

CHAPTER 4

Main Street's Failed Economy: 11 Years Of Fed Fostered Flatlining

Donald Trump is not reviving the US economy; he's just presiding over the final stretch of a stillborn recovery from the Great Recession that essentially marks 18-years of sideways for the overwhelming majority of main street households.

As we will document in Chapter 5, the problem is $70 trillion of public and private debt and a central bank that has generated fabulous paper wealth for the elites, but a tidal wave of cost inflation and financial speculation and predation — which has strangled economic growth in vast tracts of formerly industrialized Flyover America.

This baleful condition was always way beyond the Donald's pay grade. The only viable solution is to end interventionist central banking and the FOMC's usurpation of honest free market pricing in the financial system — a mission that a lifetime "low interest man" and leveraged real estate speculator would hardly find compelling or congenial.

Nevertheless, a badly impaired flatlining main street economy is the legacy of Washington's failed economic statism. And there is no better proof than the fact that virtually every core measure of industrial life has pancaked during most of the 21st century to date.

Core US Industrial Economy: 11 Years Of Unprecedented Flatlining

Thus, when it comes to the fundamental metrics of long-term economic growth and prosperity, there are no better core indicators than manufacturing output and electrical power production. The rise of the so-called services economy notwithstanding, a society which is not pumping out a healthy rate of electrical power and manufacturing growth is not on a path toward sustainable prosperity.

Yet fully 11 years after the pre-crisis peak in the fall of 2007, both of these measures are still below the levels they had obtained back then. And after the modest bounce-back from the Great Recession plunge of 2008-2009, both metrics have been flatlining regardless of who was domiciled in the Oval Office.

That is to say, Obama had nothing to boast about because on his watch manufacturing and electrical power output didn't even get back to square one (2007 peak), and now the Donald is apparently taken credit for what is actually no progress at all.

And we do mean no progress. Compared to September

Flat-Lining Production Of Power And Manufactures

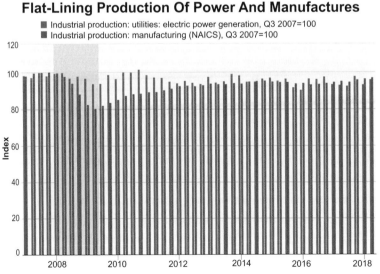

■ Industrial production: utilities: electric power generation, Q3 2007=100
■ Industrial production: manufacturing (NAICS), Q3 2007=100

Source: Board of Governors of the Federal Reserve System (US)   *Shaded areas indicate U.S. recessions*

2007, which we have indexed at 100.0, manufacturing output in September 2018 was just 98.0 and the index for electrical power production stood at 97.0

Needless to say, these are hard data which measure physical volume of core production functions at the center of the US economy. But never has the damning chart below been displayed on bubblevision because it is more than a little hard to sell stocks on the back of flat.

In fact, this chart is an indictment of the "recency bias" to which our central bank driven Wall Street casino has fallen victim. Based on cherry-picking short-run positive rates of change and ignoring the fact that the recovery of output lost during the recession doesn't constitute "growth", the talking heads have repeatedly found "encouraging" gains from the data below.

But how could they — the chart is flat as a pancake for 11 years running!

The answer, of course, is that there is no institutional memory of what a real recovery looks like anymore on either end of the Acela Corridor. So Wall Street is content to label reversible rounding error gains as progress, if it supports the case to buy stock at any given moment; and the Washington politicians — including the Eccles Building monetary politburo — boast that the born again output recovered from the recessionary bottom is the fruit of their own deft interventions to stimulate the economy.

It is not. It's evidence that ordinary capitalist growth is being stymied by Washington's monetary, regulatory and tax obstacles, and most especially by the central bank fostered strip-mining of corporate balance sheets and off-shoring of production, as we document below.

The evidence that Washington and Wall Street have conspired to asphyxiate main street growth and prosperity lies in the plain history of prior cycles. That is, during the identical peak-to-peak span of 1990-2001 and before central banking totally went off the deep-end, electrical power production rose by 25% and manufacturing output by 55%.

That was a recovery!

This is failed flat.

Nowhere Is Not Gangbusters — The Non-Recovery of Housing, Industrial Production And Construction

Perhaps nothing has been more taken out of cyclical context in this manner, or had virtually any short-run plus sign redefined as "gangbusters", than has been the case for housing and total industrial production.

But there is nothing gangbusters about it. For example, single family housing starts are still 7% below their pre-crisis level and total industrial production in September 2018 posted just 3.2% above its 11-years ago level.

And that latter midget gain, especially, is what debunks the "splendid recovery" narrative.

Housing Starts

— Privately owned housing starts: 1-unit structures, Sept 2007=100
— Industrial production index, Sept 2007=100

Sources: Board of Governors, Census   *Shaded areas indicate U.S. recessions*

In part that's because the industrial production index encompasses a large swath of the US economy including manufacturing, mining and energy (the ballyhooed shale boom) and all gas, electric, communications and other utilities. But it's also important because much of what is measured as services — retail and wholesale trade, transportation and warehousing, architectural, engineering and IT services etc. — are driven by the pace of industrial goods flowing through the economy's supply chains.

Again, once upon a time there was such a thing as "growth" over the course of a complete peak-to-peak cycle. In the identically long 1990-2001 cycle, for example, single family starts rose by 45% and industrial production by 46%.

That was growth. This isn't.

Likewise, once upon a time construction spending tended to advance smartly over the cycle, too. After all, a growing economy does take more factories, warehouses, housing units, hospitals, schools, pipelines, hotels, power plants, et al.

Accordingly, during the 1990's cycle construction spending advanced by 7.5% per year on a peak-to-peak basis, and between the February 2001 peak and the March 2006 construction peak, spending rose by 8.0% per year.

During the 12 years since then shown below, however, not so much. Construction spending has advanced by just 0.8% per year or merely a tenth of the growth rate of prior cycles.

That anemic advance over the cycle is obviously due to the deep plunge during and after the Great Recession, but that doesn't excuse the weak peak-to-peak gain this time around; it actually crystalizes the disappearing growth problem.

To wit, had construction spending rebounded strongly and commensurate with its recessionary plunge, and then stayed on the 6.0% per annum growth path registered during 1993-2007, total construction spending in 2018 would be $2.0 trillion, not the current rate of $1.3 trillion.

That is to say, owing to the recency bias and the Wall Street theory that any old advance is by definition awesome, there is in the order of $700 billion of construction spending gone missing from the current economy.

Nor can that giant gap between prior trend growth rates and post-crisis stagnation be explained by the canard that there has been less inflation during recent years — so the above nominal dollar comparison overstates the case.

Except it doesn't. If you deflate the Commerce Department's constructing spending series with the GDP deflator for fixed assets, its turns out that the comparison is even worse: The growth rate of construction spending in inflation-adjusted dollars was 7.7% per annum during 1993-2001, 7.4% per annum during 2001-2006, and 0.19% per annum between March 2006 and September 2018.

We'd say 0.19% per annum growth for 12 years running is about as close to flatling as you can get. So there, dead in the water, is exactly where another $1 trillion plus sector of the main

Construction Spending Stalls Out During This Cycle

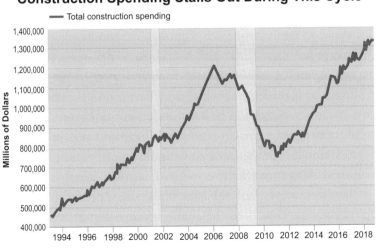

Source: U.S. Bureau of the Census   Shaded areas indicate U.S. recessions

street economy sits.

And there sits also another non sequitir about the Trumpian economy allegedly performing at an all-time highs. At $1.329 trillion in September 2018, construction spending was technically at a record high. But in constant 2018 dollars, construction spending stood at $1.300 trillion 12 years ago in March 2006.

In short, what we have in the chart above is a mere 2% real gain over the second longest business cycle in history. This core measure of economic activity, therefore, is not signaling any kind of triumph at month #115 of an octogenarian business expansion. It actually screams out failure.

Real Net Business CapEx: 17 Years Of Pancaking

The exact same point pertains when we look at total business CapEx, including plant, equipment and software and technology. Here the bubblevision boys and girls are always pointing to putative green shoots, often expressed in annualized real growth rates of 5-10%.

For instance, during the past 12 months, their favorite growth indicator, real gross private investment in nonresidential fixed assets (i. e. business CapEx), has increased by 6.4%; and is now 61% above where it stood nine years ago in September 2009.

Except you can't count highly cyclical components of the economy from the bottom of the cycle, and more importantly, you ought to consider what the "gross" term in this metric actually means. Namely, that it represents current year CapEx spending to replace what is consumed in current year production (depreciation and amortization of capital assets) plus any additional allowance for the growth of existing capacity.

Needless to say, if gross business investment is only equal to capital consumption, then the annual gain in the first number can be as big as you please. When gross investment spending is totally absorbed by replacement of worn out capital, the underlying economy is going nowhere.

And that's exactly what has happened since the pre-crisis peak in Q4 2007. At that time, annual real gross business investment was a little over $2.0 trillion per annum and current capital consumption slightly under $1.6 trillion. During the next ten years, real gross investment grew by $555 billion, but the annual rate of capital consumption was right behind, rising by $547 billion.

We'd not only call that close enough to the same for government work, but also call it powerful proof that the main street economy has been truly impaled on the flatline. As shown in the graph below, the thing that counts for growth and prosperity is net investment spending growth; and not only since 2007, but actually since the year 2000 there has been none of it!

That's right. No matter how many times the talking heads of bubblevision told you there was another good quarter for capital spending, it flat out wasn't true. What they were dispensing was talking points for their Wall Street sales and trading desks.

As we show below, there has been virtually no gain in the US economy's 73 million breadwinner jobs since the year 2000. And that's notwithstanding the BLS job count which always rises by +/- 200,000 per month come rain or shine — except during recessions and crises, which purportedly don't count.

But the flatlining breadwinner job count is really no mystery, either. How could it be growing when the nation's capital stock growth rate has been dead in the water for nearly two decades?

Needless to say, when an economy de-industrializes, the capital stock also stagnates. Even then, the full degree of US de-industrialization has been partially masked by the same central banking distortions that are responsible for the failure of the overall main street economy.

Real Net Business Investment Has Flatlined Since 2000

■ Real net fixed investment: net nonresidential

Source: U.S. Bureau of Economic Analysis

Shaded areas indicate U.S. recessions

The Fed's Double Whammy: Manufacturing Demise, Shale Oil Bubble

Oil and gas production is the only component of the domestic industrial economy that has expanded robustly since the 2007 pre-crisis peak. As shown below, output of the sector has doubled over the past 11 years, even as output of consumer goods is nearly 8% below its 2007 level and, as we have seen, overall industrial production has barely regained the flatline (up 3%).

Yet there is a reason for this radical divergence. Oil production is exceedingly capital intensive, and the booming shale sector is insanely capital intensive. That means, of course, that the Fed's drastic repression of capital costs has been just the ticket to fuel the shale boom.

Industry propagandists would have you believe, of course, that its all some kind of rocket science miracle of technology, but the truth is that the technology of horizontal well drilling and chemical, water and sand fracturing of shale formations (fracking) has been around for decades. The recent technology advances have been incremental, not radical breakthroughs.

What is new and radical is the Fed fostered scramble for yield among asset managers that resulted in upwards of $200 billion of debt, preferred stock and production financing deals flowing into the shale and E&P patch during the last decade; and then another $100 billion of E&P company equity issuance on top of that.

Yet after all of that capital and technology, the industry has produced rivers of red ink almost as fulsome as the doubling of oil production from 5.5 million to 11.3 million barrels per day since 2007. A recent study of the 33 top E&P companies, in fact, showed that they generated a stunning $100 billion of negative free cash flow between 2012 and 2017 alone.

Needless to say, an honest capital market would have shut-off the flow of negative return capital to the domestic shale industry years ago. The soaring line red line in the chart below, therefore, represents a Fake Boom fostered by radically mispriced capital.

Output has doubled by the sheer brute force of pumping capital down the well bores to fund sand, water, chemicals, power, equipment and operations even faster than the shale rocks releases their heretofore economically sequestered hydrocarbons.

In short, the shale boom is not the free market at work. It's the (virtually) free money printers at the Fed who made it all happen.

But the latter are now belatedly seeking to normalize interest rates and capital costs — a process which will puncture the shale bubble no less violently than did the Fed's belated tightening during 2004-2006 finally cause the subprime and housing bubble to splatter.

At the same time, the Fed's 2.00% inflation pumping operation has monkey-hammered the more labor intensive areas of manufacturing, such as in consumer goods. Since Q4 2007, in fact, manufacturing wage costs have risen by 30% and nearly all of that has been eaten up by domestic inflation — so its not as if it did a lot of good for the workers.

But it did further and relentlessly widen the wedge between manufacturing wage costs in the US and those in Mexico, China and other EM venues. So even after throwing all the robots and process technology at the their factories that could be rationally mustered, the output of domestic consumer goods producers is still nearly 8% below it pre-crisis level.

On the other hand, final domestic consumption of goods has proceeded apace, rising by 28% in real terms over the last 11 years. So with consumption up by more than a quarter and production down by nearly 8%, there is no mystery about how the 36% supply/demand gap was filled.

On that matter, the Donald got it right: Imports!

We examine the futility of the Donald's Trade War and tariffs in Part 2, but here it needs to be noted that the Fed has whacked US industrial production with a double whammy.

On the one hand, it has fostered a massive shale bubble that is destined to collapse into a literal black hole of economic wreckage when interest rates normalize, capital flows dry up and global oil prices get clobbered by the upcoming global recession.

At the same time, huge parts of the domestic manufacturing infrastructure have been up-rooted, off-shored and permanently disabled. Bringing them back quickly, or even at all, is not going to happen in a world where the Fed has fostered $30 per hour factory wage costs here, which must compete with $5 per hour and under levels in Mexico, China and elsewhere in the EM.

If there was ever an indictment of the Fed's financial repression and Wall Street coddling policies, it's embodied in the graph above. The speculative momo driven dynamics of the equity markets and the massive scramble for yield in fixed income sector have fueled a malinvestment spree in the shale patch which is biblical in extent.

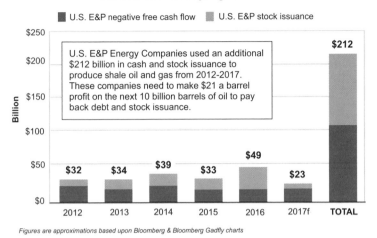

U.S. E&P Energy Companies
Cash Burn & Equity Issuance

■ U.S. E&P negative free cash flow   ■ U.S. E&P stock issuance

> U.S. E&P Energy Companies used an additional $212 billion in cash and stock issuance to produce shale oil and gas from 2012-2017. These companies need to make $21 a barrel profit on the next 10 billion barrels of oil to pay back debt and stock issuance.

Figures are approximations based upon Bloomberg & Bloomberg Gadfly charts

At length, thundering losses and write-offs will rock the industry, even as production plummets — once the artificial flow of capital stops. As is well known, production decline rates in the shale patch can be as high as 80% per annum, meaning that when the money for sand, water, chemicals and pumping rigs stops, so does the flow of oil.

By the same token, what could be more destructive to ordinary jobs in tradeable goods and services than the treadmill of rising prices, wages and costs fueled by the Fed's mindless commitment to 2.00% annual inflation?

The Bogeyman Of Deflation — The Stick With Which The Fed Has Battered Industrial America

That wrongheaded policy is the exact opposite of what the main street economy has desperately needed since the early 1990s. That is, it needed sustained deflation in order to remain internationally competitive — an outcome that would have surely happened on the free market in response to the rise of China and the EM if it had not been blocked by America's central bankers.

It goes without saying that the off-shoring that led to flatlining output in manufactured goods has also generated shrinking employment in high paying, fulltime jobs in the factories. In fact, booming economy or not, manufacturing employment stood at 12.8 million jobs in September 2018, a level still well below the 13.8 million level of September 2007.

Nor did the shale boom make even the tiniest dent in this 1.0 million loss of prime jobs. To wit, in September 2007 there were 147,200 jobs in the oil and gas extraction industries, according to the BLS. In September 2018, that figures had inched up to 153, 200 — meaning that the shale boom replaced exactly 6% of the jobs lost in manufacturing owing to the Fed's pro-inflation policies.

Indeed, the bogeyman of deflation is actually a Keynesian invention. Not only is it utterly lacking in empirical and theoretical merit, but, at the end of the day, it is what keeps Keynesian interventionism alive — especially today's central banking version.

That is, when the free market wants to deflate, it does

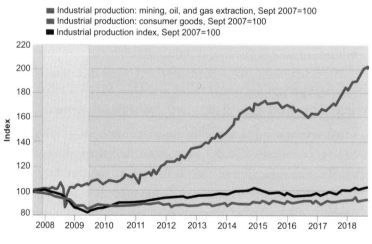

Industrial Production

■ Industrial production: mining, oil, and gas extraction, Sept 2007=100
■ Industrial production: consumer goods, Sept 2007=100
■ Industrial production index, Sept 2007=100

Source: Board of Governors of the Federal Reserve System (US)   *Shaded areas indicate U.S. recessions*

indeed take a small village of central bankers to make it inflate, instead. There is no mystery, therefore, as to why Keynesians and interventionists are rabidly and irrationally anti-deflationists.

Needless to say, the purple line in the graph above is the fetid fruit of that misguided central banks intervention in behalf of 2.00% inflation: Namely, a whole vast swath of the US manufacturing economy that has remained dead in the water for more than a decade.

It wasn't always that way. During the 1981-1990 cycle, for example, real output of consumers goods advanced at a 2.5% annual rate and it rose by 2.2% per annum during the 1990s cycle through February 2001.

Even the Greenspan mortgage/housing bubble was accompanied by a modicum of growth, with consumer goods production growing at about 1.0 per annum. Since the pre-crisis peak in Q4 2007, however, production has declined by what amounts to 0.5% per year.

There is a certain breed of free market economist, of course, who insists there is nothing to see here. The fact that oil and gas production grew at a 7.0% per year, while consumer goods output has shrunk at a 0.5% rate for the past 11 years is purportedly just the market's allocative efficiency at work.

No it isn't. Not when the capital markets have been falsified and domestic prices and costs have been artificially inflated by the central bank.

Stated differently, there is no more dangerous combination than the witches brew of free money pouring into free markets. And, of course, the Donald wants even more of the former.

The above chart, of course, is only a dramatic instance of allocative destruction caused by monetary central planning. Yet the geniuses who are now taking bows for allegedly saving the main street economy don't even look at the data which screams out the very opposite.

To wit, the gross output of the US economy has grown by

115

just *2.6%* per annum since the pre-crisis peak in Q2 2008. That is absolutely nothing to write home about — since the Fed's own sawed-off ruler for inflation — the PCE deflator — rose by about 1.4% per annum during the past 10 years.

But that's the "strong" part of the story. The real smoking gun is that manufacturing output by Uncle Sam's own carefully messaged data has grown by just *0.81%* per annum since Q4 2007.

That's right. Gross output of all manufacturing industries in the US was $5.7 trillion in mid-2008 and just $6.2 trillion 10 years later in Q2 2018. And these figures are in nominal dollars!

In true inflation-adjusted terms, the thin red bars at the bottom of the chart would be sloping steadily downward.

So has the victory lap brigade at the Eccles Building ever looked at this chart? Did it not ever occur to them that this data from hundreds of thousands of tax-paying US manufacturers is 25X more important (at least!) than the ragged BLS jobs counts about which they endlessly gum?

It surely has not. Instead, if they look at manufacturing data at all it is merely short-term dips and rips, which can be construed as "temporary" if it's a dip and "strong" if it's a rip.

In fact, most of the time, it's not either. The major cause of the short-term undulations within the punk trends shown below have been almost entirely a function of global commodity/industrial/trade sub-cycles.

Yet the latter is overwhelming driven by the starts and fits of the rulers in Beijing who are desperately trying to keep alive the greatest credit-fueled economic Ponzi in recorded history.

These Beijing machinations materialize first as massive credit surges, which ratchet-up global commodity production and prices, manufacturing output and trade volume; and then get sharply curtailed, causing contractionary waves to propagate through the world economy in the opposite direction.

In the present instance, and now that the coronation of Mr.

Xi was accomplished at the October 2017 Party Congress, the Red Suzerains have again cooled down the PBOC's printing presses; and have also administratively garroted credit expansion, especially in China's incredibly bloated and incendiary $20 trillion shadow banking system.

Then again, have the Fed heads ever noted in their post-meeting drivel that the thrashing about of the Red Ponzi is the primary force driving the short-run undulations of the world economy?

And that in attempting to tame its *$40 trillion* credit monster, Beijing has again materially slowed global growth, as is starkly evident in plunging industrial production in South Korea and cooling exports in Germany.

Needless to say, the Fed views the US economy through the faulty lens' of their Keynesian beer-goggles. They have dumbed down their monitoring board to the GDP accounts, which are highly unreliable, backward-looking Keynesian constructs; and the BLS data, which is so primitive and faulty that it could be eliminated completely and no one in the real capitalist economy would know the difference or care.

Gross Output

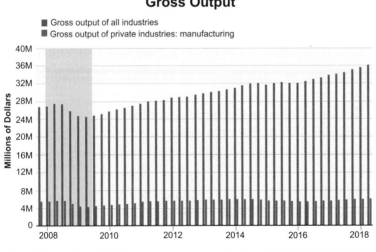

■ Gross output of all industries
■ Gross output of private industries: manufacturing

Source: U.S. Bureau of Economic Analysis   *Shaded areas indicate U.S. recessions*

Meanwhile, the fact that the gross output of the American economy has been in creeper-gear for the entire past decade seems to have escaped their attention entirely.

So does an even more fatal point: As we show elsewhere in this book, domestic inflation and employment are heavily driven by the tectonic forces coursing through the global economy. Yet the primitive tools available to the Fed no longer even reach beyond the canyons of Wall Street — to say nothing of the $20 trillion economy of main street USA or the $80 trillion economy of the planet.

The Shocking Plunge In The Growth Rate Of Labor Hours

Not surprisingly, the same central banking bias in favor of goods, services and asset price inflation that has crushed industrial growth has also resulted in a sharp reduction in the growth rate of total labor hours employed.

As shown in the right panel of the chart below, total labor hours increased by just 7.9% during the 11 years since the pre-crisis peak in September 2007. And even those additional 18.6 billion hours, as further detailed below, are heavily weighted to the low-pay, part-time economy in leisure, hospitality, retail, temp agency and other personal services.

Needless to say, on a 11-year peak-to-peak basis that is nothing short of punk. It amounts to a labor input gain to the US economy of just 0.7% per annum.

By way of comparison, during the nine-year peak-to-peak cycle between 1981 and 1990, labor hours employed grew at 2.0% per annum and during 1990-2001 the gain was 1.8% per year.

But after the turn of the century, when heavy money pumping by the Fed became the norm, the labor growth rate has taken a step change lower to just 0.64% per year; and that sharp deceleration is not due to the demographics of aging, either, as the Fed's apologists continually insist.

Wage and Salary Worker Hours

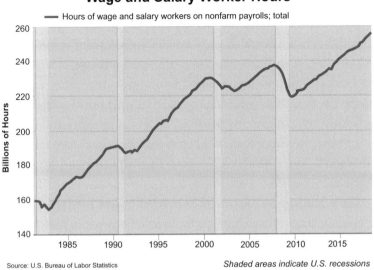

Source: U.S. Bureau of Labor Statistics

Shaded areas indicate U.S. recessions

As we saw in chapter 2, the population age 20-69 currently represents 425 billion potential labor hours. So at the comprehensive unemployment rate of 34.6% which prevailed in the year 2000, 282 billion labor hours would currently be employed, representing a growth rate of 1.2% per annum during the last 18 years.

In short, something has cut the labor growth rate in half compared to the labor hours utilization rate which prevailed at the the turn of the century. Stated differently, there are 26 billion labor hours that have gone missing, representing potentially $830 billion in foregone wage and salary income at current average rates of compensation.

Needless to say, we do not think the culprits are the 20-something Chinese girls working in Foxconn factories, who purportedly "save" too much per the Bernanke "savings glut" thesis; or Mexican workers building Ford cars at its vast state of the art auto complex in Hermosillo, as implied by the Donald's phony NAFTA "reform" that actually amounted to nothing more than a requirement to raise Mexico's auto wages to $16 per hour.

To the contrary, the culprit is domiciled only a few blocks from the White House. If the Donald really wanted to make MAGA, he would have had a top-to-bottom house-cleaning in the Eccles Building months ago.

So the fact that he has charged off in the opposite direction — noisily attacking even the timid efforts of its current incumbents to crawl back to a semblance of monetary sanity — tells you all you need to know about the dead end of Trump-O-Nomics.

As it has happened, the labor market failure fostered by Keynesian central banking is actually even more severe than implicated in the aggregate numbers above. What has actually occurred is that the quality mix of labor hours employed has also gone to hell in a hand basket.

To wit, since the peak in Q3 2007, labor hours employed in

Hours of Wage and Salary Workers

— Hours of wage and salary workers on nonfarm payrolls: leisure and hospitality, Q3 2007=100
— Hours of wage and salary workers on nonfarm payrolls: education and health services, Q3 2007=100
— Hours of wage and salary workers on nonfarm payrolls: government, Q3 2007=100
— Hours of wage and salary workers on nonfarm payrolls: manufacturing, Q3 2007=100
— Hours of wage and salary workers on nonfarm payrolls: construction, Q3 2007=100

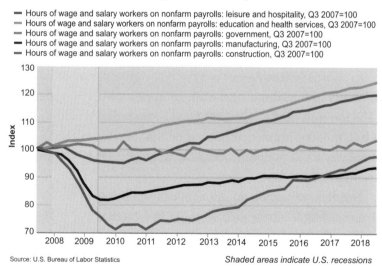

Source: U.S. Bureau of Labor Statistics   *Shaded areas indicate U.S. recessions*

manufacturing have declined by 6.2% (dark green line) while the construction sector declined by 2.4% (purple line) and mining and energy hours (not shown) have been essentially flat.

In round terms, there were 44.6 billion labor hours employed in these high productivity, high pay sectors on the eve (Q4 2007) of the financial crisis. Yet notwithstanding all the brouhaha about the strongest labor market ever, total hours employed in these core sectors have actually shrunk to just 42.7 billion hours as of September 2018.

By contrast, the number of hours employed in government, leisure and hospitality (bars, restaurants, motels and Disneyland) and health and education have increased by 2.5%, 20.0% and 24.5%, respectively. In the aggregate, these three sectors employed 88.4 billion hours in Q3 2007 at annualized rates, which figure had grown to 100.9 billion hours by Q3 2018.

But here's the thing. The current $1.2 trillion per year wage bill for the 44.6 billion hours in manufacturing, construction, energy and mining (the "goods" sector) generates for more productivity and economic value added than does the $2.7 trillion per year wage bill for 100.6 billion labor hours employed by government, leisure and hospitality and education and health services.

Nevertheless, the 12.3 billion labor hours gained since Q3 2007 in these low productivity sectors accounts for fully 63% of the total 19.5 billion labor hour increase during the last 11 years.

So there is a reason why average productivity has been deteriorating and the trend rate of economic growth has been bending toward the flatline.

And the culprit is not a failure of private capitalism: The monetary and fiscal interventions of the state, in fact, are what explains stark divergences in the chart below.

For example, consider the total HES Complex, which encompasses health, education and social service functions of the both government and private employers. The official BLS count for these sectors has grown by just under 8 million jobs or 32% since the turn of the century.

Accordingly, a sector which overwhelmingly depends upon the government fisc — $2.8 trillion of direct spending for health and education plus $200 billion per year in tax subsidies — accounts for fully 42% of the gain in the BLS employed headcount since January 2000.

Nevertheless, whether the government fisc is funded with current tax extractions — or future ones via deficit finance — there is an obvious circularity to this kind of "growth."

In fact, if governments funded the roughly $3 trillion per year of demand that they pump into the HES Complex with strictly current tax extractions, the crowding-out of production elsewhere in the economy would be far more severe and evident.

So when the HES Complex typically accounts for two-fifths or more of the headline gain on Jobs Friday, it is actually not good news at all, but another warning that that the main street economy is not all that healthy because it is growing by chewing its own tail.

HES Complex

Health, Education & Social Service. Fiscally Dependent. Growth Slowing Sharply. Pay rate=$35k/yr.

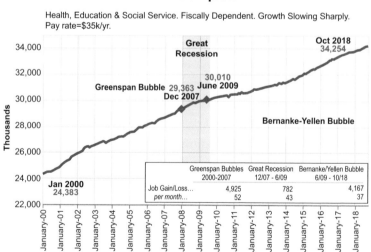

Breadwinner Economy — Flat As A Pancake Since 2000

That truth is readily evident in our measure of full time, full pay Breadwinner Economy. These are the highest productivity jobs in the US economy and in current dollars (2018) average $55,000 in annual wages.

As indicated in the chart, the 74.2 million jobs in this category reported for October 2018 include positions in manufacturing, construction, mining and energy, white collar professions, business management and support, transportation, wholesale trade and distribution, finance, insurance, real estate, communications and information technology. Altogether this cohort of workers accounts for about 49.6% of the 149.8 million nonfarm payroll jobs reported by the BLS that month.

The giant problem, however, is that the total nonfarm payroll reported by the BLS nearly 18 years ago at the January 2001 cycle peak (and the month Bill Clinton was packing his bags to shuffle out of the White House) was 132.7 million. This means that the average monthly job gain over the span was 85,000, which compares to the 194,000 per month gain in the working age population is not some kind of banner achievement.

But here's the real skunk in the woodpile. During that same period, the number of jobs in the Breadwinner Economy has risen by just 7,000 per month. That is, a pittance compared to overall job growth and a rounding error compared to the growth of the working-age population.

So if the monetary central planners domiciled in the Eccles Building wish to pat themselves on the back for achieving "full employment", as they do at every available opportunity, it amounts to about the closest thing we can think of to a self-indictment.

To be sure, they would undoubtedly counter that they Fed has no tools to generate good jobs, real work or high productivity — just job "slots" guestimated, massaged and modeled at the BLS.

But that is exactly the point. The Fed has manipulated, mangled, falsified and inflated the financial markets to a far-the-well — to the tune of printing $4.0 trillion of fraudulent credit since the turn of the century. But for what?

Apparently, in order to maximize a bureaucratically-defined labor statistic which is essentially meaningless, not within its power to control and has absolutely nothing to do with the actual economic growth and wealth of the nation's economy.

To be sure, not everything has flat-lined since the pre-crisis peak in the fall of 2007. For example, spending on education services is up by nearly 50% in the last decade.

Likewise, health care consumption is up from $1.4 trillion to $2.4 trillion or by 58%

Similarly, government social program transfer payments have grown at an even more robust pace, rising from $1.7 trillion per annum on the eve of the crisis to $2.9 trillion at present.

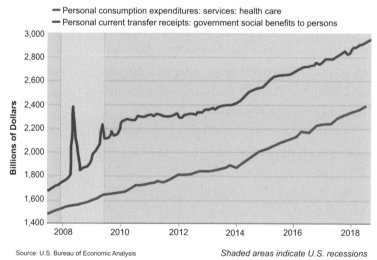

Personal Consumption

— Personal consumption expenditures: services: health care
— Personal current transfer receipts: government social benefits to persons

Source: U.S. Bureau of Economic Analysis   *Shaded areas indicate U.S. recessions*

That's a gain of 70%. There's that.

There is also the abject failure of our monetary central planners to even notice that the quality of the GDP they claim to be deftly shepherding has been falling steadily for most of this century. Compared to the disastrous implications of the chart below, the forgettable short-term squiggles in the post-meeting economic weather reports they spend hours crafting aren't even worth the paper they are printed on.

When an economy is stumbling forward at the slowest aggregate rate in modern times, and when even the growth within that envelope is dominated by health care, education and government transfer payments, you have a profound failure of state policy. That's not what free market capitalism does when left to its own devices.

The chart below is the smoking gun. It uses a 10-year moving average of real GDP growth to remove the short-run squiggles and the longer business cycles. And after one-decade of the most massive combined monetary and fiscal stimulus in US history, the real growth rate at 1.5% per annum is lower than its ever been, even during the 1930s.

Indeed, did Bernanke's unctuous claim that he had the

10-Year Average Real GDP Growth

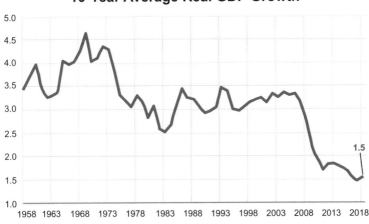

courage to print have anything at all to do with more spending on education, health care and social services?

Obviously not. What the Fed has fostered instead is a fabulous financial bubble for the top 1% and 10% of households which hold most of the financial assets. As for main street America — it was flat-lining, at best.

Real Median Household Income — Flatlining For More Than Two Decades

At the end of the day, the entire Fake Recovery ballyhooed by the Fed and Wall Street is ratted-out by the statistics on real median household income. The have gone nowhere for the entirety of this century, and that is indictment enough when it comes to the profound failure of the American economy thus far in the 21st century.

Once again, however, the recency bias on both ends of the Acela Corridor does its best to obfuscate the profound failure of economic performance implicated in the graph below. If you pick the right months for comparison, and the right point in the short-run inflation cycle, you can make flat look like up.

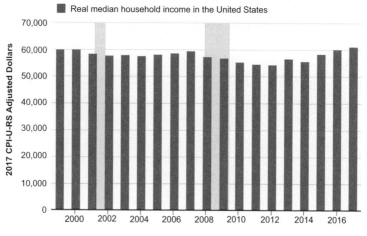

Stagnant Real Median Household Income

Sources: U.S. Bureau of the Census   *Shaded areas indicate U.S. recessions*

But it was not that many decades ago that up was actually up. For example, in 1953 real median family income in 2017 dollars of purchasing power was $34,180. Exactly 17 years later — the same span as the chart above — that figure had risen to $55,750.

So the gain amounted to nearly 3.0% per year for nearly two decades.

That was what "up" once looked like. That's what happened when Flyover America was prosperous. And that's how American capitalism rolled before it became a ward of the fiscal and monetary branches of the state.

On the contrary, the chart below is what's happening now. It explains how the Fed wrecked Flyover America and brought Donald J. Trump to the White House.

If there be any doubt that the Greenspan-launched era of Keynesian monetary central planning has been a complete disaster for main street America, the chart below should remove all doubt.

It focuses on median real net worth of America's households, thereby removing the average net worth number

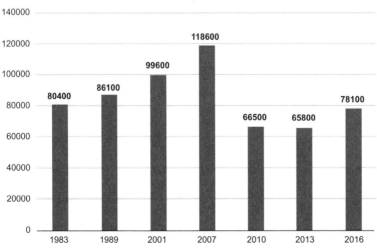

Median Wealth, 2016 Dollars

that is radically biased upward owing to the monumental financial wealth that has accrued to the top 1% and the top 0.1%.

In the year 1989, shortly after Greenspan had bailed out Wall Street after the thundering meltdown of October 1987, the real median net worth of American households was $86,100.

After 27 years of massive money pumping at the Fed — which had expanded its balance sheet from $200 billion to $4.5 trillion or by 22.5X — real median household net worth was $78,100.

That's even less than flat. But that's why they are coming, figuratively, with torches and pitchforks to join the Donald's attack on the status quo, and why the ruling elites deserve every bit of the populist onslaught which is coming their way.

CHAPTER 5

Inside The Canyons Of Wall Street: The Everything Bubble

During the 40 months after Alan Greenspan's infamous "irrational exuberance" speech in December 1996, the NASDAQ 100 index rose from 830 to 4585 or by 450%. But the perma-bulls said not to worry: This time is different — it's a new age of technology miracles that will change the laws of finance forever.

It wasn't. The market cracked in late March, plunging by a heart-stopping 32% in just 15 trading days, and then did not stop cliff-diving until the NASDAQ 100 index hit 815 in early October 2002.

During those 30 months of free-fall, all the gains of the tech boom were wiped out in an 84% collapse of the index. Overall, the market value of household equities sank from $10.0 trillion to $4.8 trillion — a wipeout from which millions of baby boom households have never recovered.

Likewise, the second Greenspan housing and credit boom generated a similar round trip of bubble inflation and collapse. During the 57 months after the October 2002 bottom, the Russell 2000 (RUT) climbed the proverbial wall-of-worry — rising from 340 to 850 or by 2.5X.

And that time was also held to be different because, purportedly, the art of central banking had been perfected in what Bernanke was pleased to call the "Great Moderation."

Taking the cue, Wall Street dubbed it the Goldilocks Economy; it was allegedly a macroeconomic environment so stable, productive and balanced that it would never again be vulnerable to a recessionary contraction and the resulting plunge in corporate profits and stock prices.

Wrong again!

During the 20 months from the July 2007 peak to the March 2009 bottom, the RUT gave back 100% of its gains. And we mean every bit of it — as the index bottomed 60% lower at 340.

This time the value of household equities plunged by $6 trillion, and still millions more baby-boomers were carried out of the casino on their shields never to return.

When Monetary Stimulus Got Trapped In The Canyons Of Wall Street — The Everything Bubble

Now has come the greatest central bank fueled speculative mania ever — the Everything Bubble.

This time even more than in the dotcom and subprime bubbles, the Fed's massive stimulus never left the canyons of Wall Street because as is explained in Part 2, the household sector had already reached Peak Debt in 2007; and because the C-suites of Corporate America had come to realize that cheap debt could do more for the value of their stock options when plowed back into Wall Street to fund stock buybacks, M&A deals and fattened dividends than if invested in productive capital on main street.

So in essence the $3.6 trillion of monetary firepower the Fed injected into the hands of Wall Street dealers — as it expanded its balance sheet from $900 billion on the eve of the Lehman meltdown to $4.5 trillion at the QE peak in 2014 — caused a massive inflation inside the Wall Street vertical.

That is, it drove stock and bond prices ever higher in a nearly parabolic ascent, thereby decoupling financial asset prices from any rational income and risk-based anchor to the real economy. In turn, soaring stock prices encouraged the C-suites to strip-mine their balance sheets and cash flows even more intensively in order to recycle even more cash back into the casino, which only added to the "bid" and boosted prices still higher.

By any reasonable meaning of the term, therefore, the radical QE and ZIRP experiments of the Fed unleashed a vicious inflation of financial asset prices, causing the equities owned by US households to explode still higher — this time by $12.5 trillion.

Self-evidently, this eruption, like the prior two, was not a reflection of main street growth. The relentless flat-lining of the main street economy described in chapter 4 powerfully attests to the contrary.

Instead, the rampant Wall Street speculation fostered by the Fed's huge liquidity injections and price-keeping operations (i. e. the Greenspan/Bernanke/Yellen "put") have essentially inflated a massive financial time-bomb that is fixing to implode.

Needless to say, that will touch off another panicked round of asset and worker dumping in the C-suites. The latter, in turn will trigger what will be the third consecutive recession of this century which the Fed heads and Wall Street speculators alike did not remotely see coming .

Alas, neither does the Donald. After correctly labeling this financial monstrosity as "one, big, fat ugly bubble" during the 2016 campaign, he threw caution to the wind with days of occupying the Oval Office. Indeed, he even strapped-on the Fed's financial bomb vest with the alacrity of a young jihadist anticipating 72 virgins in the paradise to follow.

The Donald's not heading for any paradise, however, not in this world nor likely the next. By embracing the Everything Bubble without reservation — and given the fact that the entire Acela Corridor establishment and MSM media nexus has come to loath him with a purple passion — the Donald has effectively signed his own political death warrant.

That is to say, when the Bubble splatters they will come after him with guns blaring and malice aforethought; and when 401Ks are again emptied out, no amount of demogoguing about "invasions" from south of the border will fill the Red State stadiums with cheering throngs.

Moreover, no matter how strident that Donald becomes in his attacks and blame-shifting to the Fed, it will be to no avail — except to further batter confidence in what will be fearful pandemonium in the casino.

That's because this time is very different, and the fact of it will be impossible to hide once the bubbles implode.

Booming Wall Street, Stagnant Main Street

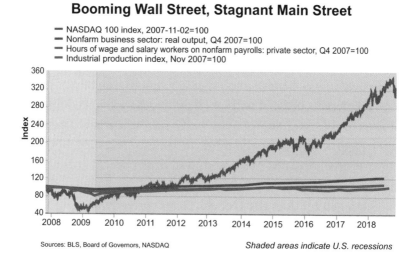

- NASDAQ 100 index, 2007-11-02=100
- Nonfarm business sector: real output, Q4 2007=100
- Hours of wage and salary workers on nonfarm payrolls: private sector, Q4 2007=100
- Industrial production index, Nov 2007=100

Sources: BLS, Board of Governors, NASDAQ   *Shaded areas indicate U.S. recessions*

What's Very Different This Time?
Central Banks Out Of Dry Powder

The Fed and other central banks are out of dry powder and are way behind the curve. They will therefore be in no position to effect a rapid V-shaped reflation of the financial markets like they did in 2009-2010. What lies ahead for Wall Street, instead, is a long painful sojourn along an L-shaped bottom — one that will last for years, not months.

By contrast, it needs be recalled that during the Greenspan housing bubble driven expansion, at least the Fed had gone about its tightening work with methodical diligence. It raised the Federal funds rate at every meeting between June 2004 and the spring of 2006 until it had gotten it up from 1.0% to 5.25%, and still had upwards of a two-year window before the Greenspan housing bubble finally burst.

Not this time. Thanks to Bernanke's sophistry and Yellen's timidity, this time the Fed heads have stranded themselves on what amounts to the true zero bound — their target rate is still barely above inflation — and they are humping a massively bloated balance sheet that they now desperately wish to shed.

We are quite certain, of course, that the Donald gets not a whit of this and that as the Everything Bubble he has so exuberantly embraced causes his political fortunes to circle toward the drain, he will attack the Fed with a reckless vengeance that is even now utterly unappreciated in the casino.

Indeed, a White House which claims it can modify the Fourteenth Amendment to the constitution (concerning citizenship of the native born) by executive order is likely to come up with an institutional assault on the Fed which will make FDR's 1937 Supreme Court packing ploy look like a Sunday school picnic.

In any event, the nearly vertical orange line in the upper-right of the chart is heading for a deep plunge, and the Donald's trashing and the Fed's thrashing about in its self-imposed trap will only make it all the more traumatic and long-lasting.

When The Wall Street Bull Turned Out To Be A Body Double.

The truth of the matter is that there was no basis whatsoever for the bullish recovery — let alone the record run — after the 2008 Wall Street meltdown. That's because the main street economy by then had been freighted down with excessive

Households and Nonprofit Organizations

— Households and nonprofit organizations; corporate equities; asset

Source: Board of Governors of the Federal Reserve System (US)   *Shaded areas indicate U.S. recessions*

household and business debts, and a Fed driven inflation of domestic prices, wages and costs that insured a continued, accelerated off-shoring of big swaths of the American economy — including the massive shift of back office and technology services in response to the India Price.

Indeed, the Bernanke-Yellen Bull was such a blatant imposter that it puts you in mind of the recent attempted Saudi cover-up of their brutal and heinous assassination of Jamal Khashoggi.

It seems that MBS not only sent to Istanbul 15 elite members of the Royal Guard (MBS' body guards which report directly to him) special forces, top intelligence officers and Royal Air Force personal, but among them was Dr. Bonesaw and Mr. Body Double, too.

That's right. The latter was garbed in the still warm jacket, shirt, shoes and trousers of the late Mr. Khashoggi — coming out the back door of the consulate just like they said. And compared to his picture going in, Mr. Body Double (aka Mustafa al-Madani) appears to have grown an instant beard, too.

Yet is this phony body double gambit any different than the

purported bull market which came roaring out of the financial slaughter-house after the March 9, 2009 bottom?

Perhaps the bull was actually dead all along, as should have been the case; and what has been pawing and snorting down in the casino is just a Fed confected simulacrum — the financial equivalent of a body double that has been injected with so many monetary steroids that it kicks, snorts and bucks like the real thing.

One rather powerful suggestion to that end lies in the 75:1 ratio of Wall Street to main street performance.

To wit, the NASDAQ 100 was recently up nearly 200% in inflation-adjusted terms since the pre-crisis peak in 2007. This rocket-like ascent compares, well, preposterously to the mere 3% gain in industrial production over the same 11 year period which we documented in chapter 4.

And we are talking apples-to-apples here: Constant dollar stock prices versus real physical output; and also from the prior peak, not the March 2009 stock market bottom.

So either the NASDAQ 100 had been savagely repressed at the peak of the housing bubble in November 2007 or the 75:1

Jamal Khashoggi caught on security camera entering the Saudi embassy in Istanbul; a "body double" Mustafa al-Madani is seen leaving in Khashoggi's clothes.

ratio of Wall Street versus main street gain in the interim makes no sense whatsoever.

We will go with the bull market body double narrative.

In fact, at the pre-crisis peak in 2007 the stock market was already suspended in the nosebleed section of history. As shown in the chart below, prior to the Greenspan era of money-pumping, the US stock market capitalization amounted to about 40-50% of GDP, but had reached 144% by the dotcom peak in the spring of 2000; and had then regained that aberrational high again by late 2007.

So the question recurs: How has the stock market capitalization continued to soar even higher — to 160% of GDP at the recent high — when the main street economy has literally flat-lined since November 2007?

And as we documented above, we do mean flat line. The core measures of the real economy show that main street has been on a round-trip to essentially nowhere during the past 11 years, including a mere 8% gain in total hours worked, flat real net investment spending and median household income and negative net change in single family housing and manufacturing.

In sum, there was precious little reason for stock market capitalization to be above 140% of GDP in late 2007 at the end of the housing/subprime bubble, and no reason whatsoever for the even further gain to nearly 160% at the recent market highs.

Financialization — The Fed Fruit Of Rampant Money-Pumping

What we are saying is that the effect of Greenspanian central banking has been to financialize the economy and drive a giant, unsustainable wedge between values on Wall Street and economic performance on main street. That has been going on for nearly 30 years now, and with each Fed-driven bubble cycle the de-coupling of Finance and Economy has become ever more tenuous.

Record Stock Market Capitalization Versus GDP

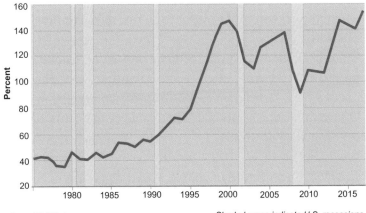

— Stock market capitalization to GDP for United States

Source: World Bank   *Shaded areas indicate U.S. recessions*

In that sense, yes, the real Bull Market was dead long ago. And it is only a matter of time before the Fed-confected and disguised Body Double meets the same fate as Mr. Mustafa al-Madani. That is to say, it gets exposed for the nasty Fake it actually is.

As shown in the chart below, household net worth (purple line) has grown by the staggering sum of $102 trillion since

Household Assets Versus GDP, 1987-2017

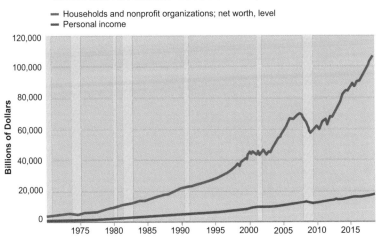

— Households and nonprofit organizations; net worth, level
— Personal income

Source: BEA, Board of Governors   *Shaded areas indicate U.S. recessions*

Greenspan discovered the printing press in the basement of the
Eccles Building in the fall of 1987 amidst the Black Monday
meltdown (6,000 current Dow points in one day). And that is
trillions with a "T."

By contrast, nominal GDP is up by only $15.5 trillion
during the same 31 year period — meaning that asset values
have grown 6.5X faster than economic production.

Do we think this is rational, sustainable or indicative of free
market capitalism at work?

We do not!

The Wall Street retort, of course, is that regardless of the
evident grind on main street, corporate profits are soaring and
that explains the sky-high stock averages and rising net worth.

Except, it doesn't.

The key variable in the chart below is corporate profits
before tax (blue line) because its reflects an apple-to-apples tax
rate, and therefore captures organic growth, not the one-time
boost from the 21% rate now in effect.

What it shows, of course, is that there has been no growth

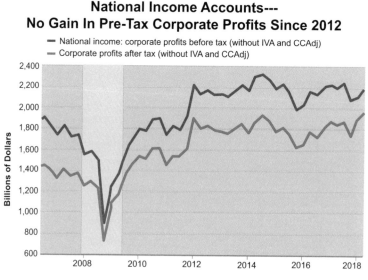

National Income Accounts---
No Gain In Pre-Tax Corporate Profits Since 2012

— National income: corporate profits before tax (without IVA and CCAdj)
— Corporate profits after tax (without IVA and CCAdj)

Source: U.S. Bureau of Economic Analysis   *Shaded areas indicate U.S. recessions*

in pre-tax corporate profits to speak of since the 2006 peak at $1.9 trillion per year for the entire business sector (i. e. corporate and noncorporate). At $2.2 trillion *in* the most recent annualized measure, the growth rate over the past 12 years has been a paltry ***1.23%*** per annum.

This is not "booming" in any known universe. In fact, when you squeeze out the inflation there has been hardly any growth at all in real terms.

The profit "growth" boom is really just typical Wall Street snake oil. It counts as "growth" the one-time tax cut, which will anniversary out of the numbers by Q1 2019, and ignores the deep plunge that earnings took after 2014.

What Profits Boom? More Wall Street Snake Oil

During the LTM period ending in September 2014, the S&P 500's reported earnings (i. e. GAAP or the kind CEOs and CFOs certify to the SEC on penalty of jail time) were $106 per share. By contrast, reported LTM earnings for September 2018 were about $130 per share, which equates to $124 on a tax rate basis comparable to the level which pertained four years ago.

So the organic growth rate during the last four years — and at the top of the business cycle, which can only go down from here — was just ***3.8%*** per annum!

What the sell-side stock peddlers never mention, of course, is the dips in-between when they are happening. Thus, between September 2014 and March 2016, the S&P 500's reported LTM earnings plunged by 18.5% to just $86 per share.

That is to say, most of the "gangbusters" earnings gains of recent quarters were just a recovery from the dip. That is, born-again profits plus the aforementioned one-time tax reduction courtesy of Uncle Sam's credit card.

The litmus test, again, is the growth rate over the cycle. And back in Q2 2007 at the pre-crisis peak, S&P 500 reported earnings posted at $85 per share on an LTM basis.

So during the past 11 years, the peak-to-peak growth rate (CAGR) has been just 3.4% per annum; and when you vacate the inflation from the CAGR, it computes to less than 2% per year.

Nevertheless, PE multiples now levitate at top-of-the-world highs. At the late September highs, the Russell 2000 was valued at 51X reported earnings, while the NASDAQ 100 and S&P 500 were valued at 25X and 23X reported earnings, respectively.

Yet why would you want to pay 23X-50X for earnings growth at a trend growth rate of just 3.4% per annum, and at the octogenarian phase of the business cycle to boot?

That is to say, all PE multiples are not created equal, notwithstanding the fact that the talking heads of bubblevision never even remotely acknowledge that crucial point. But obviously, a high PE multiple appropriate to an environment with strong tailwinds and which is posted during the second year of a business recovery is not relevant at all to year #11 of an aging expansion when gale force headwinds are everywhere evident.

In this regard, we are absolutely confident that recessions have not been outlawed and that one is due in the next year or two. Accordingly, GAAP earnings are likely to hit $70 per share at the next recession bottom long before they hit $170 per share as projected by the current two-year forward Wall Street hockey sticks.

Fed Fostered Crash Ahead — And This Time A Doozy

Needless to say, with respect to the financial crash ahead, the Fed's monetary politburo has ordered up a doozy.

As we have indicated, it is now plowing full speed ahead with QT (quantitative tightening) at a $600 billion annual rate, dumping more bonds into the trading pits than the entire size of its balance sheet as recently as July 2001. And it is aggressively dumping these massive quantities of existing government paper at the same time that the US Treasury will be borrowing $1.2

trillion this year to fund the official deficit plus all of the off-budget loopholes.

Moreover, these Keynesian monetary central planners are steaming ahead into this bubble-killing QT pivot in a kind of victory lap mode. They are wearing their "mission accomplished" bomber jackets and mistakenly think they have brought the nirvana of Full Employment to a US economy, which is purportedly stronger than an ox.

So they are hell bent on reloading their dry powder to be in position to bailout the next economic downturn; and to thereby retain their institutional mandate to function as the unelected overlords of the US financial system and economy.

We are referring to the Fed's implicit political contract which gives them unfettered power to peg, manipulate and falsify virtually every price in the financial markets — the very signaling system that is the lifeblood of free market capitalism. Yet they get all of that power merely for appearing to function as the nation's economic savior in the face of recessions and financial crises — disruptions which occur after their own handiwork sends serial bubbles crashing and the main street economy careening into the ditch .

In fact, it is becoming more evident by the day that the ECB will shut down its QE printing press in December; that the People's Bank of China will have no choice except to dump dollar reserves and buy yuan to stem capital flight and parry the Donald's insane no holds barred Trade War; and that even Japan is being forced to taper its massive QE policy owing to the crushing effect on banks and savers of its massive bond-buying spree at essentially zero long-term yields.

Furthermore, even if the Keynesian posse domiciled in the Eccles Building should wish to get cold feet in the implementation of the their interest rate normalization and QT campaign, the Donald is simultaneously pounding them from their flanks — forcing up the inflation rate and thereby diminishing their room to chicken out on their tightening campaign.

That is, we think there is an overwhelming probability that his threat to impose a 25% tariffs on all $517 billion of Chinese imports will materialize after the current desultory negotiations fail by early March 2019.

Yet as we demonstrate in Part 2, the half trillion dollars per year of Chinese imports constitutes the the price-setting marginal supply to the US economy: They account for an average of 30% (with a range of 10% to 80%) of the goods sold in America in the categories in which China competes.

So what is coming down the pike is a large pick-up in inflation on $1.7 trillion of US consumption goods where Chinese-imports are concentrated; and that's 40% of all goods consumed annually by the US economy ($4.2 trillion per annum).

If even half of the 25% tariff umbrella on this massive supply of goods is passed through to wholesalers and retail consumers, it would amount to a $200 billion per year inflationary shock.

In short, the Fed painted itself in a corner with eight straight years of negative real interest rates and massive monetization of the debt. Now the Donald's Trade War and the GOPs descent into abject Fiscal Profligacy leaves the Fed with no choice except to keep on normalizing rates and shrinking it balance sheet until the greatest Everything Bubble of all time finally splatters.

That the resulting economic downdraft will be considerable is underscored by a final piece of the Fed's immense distortion of Finance versus Economy.

The Everything Bubble — $107 Trillion Of Vastly Inflated Household Net Worth

In the context of a main street economy that is struggling to escape the flat-line relative the 11-years ago pre-crisis peak, the marked-to-market net worth of the household sector has literally shot the moon, reaching $107 trillion during Q2 2018.

That's up by an astonishing $38 trillion from the pre-crisis peak in Q3 2007 and nearly $50 trillion from the bottom in Q1 2009.

Who would have thunk it?

Apparently, when household net worth bottomed at $57 trillion during the dark days of March 2009, the whole Armegeddon-like Great Financial Crisis was just some sort of national fire drill, not the real thing. It had to be because in a flatlining economy you do not double household net worth in a mere 115 months.

Then again, when the central bank brings a massive $3.5 trillion barrage of fraudulent bond-buying (i. e. paid for with fiat credits snatched from thin air) to bear on financial asset prices in the canyons of Wall Street that's exactly what did happen; and that's also exactly why the post-crash carnage this time will clobber the top of the income ladder with malice aforethought.

Last time, as we showed in chapter 1, the bubble was fueled by mortgage debt and a multi-trillion MEW spree as middle and upper income homeowners hocked their castles for cash-out money. And a goodly portion of that MEW brigade have been living under severe financial stringencies — if not hand to mouth — ever since.

By contrast, the spending bubble this time has been concentrated in the higher reaches of the tree tops where ownership of stocks, investment real estate, unincorporated businesses and proprietorship are concentrated. In the case of equities, fully 40% are owned by the top 1% of households and 84% are owned by the top one-tenth of households.

Needless to say, when the Russell 2000 went from 350 in early of March 2009 to the recent peak of 1740, the animal spirits of the wealthy were unleashed like never before. And that's exactly why the most robust part of the retail spending revival has been for aspirational brands, luxury goods, high-end travel and entertainments, expensive homes improvement projects etc.

So when the stock indices crater for the third time this century, it will be Tiffany's and BMW that take it on the chin.

Indeed, the disconnects between Economy and Finance embedded in the net worth numbers are so egregious that the full import can only be appreciated by way of comparison with the time before Bubble Finance.

Thus, during the 30 years of halcyon prosperity in America between Q2 1957 and Q2 1987, real GDP grew at a *3.54%* compound annual rate, while real household net worth rose at a nearly identical *3.42%* annualized rate.

The one tracked the other, of course, because during any sustained period of time, the real wealth of a society cannot grow any faster than the growth of production and income. Not surprisingly, therefore, household net worth weighed in at 4.8X personal income in 1957 and posted in exactly that zone at 4.6X on the eve of Alan Greenspan's arrival at the Fed.

But that's where the skunk in the woodpile comes in. In a word, the regime of Keynesian monetary central planning or Bubble Finance ushered in by the Maestro, and then aggravated by Bernanke and Yellen, caused the iron linkage between long-term growth of production and wealth to be temporarily suspended.

Consequently, household wealth — which soared from $18 trillion to $107 trillion between Q2 1987 and Q2 2018, as shown in the purple bars below, grew far faster than GDP. Accordingly, it now stands at an off-the-charts 6.1X personal income.

Stated differently, when Greenspan arrived at the Fed, the trailing 10-year real GDP growth rate was 3.4%, but as shown in chapter 4, it has fallen sharply during the last 30 years to just 1.5%.

What that means, of course, is that something is very rotten in Denmark. There is no logical or sustainable economic model in which income growth is cut in half — and to the lowest 10-year rate since 1870 — while the wealth capitalization rate of the household sector soars into the wild blue yonder compared to all prior history.

The irony is that for the most part the Donald's red state partisans have been pinned down below the slowly growing red

Household Assets Versus GDP

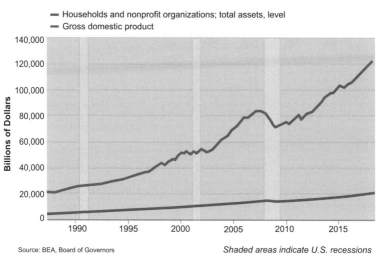

— Households and nonprofit organizations; total assets, level
— Gross domestic product

Source: BEA, Board of Governors   Shaded areas indicate U.S. recessions

line for GDP in the chart above. It is the blue county elites who have been aboard the purple line express to fabulous (paper) wealth.

Needless to say, the chart above suggests why these staggering gains in purported household wealth are not what they are cracked-up to be.

Why America Ain't Really That Rich

Real median household income during the past 30-years has crept higher at just a 0.4% annual rate compared to the 3.6% per annum inflation-adjusted rate of net worth. That means, in

Top 1% Own 40% of Stocks
Held by Households

Concentration of stock ownership by wealth class, 2016

turn, that real wealth, as reported by the Fed's flow-of-funds series, has grown nine times faster than real median household incomes in America.

To be sure, on the surface that reflects the reverse Robin Hood effect of Bubble Finance at work. The inflation of financial and real estate assets have overwhelming gone to the top 1% and 10% of households, as shown in the chart above.

But at the end of the day, that giant gap cannot be explained away by the notion that there has been a permanent redistribution of the wealth to the top of the economic ladder.

To the contrary, the truth of the matter is that the $107 trillion of household wealth reported for the most recent quarter is neither real nor sustainable; it's merely another flashing red warning sign that financial asset inflation has reached dangerous asymptotic heights.

For instance, if the household net worth-to-personal income ratio had remained at its pre-Greenspan level through the present, household net worth today would be just $80 trillion, implying that the Fed has generated at least $27 trillion of bottled air since 1987.

In fact, the overstatement of household net worth is far larger than even that figure. The burgeoning demographic/fiscal crisis in America will actually grind economic growth toward the zero bound during the decade of the 2020s as massive public sector borrowing forces bond yields dramatically higher.

And that will reveal the ugly underside of the recent flow-of-funds report. Namely, that the nation is now saddled with $70 trillion of public and private debt compared to $10.7 trillion when the era of Bubble Finance incepted back in October 1987.

In combination with 80 million retirees (by the end of the next decade), this debt albatross will smoother American capitalism in high taxes, high interest rates and battered balance sheets in both the household and business sectors. As that outcome unfolds, the current absurdly inflated stock market PE multiples will get monkey-hammered by the reality of stagnant growth and struggling profits.

That is to say, America ain't nearly so rich as the Fed's fantasy figures suggest.

What Our "Low Interest Man" In The Oval Office Doesn't Get

And that's a truth the bubble-hugging interloper in the Oval Office does not even remotely understand.

Nor does the Donald understand that attacking the Fed from the left is not going to keep the Bubble Finance party going because financial asset inflation and high domestic costs and wages are what ruined in the economy of Flyover America in the first place.

Still, America's "low interest man" was at it again in early October as the stock averages began to wobble, chiding the Fed for it's baby steps toward quasi-honest interest rates. Self-evidently, the Donald thinks the route to MAGA is via thoroughly crooked money rates — the kind that don't even cover the cost of inflation and which help developers and speculators pay back their debts in depreciated money.

We are referencing the chart below, which shows that for the past eight years running, the Federal funds rate (red bars) has been deeply underwater relative to CPI inflation (blue bars). Even with the Fed's latest 25 bps raise to *2.38%* in December, money market rates are still barely positive in real terms with the CPI running at **2.3%** on a year-over-year basis.

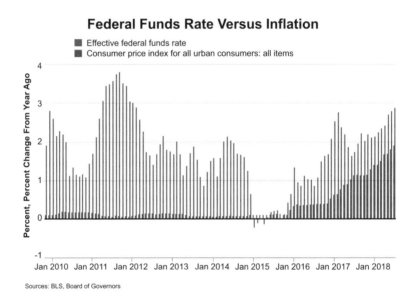

Federal Funds Rate Versus Inflation

■ Effective federal funds rate
■ Consumer price index for all urban consumers: all items

Sources: BLS, Board of Governors

To be sure, the Donald did not actually advocate negative real money market rates, nor did he endorse the resulting implicit subsidy to speculators. Instead, he just asserted that there is no inflation!

Well, I like to see low interest rates. The Fed is doing what they think is necessary, but I don't like what they're doing. Because we have inflation really checked, and we have a lot of good things happening.....I don't want to slow it down even a little bit, especially when you don't have the problem of inflation. And you don't see that inflation going back.

Well, we don't say the Donald lies; it's just that he doesn't

know what in the hell he is talking about much of the time.
The fact is, since November 2016, producer prices for finished goods are up by *6.1%* and the CPI is *4.1%* higher. Even for those ascetics in the US population who use neither food nor energy, their cost of living is up *3.6%*.

We'd call that inflation — and not especially all that benign. After all, average wages are up just *4.7%* (green line) since the Donald's election, meaning that paychecks have essentially been treading water.

Inflation Gain Since November 2016

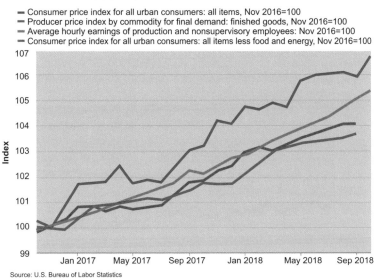

— Consumer price index for all urban consumers: all items, Nov 2016=100
— Producer price index by commodity for final demand: finished goods, Nov 2016=100
— Average hourly earnings of production and nonsupervisory employees: Nov 2016=100
— Consumer price index for all urban consumers: all items less food and energy, Nov 2016=100

Source: U.S. Bureau of Labor Statistics

When it comes to central banking, of course, it is not hard to see where the Donald is coming from. Unlike the PhDs and bankers at the Fed, the man from Trump Tower at least has some reason to be confused about the scourge of "low interest."

To wit, since 1995 the prices of New York City condos are up by *260%* compared to just *67%* for the CPI. And if you were the self-proclaimed King of Debt (or just another developer), the cost of real estate leverage would have plunged by nearly

70% over the same period, at least as measured by the yield on the benchmark 10-year UST (black line).

In other words, with standard leverage (80%) and sharply falling interest carry costs, you would have made *15X* your money riding the condo price index in barely two decades; and you might well be a convicted "low interest man", too.

The problem, of course, is that the massive asset inflation and financial repression fostered by the Fed is not sustainable; and the interim leveraged bubbles it generates do not constitute real wealth.

NYC Real Estate Speculator's Dream

— Condo price index for New York, New York, Jan 1995=100
— Consumer price index all urban consumers: all items, Jan 1995=100
— 10-year Treasury constant maturity rate, 1995-01-01=100

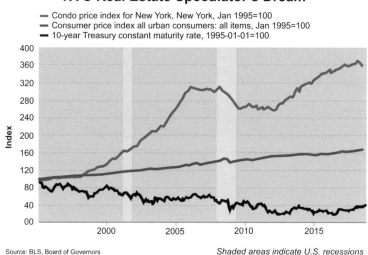

Source: BLS, Board of Governors   *Shaded areas indicate U.S. recessions*

The Evil Of Bubble Finance — Strip-mining Of Corporate Balance Sheets

Indeed, the real problem ailing America's main street economy is actually roaring inflation on Wall Street. That's because unhinged stock prices have lured the C-suites of corporate America into massive financial engineering campaigns, which have strip-mined corporate cash flows and balance sheets in order to pump a tsunami of cash — via stock buybacks, M&A deals and excess dividends — back into the canyons of Wall Street.

There they get recycled into even more speculative inflation of financial assets, which begets even more malinvestment and disgorgement of corporate assets back into the casino. We estimate this massive raid has pumped *$15 trillion* into Wall Street just since 2006.

This year alone, corporate financial engineering is heading for **$2.5 trillion** — in part goosed by Trump's giant corporate tax rate cut funded on Uncle Sam's credit card.

Moreover, the Wall Street and GOP cheerleaders, who claim that the resulting explosion of M&A deals and stock buybacks is all to the good because it represents the free market at work, couldn't be more deluded. The massive falsification of stock prices in the casino totally outweighs and overwhelms the so-called market for "corporate control"; and C-suite allocation of cash flows to financial engineering speculation does not represent the "highest and best uses" of company resources.

When the financial markets are overtaken by speculative mania and C-suites become stock trading rooms — as has been the case for years now — capitalism doesn't grow; it consumes its own financial lifeblood.

At the end of the day, of course, sustainable economic growth depends on strong net investment in the tools of production and productivity growth — plant, equipment and technology. That is to say, CapEx over and above the $2.2 trillion consumed in current production in the US economy annually, and to compensate for the effects of the Fed's foolish pursuit of 2.00% annual inflation or more.

Needless to say, that has not been happening. As we have seen, real net investment was $500 billion per year at the turn of the century, and has remained below that level — sometimes dramatically so — every year since, including 2017 when it came in at $494 billion in constant dollars.

The above two data points — $2.5 trillion of financial engineering in 2018 and just $494 billion in real net business investment — are worth well more than a year of Fed head gumming about the "incoming data", which allegedly guides their deliberations.

These two figures say that the entire system is broken — that the effect of massive central bank intrusion into the money and capital markets has been to hollow-out the main street economy in favor of rampant speculation and gambling in the casino.

R-Star — The Fed's Latest Idiotic Fetish

Yet the Fed heads don't get the big picture in the slightest. In fact, they have become ever more obsessed with the ethereal marginalia of a monetary priesthood that has completely lost touch with reality. We are referring to the so-called "r-star" (r*) or *neutral rate of interest*.

The fact is, there ain't no such thing. It's a completely unobservable, unknowable, subjective figment of central banker imaginations, which gives them an excuse to indefinitely peg interest rates at the artificially low levels that are responsible for the hollowing out of the main street economy described above.

Indeed, owing to the eight straight years of negative real money market rates displayed in the chart above, the US economy has been starved for honest price signals with respect to the carry-cost of speculation and the true economics of long-term debt and equity capital. It desperately needs free market pricing of interest rates and risk asset prices; and an opening for fear to come back into the financial markets to off-set the rampant greed and unhinged speculation that now prevails on Wall Street.

But what we get from the Fed is just gibberish about the neutral rate of interest — a convenient chimera that keeps the boys and girls and robo-machines of Wall Street hitting the "buy" key on the belief that the Fed is almost done tightening, and that an outbreak of honest pricing of money and debt is not remotely possible.

Just compare the meaningless blather quoted below from Dallas Fed president, and former Goldman partner, Robert Kaplan, with what happened in the money markets in the days of yore when capitalism boomed and there was no Fed to help it along at all.

During the famous panic of 1907, for example, the call money rate — which was the money market rate of the day and the price that speculators paid to carry stock on margin — would often fluctuate by 300 basis points in a single day. Call money rates, in fact, often reached 30% and even 60% when money got scarce because lenders feared markets were over-extended and that a sharp break in the stock averages was imminent.

In those supposedly antediluvian times — which were actually far more enlightened than today — interest rates did god's work of quelling speculation and fostering disciplined two-way trading for one overwhelming reason: To wit, the call money lenders were putting their own capital in harm's way, and accordingly demanded a price — even if 30-60% at moments of extreme financial stress — that compensated for the perceived risks.

Needless to say, when J.P. Morgan organized his syndicate of lenders in his Madison Avenue library that famously ended the panic of October 1907, his men did not spend long nights debating the existence and level of r*.

Instead, they put on their green eyeshades and burned the midnight oil until the wee hours parsing through balance sheets and financial statements to determine which supplicants for scarce money could be salvaged and which ones needed to be relegated to the bankruptcy courts come the break of day.

As it happened, over-extended copper barons, real estate speculators, insolvent railroaders, high-flying trust bankers and many more like and similar speculators were carried out on their shields. Indeed, J.P. Morgan's men were merciless in shooting the wounded, but not because they were misanthropic; it was because unlike the Fed of today, they had their own capital on the line.

But here's the thing. After the financial rot had been purged and capital and money began to again flow into the real economy, American capitalism was soon booming like never before. Two years latter the US economy was expanding at 4-5% rates and didn't falter until it was stopped by the folly of the Great War in the summer of 1914.

As fate would have it, the Fed opened its doors for business a few months later, but even then it had no authority to buy a single bill or bond from Uncle Sam; or to fiddle with any interest rate or financial asset price on Wall Street; or to target any main street variable like inflation levels, unemployment, real GDP, housing starts or anything else.

The original Fed, as designed by the great Carter Glass, was a decentralized "bankers' bank" that could only lend against sound and liquid business collateral called real bills — such as finished inventories and receivables — and only then at a penalty spread above market rates of interest. It did not manage, peg or distort financial markets, only liquefied them during periods of seasonal or cyclical stress.

Only when Woodrow Wilson foolishly plunged America into Europe's war in April 1917, did the Fed become the financing arm of the state, pegging interest rates and funding War Bonds with fiat credit; and, at length, expanding its remit to today's plenary dominance of the financial system.

Perhaps the greatest irony is that the New York Fed, which conducts the Fed's massive open market operations and is the legatee of J.P. Morgan's' Madison Avenue syndicate, is now run by a Keynesian scribbler and Fed lifer named John Williams.

He's the father and leading theoretician of the obscurantist idiocy symbolized by r* and he has never had to risk a single dime of his own capital during a lifetime of money-pumping by the trillions.

> It'll take probably three rate increases from here, which would get us in the range of 2¾ to 3 [percent]. That, for now, is probably my best — that gets us in the vicinity — and I would underline the word "vicinity," "neighborhood," whatever adjective you want to use there — that gets us in the vicinity of neutral.
>
> - Dallas Fed President Robert Kaplan,

You can be sure of this. In the era before r* you wouldn't have had the recent announcement that a speculative trainwreck called WeWork, which is losing money at a billion dollar annual rate, is fixing to get a capital injection of $15-$20 billion; and at a total valuation of $40 billion from another speculative trainwreck called Soft Bank, which has managed to bilk global punters of some $95 billion to be channeled into like and similar cash burning machines.

As is self-evident, WeWork is the Lehman of the current bubble, running an epically mismatched book that makes the latter appear to be a paragon of financial prudence.

Its core business is taking on long-term office leases, lavishly renovating the spaces and then subletting them for a week or month at a time; and mostly to start-up tenants with no profits and usually no revenue, which pay their rent by burning venture capital, even as they demand perks such as free-flowing cucumber water or craft beer.

When WeWork raised *$700 million* in a junk bond sale a few months ago, it explained away its massive red ink hemorrhage with something it called "community adjusted Ebitda."

The latter figure not only excluded interest, taxes, depreciation and amortization, but also basic expenses like marketing, general and administrative costs, development and design costs and most it is employee compensation, which it provides through stock options.

That is to say, its regular way EBITDA of negative $769 million in 2017 was miraculously transformed into $233 million of purported profit (community-adjusted Ebitda)!

So we'd say WeWork is the poster boy for the idiocy of r*.

Needless to say, J.P. Morgan's men would have never let WeWork through the library door, but it is exactly what the trillions shoveled into the canyons of Wall Street by the Fed have fostered and kept alive.

Yet the silver lining is this: When the Everything Bubble finally crashes, the Donald will turn on the Fed with a vengeance.

Bringing the baleful regime of the Fed into disgrace and disrepute is the one constructive step we expect from the Donald. So doing, the Great Disrupter will be carrying out his most important mission of all—even as they carry him out on his political shield.

PART 2

The Folly of Trump-O-Nomics

CHAPTER 6

The Donald's Real Bleep-Hole Moment — $41 Trillion And Counting

Earlier this year the Donald provoked a bleep-hole moment on the Fox "family channel" or what was otherwise known as the shit-hole moment across the rest of the MSM.

But whatever you called the contretemps spurred by the president's crude utterance with regard to certain countries on the African continent, the claim that this was evidence that he's an incorrigible racist was beside the point. Actually, we already knew that the Donald is a semi-literate bully, who never got (read) the memo on racial comity — to say nothing of political correctness.

Still, there is a not inconsiderable share of Washington's preening, self-important ruling class that indulges in that very same kind of gutter talk on a regular basis when puffing their chests and marking the objects of their displeasure. That's why the shaming chorus which sprung up from all corners of the Swamp was enough to give hypocrisy a bad name.

But if we have to have a shaming of politicians, there is a far better reason for it than that unfortunate presidential slur.

To wit, Trump and the GOP deserve everlasting ignominy for literally shit-canning fiscal rectitude. So doing, they have completely abandoned the GOP's fundamental reason for being — watch-dogging the US Treasury — in favor of immigrant-bashing, border hysteria and what boils down to crude nativism by any other name.

You do not drain the Swamp and shackle Leviathan, however, by obsessing on and demogoguing about a non-problem that requires muscling up the state's internal control apparatus and wasting tens of billions more on Mexican Walls, border enforcement armies and deportation dragnets across the length and breadth of the land.

The fact is, five pro-liberty and pro-free market steps would make the whole trumped up border "invasion" bunkum and balderdash go away in a heartbeat. These would include:

- Legalizing all drugs and turning the distribution job over to nonviolent operators like, say, Phillip Morris;
- Freely handing out guest worker permits at the 48 border control stations and regularly renewing them on demonstration of gainful employment (W-2 forms);
- Denying any and all forms of Federal welfare to non-citizens;
- Providing guest workers a ten-year route to citizenship if they hold a steady job, don't break the criminal law (speeding tickets ok) and pay an admission fee based on a modest percentage of their cumulative W-2 wages; and
- Permitting all so-called illegals already here to obtain a guest worker permit at the nearest Federal courthouse and to embark on a 10-year route to citizenship if they hold a job, observe the law, pay the admission fee and also a reasonable fine for their original misdemeanor (crossing the border illegally).

That would end the drug-cartel related violence at the border once and for all and bring America what it desperately needs: Namely, more strong backs to supplement what is a declining pool of native born workers, which peaked in 2015 and is now shrinking per the chart below. And, also, to put it baldly, provide more young tax-mules to help fund the crushing Welfare State burden implicit in the impending tsunami of Baby Boom retirements, which will double the benefit rolls from

55 million to 100 million over the next several decades.

And that brings us to the true bleep-hole moment of the Trump presidency: Namely, the fact that he and the Congressional GOP have spent 24-months literally desecrating every principal that the once and former party of fiscal responsibility, balanced budgets and minimal public debt ever stood for.

The U.S. Workforce, With and Without Future Immigrants

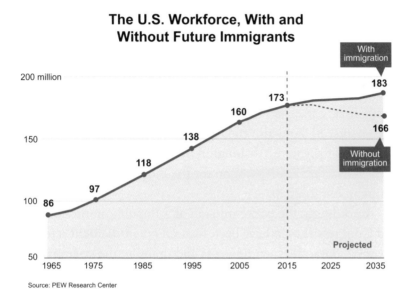

Source: PEW Research Center

The Winter Of Fiscal Infamy

Yes, the GOP had been straying from its philosophical north star for decades — ever since Ronald Reagan broke the taboo and massively increased the Federal deficit on purpose in the absence of a WW II type emergency. But last winter's one-two punch of a $2 trillion unpaid for tax cut (including added debt service) and the $400 billion two-year spending spree embodied in the Horribus appropriations bill truly broke the glass.

That's because the offense far transcended just the

magnitude of the incremental red-ink attributable to these measures, which we would put at about $5 trillion over the next decade.

The truly unforgiveable sin was to do it in the specific years 2017-2018, which represented the top of a long business cycle expansion, not the recessionary bottom; and, more importantly, the foreground of a new decade which is guaranteed to experience the next deficit-swelling recession, soaring interest expense on a massive and growing public debt and the aforementioned demographically driven explosion of Social Security, medical and other transfer payment spending.

Stated differently, these two years actually represented the last train out of the legislative station ahead of the on-rushing 2020s' fiscal cataclysm that was already baked-into-the-cake (see chapter 8). And also the last chance ahead of the coming two years of absolute Washington dysfunction and nasty partisan warfare in preparation for the mother of all presidential donnybrooks in 2020.

Accordingly, the entire mission of a Republican president and Congress should have been focused on entitlement reform, sweeping domestic spending cuts and draining the swamp of waste on the Pentagon side of the Potomac. Given today's baleful fiscal circumstances, the very idea of piling more borrowings on top of the inherited structural deficit of $700 billion for the current year (FY 2019) should have been treated as rank heresy.

Once upon a time, in fact, only the Dems would have entertained that kind of gross fiscal irresponsibility!

So what has actually transpired through it all is that the Donald has dropped the equivalent of a neutron bomb on the GOP. Its edifice is still standing but what used to be inside is dead to the world.

Worse still, those now departed legions of GOP budget hawks have been replaced by an unseemly coalition of militant border patrollers, neocons blood-lusters and military pork barrel servitors of the Warfare State. That is to say, a predatory gang of self-serving swamp-dwellers who couldn't defend the taxpayers or the nation's solvency if their lives depended upon it.

So American fiscal governance is now absolutely dead as a doornail. The Great Disrupter came to Washington to monkey-hammer the status quo and spark breakdowns and crises. And on the fiscal front, at least, he has succeeded beyond all expectations.

For reasons which are not hard to grasp and which are laid out below, the nation's Fiscal Doomsday Machine is now unstoppable; and most especially because the post-midterm Trump White House will have zero legislative power and therefore maximum inclination to barnstorm Red State America in behalf of Trade Wars and Border Wars, which can be prosecuted to a considerable extent under executive authority.

In that context, the untoward effects of the Trade War piece is obvious enough. As indicated previously, China's $526 billion of imports to the US are the marginal price-setter for roughly $1.7 billion of goods in the categories they supply, with the balance provided by domestic producers and other exporters.

But when it comes to pricing, China's got the conn. By both hook and crook it is the low-cost supplier. The Donald's 10%-25% tariff on its share of the $1.7 trillion, therefore, will create an immediate price umbrella under which the balance of suppliers will be able to lift their offers significantly — and yet still capture market share if they don't raise all the way to the landed Chinese price plus 10%-25%.

So consider a 15% lift on what might be termed the China goods aisle of the US supermarket, which happens to account for 40% of the entire $4.2 trillion of annual goods consumption in the US from all sources. That would equate to a $250 billion inflationary bow-wave, which, in turn, would force the Fed to stick with its normalization campaign, even if it otherwise wanted to chicken out.

By taking the wrong fiscal path in 2017-2018, therefore, the Trumpite/GOP has set up a perfect storm in the bond pits.

To wit, a $1.2 trillion new borrowing requirement for the current fiscal year is fixing to slam hard upon the $600 billion of old debt the Fed will be dumping. On top of that there will be hundreds of billions more of homeless treasury paper that will be on offer from carry trade speculators getting whacked by rapidly increasing repo rates and by foreign investors getting clipped by the rising dollar and prohibitive currency hedging costs.

Financial repression sure looked easy, of course, when the world's central bankers had their Big Fat Thumbs on the scales during the last 14 years as they collectively scooped up $21 trillion of government bonds and other paper and salted it away on their cost free balance sheets. But if the economic god had a son, perhaps he too would look to the heavens and ask they be forgiven on the grounds that "they know not what they do."

That is, these fools have so bludgeoned and distorted the bond markets that the latter have mutated into coiled springs of instability. In hundreds of different ways, speculators have been buying on leverage what the central banks have been buying, and now that the latter — led by the Fed — are pivoting to QT, they will be selling what the central banks are selling in what will amount to a global margin call.

That's the implosive catalyst that has been implanted in the bond markets by the foolish attempt of Keynesian central bankers to improve upon the natural growth propensity of market capitalism by systematically and deeply falsifying interest rates.

So when that coiled spring of mis-pricing up-chucks the benchmark 10-year Treasury note toward the 4.00% marker, it will be all over except the shouting.

By that we mean the Everything Bubble will splatter in the casino, bringing on a fierce new onslaught of "restructuring" campaigns from the corporate C-suites as they desperately heave workers, inventories and impaired assets overboard — like they did in the fall and winter of 2008-09 — to appease the trading gods and rescue their immolating stock options.

The outcome of this is otherwise known as "recession," Bubble Finance style. And once the recessionary red ink starts flowing on top of the already hideous Trumpite/GOP Fiscal Debauch, Washington's budgetary veins will be opened wide for the terminal blood-letting.

A recession-driven deficit will quickly breach the $2 trillion per annum level, and from there it's just the dismal math of soaring debt and interest compounding upon themselves.

The Donald's Xenophobic Militancy — To What End?

What's worse, even as this forbidding scenario is unfolding in plain sight — 10-year yields are up 160 basis points from their 2016 low — the Donald has taken the GOP off the deep-end of xenophobic militancy. Consequently, they won't even notice the fiscal typhoon coming until they are engulfed by it, and then the "low interest" man in the Oval Office will launch an all-out war on the Fed, which will only make the conflagration worse.

Meanwhile, it might well be asked what exactly was the great immigration bogeyman that caused the conservative party to jettison its core principals and policy mission in order to confront.

For sure, it's not crime and violence. The latter evils were legislated in Washington and are nurtured by its ludicrous Drug War. That is, drug cartel violence needs to be fought on the floor of the House and Senate in the form of prohibition repeal legislation, not on the borders where it begets law enforcement violence in response to the inherently violent drug cartels which exist only due to the high prices and artificial scarcity economics of prohibition.

And it's not that we have too many immigrants — legal, illegal or otherwise. The 44 million current immigrants in the US, in fact, constitute a lower ratio to the population (13%) than the 15% level which prevailed (orange line) during the heyday of American growth and prosperity in the second half of the 19th century.

Number of Immigrants and Their Share of the Total U.S. Population, 1850-2016

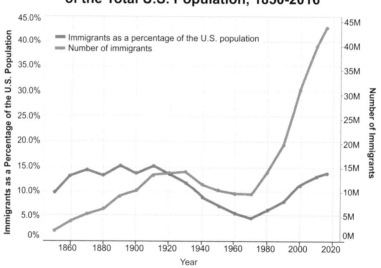

And please don't say they take Americans jobs. It's possible that even Nancy Pelosi knows better than that trade union canard; and, besides, vibrant capitalism can employ any and all workers who offer their labor if the state doesn't throw up obstacles or block the way with unreasonable minimum wage laws.

Finally, don't play the "they broke the law" card to get here, either. For crying out loud, crossing the border without papers is a misdemeanor, not an anti-social criminal act. If commission of a misdemeanor were a universal basis for deportation, the American Indians would soon have their empty continent back.

So, obviously, there is no immigration threat that requires the US military on the border, the rolling out of trainloads of razor-wire, wasting $40 billion or more on the Donald's idiotic wall or the vast mobilization of border security operations which are now driving the budget of the Homeland Security Department sky-high.

There is another basis for the Donald's Border Wars and the GOP's anti-immigration crusade, of course, and it's really not hard to figure. It's not about the 800,000 dreamers, chain migration, the diversity lottery, MS-13 gangs, the Mexican Wall and now the caravans of destitute and desperate "invaders" allegedly threatening our borders.

Underneath all these alleged immigration issues, in fact, is a bare-knuckled political war between the partisan apparatus and vote getting machines of the two political parties.

The sundry Dem caucuses want more immigrants, and the browner the better, because they see it as their only route to electoral dominance. But that's actually a good sign, not a threat, because it underscores that the modern Dem party has nothing to offer except a friendly demeanor and the hackneyed rhetoric of identity politics.

By contrast, the hard core GOP immigrant-thumpers are desperately attempting to hang-on to Red State rule in the face of the forbidding demographic math of the dwindling white and ruralish population — and the fact that not many Norwegians want to immigrate to America, anyway.

But they are dead-wrong about this kind of Alamo Politics. The 40-years of GOP dominance from William McKinley through Teddy Roosevelt, Taft, Harding, Coolidge and Herbert Hoover, too, was built on the support of immigrants who voted for the full lunch pail economics of the old GOP.

Donald Trump wouldn't have been nominated for dog-catcher in that Republican party; and he would have found the congressional nativists, immigrant-bashers and Klansman to support his "nationalist" agenda mainly on the back benches of the Democrat side of the aisle.

Alas, the Donald's Border Wars agenda and related tweet-storms, unhinged stadium rhetoric and stunts like sending 15,000 regular army forces to the Mexican border would be bad enough in terms of supplanting and displacing the GOP's traditional fiscal agenda.

But now the whole misbegotten enterprise has been completely Foxified with Sean Hannity, Laura Ingram and even Tucker Carlson competing to propagate the most shrill daily rendition of the Trumpian fear-mongering against what amounts to a Fake Invasion.

So the bottom line is this: When it comes to the nation's fiscal governance there is absolutely no one home in Washington. The upcoming deluge of red ink will meet with no resistance at all.

The $41 Trillion Debtberg Ahead

In fact, Washington is drifting rapidly into a hellacious fiscal calamity — with the nation's budgetary doomsday machine likely to drive the public debt to $41 trillion and 140% of GDP by the end of the 2020s.

Moreover, this isn't just a risk; it's a near certainty based on the built-in budgetary math and the sheer auto-pilot nature of its driving forces.

For instance, the income entitlements including Social Security, disability, SSI, food stamps, family assistance, the earned income credit, government pensions and veterans benefits cost $1.5 trillion in the year just ended, but in the absence of Congressional action will automatically soar to $2.5 trillion by 2028.

The tab for the giant open-ended medical entitlements — Medicare, Medicaid, CHIP and ObamaCare — is racing upwards even more rapidly — at nearly 7% per year. Consequently, last year's spending of $1.2 trillion on these programs will become $2.2 trillion by the end of the current

10-year budget window. And automatically so, without the legislative branch lifting a finger.

These big numbers are bad enough in the telling, but their place in the structure of the Federal budget is what screams out calamity ahead. To wit, last year outlays for the combined income and medical entitlements amounted to just under 14% of GDP, but if Congress were to go AWOL for the next 12 years, they would automatically absorb upwards of 18% of GDP by 2030 due to the huge Baby Boom retirement-driven increase in the caseload.

And that's where the rubber would meet the road. Owing to the Christmas Eve tax cut, the revenue base will drop by $280 billion in the current year (FY 2019), bringing Uncle Sam's take down to just $3.4 trillion or 16.6% of GDP — the lowest non-recession year level since the eve of the Korean War.

In other words, what is now in place owing to the combined folly of the GOP tax cut on top of 30 years of bipartisan fiscal can-kicking, is a revenue base that is not even large enough to pay for the big entitlements!

And, of course, that omits entirely the roughly $2.7 trillion that current policy would require by 2028 for national security, roads, education, agriculture, space, small business, medical research, rivers and harbors, courts and prisons, the Census Bureau, the Washington monument etc. , and also what will be at least $1.0 trillion per year of interest on the national debt by then.

To be sure, the Washington budget scorekeepers have hidden this sheer absurdity — $2.7 trillion of non-entitlement expense and zero revenue to pay for it — by papering it over with a motley array of accounting gimmicks. These cause projected revenue, for instance, to rise back to 18.5% of GDP by 2028, but this two-percentage points of GDP gain ($600 billion) is overwhelmingly fake revenue.

For instance, the individual tax cuts, which allegedly go to 90% of taxpayers, will cost $189 billion in the first full year (FY 2019).

But thanks to the disappearing ink in which they were written (i. e. the 2025 "sunset") that number swings to an $83 billion tax increase by 2027. Of course, the latter is never going to happen: The GOP tax-writers have already baldly confessed that the sunset was just a gimmick to avoid the fiscal discipline required by the budget rules.

The only thing they haven't confessed to is on the eve of which up-coming election they plan to vote to cancel the sunset, thereby noisily "saving" 140 million individual tax filers from what would otherwise be upwards of a quarter-trillion per year tax increase.

The same story pertains to the $50 billion per year or so of so-called "tax extenders." This refers to expiring tax breaks for wind, solar and biofuels — along with affordable housing and community development, Hollywood film expensing rules, NASCAR motor sports, rum producers, tuna canneries, short-line railroads and countless more.

The game here has been going on for decades. These tax subsidies get continuously put back on the statute books a few years at a time. But on the eve of expiration they are invariably given another short-term extension. That is, Lucy always jerks away the revenue football, leaving Uncle Sam to borrow the difference.

Needless to say, when you cut through all the clutter of these fake out-year spending cuts and revenue increases, and then lay on top the Trump tax cut and the February Horribus appropriations bill, the fiscal outlook literally collapses before your eyes.

Thus, just one year ago CBO's then current 10-year baseline deficit was projected at $10.2 trillion. But after the tax cut and last winter's two-year appropriations deal — which raised defense by $80 billion per year, domestic appropriations by $63 billion and also added $100 billion of disaster aid with no offsets — the 10-year CBO deficit estimate rose to to $12.4 trillion;

and that alone took the public debt to $34 trillion by 2028 via CBO's own reckoning.

But that's not close to the truth of the matter because the current official forecast still includes all the fake revenue and spending cuts and a economic forecast so hideously optimistic that it would have made Rosy Scenario of Ronald Reagan's time blush with embarrassment.

In the first place, the Horribus appropriations deal was only good for two years (FY 2018-19), and under budget scorekeeping rules the baseline reverts to the old sequester cap levels thereafter. That is to say, after an $80 billion feed to $717 billion, the military-industrial complex and its army of lobbyists and Capitol Hill porkers are going to just meekly assent to a funding plunge back to $650 billion in FY 2020.

Right. And the same goes for the $63 billion of swill that was added to the domestic appropriations side. Under the official baseline, spending authority of $724 billion in FY 2019 is supposed to plummet back to $671 billion in FY 2020 and beyond.

In the real world, of course, a US Senate crawling with GOP war-hawks and neocons is not about to take a $68 billion hit on defense appropriations in FY2020 and beyond. Nor is Nancy Pelosi's new revenge-seeking House majority about to give back a dime of the domestic pork they extracted from the Trumpite/GOP last February.

This means, in short, that there is a $2.3 trillion spending shortfall in the CBO baseline for the last nine years of the current 10-year window, representing the outyear cost of blowing the old sequester caps per the Horribus deal on a permanent basis, and the extra debt service that would result.

Likewise, when you remove the GOP's fake tax cut sunset and the phony out-year spending cuts and tax extenders you get another $2.3 trillion shortfall over the budget window. Altogether, therefore, the projected red ink swells to a cumulative $17.0 trillion during FY 2019 through FY 2028, and by the latter year the public debt rockets to $38.5 trillion.

The chart below was developed by the Committee for a Responsible Budget, and if anything it errs on the conservative side. The blue section of the deficit bars is the prior CBO baseline, the red area adds the impact of the GOP tax cut, and the dotted boxes reflect spending increases already made or promised (defense, disaster aid, border control, veterans, ObamaCare bailout subsidies etc.) and the various budget gimmicks which are used to hide the out-year deficits.

Deficits in the Updated Budget Projection

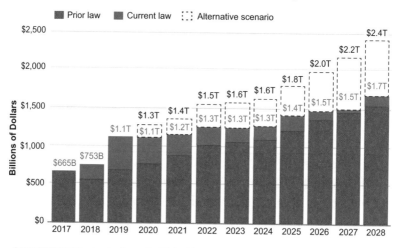

Source: CRFB calculations based on Congressional Budget Office data

There is a certain breed of conservative who is always whining that low taxes are not the problem, nor is it the deficit per se. The culprit is purportedly too much spending, which may be true in the ethereal reaches of pure philosophy, but in a Trumpified GOP its rather beside the point.

The spending share of GDP is rising rapidly and it's the Trumpified GOP which is driving it. Republicans have acquiesced to the giant entitlement programs for so may years that they own them as a normative matter — especially because

Trump has officially ruled them off limits.

But now the discretionary part of the budget is also soaring, and there is absolutely not doubt why. It's owing to the Donald's massive spending increases for defense, veterans and homeland security/border control — plus all the other domestic pork which has been proffered to line up sufficient GOP and Dem votes on Capitol Hill.

Handmaids Of The Warfare State — Why America Is Going To Hell In A Fiscal Hand Basket

Indeed, if you want to know why America is going to hell in a fiscal hand basket, it's because during the Trumpian era the last vestige of opposition to the Warfare State and the fiscal muggings of the military/industry/intelligence complex has utterly evaporated.

We are referring, in part, to the delirious Russophobia that has overtaken the Dems and the liberal media since they had the daylights shocked out of them by the 2016 election — a state of mental derangement that has degenerated into downright hysteria since the Helsinki Summit.

Accordingly, the anti-war left has abandoned the legislative playing fields. Now anti-Russian policy actions (e. g. sanctions) pass through the Congress with bipartisan greased lightening, and defense appropriations had exploded to the highest level in post-war history in real terms.

In fact, the $717 billion just approved for FY 2019 compared to a constant dollar level of just $550 billion (2018$) in FY 1990 — the final year before the Soviet Union with its 55,000 tanks and 9,000 nuclear warheads slithered off the pages of history.

So we are already spending *30% more* than at the peak of the Cold War, but you haven't seen nothing yet. Not now that Rachel Maddow and Anderson Cooper have become rabid war hawks, virtually begging for military confrontation with Russia and its pipsqueak economy and pint-sized military.

Indeed, what is lost in this anti-Putin hysteria is that the GDP of the NATO-29 is $36 trillion, and that is 26X that of Russia. Likewise, when you add the NATO-28's military spending of $280 billion to Washington's humongous defense budget, the total is nigh on to $1 trillion per year — or 16X Russia's entire military expenditure of $61 billion per annum.

We emphasize this massive imbalance of economic resources and military might as between NATO and Russia because it is the very reason why the bellicosity and fiscal largess from Capitol Hill won't diminish any time soon. That is to say, the Imperial City politicians are in a full frontal bully mode because they believe (not unreasonably) that they can huff, puff and spend with relative impunity.

This is not at all like the days of the real cold war in the 1960s and 1970s when America actually did face a deadly dangerous enemy; and when it was also evident to most rational people that rash provocations could be fatal and that the Cold War was something to be vigilantly endured, not won.

Accordingly, defense strategy was based on MAD or mutual assured destruction because all except an ultra-hawkish fringe in Washington could see that even attempting to "win" a nuclear arms race and war with the Soviet Union was a recipe for eventual incineration of the planet.

This meant, in turn, that by FY 1979 when the triad nuclear deterrent had been fully built and paid for and the folly of the Vietnam land war in Asia had been fully purged from the numbers, the defense budget totaled only *$385 billion* (in 2018$).

Significantly, that was the same *$385 billion* level (2018$) that had prevailed back in FY 1960 right after Nikita Khrushchev had promised to "bury" America. Yet the nation's greatest war general then in the Oval Office, President Dwight Eisenhower, thought that level was adequate to insure America's security, and even warned in his parting address to Congress about the dangers of excessive military spending and the insatiable fiscal appetites of the military-industrial complex.

Our point is that the sobriety of purpose and military spending restraint that went with it under Dwight Eisenhower and Jimmy Carter alike has vanished in the aftermath of the Cold War's end and the subsequent rise of the Russophobic branch of the War Party among the Dems and mainstream media.

And as this phony Cold War 2.0 has gotten agitated to a fever pitch, the military/industrial/surveillance complex surely thinks it has died and gone to heaven. After all, Washington is now spending 85% more against essentially a non-existent threat than it did during the pre-1980 era of Cold War 1.0 when the Soviet nuclear threat was palpable.

In their mindless and unhinged anger at losing the 2016 election to Donald Trump, the Dem/liberal media wing of the War Party has so demonized Putin and so grotesquely exaggerated the Russian threat that they literally cannot see straight or assess actual facts with even a modicum of rationality and proportion.

That's more than evident in their hysterical response to Trump's unwillingness to attack Russia for its purported election meddling; and in their utter incapacity to see that Mueller's grandstanding indictment of the 12 Russian spear-phishermen is not Pearl Harbor at all — and much more like the false flag hurled up from the Gulf of Tonkin by LBJ.

In ordinary circumstances it might be the case that the present Russophobic hysteria gripping the Imperial City would eventually burn itself out. At length, Chris Cuomo (CNN) and Rachel Maddow (MSNBC) would be exposed and discredited as the modern day equivalent of Betty Parris (age 9) and Abigail Williams (age 12) — the cousins who famously incited the Salem witch trials in 1692.

But the problem at the moment is that the nation's fiscal

accounts are exploding wide-open in the here and now. What is unfolding is a tripartite perfect storm consisting of:
- the Donald's primitive view that bigger is always better, as it applies in this case to defense spending;
- the endless appetite of the military-industrial-surveillance complex for more of everything; and
- the anti-Russian bellicosity of the Dems and their media megaphones.

To be sure, the deficit eruption now underway has been obfuscated by the vicious partisan warfare attendant to the Helsinki Summit and its aftermath, but the figures are published every day by the US Treasury and they do not lie — trillion dollar deficits are back and there is no prospect whatsoever that they will go away.

The Wages Of Monumental Debt — Soaring Interest Expense

Then there is the impending explosion of interest expense. The latter is virtually guaranteed to rise from $316 billion in the year just completed (FY 2018) to $915 billion by 2028. That's mainly because the low FY 2018 number was a phony artifact of decades of Fed financial repression and the massive expansion of the Fed's balance sheet under QE.

As a result, the weighted average cost of interest on the Federal debt has been well under 2.0%. And, as we described in Part 1, the Fed also paid upwards of $100 billion per year to the US Treasury as an off-setting "profit" on its money printing scheme — a windfall which will be fast disappearing as the Fed shrinks its balance sheet under QT and makes ever higher IOER payments to the banks in order to enforce its target interest rate policy.

Still, the CBO is almost certainly underestimating the future blended interest rate on Uncle Sam's rapidly expanding debt balances. The CBO, for instance assumes that the 1.8%

average rate during FY 2017 will reach 3.2% by 2028 in very slow increments.

However, when you unpack the numbers you find CBO's 10-year average for the 90-day T-bill is 3.1% and is 3.8% for the 10-year Treasury note. But the T-bill rate is already at 2.40% and the 10-year benchmark note, which is up by 160 basis points from the 2016 low, is at 3.00% and fixing to punch though its 35-year down trend.

The 37-Year Bond Rally Is Over

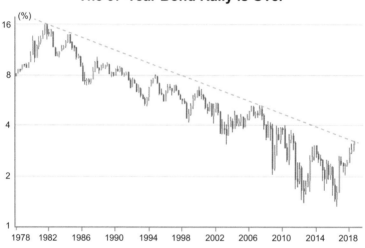

10-Year Treasury Bond Yield

Once that happens and the world's $100 trillion bond bubble bursts in the face of global QT, we'd bet its Katie-bar-the-door time.

When the machines and speculators start selling bonds because yields have broken trend and are marching back up hill for the first time on a secular basis since 1981 we think there will be a lot more upside on interest rates than the mere 70 basis points on the T-bill and 55 basis points on the 10-year that separates today's market from CBO's forward averages for the next 10 years.

In that event, the chart below — which is based on the current CBO interest rate assumptions and which already shows Uncle Sam's interest expense soaring — would go absolutely parabolic.

The truth of the matter is that interest expense on Washington's exploding debt — where annual deficits are hitting $1.2 trillion this year and $2.4 trillion by 2028 under Rosy Scenario economics — could end up far higher than *$1 trillion* annually.

Net Interest Costs are Projected to Rise Sharply

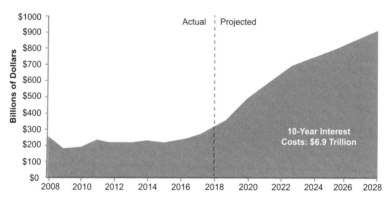

Source: Congressional Budget Office, *The Budget and Economic Outlook: 2018 to 2028,* April 2018. Compiled by PGPF

That would also push Federal spending to upwards of 25% of GDP — at which point the funding gap against a sub-17% of GDP revenue policy would become a self-fueling fiscal death spiral.

And that's what makes the GOP's asinine tax bill — a temporary break for the main street folks and a permanent 21% corporate rate which will generate trillions of stock buybacks, dividends and other financial engineering maneuvers that benefit primarily the top 1% and 10% — such a fiscal horror show.

When you strip out the gimmicks, the Trumpite/GOP tax policy amounts to a permanent revenue take of just 16.8% of

GDP. Stated less clinically, this means the Donald and his GOP collaborators have just completed the drawing-and-quartering of the nation's fiscal accounts.

America's Fiscal Accounts Are Being Drawn And Quartered

The plain fact is that the US nominal GDP has grown by just 3.9% per annum for the last 18 years. So when you are permanently borrowing 7.5% of GDP — or nearly double the trend growth rate of GDP — you will indeed bury the nation in debt. It's pure math at that point.

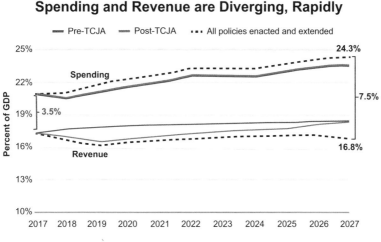

Spending and Revenue are Diverging, Rapidly

Sources: CRFB calculations based on Congressional Budget Office and Joint Tax Committee data.

In fact, the stunning irresponsibility of it couldn't be more apparent when you recall that the 18% of GDP cost of the entitlements outlined above is overwhelmingly driven by old people — including a substantial share of Medicaid costs which go to poor retirees and nursing home beneficiaries. Yet the baby-boom retirement bow wave is just getting started.

As shown below, there are presently about 55 million people 65 and over, but after 2030 that number will go parabolic, reaching 105 million eventually. So if the plan is to end the 2020s with $2 trillion plus annual deficits as shown above, it doesn't take much imagination to see where the fiscal accounts will go when the shaded area in the graph below vectors sharply to the upper right after 2030.

Entitlement Reform is as Important as Ever

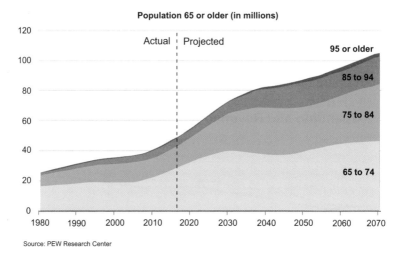

Population 65 or older (in millions)

Source: PEW Research Center

But even that's not all. The deficit chart above adopts the current CBO economic forecast which assumes recessions have been abolished from the face of the earth and that the already faltering US recovery at 115 months will just keep on trucking to a ripe old age of 232 months in 2028.

Rosie Scenario 2.0

The risible fantasy of that assumption is evident in the chart below. In the face of soaring public debts, $70 trillion of total public and private debt and an epochal pivot to QT by the Fed and other central banks, there is not a snowballs chance in the hot place of the red bar (below) ever materializing.

As it is, the CBO's official Rosy Scenario forecast assumes average annual nominal GDP growth — and that's what drives revenues and the deficit, not "real" GDP — that is 33% higher over FY 2019-2028 than during the last ten years (2007-2017). Accordingly, the cumulative nominal GDP underlying the current official budget forecast reviewed above is about $252 trillion over the next 10 years.

Duration of the U.S. Business Cycle (in Months)

That's a big number, but also a vulnerable one. If you just factor in an average recession somewhere along the line during the 10-year window ahead and also account for the obvious global headwinds from the central bank pivot to QT and slowing global growth, you can easily get a nominal GDP growth rate equal to the actual rate for the last decade.

And even that would be sporty because the last decade benefited from massive global QE and the once in world history topping phase of the Red Ponzi, which grew from $3.5 trillion to $12.2 trillion during the decade or the current output of France, England and Germany combined.

So even a 2007-2017 based "Copy & Paste" GDP growth scenario during the decade ahead would result in about $13 trillion less GDP compared to CBO's current assumptions. In turn, that would mean $2.2 trillion less revenue at the sub-17% current policy tax take; and about $2.5 trillion in additional deficits over the 10 year period when you add safety net expenses during the assumed recession and incremental interest costs from the higher deficits.

In short, when you replace Rosy Scenario with Copy & Paste in the above budget projection by the Committee for a Responsible Budget, you get $20 trillion of added debt during the current 10-year budget window. And you also get $41 trillion of public debt representing 140% of GDP by FY 2028,

Needless to say, that outcome could perversely be described as just in the nick of time. After all, shortly thereafter the Baby Boom retirement bow-wave will crest and lay total waste to the nation's fiscal accounts.

So at the end of the day, we come back to the Donald's shit-hole moment and the anti-immigrant Alamo Politics which under-pinned it.

To wit, there is only one way out of the impending fiscal catastrophe and that is to roll out the welcome wagon to tens of millions of younger and working age immigrants who can function as tax mules to carry the burden of 105 million baby-boomer and retirees.

There is virtually no other way out of the giant fiscal trap that is now closing in on the Imperial City — even as going that route is also the only way to save America's constitutional democracy.

What the GOP immigrant bashers fail to recall is that America was not based on a tribe, a folk, a people or a nation. It was a melting pot of diverse peoples who came here seeking the freedom to go their own way as guaranteed by the constitution and to pursue the opportunity to prosper as offered by free market capitalism.

And it worked without any borders at all. There were no immigration quotas until 1925 and no passports were required to enter or leave America until the exigencies of World War II in November 1941.

The truth of the matter is that in the present day and age people come here "illegally" to either: (1) sell or distribute illegal drugs; or (2) find jobs and a better standard of living for their families.

The former reason can be eliminated by the stroke of a Presidential pen on a repeal statute, and the latter can be encouraged and regularized by a large-scale guest worker program, which is the only thing left that could prevent an American fiscal catastrophe.

CHAPTER 7

The Worst Tax Bill In A Century

The Trump/Republican tax bill was not "at least something." It was not "better than nothing." And, no, we are not letting the perfect become the enemy of the good.

In truth, the so-called Tax Cut and Jobs Act was a fiscal, economic and political monstrosity. It was hands down the worst tax bill enacted in the last half-century — maybe even since FDR's 1937 soak-the-rich scheme, which helped reignite the Great Depression.

True, rather than soak them, the GOP's bill will pleasure America's wealthy with a bountiful harvest of tax relief. Owners

Buyback Explosion!
Dollar value of share repurchase announcements, by year

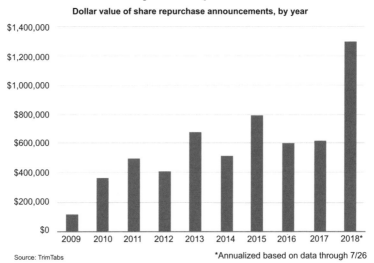

Source: TrimTabs   *Annualized based on data through 7/26

of public equities, for example, are garnering an estimated $1.3 trillion dollar shower of stock buybacks fueled by the corporate rate cut to 21%, and also massive dividend increases on top of that.

So in honor of the Christmas Eve Tax Cut of 2017 you could hand out some red baseball caps labeled "Making Wall Street Giddy Again" (MWSGA) and be done with it.

Unfortunately, there is a lot more where that came from. For example,

- 4 million top bracket ATM (alternative minimum tax) payers were relieved of about $80 billion per year of Uncle Sam's extractions;
- around 5,000 dead people per year with estates above $20 million will get to leave more behind to their heirs;
- owners of real estate will be able to deduct another 20% of property income that isn't already sheltered by depreciation and interest deductions; and
- tax accountants and lawyers will become stinking rich helping America's proprietorships (24 million), S-corporations (4 million), partnerships (3.5 million) and farms (1.8 million) convert their *"ordinary income"* into newly deductible *"qualified business income."*

Notwithstanding these facts, the commonality between the FDR's tax bill disaster and this one is that both represent exactly the wrong policy at a time which could not be worse.

In the New Deal case, business and investor confidence had finally begun to recover after the trauma of the 1929 Crash and the subsequent withering depression, but FDR's excess profits tax and punitive marginal rates on high incomes sent the economy tumbling until it was rescued by war mobilization after 1940.

In the current situation, the absolute worse thing you could do is what the Trump/GOP tax bill actually did: That is, draw on Uncle Sam's credit card to fund temporary cuts for the middle class and a permanent windfall to the top 10 percent of households which own 84% of the stock.

The reason, of course, is that America was already marching straight into the immense fiscal and demographic trap described in chapter 6. So the Christmas Eve Tax Cut amounted to the coup d'grace — a further unwarranted $2 trillion of red ink (including added interest) over the coming 10-year budget window that will cause the already monumental public debt ($21 trillion) to spiral out of control and smoother any semblance of economic prosperity as we have known it.

When all is said and done, the tax bill which passed on Christmas Eve 2017 boils down to the mother-of-all-riverboat gambles. That's the term that former Senate Leader Howard Baker tagged the Reagan tax cut with in 1981, but as it has happened, he was way ahead of his time: This one's the real stinker, emanating as it does from the modern day GOP's bogus theory that tax cuts pay for themselves.

We are speaking, of course, of the "growth dividend" fantasy, and the risible idea that driving this year's borrowing requirement to $1.2 trillion won't compound the public debt problem in the long run because the out-year revenue loss will all be made up for with surging economic growth, jobs, incomes and tax revenues.

But there is no chance whatsoever of that because Trump/GOP tax bill did not even embody a meaningful cut in marginal tax rates paid by individuals. Yet that was the core premise of the whole supply-side tax cut theory going back to Ronald Reagan, as we reprise below.

To the contrary, the Christmas Eve Tax Cut was actually a dog's breakfast of special interest nostrums and gratuities written by K-street lobbyists, the business PACs and the GOP donor networks.

For example, doubling the child credit and the standard deduction does put money in the pockets of households — about $150 billion in FY2019 — but that's purely a Keynesian demand pumping notion. It will do virtually nothing to enhances incentives to work, save, and invest. In fact, in contrast to the Reagan 25% rate cuts, the marginal rate reductions in the Christmas Eve Tax Cut amount to only 2-3 percentage points.

At the same time, the money pumped into taxpayer pockets in this manner will also be extracted dollar for dollar from business CapEx and other investment spending. That's the inherent math now that the Fed is out of the debt monetization business, and, as we saw in Part 1, has allowed "crowding-out" to re-emerge from its 35 years slumber.

Likewise, as noted above, the GOP revilers gifted AMT payers with a $637 billion tax break over the next eight years, and for that the "donor class" will surely be grateful. And the fact is, the AMT is an obnoxious tax that should be abolished completely, if replaced with a more just and benign source of revenue.

Still, thankful as the donor class may be for justice at last (Nixon put in the AMT in 1969!), we are also quite sure that the 4 million beneficiaries of this "tax cut" will not add any hours to their work schedules or invest any more productively than the have been doing. If the AMT repeal has any economic impact at all, it will be to bid up the charter rates on luxury yachts and Net Jets; and also put a few thousand tax lawyers and consultants out of business.

When all the sunsets and temporary middle class breaks are set aside, in fact, the heart of the tax cut was a $1.76 trillion revenue loss over 10 years for the 21% corporate rate and the 20% pass-thru deduction for "qualified business income."

Yet there is every reason to believe that upwards of 90% of the resulting massive increase to the Federal debt will be recirculated back to Wall Street and to the top 1% and 10% of households in the form of increased stock-buybacks, dividends and other forms of capital return.

Again, the purpose here is not to extol the corporate

income tax. It is actually a relic of your grandfather's economy and should have been abolished years ago, and replaced with spending cuts or a more benign and collectible tax, such as a direct consumption tax or VAT.

But it never should have been just cut to 21% and paid for on Uncle Sam's credit card. And especially not on the screwball theory that the lower rate will generate so much incremental investment, production and jobs that the "flowback" revenues will pay for the cut.

It won't — not in a million years. That's because the modest difference between the effective corporate rate (what companies were actually paying after the best tax planning money could buy) in the US and most other industrial economies was nothing like the magnitude implied by the old 35% statutory rate compared to much lower statutory rates in Europe and East Asia.

In fact, the US effective rate for internationally mobile US companies (e. g. excluding retailers and local service providers which can't move abroad anyway) was actually in the low 20% range; and often, such as the case of IBM and other tech giants, was in the low teens, thereby easily matching rates abroad.

What this means is that US based companies shifted volume production and employment abroad based on economic factors such as lower wage costs and proximity to end markets or supply chains. At the same time, they often shifted their tax books and token staff operations to tax havens to help lower their effective tax rate — something that cost Uncle Sam revenues, but did not materially cause the off-shoring of US jobs.

Just consider the case of Microsoft, which employs upwards of 130,000 workers worldwide — including about 200 in Puerto Rico, 700 in Singapore and 1,100 in Ireland. If headcounts in a high tech firm are a reasonable proxy for output, therefore, Microsoft's production in these three tax havens amounts to just 1.5% of its worldwide total.

By contrast, Microsoft books upwards of two-thirds of its taxable income in these three jurisdictions thanks to state of the art tax planning and the off-shoring of billions of "intangible assets" to these entities. It accomplishes the tax dodge by having the latter's units charge the company's US operations hefty royalty fees for use of such intellectual property, thereby shifting profits to the above three tax haven jurisdictions where the corporate tax rates are 2.0%, 7.3% and 7.2%, respectively.

What we mean is that Microsoft off-shored its tax books, not its production and jobs. The rate reduction to 21%, therefore, will not bring jobs and investment back to Redmond, Washington because they never really left — not for the tax havens.

By contrast, consider the case of IBM, which has massively off-shored it production and jobs. Since 1993, it has raised its job count in India from zero to 130,000 at present, while cutting is domestic employment count from 150,000 to less than 90,000.

But that huge migration was not due to tax rates in any way shape or form. In fact, in a globally mobile and competitive labor market where the US is at the top of the cost curve, wage rates on the margin are set by the India Price for back office and technology-based services and the China Price for goods; and that's exactly what happened in the case of IBM's massive off-shoring during the last quarter century.

What this means more generally is that the great off-shoring of the US productive economy (as opposed to tax books shuffled to tax shelter jurisdictions) has occurred owing to economic causes and the technological enablement of the global internet. These include dramatically lower labor rates abroad and proximity to materials, supply chains and end customer markets, not the statutory tax rate.

IBM's effective tax rate, for example, was about 11% even before the tax bill passed, and that was not atypical. Again, however, the massive number of IBM jobs went to India for low cost labor, while the tax books went to tax havens for low rates. Lowering the statutory rate, therefore, will indeed reduce the need for migrating the tax books, but will have no material impact on the economic causes behind the migration of jobs.

For example, a recent study of the largest US companies with positive net income over a six year period showed that the average effective tax rate was only 14%. That is, the big cap internationals had already given themselves a big tax cut "selfie" by moving their tax books to the Caribbean, the Channel isles, Ireland, and other tax havens in addition to the impact of economically-driven off-shoring of production and jobs.

In this context, the smiling doofus who is Trump's CEA Chairman, Kevin Hassett, peddled a real whopper in behalf of the rate cut. He claimed — contrary to all evidence and logic — that the corporate income tax is shifted onto wages and that the 21% rate is therefore worth $4,000 per household in higher earnings!

That was complete malarkey, of course. Then again, contrary to all evidence and logic, Hassett also predicted the Dow would hit 36,000 in the year 2000, right before it bottomed at 8,000 (October 2002)

At the end of the day, the GOP has set up a scheme of massive borrowing and a monstrosity of tax law sunsets, deferrals and fake "payfors" that will knock the stuffings out of what remains of Washington's capacity to manage the nation's fiscal crisis in the years ahead.

Indeed, heading for the fiscal calamity described in chapter 6, the GOP nonetheless chose to embrace a hoary theory that America's failing rate of GDP growth, investment in productive assets and real wage gains is due to the high corporate income tax.

That is pure Wall Street and K-Street poppycock, of course, and not just owing to the effective tax rate and tax planning factors described above.

Beyond that looms the Fed's massive repression of interest rates and the deductibility of debt on corporate tax returns. This means that for several decades now the after-tax cost of corporate debt has been at rock bottom levels. Accordingly, there has been no barrier whatsoever to business investment in any and all domestic projects and assets with even minimal prospective rates of return.

As indicated above, we would get rid of the corporate income tax in its entirety (i. e. zero rate) if it were replaced with permanent spending cuts or a direct tax on consumption. That's because the corporate income tax is a relic of distant industrial past when capital mobility and integrated global labor markets and supply chains were a shadow of present day reality.

Consequently, it is no longer really collectible by national governments. Despite only modest reductions in the statutory rate since the 1950s, there has been a huge decline in the revenue take — from upwards of 8% of GDP back then to only 1.5% in 2017. That's state of the art tax planning and economically driven capital mobility at work.

Indeed, today the corporate income tax has become essentially a honey pot for high-priced tax planning and shelter schemes, which is actually just a form of government induced economic waste that does not add to national economic growth or wealth.

So Trump and his GOP majority in the last Congress had a wonderful chance to enact true reform by replacing the obsolete corporate income tax with a modern day VAT (value added tax) like most of the rest of the world.

But the K-Street lobbies and GOP donor class were violently opposed. So, instead, the GOP politicians choose the path of least political resistance by pulling out Uncle Sam's credit card — in their very finest imitation of Democrat free lunch economics — and charged the corporate rate reduction to future tax payers.

The Reagan Benchmark Versus
The Christmas Eve Tax Cut

Although it was peddled as some kind of latter day incarnation of Reaganomics, the Christmas Eve Tax Cut was nothing of the kind. It actually makes a mockery of the still valid supply-side ideas and theory from the 1980s; and there is no better way to demonstrate that than to compare it with the original 1981 Reagan tax cut — as imperfect as even it was in the final execution .

The key points about "supply-side" with respect to the Reagan tax cut of 1981 are depicted in the indented box contained in the chart below.

It shows the split between

- marginal rate cuts for individuals, which was the high-powered pro-growth element;
- the business cut in the form of sharply accelerated (10-5-3) depreciation schedules, which unlike today's corporate rate cut at least had the virtue of being tied to purchase of plant, equipment and technology; and
- a medley of loopholes and special interest tax breaks ("ornaments"), such as tax credits for oil royalty owners and wood-burning stoves, that emerged from the bidding war between the Reagan White House and Congressional Republicans, on the one hand, and Speaker O'Neill's' Democrat majority in the House. The latter was determined to maintain its rule of the roost — even by trashing the nation's revenue basis if necessary for legislative victory.

Taken altogether, however, the actual 1981 tax act provides a **benchmark** for exposing the phony supply-side stimulus claims made for the Christmas Eve Tax Cut of 2017.

In the first instance, when the "bidding war" with the Dems ended in July 1981, the US Congress had cut the Federal revenue base by 6.2% of GDP in the outyears. At today's

The 1981 Reagan Tax Act: Biggest Cut as % of GDP in U.S. History

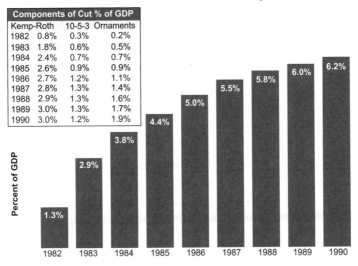

Components of Cut % of GDP		
Kemp-Roth	10-5-3	Ornaments
1982 0.8%	0.3%	0.2%
1983 1.8%	0.6%	0.5%
1984 2.4%	0.7%	0.7%
1985 2.6%	0.9%	0.9%
1986 2.7%	1.2%	1.1%
1987 2.8%	1.3%	1.4%
1988 2.9%	1.3%	1.6%
1989 3.0%	1.3%	1.7%
1990 3.0%	1.2%	1.9%

economic scale that would amount to a tax cut of $1.2 trillion per year!

By contrast, the peak year cut (FY 2019) in the Trump/GOP tax bill is just $280 billion or just 1.3% of GDP. So even if "bigness" mattered in the formulation of tax policy, which it doesn't, the hard numbers put the lie to the ridiculous claim by the Donald and his GOP acolytes that the Christmas Eve Tax Cut was the "biggest tax cut in history."

Moreover, debunking this "mine is bigger than yours" boast actually helps illuminate why the "growth" boom claimed for the current bill is so preposterous.

When all is said and done, the bill is probably anti-growth. In fact, it is actually the weirdest large scale tax cut ever enacted (to our knowledge) because it is drastically front-loaded and then shrivels wimpishly out of sight after the middle of the decade.

That is, the Trump/GOP tax bill amounts to is a temporary tax abatement gift to the middle class that will eventually turn into a fiscal nightmare; and a permanent cut of the corporate tax rate that will do virtually nothing for growth.

Obviously, this nonsensical disappearing tax cut pattern resulted from the effort to game the Congressional budget process, and to deliver the maximum wallop of tax cut goodies on election day of November 2018.

So other than the permanent 21% corporate rate, the bill's string of sunsets, temporary cuts and out-year increase amounts to a "Charlie Brown and Lucy" version of fiscal policy: After the next election, Lucy is empowered to pull back the football year after year through 2027 until there is nothing left of the "stimulus."

But for the life of us, we can't figure out what kind of economic theory is embedded in the yellow bars of the chart below — notwithstanding the diminutive size of the overall cut. It is certainly not any kind of supply-side theory which would embrace raising the tax burden on the US economy from 16.6% of GDP in FY 2019 (maximum cut year) to 18.5% of GDP in 2027 (after the net impact turns positive).

After all, that's a 13% increase in the total Federal tax burden between the front-end and the back-end of the decade ahead. Accordingly, it does not incentivize a permanent increase in supply-side resources at all — just a one-time pull forward of economic activity per the patented Keynesian "stimulus" illusion.

In fact, the steady uphill march of the Federal tax burden depicted below can only be described as some kind of Trumpian throw-back to the primitive "pump-priming" theory of the 1930s — a relic so tattered and discredited that even modern Keynesians no longer talk about it.

In the interim, of course, it will enable companies to pump trillions back into the casino in the form of stock buybacks, enhanced dividends and empire-building M&A deals — which may have been the point all along.

Measured in terms of static revenue loss, therefore, the peak tax cut occurs during the first full year (FY 2019) and amounts to the aforementioned $280 billion or 1.4% of GDP.

Thereafter, the nominal dollar cut shrinks as per the graphic below. By 2022 the tax reduction amounts to just $178 billion and then declines to $114 billion in 2025. At that point, it reverses to a tax increase of $33 billion in 2027. Relative to GDP, these figures amount to 0.8%, 0.4% and +0.1%, respectively.

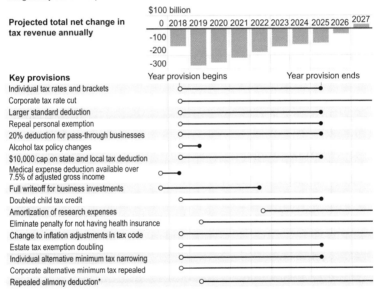

Sunset Boulevard

Republicans scheduled many of their tax cuts to expire, to stay within the $1.5 trillion, 10-year budget they set for the plan.

So in comparative terms, the peak year Reagan cut amounted to **6.2%** of GDP or **4.4 times** more than the 1.4% cut scheduled for FY 2019 in the GOP bill. More important, on a ten-year basis the Reagan cut averaged 4.0% of GDP versus 0.6% for the current bill.

Our point here, however, is not merely to effect a "gotcha" on the GOP bloviators by showing that the Reagan tax cut was actually 10 times bigger on a long term basis. Rather, it is to highlight the quantitative realities behind the rhetorical hyperventilation which continues to emanate from the Republican camp.

The truth, actually, is more nearly the opposite. What's big is not the tax cut number, but CBO's baseline GDP estimate of $253 trillion over the ten year period. Simply put: We don't think a $1.5 trillion net tax cut over that same period would move the GDP needle very much even under ideal conditions.

But most certainly not when there are huge headwinds emanating from massive treasury borrowing, the epochal central bank pivot toward QT (quantitative tightening) and the inherent frailties of a geriatric business cycle.

Indeed, the size, shape, corrections and consequences of the giant 1981 tax cut depicted in the chart above tells you all you need to know about the rhetorical baloney that was (and still is) emitted by the GOP propagandists regarding their recent handiwork.

The GOP tax bill, in fact, was actually a twisted pretzel of legislative gamesmanship designed to scam the Senate reconciliation rules, thereby enabling the unruly caucus of ideologically fragmented Republicans to obtain — one concession and compromise at a time — the magic 51 Senate votes and a GOP "win."

But this "win" will do nothing good for Flyover America — the only reason the GOP obtained power at both ends of Pennsylvania Avenue during the 2016 election. And it is already boomeranging on the pettifogging Republican pols who rammed it through without hearings or serious analysis as to its likely fiscal and economic impact.

On the matter of individual taxes and marginal rate cuts, which are supposed to stimulate work, investment and enterprise, the Reagan marginal rate cuts started at 1.8% of GDP in year #1 and reached 3.0% of GDP when the 25%

rate cut in all brackets became fully effective. At CBO's current GDP estimates for the next decade, this 3.0% of GDP individual/marginal rate cut would have amounted to $850 billion per year by 2027.

By contrast, the Christmas Eve Tax Cut reduced marginal rates by only 2-3 percentage points in most brackets and then piled on a grand shuffle of the following: A doubled standard deductions, complete repeal of the personal exemptions and a doubling of the child credit.

The net of those puts and takes for individual tax payers amounts to about $150 billion per year or just 0.7% of GDP. That means that the Reagan supply-side cut when fully effective on the individual side was more than 4X larger than those in the Christmas Eve Tax Cut ; and even then, the GOP's current pale imitation of marginal rate cuts disappears entirely after 2025, when the sunset provision triggers in.

Moreover, these calculations essentially obscure the impact on taxpayers at the very top of the income pyramid, where supply side incentives are logically the most potent. That's important because top bracket taxpayers are getting a huge windfall cash gift from the corporate rate cut and the resulting massive increase in stock buybacks and dividends, but not from the direct individual income tax provisions, which are far more consequential for incentives and investment behavior.

Thus, the impact of repealing the aforementioned AMT for 4 million wealthy tax payers, the $670 billion tax increase owing to capping the SALT deduction (state and local income and property taxes) at $10,000, closing other so-called loopholes over the period, and the 20% deduction for "qualified business income", which will mainly impact higher income taxpayers who itemize, is pretty much a wash.

By 2025, before the entire 500 pages of the bill impacting individual taxpayers reverts to the status quo ante of 2017, the impact of these three big features primarily effecting the upper brackets is a net reduction of just $24 billion. That is, a $100 billion annual increase for loophole closings less $90 billion of relief from the AMT changes and a $34 billion net cut from the pass-thru deduction changes.

Given that the top 5% of taxpayers will have a projected $5 trillion of adjusted gross income in 2025, we don't think this so-called giveaway to the wealthy — which would amount to 0.5% of pre-tax income — is going to move the growth needle very much, either.

Indeed, when all the individual income tax puts and takes are netted out, the reduction for all 150 million filers in all brackets during the best year (2025) is just $100 billion, representing only 6.5% of the $1.53 trillion current law baseline for individual income tax collections that year.

And then the bottom drops out: Everyone is hurtled back to their 2017 position — save for the fact that $32 billion extra will be extracted from individual taxpayers owing to a less generous inflation adjustment index which the bill makes permanent.

The comparison with the Reagan business cuts shows the same disproportion. When fully effective, the 10-5-3 depreciation schedule reduced business taxes by 1.3% of GDP or about $300 billion per year in today's economic scale, and these changes were permanent.

Also, as indicated, the Reagan business cuts were based on the principle of "no ticky, no washy." That is, if you didn't add to your productive capacity or process efficiency by purchasing new plant and equipment, there was no tax benefit.

None of Reagan's giant business cut, therefore, went back into the canyons of Wall Street as stock buybacks (which weren't even legal until 1983) or dividends: The benefits flowed to suppliers of capital goods and their workers, instead.

In that context, the plant and equipment linked cuts in the current bill are small potatoes by comparison. They disappear entirely after 2022, and amount to only $37 billion in the peak year of FY 2019.

In round terms, therefore, the Reagan bill's incentive for CapEx was about 8X larger relative to the size of the economy. Beyond that, since the current bill's deprecation incentives disappear abruptly, their primary impact will be to pull forward in time existing business CapEx plans, not stimulate higher long-term investment.

At the end of the day, the Christmas Eve Tax Cut is no supply-side policy measure at all. There is virtually no potential for stimulus or enhanced, sustainable economic growth in the overwhelming bulk of the GOP's 500 pages of gifts to K-Street and Wall Street.

To be sure, the far larger Reagan tax cuts for both individuals and business ended up being an excersize in unprecedented fiscal irresponsibility, as well. That's because the off-setting spending cuts in the original Reagan fiscal blueprint of 1981, which were intended to pay for a goodly part of the revenue loss from the tax cuts, did not happen.

Once the giant tax cut was enacted in August 1981, however, the GOP promptly forgot about the "payfors" it still owed. But at least the large marginal rates cuts and sharply accelerated depreciation features, which accounted for two-thirds of the so-called "static revenue loss" as shown in the chart above, did have a strong pro-growth impact.

Needless to say, even the pro-growth part of the Reagan cuts is not even remotely replicated in the Christmas Eve Tax Cut, and that makes the current resort to credit card based "stimulus" all the more condemnable.

That's because there's a crucial fiscal difference between today and 1981. Back in the early 1980s, Uncle Sam could afford to borrow (not wisely) to fund the kind of supply-side oriented tax cuts which dominated the 1981 act — since the public debt only amounted to $930 billion and 30% of GDP.

By contrast, today the Treasury balance sheet reflects 35

Draining the Debt Swamp: Reagan Vs. Trump

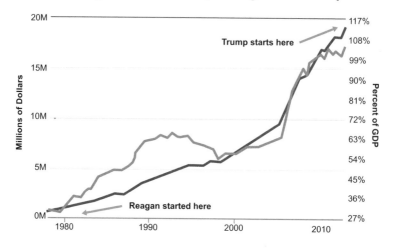

years of reckless fiscal policy and labors at 106% of GDP.
And that's before adding on the roughly $20 trillion of new
deficits over the next decade, as essayed in chapter 6, which are
built into current law and the Trump/GOP tax and spending
programs.

Even then, as shown below, the huge Reagan supply-side
tax cuts did not appreciably move the needle of GDP growth
relative to the then embedded trend of 3.5% per year trend that
had prevailed since the end of the Korean War.

You might wonder, therefore, what the GOP pols had been
smoking when they essentially voted to borrow $1.7 trillion
to finance stock buybacks and M&A deals under the far more
challenging fiscal and monetary conditions of the present time,
and the worsening trends that are already baked into the cake
for the coming decade.

Even The Reagan Supply-Side Tax Cut
Did Not Stimulate Extra Growth

The heart of America's economic growth problem, of course,
lies in the Eccles Building, not the IRS code. But even then it
is important to clarify the revisionists myths about the 1980s

200

THE WORST TAX BILL IN A CENTURY

because, in truth, even the considerable supply-side stimulus of the 1981 Tax Cut did not cause any extra economic growth at all.

And the reasons for this are absolutely pertinent to the present situation. Back then, the supply-side incentives of the Reagan tax cut were heavily neutralized by the resulting calamity of paying for this massive tax cut with borrowed money.

In the first instance, the Treasury began to bleed so drastically that even the Gipper signed three sequential tax increases in 1982, 1983 and 1984 — which recouped about 40% of the original cut and thereby undoubtedly created some headwinds to growth. Supply side cultists, of course, thought these tax increase bills were the work of the devil and never ceased denouncing your author as a nefarious "tax grabber" for helping to engineer them on Capitol Hill and convince Reagan to sign the bills.

But the alternative would have been not the *6%* of GDP deficits that were actually realized, but 10% of GDP deficits, which, under the interest rate levels of the time, would have spiraled out of control in a feedback loop of exploding debt service costs.

Eventually there would have been a thundering bond market collapse because the financial system was still operating under a reasonably honest central banking regime. Paul Volcker's resolute monetary discipline did not brook with accommodating reckless fiscal deficits, and in the end did crush the roaring commodity and CPI inflation fostered by his two immediate predecessors (Miller and Burns).

Accordingly, the giant Reagan deficits which broke out in the mid-1980s were not being monetized — as has been the case during the most recent two decades. In turn, the law of supply and demand in the bond market resulted in soaring interest rates during 1987 and the eventual crash of the bond markets and, more famously, the stock market meltdown in October 1987.

Had not Greenspan discovered the Fed's printing press in the basement of the Eccles Building on Black Monday and run it at full speed, Reagan would have left office in the midst of soaring yields and a massive crowding out of private investment in the bond market, and a subsequent crippling recession. Yet even with the Fed's monetary rescue, average real GDP growth during the Gipper's eight years ended up at *3.58%* per annum, thereby matching to nearly the second decimal place the 27-year average of *3.55%* recorded from 1953 through the end of 1980.

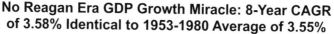

No Reagan Era GDP Growth Miracle: 8-Year CAGR of 3.58% Identical to 1953-1980 Average of 3.55%

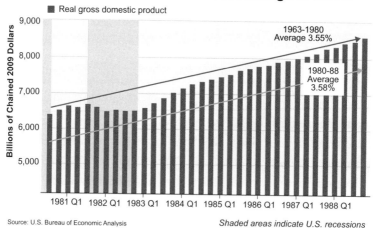

Source: U.S. Bureau of Economic Analysis   *Shaded areas indicate U.S. recessions*

To be sure, there were about 12 quarters of 4-5% growth in 1983-1985 when the US economy bounced back from the deep recession that Volcker had unavoidably induced to crush double-digit inflation. But that amounted to recapture of lost GDP during the contraction — not a permanent increase in the US economy's growth capacity.

What this means for the present is straight forward. The three-decade interregnum of massive monetary expansion, and therefore monetization of the public debt, is now over and done. Indeed, it ended in October 2017 — almost 30-years to to the date of Black Monday — when the Fed launched the first month of balance sheet contraction, and began an epochal pivot toward long-term QT (quantitative tightening).

Accordingly, like in the case of the Reagan Tax Cut of 1981, the large increases to the public debt resulting from the current GOP tax bill will not be monetized by the Fed; nor, in our judgment, will they be monetized by foreign central banks or absorbed by offshore investors driven into dollar bond markets by insufficient yield in their own domestic markets, as has been the case with Draghi's mad monetary expansion of the past 30 months.

The ECB will soon be out of the bond-buying business, as is the PBOC already and the BOJ not too far down the road. Yet without the big Fat Thumb of the central banks on the fixed income supply/demand scale, yields will rise sharply to clear the bond markets, and it will happen soon.

As we showed in Part 1, Uncle Sam's borrowing requirement under the now enacted tax bill and with the huge pending increase for defense, disasters and health care, will total upwards of *$1.20 trillion* during the current fiscal year (FY 2019), and continued to rise beyond $2.0 trillion per year from there.

In that environment, we believe the Bubble Finance-diseased C-suites will show the ugly legacy of 30-years of Keynesian monetary central planning. When the stock market breaks owing to the fact that a presumption of permanent, ultra-low bond yields are "priced-in" at today's nosebleed PE multiples, the C-suites will engage in another orgy of disinvestment.

That is, the increased after-tax cash flow owing to the 21% rate, which will amount to *$125 billion* in FY 2019 and *$1.4 trillion* over the decade, will be used to pay-down some of the suddenly higher cost debt — liabilities that US businesses took on over the last decade to fund financial engineering; and some will be used to desperately buy-in stocks and otherwise propitiate the snarling trading pits of Wall Street, which will demand sweeping "restructuring" actions (i. e. mass firings) and intensified financial engineering maneuvers to prop up stock prices (return of the tax bill-enhanced after-tax cash flows).

In this context, it should not be forgotten how deeply the corporate sector has buried itself in debt under the financial repression regime of the Fed and the hysteresis that has enveloped the C-suites. That is to say, the current generation of corporate leaders have forgotten how to grow companies organically via heavy "investment" in both capital items and in their operating P&Ls in the form of R&D, employee training, operational efficiencies and other capital improvements which get charged to current expense (and diminish reported profits under GAAP).

Instead, their idea of growth centers on borrowing money and diverting cash flows into financially engineered earnings per share gains. That is, shrinking the float on Wall Street and satisfying the demands of the casino gamblers for maximum current returns.

Indeed, reduction of the $14.3 trillion albatross of credit market debt now sitting on American business is sure to function as an alternative magnet for cash flow as interest rates and bond yield steadily normalize (rise) in the years ahead.

In fact, the same front-loaded taper that afflicts the general shape of the GOP tax bill is also operative on the business side. The actual net corporate tax cut in FY 2019 is just *$92 billion* when you factor in all of the "payfors" such as the foreign cash recapture, the cap on interest deductibility and a multitude of loophole closings, and then flips-over to a *$25 billion* net increase by 2025.

Even when you throw in the pass-thru tax cuts which get booked on the individual side, the gains in after-tax cash flow plunge sharply after the first year — when gimmicks like 100% first year depreciation expire. To wit, the net cut in FY 2019 is

$120 billion but this figures drops to nearly zero by FY 2022 and remains at that level thereafter.

In all, domestic business profits are estimated by CBO to total $18.2 trillion over the decade. But the net gain to after-tax cash flow for corporate and pass-thru businesses combined nets to just $600 billion or barely 3.3% of pre-tax profits.

That's not going to cure the rampant financial engineering in the C-suites. Not by a long shot.

CHAPTER 8

The Lost Decade of 2010-2020: How Washington Squandered The Last Chance For Fiscal Redemption

A relentless march toward financial calamity is now underway because the Fed's massive intervention in the bond market and radical suppression of interest rates resulted in a Lost Decade on fiscal policy. For all intents and purposes, the period between 2010 and 2020 was the last time to redress the massive spending bow wave that will be unleashed by the Baby Boom generation's entry onto the retirement rolls and the generous Welfare State income and medical entitlements which they will be eligible to draw upon.

As shown previously, during the last 10 years the US population 65 years and older has risen from 40 million to 55 million, and will reach more than 70 million by the end of the 2020s. Thereafter it continues to rise, as was shown in chapter 6, to more than 100 million a few decades down the road.

Self-evidently, the time to get a head of this enormous Welfare State ballooning bow wave was during the past decade and as a last resort, exactly now. But rather than take preventative budgetary action while there was still time, Washington spent these pivotal years ignoring Welfare State entitlements, ramping-up the Warfare State budget and cutting taxes whenever it could.

And then came along Donald Trump who doubled down on

this embedded fiscal default, demanding more Warfare State, no tampering with the Welfare State and lower taxes, too.

Accordingly, the public debt has already doubled from $10 trillion in 2008 to $21.8 trillion at present and will reach $25 trillion by the end of the Donald's term. Yet the retirement spending bow wave is just beginning its long-term ascent.

In this context, the chart below underscores why the Fed's massive falsification of interest rates has been so destructive. Notwithstanding the aforementioned $12 trillion increase in the public debt during the past decade, annual interest costs during 2017 were essentially the same as they were back in 2008 ($260 billion).

So the political significance of the chart below cannot be gainsaid. In essence, the Washington politicians had their cake and ate it, too, with the interest expense rising by only 13% even as the public debt grew by 110% over the past decade.

Federal Debt Has Risen Far Faster Than Interest Expense

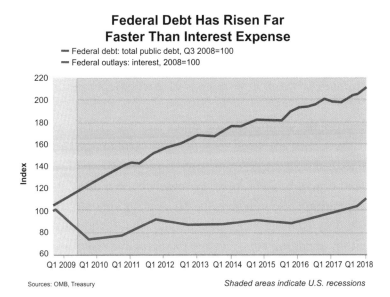

━ Federal debt: total public debt, Q3 2008=100
━ Federal outlays: interest, 2008=100

Sources: OMB, Treasury   *Shaded areas indicate U.S. recessions*

Needless to say, that caused a fatal disconnect on both ends of Pennsylvania Avenue. To wit, we learned long ago from first hand experience in the Imperial City during the 1970s and 1980s that the one thing that finally does impart some fiscal backbone among politicians is the fear of soaring interest rates. Politicians know that means a painful budget squeeze because the interest has to be paid, and that their favorite constituencies and pork barrel projects eventually will get short-changed in order to cover the debt service tab. So rising expense for the latter is effectively the signaling system for America's process of fiscal governance.

During the crucial decade for addressing the Baby Boom/Welfare State time bomb, therefore, Washington got all the wrong signals. Rather than fearfully developing a fiscal cushion for the post-2020 spending storm, it insouciantly ran giant, continuous deficits during what will soon be the longest peacetime expansion in history.

From a purely cyclical point of view that lapse was bad enough. Now that the Fed has much belatedly begun the monetary normalizing process, the falsely suppressed interest costs of the past decade will soar. That's owing to rising yields, the already doubled public debt and the long-neglected structural deficit that now exceeds $1.2 trillion per year and 6% of GDP.

During the coming decade alone, therefore, CBO projects that debt service costs will total nearly $7 trillion or three times more than the $2.3 trillion incurred during the last 10 years.

And even that assumes an extremely benign interest rate normalization cycle in which the 10-year treasury yield by 2028 is only 70 basis points above today's level; and also that the phony spending cuts, revenue increases and Rosy Scenario 2.0 economic assumptions dissected in chapter 6 actually materialize.

Stated differently, based on honest budget accounting and sober economic and interest rate assumptions, the public debt is likely to soar by $20 trillion to $41 trillion during the coming decade, as we demonstrated in chapter 6.

Accordingly, in the likely event of a real "yield shock" in the bond pits, the steep rise of interest expense already projected by CBO would go absolutely parabolic — soaring toward $10 trillion during the 10-year budget window ahead. That's 4X the tab paid during the last decade.

In turn, soaring debt and interest expense during a time when most of the 78 million Baby Boom will already be in benefit payment status would cement the political paralysis that is the essence of the fiscal catastrophe now rumbling down the pike. That is to say, the Donald inherited a fiscal disaster and has quickly turned it into an epic generational calamity.

Literally, it is both too late and utterly infeasible under current political alignments to stop what amounts to a fiscal Armageddon. What we are referring to is the fact that after 2020, the sheer mathematics of Baby Boom retiree numbers, entitlement benefits per retiree and the voting firepower of the swelling elderly population will rule the roost.

The Soaring Value Of Benefits Per Recipient

The above referenced demographics are forbidding enough, but that was not the only thing baked into the cake during the Lost Decade. Owing to the Social Security benefit formula, average benefits per recipient in real terms (2018 dollars) will *double* over the next several decades and ultimately *triple* in the longer run.

For instance, constant dollar benefits (2018 $) for medium earners (light blue bars) will rise from *$20,000* per year today to nearly *$30,000* by 2040 and then *$50,000* in the longer run. Likewise, constant dollar annual benefits for top earners (green bars) are projected to rise from $33,000 at present to $88,000 eventually

In short, there is a doubly whammy built into the Social Security entitlement system: Both the retired population and

Annual Social Security Benefits in 2018 Dollars
With Retirement at Normal Retirement Age

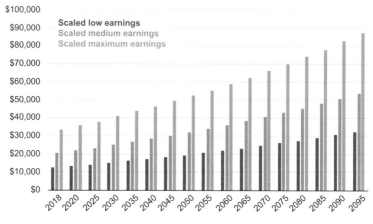

Source: Excerpts from Table v.c7 of the Social Security Trustees Report, page 150

benefits per retiree are slated to soar during the decades ahead.

The actual dynamics of this demographic/Welfare State bow-wave, however, are considerably worse than implied by the doubling of the rolls and benefits during the decades immediately ahead.

That's because the wage economy of the active work force has been deteriorating in terms of secular trends in productivity growth and output per worker. This trend, in turn, interacts in an exceedingly perverse manner with the Social Security benefit formulas, which effectively go in the opposite direction.

And as amplified below, that's why the nation is now saddled with what can only be described as a fiscal doomsday machine. But to appreciate its terrifying implications a succinct review of recent Welfare State history is essential.

The knock-out blow happened between 1946 and 1977. In the first instance, the 78 million member Baby Boom generation was born between 1946 and 1962. After that, the final costly flourishes on today's giant retirement-driven Welfare State were legislated during the subsequent 15 years.

These huge long-term fiscal inflators included LBJs

Medicare program in 1965; Tricky Dick's disastrous 1972 Social Security amendments that indexed earnings for wage growth; and Jimmy Carter's so-called progressive reform package. The latter made the benefit amount calculation steeply progressive — thereby, as it happened, giving your author a chance to cast a very loud "nay" vote in the well of the U. S. House of Representatives.

In any event, the great Baby Boom/Welfare State fiscal tsunami has been baked into the cake since 1977. But unsurprisingly, Washington utterly ignored this readily measureable ticking time bomb for the next four decades, including the Greenspan Commission package of 1983, which essentially raised the payroll tax rates in order to generate the appearance of solvency during the interim years.

As we have indicated, the Lost Decade of the 2010-2020 period was obviously the very last time to tackle the problem owing to the great wave of 1950s babies slated for retirement after 2020, and the fact that once they were on or near benefit status they would form an insuperable bloc of political resistance to reform.

Moreover, during that period this built-in fiscal bow-wave was actually being made considerably worse by the weakest macro-economic recovery in history; and especially owing to the adverse developments in the wage economy as reflected in deteriorating secular trends in productivity growth and output per worker.

The latter trends are indisputable as an empirical matter per the chart below. But their significance for the topic at hand requires brief reference to what the Nixon and Carter amendments actually did to the cost and benefit structure of Social Security going forward.

The Nixonian Curse Of Wage Indexing

The Nixon amendments established *wage indexing* and essentially reflected the industrial glory days of the US economy at its peak. That is, an assumption that the strong productivity and real wage growth of the 1950s and 1960s would continue forever, world without end.

As a technical matter, these amendments basically provided that your covered earnings at, say age 20, would get inflated for the next 40 years by the average growth in US wages. The latter is reflected in a government published measure called the Average Wage Index (AWI).

Since nominal wage growth almost always covers at least the going rate of inflation in the general price level as measured by the CPI, that part of the AWI index is fair enough because it maintains the purchasing power of wages earned and recorded during the employee's working years. But the skunk in the wood pile is that the AWI also incorporates annual gains in real wages reflecting productivity improvements and real economic growth.

Even under ordinary steady-state macroeconomic conditions, the "real" component of the AWI is a pretty generous windfall. It basically says that all the good things which happen to real economic growth until a 20 year-old worker turns 60 years of age gets retroactively factored back into his wage record.

Stated differently, wage indexing thoroughly debunks the canard that retirees are only getting back what they earned. In fact, they get retroactively awarded a big fat bonus for the gains generated by society for decades after their actual wages were recorded and taxed.

This has been described as an intergenerational ponzi scheme, and recent developments prove that characterization to be more than apt. To wit, under conditions of declining long-term productivity growth, current recipients are getting benefits based on the high-productivity wage growth of past decades, while current payroll tax collections reflect the weaker, low-productivity wage growth of the present period.

So in a pay-as-you-go financing system like Social Security, the fiscal math soon becomes daunting; wage indexing becomes a downright fiscal albatross.

For example, since about 1992 the general inflation rate as measured by the CPI-W(used to make the annual COLA adjustment) has increased by an average of about 2.0% per year, with the normal cyclical variations around that trend.

However, during the seven years ending in 2000, the AWI rose by an average of *4.4%* per year, meaning that the real wage component rose by 2.4% per annum and was duly reflected in indexed wage records. By contrast, during the seven years ending in 2016 the average annual gain was only *2.1%*, meaning virtually no gain at all in real wages and in the current payroll taxes levied upon them.

So even within this quarter century long example it is obvious that the intergenerational Ponzi is loosing ground. That is, the class of 2016 retirees got a 2.1% per year benefit boost from their earnings during the 1990s, while the pay-as-you-go payroll taxes coming into the trust funds in 2016 reflected real wage gains of a mere 0.1%.

Needless to say, when a secular trend of diminishing real wage growth is extended out to the typical 75-year actuarial horizon — that factor alone tends to make the system go tilt. The official Social Security trustees report, however, obfuscates this fatal problem by, well, assuming it away.

To wit, the average productivity growth rate (real GDP per worker) during the 44 year period between 1966 and 2007 was *1.73%* per annum. And for the next 75 years, the trustees assume almost exactly the same rate — *1.68%* per annum.

In fact, the productivity growth rate since the financial crisis has been less than half of that (*0.8%* per annum) and shows no sign whatsoever of reversing. And why would it in a context in which the Fed and other central banks around the world are belatedly normalizing interest rates?

After all, they will be potentially draining trillions of cash from the bond pits under their pivot to quantitative easing (QT) at the very time that Federal borrowing is exploding by $20 trillion over the coming decade, meaning that the already listing

Real GDP Per Worker Employed
1947Q1 to 2017Q2

Prices of 2009, seasonally adjusted annual rates

Sources: BEA, BLS via FRED

US economy will be slammed by a thundering "yield shock."

Needless to say, when this baked-into-the-cake yield shock hits America's $70 trillion economy-wide public and private debt mountain, a return to historic real growth and productivity rates is not the first thing that comes to mind.

To the contrary, if the current 0.8% productivity growth trend prevails for the longer term future — which is probably the best that can be expected — currently projected budgetary shortfalls will be drastically amplified.

Stated differently, Watergate was dismissed as a third-rate burglary at the time, and perhaps it was. The real Nixon heist, however, was the 1972 Social Security amendments which hostaged future generations to the fundamental scam of intergenerational wage indexing.

Jimmy Carter's Gift Of The Progressive Benefit Formula

Not long after Nixon's lamentable fiscal deed was accomplished, Jimmy Carter came along to add insult to injury

214

by chiseling into statute the sharply progressive benefit structure shown in the graph below.

The graph is presented on an indexed monthly earnings basis — so for purposes of visualization we translate it to annualized earnings equivalents, as well. As can be seen, there are three rate tiers for calculating monthly benefits from the worker's indexed wage record — 90%, 32% and 15% from bottom to the top of the wage scale.

Accordingly, the retiring worker illustrated in the first box (based on 2015 rates, which have been adjusted slightly higher for inflation since then) earned an average of $826 per month (AME) or $10,000 per annum. So what would amount to a low-wage part-time worker in today's gig economy would get a benefit of $743 per month or $8,916 annually, representing a *90%* replacement rate on his earnings.

The $4,890 per month worker in the second box ($58,700 per year) would get a blend of 90% and 32% on his earnings for a weighted average *42%* replacement rate ($2,073 per month/$24,876 per year). That's pretty much the average for full

How Social Security Disability Benefits are Calculated Base on Income

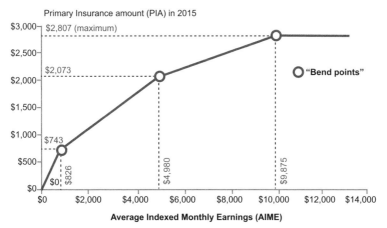

Sources: Social Security Administration, Fact Sheet, "2014 Social Security Changes," http://www.ssa.gov/pressoffice/factsheets/colafacts2014.pdf, and Social Security Administration, "Primary Insurance Amount," http://www.ssa.gov/OACT/cola/piaformula.html

time jobs in the US currently.

Finally, the worker in the largest box, who is at the top of the covered wage scale ($119,000 per annum), would receive $2,807 per month or $33,684 per annum. That reflects all three tiers and amounts to a blended wage replacement rate of just *28%*.

Here's the thing. In recent years, the overwhelming share of new jobs, and, more precisely, covered hours worked and subjected to the payroll tax have been on the low end of the wage scale. Thanks to Jimmy Carter's steeply progressive rate structure, therefore, average replacement rates will be rising over time — and that means the benefit cost of the system relative to the wages being taxed will also be steadily rising.

In fact, as we previously discussed, the "job" gains being reported for the US economy are largely in the Part-Time Economy ($20k earnings per year or less) and the HES Complex (Health, Education and Social services), which generally pay in the middle and lower end of the wage scale ($35k per year average).

So wage replacement rates going forward are likely to be heavily bunched in the *40-60%* range rather than *25-30%* from what we have described as full-time, full-pay Breadwinner jobs.

Replacement Rates for Retired Worker Age 65, 2017

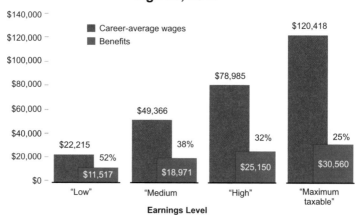

Since the year 2001, in fact, the number of Breadwinner jobs has grown by only *1.9%* in total. That means there has been virtually no growth in future entrants to the two low wage replacement rate categories (32% and 25%) on the right of the graph above.

Another way to look at it is that over the last 18 years the US economy has generated only 6,400 full-time, high-pay breadwinner jobs per month, and there is no sign of a sustainable acceleration. Yet there are currently 105,000 workers and their dependents joining OASI (old age and survivors insurance) rolls each month.

Breadwinner Economy

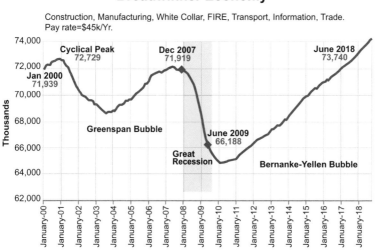

Construction, Manufacturing, White Collar, FIRE, Transport, Information, Trade. Pay rate=$45k/Yr.

Accordingly, the system is going tilt on a long-term basis. That's because it is the high taxes of highly paid, low-replacement rate workers upon which the progressive benefit structure is built, yet the US economy is producing fewer and fewer of the former.

By contrast, 88% of the net growth of the 19 million payroll jobs created over the last 18 years has been in the Part Time Economy (35%) and the HES Complex (53%). These will skew future beneficiaries heavily toward to the "low" and "medium" earner boxes in the graph above, where benefits range between *38% and 90%* of AIME.

In short, owing to the progressive benefit structure and the deteriorating US labor market, the benefit cost of the system is running ever further away from the payroll tax base on which its funding depends. That means the social security trust funds will soon be insolvent and far sooner than the Rosy Scenario worshipping trustees of the system are projecting.

Needless to say, insolvent trust funds sometime during the latter half of the 2020s will generate a political "hard stop" in America. That's because benefits under current law would be automatically slashed to the level of in-coming payroll tax revenue, which is likely to fall short of benefit costs by 30% or more.

Part-Time Economy

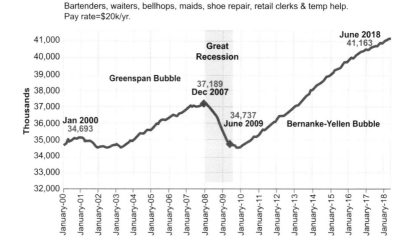

Bartenders, waiters, bellhops, maids, shoe repair, retail clerks & temp help.
Pay rate=$20k/yr.

In the alternative, the vastly enlarged high-voting retirement population could attempt to force through Congress staggering tax increases to keep the benefits of 78 million Baby Boomers flowing. But either way, the economic and political dislocations will be monumental.

HES Complex

Health, Education & Social Service. Fiscally Dependent. Growth Slowing Sharply.
Pay rate=$35k/yr.

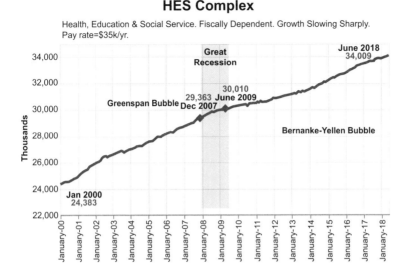

If that weren't bad enough there is one more fillip in the system that is making the fiscal equation even worse. Namely, in what is increasingly a part-time, gig-based, contract-by-the-hour labor system, year-to-year earnings **variability** is rising sharply; and that contrasts markedly with the 40 hours per week, 50 weeks per year job model for which the Social Security system was designed decades ago.

This rising level of annual earnings variability, too, will drive up the cost of benefits relative to current wages being taxed. That's because workers get to choose their highest 35 earnings years and drop out the rest.

The chart below shows how this works and was designed for a typical lifetime earnings cycle. In the current gig-based labor market, however, the impact of the drop-out years on lifetime earnings will be far more extreme, thereby raising the worker's AIME (average indexed monthly earnings) relative to his total lifetime wages being taxed.

In short, the Baby Boom retirement wave is plowing right into a Welfare State benefit structure that was designed for your grandfather's economy based on 3-4% annual GDP growth and a stable full-time labor market.

Top 35 Earnings Years Included in AIME Calculation

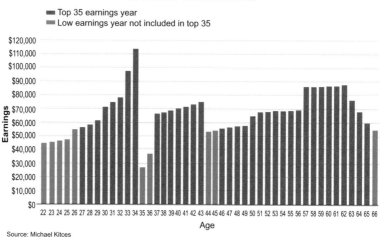

Source: Michael Kitces

As demonstrated above, that is not remotely close to the debt-burdened, low-growth, low-productivity economy and gig-driven labor market that actually exists in the US economy today and is likely to prevail for the indefinite future.

After all, the Trumpite/GOP policy of Trade Wars and Border Wars and essentially wanton fiscal debauchery can hardly be expected to make it any better.

So the ultimate fiscal calamity from this collision is barely reflected in the official long-term projections. The latter largely assume, as shown above, a reversion to historic growth and productivity performance metrics.

Even then, however, the outlook beyond the disastrous 10-year period reviewed in Part 1, which shows the public debt doubling to *$41 trillion* and *150%* of GDP by the end of the 2020s, only gets steadily worse thereafter.

In its latest projections, for example, the CBO shows the medical and Social Security entitlements alone will nearly double from *10%* to *18.6%* of GDP in the decades ahead.

To be sure, it might be argued that the prospective public debt explosion could be cured with some combination of

Federal Entitlement Programs are Projected to Nearly Double as a Percentage of GDP Under Current Law

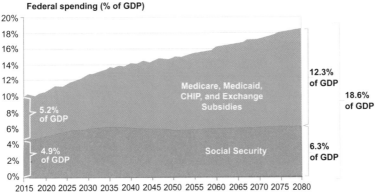

Federal spending (% of GDP)

Source: Congressional Budget Office, *The 2015 Long Term Outlook*, June 2015. Compiled by PGPF. Note: Current law projections are from CBO's extended baseline scenario. CHIP is the Children's Health Insurance Program and helps pay for health insurance for uninsured children. Eligibility for CHIP is based on household income and varies by state.

sweeping entitlement reforms and major tax increases designed to close this yawning fiscal gap. But there is one over-powering reality that says essentially: No mas!

To wit, since the turn of the century there has not been a *single meaningful entitlement reform or permanent tax increase* enacted on Capitol Hill. And now that the window is closing on the Lost Decade, the prospects are only diminishing and rapidly so.

In part, that's because the Trumpified GOP has given up on fiscal rectitude entirely, and has actually taken Social Security and Medicare off the budget table.

Yet that posture is not about to change in the foreseeable future owing to the raw political facts of life. To wit, in the decade ahead there will be upwards of 100 million voters in retirement status or within shouting distance of retirement age — meaning that the political force against benefits cuts will be insuperable.

At the same time, the work force relative to the retired population is rapidly shrinking, as shown in the graph below. Within a decade, the level of tax rate increases needed to meaningfully close the gap would be flat-out prohibitive from

A Shrinking Base to Support Retirees

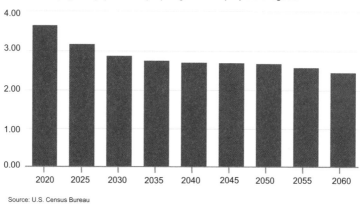

Ratio of projected population of people age 18-64 to people over age 65

Source: U.S. Census Bureau

both a political and economic incentive point of view.

So what is coming down the pike is a fiscal calamity. The Baby Boom/Welfare State tidal wave plus the exploding net interest expense of what will be a $41 trillion public debt will inexorably drive Federal outlays toward *30%* of GDP.

By contrast, the current policy revenue baseline — including the overwhelming GOP insistence that the Trump

Federal Debt Held by the Public

Percentage of gross domestic product

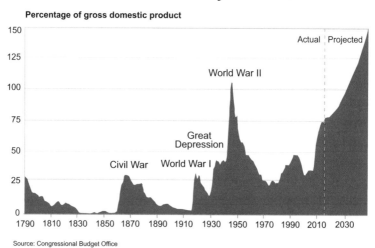

Source: Congressional Budget Office

222

Tax cuts be made permanent — would not even reach *17%* of GDP.

At bottom, therefore, double digit annual deficits are baked into the fiscal cake as far as they eye can see.

It does not take a lot of "big data" calculations to see what happens in a low growth economy saddled with permanent double-digit fiscal deficits. Namely, the cumulative debt build-up goes parabolic and insolvency is only a matter of time.

CHAPTER 9

Bombs Away Over Quebec

The Great Disrupter's rebuke of the keepers of the G-7 "consensus" at this year's meeting could not have been more welcome. That's because these so-called globalist multilateral institutions are the real enemy of democracy, capitalist prosperity and human liberty in the world today.

The G-7, the G-20, NATO, the IMF, the World Bank, the WTO (World Trade Organization) and the rest are the vehicles through which the permanent political class rules and ruins the world.

That is, elected presidents, prime ministers and parliamentarians come and go. But mostly they get led around by the nose by the bureaucrats and apparatchiks who run their governments, populate their think tanks, NGOs and lobbies and propagate their group-think through the likes of G-7.

Needless to say, the agenda of the global political class is statist through and through. That's what they do: relentlessly invade markets, society and private life in order to impose their purportedly superior wisdom and morality upon the unwashed masses and to correct the supposed imperfections of the free market.

The result, of course, is today's sprawling leviathan states which are choking-off both prosperity and liberty in a rising tide of taxes, regulation, redistribution, speculative finance and debt.

That the latter has drastically shrunk the sphere of personal liberty cannot be gainsaid. Most recently, for example, it even took a weasel-worded ruling by the Supreme

Court to ensure the right of a Colorado baker to reject a wedding cake order that was offensive to his beliefs about marriage.

Nor can it be doubted that capitalist prosperity has gone AWOL under the baleful rule of the very statists and globalists who had gotten themselves all balled-up into a snit in preparation for their confrontation with the Donald.

Thus, during the 20 years before the formation of G-7 in 1975, US real GDP grew at a *3.9%* compounded annual rate and real family income rose by *2.8%* per annum.

Median Family Income

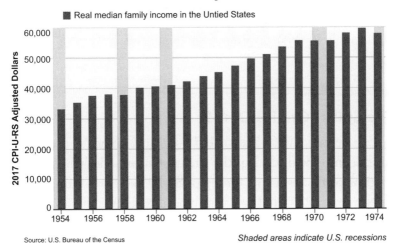

■ Real median family income in the Untied States

Source: U.S. Bureau of the Census   *Shaded areas indicate U.S. recessions*

By contrast, since the year 2000, the real GDP growth rate has averaged only *1.8%* per year or just *46%* of the growth rate that was recorded during 1954-1974.

More important, real family income has been essentially dead in the water. To be exact, it has crept higher at a *0.17%* annual rate — and you only get that rounding error of gain if you believe the BLS' sawed-off inflation ruler accurately measures the cost of living faced by families in Flyover America.

The truth of the matter is that the actual living standard of the median American family has been shrinking for the entirety of this century to date.

Median Family Income

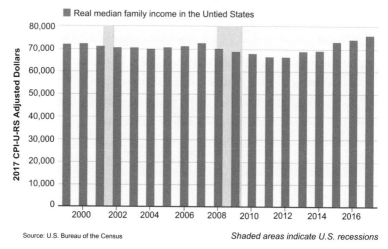

■ Real median family income in the Untied States

Source: U.S. Bureau of the Census   *Shaded areas indicate U.S. recessions*

The Statist Origins Of G-7

To be sure, the G-7 alone did not cause America's prosperity to slide into the ditch. But the circumstances under which its original predecessor (the Group of Six or G-6) was formed back in November 1975 tell you all you need to know.

To wit, Tricky Dick Nixon had sabotaged the relatively stable and automated international order of the Bretton Woods gold exchange standard at Camp David in August 1971 when he defaulted on America's obligation to convert dollars into gold at $35 per ounce.

In turn, that unshackled the Fed (and at length other central bankers) to create money and credit at will and thereby foment economic and financial mayhem in the name of discretionary macro-economic management and betterment.

In short order, the Fed — newly liberated from its anchor to gold — unleashed a previously unimagined peacetime inflation. Energy and commodity prices soared and the CPI hit double digit rates, thereby causing newly floating exchange rates to swing wildly and to wantonly disrupt well established patterns of trade and financial flows.

For example, CPI inflation had averaged a mere *1.5%* per annum between 1954 and 1965—before the inflationary disturbance triggered by LBJ's giant "guns and butter" deficits (which were out-sized for the times but actually only 3% of GDP). And with the economy humming along at 4.0% real growth, nary an economist in the land — even the "saltwater" Keynesians at Harvard — averred that there wasn't enough inflation or that 2.00% would be some kind of economic godsend.

But with Bretton Woods ash-canned and printing presses at the Fed unthrottled, the first round of bad money uncorked the commodity and consumer price levels. Between 1971 and 1975, the CPI soared to an average annual gain of *7.5%*, peaking at *11.5%* in in the first 10 months of 1974.

Eventually, and notwithstanding various experiments in voluntary "incomes policy" and more explicit and coercive Nixonian wage, price and capital controls, inflation got so out of hand that the Fed had to slam on the monetary brakes in 1974.

That eventually threw the US and global economy into the deepest recession since the 1930s. The trauma of stagflation, roiling FX markets and disrupted trade also generated strong protectionist pressures for the first time in the post-war era.

In effect, G-6 was born when the politicians of the day took it upon themselves to fix — via multi-lateral gabfests and policy interventions — the serviceable monetary order which Nixon broke in his maniacal quest for a massive 1972 election landslide.

Needless to say, the six heads of state who gathered at a medieval castle in Rambouillet France in November 1975 were more than just mouthpieces for the policy wonks and apparatchiks who organized and prepped the confab. Nearly

The first G-6 meeting Nov. 7, 1975, Rambouillet Castle close to Paris.

to a man they constituted a rogues gallery of statists and interventionists.

Among them were two outright socialists in the persons of Chancellor Helmut Schmidt of Germany and Prime Minister Harold Wilson of the UK. Likewise, the president of France, Valery Giscard d'Estaing, was a confirmed statist advocate of French dirigisme — as was the Christian Democrat prime minister of Italy, Aldo Moro.

At that point in time, the Japanese export machine was also ramping at full speed. Its milquetoast prime minister, Takeo Miki, presided over an LDP government that was dedicated to harvesting crony capitalist spoils at home and promoting export mercantilism abroad.

The only non-statist in the group was Gerald Ford, the Michigan Congressman and House GOP leader who had become an accidental president upon Nixon's demise.

But according to legend, Ford had played center too long on the University of Michigan football team in the days before

228

proper helmets. And according to fact, he had spent nearly three decades in Washington as a Congressman being house-broken by the machinery of state.

Even more importantly, he had inherited a team of economic advisors enthrall to the fresh water Keynesianism (otherwise known as "monetarism") of Milton Friedman. Rather than recognizing that the Camp David default on the Bretton Woods gold standard was the problem, they stubbornly held that floating exchange rates and deft management of the money supply growth dials at the Eccles Building would bring order and stability to the world economy.

All that was needed beyond that was reliable Full Employment budget policy (i. e. deficits when the economy was operating below its "potential", which was most of the time) and well-orchestrated coordination of trade, energy and other macro-economic policies among the major nations.

Thus, the new monetary order was to be based on wise central bankers, busy-body economic policy apparatchiks from the elected governments and a wholly fanciful belief that through something vaguely called "policy coordination" the G-6 government could actually improve on the performance of capitalism.

State-centered Keynesianism and globalism, in fact, were to become the surrogate for capitalist prosperity governed by the Bretton Woods system of essentially universal, interchangeable monies anchored to the automatic stabilizer of gold.

Needless to say, central bankers, economic policy bureaucrats and the sherpas of multilateralism were not up to the task.

At length, Keynesianism and globalism brought about a calamity of massive trade deficits, off-shored production and borrowed but unsustainable consumption and spending that chronically exceeded domestic production and income.

The simple fact is, under a regime of sound gold-backed money the chart below could have never materialized. Under a gold-backed monetary regime, trade deficits generated a loss of gold reserves, which, in turn, curtailed domestic credit formation and demand, causing wages, prices and costs to deflate.

The consequences were automatic macro-adjustments and renewed competitiveness in the global economy. That is, exports rose and imports shrunk in response to domestic cost deflation.

By contrast, the chart below is the smoking gun. Under G-6/7 style Keynesian globalism, trade accounts never adjust or clear, and perhaps that's exactly the point. It allows current office-holders to take credit for debt-fueled prosperity that is simply economic activity stolen from the future, while giving them endless — albeit artificial — economic and trade imbalance problems to solve through policies of statist intervention.

43 Straight Years Of Increasing US Merchandise Trade Deficits

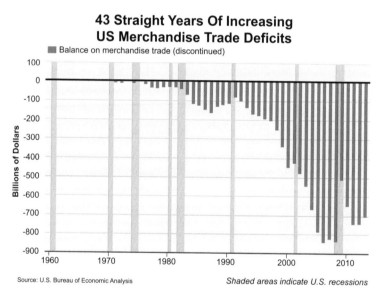

Source: U.S. Bureau of Economic Analysis   Shaded areas indicate U.S. recessions

More important, the above chart is not the product of bad trade deals as averred by the Donald; it's the step child of bad money, as we amplify in chapter 10.

It came about because central bankers in America

230

systematically and chronically inflated domestic costs, prices and wages on the misbegotten Keynesian predicate that inflation is the handmaid of economic growth and prosperity; and that nothing less than 2.00% inflation is the very elixir of prosperity.

To the contrary, the Fed's pro-inflation policies have functioned as a destroyer of competitiveness, good jobs and real production-based wealth in the US economy. That's because after the inflationary blow-off of the 1970s, America's heavily unionized industrial wages were already increasingly disadvantaged in the global economy.

But when Greenspan went all-in for central bank driven prosperity management after 1987, a fatal process was unleashed. As hundreds of millions of new low cost industrial workers were recruited from the rice paddies of China and east Asia, the natural tendency was for domestic US wages and prices to deflate in order to preserve international competitiveness.

But the Maestro and his money printers were having nothing to do with sound economics — electing instead to counteract the natural deflationary forces at loose in the world with massive expansion of domestic credit designed to keep domestic wages and prices continuously rising.

As is evident from the chart below, however, Greenspanian pro-inflation policies back-fired. Real wages have been stagnant or slightly shrinking for 30 years, even as nominal wages — what really matter in global markets dominated by the China Price for goods and the India Price for services — have nearly tripled.

In short, the post-1971 regime of central banking and globalism delivered an off-shored and hollowed-out domestic economy, not a rising level of real wages and domestic prosperity.

They also eventually brought American politics full circle by the election of a bombastic, incorrigible protectionist to

Average Hourly Earnings
Production and Nonsupervisory Employees

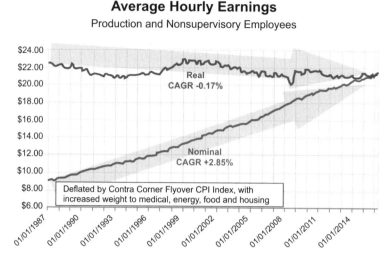

the Oval Office. As one MSM commentator gummed at the time, the Quebec summit may prove to be the death knell for the rotten regime of bad money and globalist statism which incepted in the 1970s.

The stinging rebuke of Treasury Secretary Steven Mnuchin over the weekend at a Group of Seven finance ministers meeting may mark the beginning of the end of the organization, experts fear.

There is "a growing concern that the entire rules-based international system and the institutions that underlie it are increasingly at risk," William Reinsch, a senior adviser at the Center for Strategic and International Studies, told reporters on a conference call Monday.

After an unsuccessful charm offensive to try to convince President Donald Trump that a trade war was not in anyone's interest, the leaders of the other six nations of the G-7 group are going to "try something else" and be more confrontational, added Heather Conley, a former U. S. State Department officials now with the CSIS.

Needless to say, whatever they tried didn't work. Instead, the Quebec summit brought Trump's pre-eminent virtue to the fore.

BOMBS AWAY OVER QUEBEC

That is, he stubbornly refuses to be instructed, mediated, scripted and sherpa'd by the political class. So however misguided and superficial his policy stances might be, he does represent a direct intrusion by the electorate into their own process of purportedly democratic governance; and in a disruptive manner that has not issued from the Oval Office since the early days of Ronald Reagan before he, too, (like Gerald Ford) became house-trained by the system.

To be sure, the Donald has got it all wrong on the trade question as a substantive matter. As we demonstrate in chapter 10, America's massive trade, jobs and growth deficits are not due to rising tariff and non-tariff barriers abroad.

Moreover, even if there are higher tariffs on some products and in some countries, the answer is not filling our harbors with rocks to match theirs or punishing our consumers to order to strike at their stupidity for sending subsidized goods and services to America.

Nevertheless, the Donald went to Canada on an important mission, packing a bogus protectionist agenda. And, ironically, the latter is so primitive and nonsensical that it promised a fair chance to actually accomplish the job immediately at hand — blowing up the G-7 and the whole misbegotten Keynesian project of global policy coordination.

Still, only an unreconstructed 18th century mercantilist could argue that national security requires protectionist steel and auto tariffs. After all, the world is drowning in upwards of 700 million tons of excess steel capacity (compared to DOD requirements of less than 2 million tons per year) and has the capacity to produce millions of excess auto units annually.

So it was bombs away over Quebec:

The United States must, at long last, be treated fairly on Trade," Mr. Trump tweeted as G-7 finance ministers finished the pre-summit meeting in Canada last weekend. "If we charge a country ZERO to sell their goods, and they charge us 25, 50 or even 100 percent to sell ours, it is UNFAIR and can no longer be tolerated. That is not Free or Fair Trade, it is Stupid Trade!"

It's hard to think of anything more foolish than the above statement, albeit well-intended as the Donald might be.

Actually, in fact, there is one thing decidedly more foolish: The utterly naive wishful thinking down in the canyons of Wall Street that on trade the Donald is all bark and no bite.

CHAPTER 10

Bad Money, Not Bad Trade Deals Is The Cause Of America's Trade Disaster

The global trading system's newly activated one-man wrecking crew was at it over Oscars weekend last spring. Mustering up his best Clint Eastwood impression, Trump invited his target of the moment — the Brussels trade bureaucrats — to make his day.

Retaliate against Harley's Hogs, Jim Beam's bourbon and Levi's Skinny Jeans, proclaimed the Donald, and you folks are going to find yourself neck deep in BMW's:

> *If the E. U. wants to further increase their already massive tariffs and barriers on U. S. companies doing business there, we will simply apply a Tax on their Cars which freely pour into the U. S. They make it impossible for our cars (and more) to sell there. Big trade imbalance!*

Let us reiterate what we said in chapter 9. This is not just another case of Trump banging on a twitter keyboard that doesn't push back — unlike the courts, most of the Dems, much of the Congressional GOP and a goodly part of his cabinet.

On the matter of trade policy, by contrast, the Donald has considerable unilateral running room owing to the vast presidential powers bestowed by section 232 of the 1962 trade act and section 301 of the 1974 trade act. The former authorizes protectionist measures, including tariffs, to safeguard "national security" and the latter authorizes such measures in order to enforce US trade agreements or to counter "unfair" foreign trade practices.

To be sure, the rubbery definitions of the quoted terms (national security and unfair practices) were meant to be parsed and activated narrowly by mainstream White House occupants, not to be used as a protectionist blunderbuss by a raging wild man intoxicated with 18th century notions of mercantilist economics.

Steel And The Fig Leaf Of National Defense

For example, consider the national defense fig leaf under section 232 that Trump tapped for his across-the-board 25% tariff on $29 billion of annual steel imports.

Last year the US produced an estimated 82 million tons of steel domestically and imported another 14 million tons from Canada, Brazil and Mexico, which are the #1, #2 and #4 steel importers to the United States, respectively. So that's 96 million tons of availability — assuming that our hemispheric neighbors, who have no nukes, are not foolish enough to declare war on Washington and embargo their steel exports to the US.

Somehow 96 million tons seems more than adequate to cover the 2 million tons per year needed for the current US war machine, according to the Pentagon; and in truth the real requirement would be far less — perhaps a few hundred thousand tons per year to protect the actual safety and security of the US homeland.

After all, under the present state of affairs true national security is purely a matter of nuclear deterrence — since no country in the world has an even remote capacity to invade North America with conventional forces. Moreover, the steel used in our current massive nuclear retaliatory force (Trident subs, Minutemen missiles and strategic bombers) was produced long ago.

That is, we actually don't need no more stinkin' nukes nor any more steel to launch them.

In fact, if Washington stopped wasting money on aircraft carriers, tanks, amphibious landing ships, TOW missiles, airlift planes and bunker buster bombs, among other weapons of foreign invasion and occupation, the national defense really wouldn't need much more steel annually than is produced by Denmark (70k tons). In today's world, in fact, military steel is about empire, not homeland security.

At least in his tweet storms, the Donald hasn't hidden behind this lame national security defense — even if it is the source of his authority to scare the bejesus out of the rest of the civilized world.

Nope. Trump came right out and said he loathes the outcome of the current global trading system and is now launching drastic actions with protectionist malice aforethought. In fact, not even the Oscars could slowed him down, as he further tweeted on that Sunday night:

> *The United States has an $800 Billion Dollar Yearly Trade Deficit because of our "very stupid" trade deals and policies. Our jobs and wealth are being given to other countries that have taken advantage of us for years. They laugh at what fools our leaders have been. No more!*
>
> *We are on the losing side of almost all trade deals. Our friends and enemies have taken advantage of the U. S. for many years. Our Steel and Aluminum industries are dead. "*

The funny thing is that Trump has an overwhelming case. Almost to the year that the foolish Trade Act of 1974 was put on the books, the US experienced its last annual trade (goods) surplus in 1975.

Since then, there has been a continuous and deepening of

the US trade deficit. That is, a 43-year plunge into the red that marks the vast off-shoring of US production, jobs, and wages.

In all, it cumulates to about *$15 trillion* more of stuff America bought versus what it sold to the rest of the world since 1975. And needless to say, that doesn't happen on a level playing field.

In that respect, at least, the Donald's so-called free trade critics have their heads buried deeper in the sand than even the orange comb-over. That's because most of them are Saltwater Keynesians of the Harvard/IMF/Brookings school or Freshwater Keynesians of the Friedman/Chicago/AEI persuasion.

Either way, the establishment free-traders seem to think that America can borrow its way to prosperity forever and ever, world without end; and that the mangled state of the US economy after four decades of this kind of trade mayhem is a natural outcome of relatively free markets at work.

No it isn't!

Even when you throw in the $4 trillion surplus on the services account (tourism, transportation, insurance, royalties and business services) during the same 43-year period, the deficit on current account with the rest of the world is still $11 trillion, and that's in then-year dollars. Inflated to 2018 purchasing power, the balance with the rest of the world since 1975 amounts to upwards of $19 trillion or nearly the current GDP of the US.

So notwithstanding his rhetorical bombast and primitive mercantilism, the Donald is on to something. In fact, it's why his candidacy rallied large swaths of voters in Flyover America, and it is ultimately why he won the electoral college, effectively, in the swing industrial precincts of Pennsylvania, Ohio, Michigan, Wisconsin and Iowa.

Alas, the *$11 trillion* economic enema depicted on the next page (between the blue and orange lines) is not the work of

43-Year Cumulative Current Account Deficit----$11 Trillion

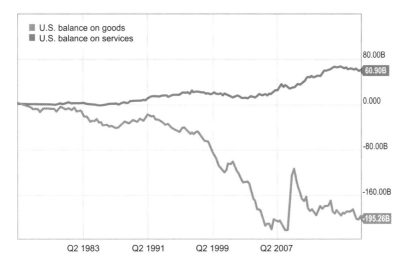

fools, knaves or traitors in the trade negotiations departments of the US government. That is to say, the USTR (US trade representative), the Commerce Department and the State Department trade apparatchiks had comparatively little to do with it; nor can it be pinned on NAFTA, the WTO (world trade organization) or even the globalist minions at the IMF and World Bank, either.

Instead, the malefactors names are Alan (Greenspan), Ben (Bernanke) and the Two Janets (Yellen and Powell). America is losing it shirt in trade owing to bad money, not bad deals.

That's because Keynesian monetary central planning has it upside down. It seeks to **inflate** domestic prices, wages and costs at **2%** per year (or more if correctly measured) in a world teeming with cheap labor — when a regime of honest money would have generated **deflationary** adjustments designed to keep American industry competitive.

Likewise, Bubble Finance has resulted in drastic financial repression, ultra-low, sub-economic interest rates and debt fueled consumption and financialization — when sound money would have caused the opposite. To wit, high interest rates, low consumption and enhanced levels of savings and investments in order to maintain sustainable equilibrium with the rest of the world.

Above all, America's greatest export historically was not merely the continuous trade surpluses racked-up every single year between 1893 and 1971, but actually the ideas and institutions of free enterprise and capitalist invention. Yet it all went wrong after Tricky Dick's disastrous lurch into 100% state controlled money at Camp David in August 1971.

America's Leading Post-1971 Export — Monetary Inflation

By unleashing the world's leading central bank to print money at will, Nixon paved the way for the Eccles Building to become a massive exporter of monetary inflation.

At length, these floods of unwanted dollars mightily encouraged the mercantilism-prone nations of the East Asia, the petro-states, much of the EM and sometimes Europe, too, to buy dollars and inflate their own currencies. They did this in order to forestall exchange rate appreciation and the consequent short-run dislocations in their own heavily subsidized export sectors.

Below we track exactly how the Fed's great export contraption of monetary inflation brought about the hollowing out of industrial America as per the Donald's case of mistaken blame. But suffice it to say that in the pre-Keynesian world in which a monetary settlement asset governed the flow of trade and international finance, and which was anchored in gold rather than the fiat credit of national central banks, there would have been no such thing as $15 trillion of continuous US merchandise trade deficits over 43 years running.

Instead, the large trade deficits caused by the mobilization of cheap labor from the Asian rice paddies and cheap energy from the sands of Arabia would have generated their own correction.

To wit, large US current account deficits would have caused a painful outflow of the settlement asset (gold),which, in turn, would have caused domestic interest rates to rise, domestic credit to shrink and prices, wages and costs to deflate.

At length, imports would have been declined, exports would have increased and the US current account would have returned to sustainable equilibrium, thereby bringing about a reflow of the settlement asset (gold) back to the US.

As it happened, however, the Fed's destructive monetary inflation spread like an infectious disease, and nowhere is that more evident than in the case of the Donald's favorite whipping boy, NAFTA. The latter is an arrangement that Trump does not even vaguely understand — attested to by the fact that his recently ballyhooed "deal" after months of huffing and puffing amounted to nothing more than a name change.

As to the underlying substance, however, nothing has changed because the central banking source of the problem has not been addressed in the slightest.

Thus, the real source of the drastic current trade imbalance

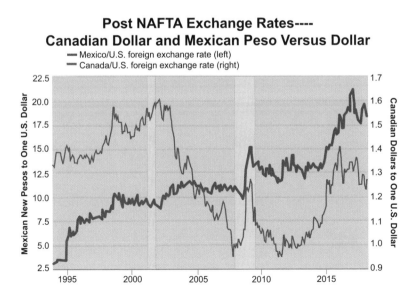

Post NAFTA Exchange Rates----
Canadian Dollar and Mexican Peso Versus Dollar
— Mexico/U.S. foreign exchange rate (left)
— Canada/U.S. foreign exchange rate (right)

with Mexico is that it went whole hog trashing its own currency in response to dollar inflation after the inception of NAFTA and the peso crisis in the early 1990s. Since then, the peso's exchange rate versus the dollar has plunged from about *3:1 to 20:1*.

Not surprisingly, Mexico's already cheap labor become that much cheaper in dollar terms, meaning that the Donald actually hit the nail on the head.

In 1991, US exports to Mexico slightly exceeded imports, meaning there was an actual bilateral surplus with Mexico. By contrast, in 2017 the US incurred a whopping $71 billion trade deficit. US exports to Mexico, in fact, were just $243 billion or 77% of the $314 billion of US imports from Mexico.

Still, that huge imbalance wasn't owing to removal of tariffs and other barriers under the NAFTA deal which became effective on January 1, 1994 — nor was it owing to Mexican trade machinations since then. It was and remains a monetary and relative cost phenomena.

The evidence for that lays in the other half of the Donald's

US/Mexican Exports and Imports Since NAFTA

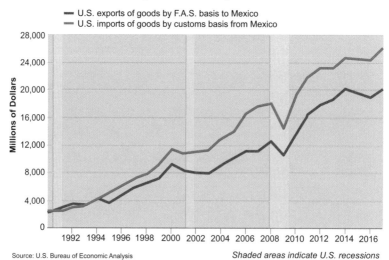

— U.S. exports of goods by F.A.S. basis to Mexico
— U.S. imports of goods by customs basis from Mexico

Source: U.S. Bureau of Economic Analysis   *Shaded areas indicate U.S. recessions*

anti-NAFTA crusade concerning Canada, which he's gotten all wrong.

Whatever games the Canadians have played in mercantilist promotion of individual commodities such as forest products, the Canadian exchange rate is not much different today than it was in the early 1990s. Nor has its internal prices, wages and costs changed much relative to the domestic US economy.

Not surprisingly, there has also been no trend change in the US trade balance with Canada. Both imports and exports have grown by about *4X* compared to their pre-NAFTA levels in the early 1990s. In fact, during 2017 US exports to Canada totaled $282 billion and imports from Canada were $300 billion. With exports at 95% of imports, we'd say that's close enough to zero for government work.

Stated differently, an allegedly "bad" trade deal led to wholly different outcomes as between the NAFTA partner to the north versus the partner to the south. So the cause of the imbalance with Mexico was not in the mechanics of NAFTA; it originated in FX differentials and their impact on relative wages, costs and

US/Canada Exports and Imports Since NAFTA

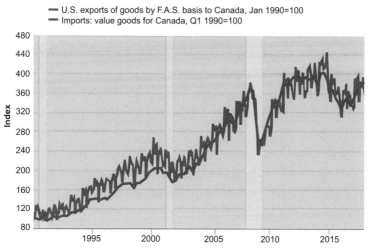

— U.S. exports of goods by F.A.S. basis to Canada, Jan 1990=100
— Imports: value goods for Canada, Q1 1990=100

Sources: BEA, OECD   Shaded areas indicate U.S. recessions

prices between the two economies.

Nor is the NAFTA case an isolated example. More generally, America's massive trade deficit problem and the resulting drastic decline of the US industrial economy during recent decades is a function of bad money, not bad trade deals. The divergent exchange rate history of these two NAFTA partners — Mexico depreciated and Canada didn't — since 1993 provides a pretty good illustration of this phenomenon.

When mercantilist nations used the flood of Fed dollars as an excuse to engage in persistent exchange rate suppression and dirty floats, they did in fact steal production and jobs from American workers.

But as we will see below, the solution to that is a hard dollar at the Fed, not loud hollering through a Twitter account from the Oval Office.

So the Donald is right about the horrific results of US trade since the 1970s: To repeat, the Keynesian "free traders" of both the saltwater (Harvard) and freshwater (Chicago) schools of monetary central planning have their heads buried far deeper in the sand than does even the orange comb-over with his bombastic affection for 18th century mercantilism.

The fact is, you do not get an $810 billion trade deficit and a 66% ratio of exports ($1.55 trillion) to imports ($2.36 trillion), as the US did in 2017, on a level playing field. And most especially, an honest free market would never generate an unbroken and deepening string of trade deficits over the last 43 years running, which cumulate to the staggering sum of $15 trillion.

Better than anything else, those baleful trade numbers explain why industrial America has been hollowed-out and off-shored, and why vast stretches of Flyover America have been left to flounder in economic malaise and decline.

But two things are absolutely clear about the "why" of this $15 trillion calamity. To wit, it was not caused by some mysterious loss of capitalist enterprise and energy on America's main street economy since 1975. Nor was it caused — contrary to the Donald's simple-minded blather — by bad trade deals and stupid people at the USTR and Commerce Department.

After all, American capitalism produced modest trade surpluses every year during the 80 years prior to 1975. Yet it has not lost its mojo during the 43 years of massive trade deficits since then. In fact, the explosion of technological advance in Silicon Valley and on-line business enterprise from coast-to-coast suggests more nearly the opposite.

Likewise, the basic framework of global commerce and trade deals under the WTO and other multi-lateral arrangements was established in the immediate post-war years and was well embedded when the US ran trade surpluses in the 1950s and 1960s.

Those healthy post-war US trade surpluses, in fact, were consistent with the historical scheme of things during the golden era of industrial growth between 1870 and 1914.

During that era of gold standard-based global commerce, Great Britain, France and the US (after the mid-1890s) tended to run trade surpluses owing to their advanced technology, industry and productivity, while exporting capital to less developed economies around the world. That's also what the US did during the halcyon economic times of the 1950s and 1960s.

What changed dramatically after 1975, however, is the monetary regime, and with it the regulator of both central bank policy and the resulting expansion rate of global credit.

In a word, Tricky Dick's shit-canning of the Bretton Woods gold exchange standard removed the essential flywheel that kept global trade balanced and sustainable. As we have seen, without a disciplinary mechanism independent of and external to the central banks, trade and current account imbalances among countries never needed to be "settled" via gains and losses in the reserve asset (gold or gold-linked dollars).

Stated differently, the destruction of Bretton Woods allowed domestic monetary policies to escape the financial discipline that automatically resulted from reserve asset movements. That is, trade deficits caused the loss of gold, domestic deflation and an eventual rebalancing of trade. At the same time, the prolonged accumulation of reserve assets owing to persistent current account surpluses generated the opposite — domestic credit expansion, price and wage inflation and an eventual reduction in those surpluses.

Professor Friedman's Giant Mistake: Dirty Floats, Not Free Market FX Rates

Needless to say, as the issuer of the gold-linked "reserve currency" under Bretton Woods, the Fed was the first to break jail when Nixon deep-sixed America's obligation to redeem dollars for gold in 1971-1973. At the time, however, the freshwater Keynesians led by Milton Friedman and his errand boy in the Nixon/Ford White House, labor economics professor George Shultz, said there was nothing to sweat over.

That's because the free market would purportedly generate the "correct" exchange rate between the dollar and D-mark, franc, yen etc; and then these market-determined FX rates, in turn, would regulate the flow of trade and capital.

Very simple. Adam Smith's unseen hand all over again.

In fact, not in a million years!

The giant skunk in the woodpile actually smelled of state-driven monetary emissions or what was called the "Dirty Float."

The latter threw everything into a cocked hat. Unlike under Bretton Woods or the classic pre-1914 gold standard, the new regime of unanchored money allowed governments to hijack their central banks and to use them as instruments of mercantilist trade promotion and Keynesian domestic macroeconomic management.

To be sure, it took some time for traditional central bankers to realize that they had been unshackled. For example, during the final years of his tenure (1970-1978) Arthur Burns caused a pretty nasty recession in 1975 trying to reclaim his reputation for monetary probity after meekly capitulating to Nixon in fueling the 1972 election year boom that finally destroyed the remnants of Bretton Woods entirely.

At length, however, Alan Greenspan inaugurated the era of Bubble Finance in 1987, and the die was cast. During his 19-years at the helm of the Fed, Greenspan massively inflated the Fed's balance sheet (from $200 billion to $830 billion) and the cost structure of the US economy at a time when the mobilization of cheap labor from the rice paddies of China and east Asia demanded exactly the opposite policy. That is, a policy of Fed balance sheet shrinkage and domestic deflation.

Accordingly, a destructive pattern of reciprocating monetary inflation within the global convoy of central banks was set in motion: The Fed inflated and then its counterparts around the world inflated in a continuous loop. So doing, the central banks of the world locked into a permanent condition of unbalanced trade.

The latter originated in the Fed's flood of excess dollars into the international financial system in the 1990s and thereafter.

China Central Bank Balance Sheet

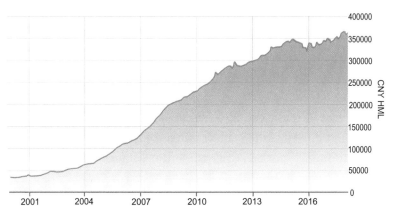

Source: Tradingeconomics.com | Peoples Bank of China

This, in turn, caused central banks in Asia, much of the EM, the petro-states and sometimes Europe, too, to buy dollars and sequester them in US treasury paper (and GSE securities). This Dirty Float was undertaken, of course, to stop exchange rate appreciation and to further mercantilist trade and export-based domestic economic policies in China, South Korea, Japan and elsewhere.

But what is also did was enable a sustained debt-based consumption boom in the US that was not earned by current production. The excess of US consumption over production, which showed up in the continuous US current account deficits, was effectively borrowed from central banks (and often their domestic investors).

That happened because these central banks, for example, as in the case of China displayed above, were willing to swap the labor of their people and the endowments of their natural resources for US debt paper rather than face rising exchange rates and temporary headwinds to their mercantilist growth strategies.

In short, the $15 trillion plague of US trade deficits since 1975 is the bastard step-child of the Dirty Float maintained in Asia and elsewhere as a defense against the Fed's profligate money printing. Over time, it morphed into a back-door form of de facto export subsidies that would otherwise be illegal under the current WTO rules of global trade.

So when the Donald declaims that pointy-head bureaucrats are the culprits behind the US trade disaster, the part that he gets wrong is only the names of the miscreants. To wit, the real malefactors of trade stupidity are named Greenspan, Bernanke, Yellen and Powell. America has suffered a trade calamity owing to their bad money, not bad deals cut at the Commerce Department or Foggy Bottom (State).

As we indicated above, Keynesian monetary central planning has it upside down. It seeks to inflate domestic prices, wages and costs at 2% per year in a world teeming with cheap labor — when a regime of honest money would have generated deflationary adjustments designed to keep American industry competitive.

Had the Fed conducted a regime of sound money, it would have denied much of the incentive for and rationalization of the Dirty Float. Indeed, had the US maintained a regime of high interest rates, low consumption and enhanced levels of savings and investments in order to maintain sustainable equilibrium with the rest of the world after 1990, it is doubtful that the Dirty Float would have become massive, near-universal and quasi-permanent.

That's because in a world of hard dollars, money-printing, low-interest rate central banks would have caused soaring domestic inflation and destructive capital flight. The People's Printing Press of China, for example, would have been caught short decades ago.

Indeed, in a world of hard money, the egregious *9X* expansion of its balance sheet, which fueled the Red Ponzi's runaway capital spending mania, could never have happened.

Needless to say, China was not the only Dirty Float malefactor. The Japanese have been far worse.

Japan Central Bank Balance Sheet

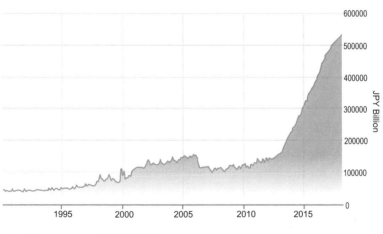

Since 1990 the balance sheet of the BOJ has expanded by *20X*, thereby insuring that the yen exchange rate versus the dollar remained uneconomically low, and that Japan's egregiously mercantilist trade policy would remain undisturbed by honest yen selling prices for its goods sold on the international markets.

The story is much the same throughout the lands of cheap labor and/or Dirty Floats. As we pointed out above, Mexico's exchange rate has fallen from *3:1* prior to NAFTA's inception to *20:1* at present. Therefore, it wasn't a bad trade deal that caused the current $71 billion US trade deficit with Mexico; it was bad money.

After all, about the only thing more profligate than the Fed's *20X* balance sheet growth since 1990, is the *40X* expansion by the Mexican central bank.

Mexico Central Bank Balance Sheet

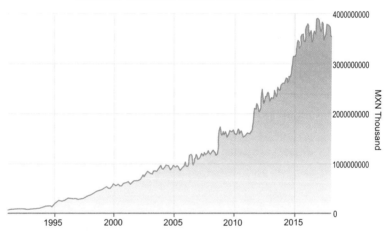

Source: Tradingeconomics.com | Banco de Mexico

90% Of The US Trade Deficit Is Due To Dirty Floats

Not surprisingly, it turns out that the land of Dirty Floats accounts for the **90%** of the $810 billion trade deficit incurred by the US last year (2017).

That's right. The overall trade problem is that the US

exported only $1.55 trillion of goods, materials and energy last year, or just *66%* of the $2.36 trillion of merchandise that it imported. Yet just 10 countries account for nearly all of that huge imbalance.

These countries are China, Vietnam, Mexico, Japan, Germany, South Korea, Taiwan, Malaysia, Thailand and India. As a group, these countries bought just $627 billion of US exports, while sending $1.35 trillion of imports to the US.

Accordingly, the combined deficit was $725 billion, representing 90% of the total US trade deficit.

Moreover, the US export-to-import ratio was just 46% for the 10 countries as a whole, and far worse among the most egregious Dirty Floaters.

Thus, China's $130 billion of exports from the US represented just 25% of its $527 billion of imports to the US. In the case of Vietnam, the export ratio was only 17% ($8 billion of US exports versus $46 billion of imports to the US).

As we indicated, the massive trade deficit with these 10 countries is largely a product of the Eccles Building and the Dirty Floats it has fostered among these mercantilist countries.

And that's true even in the case of Germany, which sent $118 billion of goods to the US last year compared to US exports to Germany of just $53 billion. The latter amounted to only *45%* of imports from Germany, and resulted in a staggering $65 billion trade deficit with the US.

Were Germany not a part of the EU, the exchange rate for the D-mark would be far higher than the euro's, and Germany's trade surplus with the US (and the rest of the world) would be far smaller. In effect, the mad money printer, Mario Draghi, has actually effected a hidden Dirty Float that has been a tremendous windfall to German industry.

By contrast, the US trade accounts are functionally in balance with the entire rest of the world. As we showed above, for instance, US exports to Canada are *95%* of imports from our giant trading partner to the north.

Indeed, for the rest-of-the-world as a whole, the trade numbers are quite striking and sustainable. Overall US exports to these 130 destinations amounted to $924 billion during 2017 compared to $1.0 trillion of imports from these suppliers.

Accordingly, exports amounted to *92%* of imports, and the total $76 billion deficit at just *4%* of two-way trade (nearly $1.92 trillion) was close enough to zero for big picture purposes.

And that gets us to the big fat skunk in the Donald's woodpile of trade delusions. Self-evidently, trade deals and the WTO did not produce a healthy balance with 130 countries and a disaster with just 10 bilateral partners.

Stated differently, the same "bad" and "dumb" trade deals did not generate a deficit of just $76 billion and 4% of total turnover with the preponderant share of US trade partners, but a deficit of $723 billion or 37% of two-way turnover among the ten big Dirty Floaters.

Instead, we are dealing here with bad money, but, alas, neither the protectionist inside the White House nor the free traders shouting at the front gate have explained that to the Donald.

Ironically, the only way out of the Donald's crude protectionism is a return to sound money. Yet that's the last thing the Wall Street and Fortune 500 "free-traders" are about to embrace.

In effect, they wish to perpetuate a monetary regime that swaps American labor and living standard in Flyover America for massively inflated financial asset prices on Wall Street. That is, for unspeakable windfalls to the top *1%* and *10%* which own 45% and 85% of financial assets, respectively.

No wonder the people out there in Rust Belt America are mad!

And it's also no wonder they put a madman in the Oval Office to attack a system that truly is "rigged" against them.

CHAPTER 11

Smoot-Hawley Redux

The Donald apparently believes that ever since Smoot-Hawley worked out so well in the 1930s that the US has been foolishly engaged in unilateral disarmament on the trade front.

In fact, if trade is all about bilateral export/import scoreboards and whose tariff is bigger, then to hear the Donald tell it you would think America has the shortest one on the planet at barely **2%** of imported goods' value.

You could call it the Tiny Tariff Syndrome (TTS). But it's not the source of America's massive trade imbalances as we demonstrated in chapter 10.

The steady reduction of US tariff levels from the 30% level of the McKinley Tariff at the turn of the 20th century has been an unequivocal boon to domestic prosperity and wealth generation. In fact, during the last 30 years worldwide tariff rates have fallen by a stunning 80%.

On the current $17 trillion of worldwide two-way merchandise trade, the average tariff is now just 2% or virtually identical to that of the US.

Besides, tariffs are taxes on domestic consumers since they tend to create an above market *price umbrella* for products where imports form a significant share of the market. So the burden on commerce is not just the tariff dollars collected at the border; it's the tariff rate times the totality of domestic consumption, which includes the windfall transfer to domestic producers resulting from tariff-bloated selling prices.

To be sure, some countries do subsidize their exports through currency repression or direct government fiscal and tax aids.

But at the end of the day, that amounts to a transfer of foreign aid to the US or other importing countries. It's a windfall gain to domestic welfare that shows the stupidity of mercantilist export promotion, but most certainly does not merit taxing domestic consumers in retribution for the economic sins of foreign governments.

The above World Bank graph on the steady descent of average global tariff levels also debunks the Donald's calamity-howling about Canada's 270% tariff on milk and Germany's 10% tariff on cars. In citing these examples, he's basically grasping at non-representative outliers. Otherwise the 2.0% average tariff level shown above would not compute.

The Donald's Trade Views Are Based On Fake Facts

Worse still, he often just makes it up as in this infamous riff before the June G-7 meeting:

"The United States must, at long last, be treated fairly on

Century Long Decline In Average US Tariff Rates

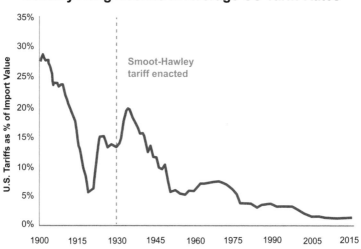

Trade," Mr. Trump tweeted as G-7 finance ministers finished the pre-summit meeting in Canada last weekend. "If we charge a country ZERO to sell their goods, and they charge us 25, 50 or even 100 percent to sell ours, it is UNFAIR and can no longer be tolerated. That is not Free or Fair Trade, it is Stupid Trade!"

In fact, Trump's proficiency at finding these tariff rate aberrations puts you in mind of the keen-eyed young boy looking for bubble gum in the chicken coop!

At least, that's what the data below suggests.

Thus, at **1.70%** of imported value, the average US tariff is virtually identical to the "massive tariffs" Trump claimed to be imposed by France, which actually average out to just *1.96%*; and that figure happens to be the same as Germany's weighted average rate of *1.96%*, as well.

Actually, Canada's weighted average tariff is a tiny tad lower than the US rate — just *1.56%* of the value of goods imported. Moreover, even today's minuscule tariff rates for all four countries have been steadily declining for decades.

More important, these differences are rounding errors — great big nothing burgers in the scheme of things.

Average Global Tariff Rate (%)

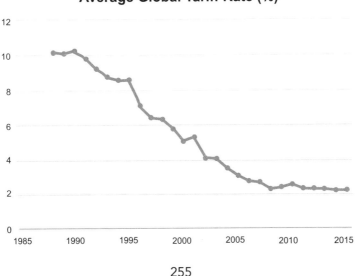

Contrary to the duplicitous rhetoric of Larry Kudlow and other White House free trade shills, you could get rid of all tariffs in the world today — and it would have virtually no impact on America's *$800 billion* annual deficit in merchandise trade or add a blip to US growth and jobs.

So the facts are absolutely clear: It is beyond lunacy to launch a global trade war based on "unfair" tariffs or to cite outlier examples as proof of nefarious foreign practices.

Consider, for example, the de minimis role of tariffs in the $720 billion of combined two-way trade between the US and the EC in 2017. Fully 50% or $360 billion of that trade turnover was subject to zero tariffs, and the total levy on $283 billion of US exports to Europe was well less than $5 billion.

The Donald's doddering old Commerce Secretary, Wilbur Ross, is always talking about how the Administration's idiotic 25% tariff on steel amounts to less than one penny per can of Campbell soup. But here's the real empty soup can: The total annual tariff levied on US exports by Canada and the EC — the Donald's targets at the G-7 meeting — amounts to *0.03%* of US GDP!

The truth is, what gets the Donald (and other protectionists) aroused on the matter of tariffs is one-off situations where powerful domestic lobbies have built a wall of protection over the years — even though they amount to rounding errors in the total value of trade.

For instance, Trump is always harrumphing about the EC's 10% tariff on passenger car imports compared to only 2.5% for the US.

Yet he has never mentions that the US has a 25% tariff on pick-up trucks. Perhaps that's because the so-called free trade US auto industry would literally attack the Oval Office door with tire irons if he ever tried to reduce it.

After all, the Chevrolet Silverados, Ford F-150s and Dodge Ram trucks thus protected account for virtually all of the Big

Three's North American profits.

Likewise, when it comes to train carriages, the shoe is on the other foot: The US imposes a 14% duty versus a EU duty of just 1.7% on imports from the US.

Then it's also true that the EU imposes a 30% tariff on shoes and clothes — but those are obviously aimed at China and Vietnam, not the US — which doesn't make these products anymore, anyway.

Likewise, the US imposes duties of 350% and 130% on tobacco and peanuts, respectively, and its not hard to see the fine hand of the farm lobby's crop-by-crop log-rolling operation at work. Still, we doubt whether these US lobbies take much skin off the back of European farmers, who essentially don't grow these crops.

In any event, this zero-sum game has fallen out of favor around the world. Based on a somewhat different measure of global tariffs than shown above, World Bank data shows the steady drop from an average worldwide tariff rate of 30% in the early 1980s to well into the low single digits today; and in the case of the so-called rich countries (yellow line), the average rate is approaching the vanishing point.

Trends in Tariff Rates (%)

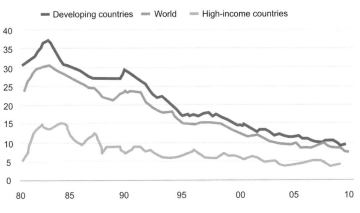

Source: World Bank

Even the statist and socialist authorities who run trade policy in most countries today have recognized that tariffs do not create net domestic jobs and growth — just an arbitrary re-allocation of the pie.

Ntbs Can't Be Eliminated By Tariff Wars, Either

Yes, we do know about non-tariff barriers (NTBs). These are more subtle forms of discrimination against foreign goods used by mercantilist governments around the world — such as "health and safety" regulations that are biased against foreign suppliers or require a license or certification that never seems to be forthcoming from the host government.

In fact, that was one of the original research assignments we got from our boss, Congressman John Anderson, way back in 1970. He represented Rockford, Illinois, and in those days the area was a powerhouse exporter of corn, soybeans, machine tools and much else.

He also had Nixon's ear on trade — so our job was to dig up NTBs that could be waved at the Japanese and others during negotiations to open up foreign markets for US export products.

Admittedly, most of these NTBs are blatantly protectionist in purpose and often so far-fetched as to strain credulity. For instance, a Japanese agriculture minister of that era insisted that Japanese intestines were much smaller than American ones, and that US beef was therefore a dire health hazard!

In any event, even NTB's have been steadily chipped away since the 1970s owing to several rounds of world trade negotiations, and are far less significant obstacles to trade flows today.

And that gets to the heart of the matter. The trend growth rate of the US economy has been steadily falling since the 1970s — virtually in tandem with the decline of tariff and non-tariff barriers to commerce. So unfair trade practices abroad absolutely do not explain why growth is faltering at home.

The previously presented chart below helps to crystallize this point by showing the rolling 10-year average GDP growth rate in order to even out the cyclical fluctuations. Self-evidently, what was a 4.0% per annum growth trend between 1954 and 1974 (i. e. after the distortions occasioned by WW II and the post-war demobilization worked out of the 10-year average) has steadily diminished , and in recent years has actually bottomed at just *1.3%*.

Indeed, what the chart below actually correlates with is not bad trade deals and rising unfair trade practices, but the arrival and apotheosis of bad money after Richard Nixon shit-canned the Bretton Woods gold exchange standard in August 1971.

10-Year Average GDP Growth Rate

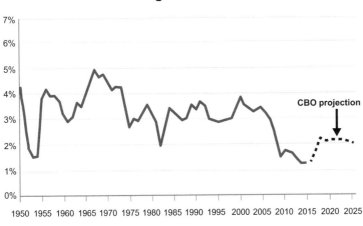

Sources: Bureau of Economic Analysis, CBO January 2016 baseline, CRFB calculations
Note: These are compound averages over 10 years. The CBO projection line includes historic data to maintain 10-year average.

And that gets us to the heart of the Donald's incorrigible trade protectionism. In fact, it has nothing to do with economic analysis, policy principles or the observable empirical trends with respect to trade barriers — which all go the other way.

Instead, it all about the *Art of the Deal* — the lens through which Trump views the entire world and which informs everything he does.

That this winning versus losing worldview boils down to a crude form of tit-for-tat tariff math was made crystal clear in the above cited tweet storm. The Donald falsely claimed that America's tariffs are low and foreign tariffs are high owing to decades of stupidity in Washington and the nefarious dealings of dumb trade negotiators. That is to say, America's crushing $800 billion trade deficit is due not to economics and monetary influences, but sheer incompetence in the realm of international trade negotiations—something the Donald's superior skills at the latter can easily remedy. No sweat!

Of course, what is actually "Stupid" here is the presumption that the trade issue boils down to a 10% tariff on passenger car imports in Europe versus a 2.5% rate on imports to the US.

As demonstrated above, that kind of tariff rate differential is far more the exception than the rule and it's off-set by an equal number of examples that go the other way. The fact is, the relevant tariffs in the world today range between zero and 5%, and thereby have virtually nothing to do with the America's $800 billion deficit in traded goods.

How The Donald Got Milk

Nevertheless, when it comes to the Donald's Art of the Deal framework any number will do, and the dairy industry provides a whopper.

Trump essentially won the electoral college on the margin in the once and former "Dairy State" of Wisconsin. During the course of his campaigning there, he surely found his mark.

As one writer recently noted:

Canada's 270% milk tariff is Trump's favorite whipping boy and hit in his Wisconsin speech, but its to protect a relic of New Deal cartelism: It's not unfair, it's stupid and a massive penalty to its own citizens.

But that has not held Trump back from speaking out about trade with Canada. At an event in Wisconsin last week, Trump called Canada's dairy pricing scheme a "disgrace" and "another typical one-sided deal against the U. S." He has promised to "stand up for our dairy farmers" and "get the solution," though he has not specified what that solution is.

As it happens, even FDR's down on the farm socialism was never as absurd as Canada's cartelized diary industry. Every one of its 12,000 dairy farms has a production quota in gallons of milk that can be sold legally.

In return, it is illegal to sell milk in Canada below a government mandated support price that is way above the world price — nor to import it at the drastically lower world price without paying the 270% tariff upcharge.

Obviously, without the high tariff, the whole cartel arrangement would collapse in a heartbeat.

So Canada's 36 million milk consumers are getting hosed to a fare-the-well by a tiny but politically powerful phalanx of dairy farmers, who are supported by all three political parties. In fact, less than 1,000 large farms account for a signification share of Canada's total production, and undoubtedly laugh all the way to the bank with their fulsome monthly milk checks.

The question recurs, of course, as to why Canada's wanton punishment of it's own milk consumers would merit starting a trade war.

After all, Canada's total milk production is worth only $6 billion annually compared to $38 billion in the US; and like the case of Canada (at wholesale), the US dairy industry has been coddled with heavy subsidies and production controls ever since the New Deal.

In any event, even a 25% share of Canada's market for US producers would amount to only $1.5 billion per year — compared to $282 billion of existing US exports of other products to Canada.

So we are not sure what kind of "deal" the Donald was after in this instance — but surely the cure would have been far worse than the disease.

Moreover, it turns out that what US dairy farmers were actually squawking about is very, very small beans. To wit, they wanted the Donald to obtain a reopening of an arcane loophole in Canada's protective wall for its domestic milk cartel.

That is, the 270% tariff rate applies to whole milk and certain products, but not "unfiltered milk" which is used in cheese-making and for which the tariff is *zero*. Not surprisingly, U. S. dairy processors used to export this essentially dewatered milk product to Canada — generating about $500 million per year in sales.

However, that unfiltered milk trade began to taper off recently, when the socialist dairy farmers in Canada's largest province, Ontario, finally woke up: They simply got government's approval to drop the price of domestic *unfiltered* milk to a point that priced out U. S. competitors.

As a result, Canadian cheese-makers stopped doing business with several U. S. dairy processors, and 75 farmers in Wisconsin lost their processing contracts.

And there you have it.

After having been snookered by 75 US dairy farmers about a non-problem, a revised provision in the new deal means that the Donald finally got milk!

In a word, the Donald has an unblinking eye for the marginalia when it comes to trade. How could NAFTA have actually been the "worst

trade deal in history" and an instrument by which Mexico and Canada were"robbing the American economy blind", as he has consistently declaimed, if absolutely nothing material will change in the two-way flow with Canada as a result of the Donald's ballyhooed 11th hour deal with Canada?

Not surprisingly, however, the Donald wasted no superlatives praising what amounts to the same deal with a new name.

Late last night, our deadline, we reached a **wonderful new Trade Deal** *with Canada. . . . These measures will support many - hundreds of thousands - American jobs. . . . . It means far more American jobs, and these are high-quality jobs. "*

Well, actually, he's talking about a few hundred dairy barn jobs in Wisconsin and other border states. In all other instances, jobs and pay levels will remain exactly the same.

For instance, the massive flow of automotive materials, parts, sub-assemblies and final assemblies is currently almost perfectly balanced between the two countries. Thus, during 2017 the US exported $51.4 billion of finished vehicles and parts to Canada and imported $56.4 billion from Canada.

Needless to say, there is not a word in the new deal that will alter that relative balance. In fact, there is probably no better testimonial to the virtues of market driven free trade than is embodied in the auto supply chain and final assembly networks which overlay both sides of the Ontario border.

The pricing system is driven by the auto OEMs — all of whom operate on both sides of the border — and wages are driven by the UAW and its sister CAW in both cases. Beyond that, other costs — such as logistics, utilities, taxes, vendor services — are essentially common.

Stated differently, the US/Canada trade system wasn't broke in the first place, and thankfully Trump didn't fix it.

Indeed, when you set aside the obvious case of crude oil and products, the US exported $263 billion to Canada last year and imported only $229 billion — meaning that under normal arithmetic it had a *$34 billion* non-oil surplus with Canada!

As we have previously indicated, we don't put much stock in bi-lateral trade balances, but in this case you have a pretty good illustration of why the Donald's anti-NAFTA fulminations were always a crock.

The only part of the US/Canada trade that was badly imbalanced on a statistical basis is the petroleum and related fuels account. During 2017, Canada exported $77.3 billion to the US, but imported only $19.6 billion.

But that $58 billion oil trade deficit with Canada had nothing to due with "bad trade deals", stupid previous presidents or nefarious trade practices by Canada.

To the contrary, it's a function of the fact that owing to the structure of the in-place pipeline and ocean transportation systems, the petroleum commodity essentially flows south. That is, Canada's western heavy oil and tar sands fields feed into the US midwest refineries, while some of the soaring production from the Texas shale patch flows into the export ports on the Gulf and into world trade.

Accordingly, Canada's $77 billion of oil and fuels exports to the US in 2017 was more than offset by US oil exports of $138 billion to the rest of the world. But aside from this geographically based Adam Smithian division of productive activities, there is now and never has been anything remotely "unfair" about the facts of US/Canada trade.

And the fact is, the imbalances go both ways as might be expected in a dynamic, comparative advantage driven free market. Thus, the US exported $43 billion of machinery, mechanical appliances, boilers equipment and nuclear reactors to Canada in 2017, but imported only $22 billion in this category.

Similarly, US electrical machinery and related products exports to Canada totaled $25 billion last year compared to only

$7.6 billion of imports from Canada.

And that gets us to the real joker in the Donald's "art-of-the-deal" compromise with Canada. The principal concession made by the Trump White House was that if it decides to wreck the global auto supply chain with a steep tariff under section 232, Canada will be given an annual tariff free quota of 2.6 million finished light vehicle assemblies and $32.4 billion of auto parts.

Say what?

There is now zero tariff on autos from Canada because that's the whole point of NAFTA — it's a free trade zone!

And what the "compromise" really means is that if the Trump administration goes off the deep-end and puts tariffs on the global auto industry on the grounds that Beemers and Lexus' threaten national security, then Canada does not have to go to the time and expense of getting itself exempted under the Section 19 disputes resolution machinery.

Needless to say, what Trump doesn't have is a plan to deal with the real source of America's yawning trade deficit and failing industrial economy.

But as a reminder, here's the real problem: massive monetary expansion and the relentless inflation of America's domestic prices, wages and costs since Alan Greenspan inaugurated Keynesian monetary central planning in 1987.

In fact, the CPI has risen by 120% during that period and nominal wages by 140%. Not surprisingly, the number of jobs in goods-producing industries has declined by 17%.

China's Communist Economy Is Their Problem — We Don't Need A "Trade Nanny" In Washington To Hector Them

That gets us to the Red Ponzi — but even there the nation's weighted average tariff rate is just 3.5% currently, and that represents a considerable drop from the 32% rate which prevailed back in 1992 when Mr. Deng announced that it "is glorious to be rich" and that the route to that blessed state was through a dramatic increase in trade with the rest of the world.

Stated differently, almost everyone seems to "get it" on the tariff matter except for the Donald's Three Stooges of Protectionism — Wilbur Ross, Peter Navarro and Robert Lighthizer — who advise him on trade and have thereby managed to keep their White House passes in good standing.

Still, the Donald has declared a tariff war on China like no other in modern history. After all, the currently threatened 10-25% tariffs on China's $517 billion of exports to the US would amount to a $50 billion to $130 billion unguided economic missile.

In some instances it would smash US consumers and in other cases it would reduce Chinese netbacks (profit margins) to the vanishing point — even as it created a massive price umbrella which would generate windfall profits for other suppliers, both foreign and domestic.

Regardless of the degree to which the Trump tariff threat is actually implemented, it in no way shape or form resembles the art of the deal; it's actually an exercise on plain old economic lunacy and mayhem.

And that includes the White House attack on China's alleged non-tariff barriers (NTBs). As indicated above, these are more subtle forms of discrimination against foreign goods used by mercantilist governments around the world — such as "health and safety" regulations that are biased against foreign suppliers or require a license or certification that never seems to be forthcoming from the host government.

Among the major NTBs are "buy national" style preferences for government procurement. Everybody does it, but the US is the grand champion because its massive military spending plus domestic infrastructure and other procurements amounts to $1.5 trillion per year at all levels of government. And virtually all of it is under "buy America" type strictures.

Still, the fact of life is that on an overall basis even these traditional NTBs have been considerably reduced in recent decades; and if the truth be told, the US isn't much cleaner on the NTB front than most of its major trading partners.

Greenspanian Monetary Central Planning: More Inflation, Fewer Good Jobs

— Consumer price index for all urban consumers: all items, Jun 1987=100
— All employees: goods-producing industries, Jun 1987=100
— Average hourly earnings of production and nonsupervisory employees:total private, June 1987=100

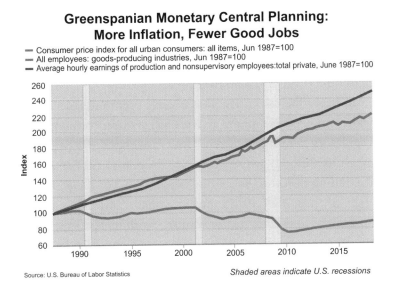

Source: U.S. Bureau of Labor Statistics   *Shaded areas indicate U.S. recessions*

But even these traditional NTBs are not exactly the essence of Trump's beef with China, anyway. What he and his Three Stooges of Protectionism actually object to (besides the drastic $375 billion bilateral trade deficit) is that China runs, well, a communist economy!

That's right. They don't call it Red Capitalism for nothing. The entire financial system is rigged via giant government controlled banks and limitless credit fostered by the People's Printing Press of China (PPOC) and back-stopped one way or another by the state.

Moreover, that's to say nothing of the massive fiscal subsidies operated through local governments and the trillions of debt they have issued in behalf of developers and industrialists. Even more significantly, the PBOC has essentially fueled a $40 trillion mountain of printing press credit (implicitly subsidized) on which the whole so-called China miracle is based.

By the same token, the Chinese communist party also controls the non-financial economy top-to-bottom via a licensing and regulatory dragnet that pales into insignificance the Washington regulatory dragons incessantly slayed by GOP orators. And that includes extremely nationalistic controls on foreign direct and portfolio investors.

But here's the thing. The Red Ponzi's fiscal and currency subsidies on exports amount to a wealth transfer to the US. And its regulatory controls on foreign investment and imports cause as much harm to its own economy as they do to the US and other trading partners.

The truth is, if US based multinationals don't like China's requirements to establish joint ventures with local Chinese companies or agree to transfer proprietary technology to them — there is a simple solution: Don't invest in places where you are not treated fairly and don't go on CNBC bragging about your "high growth" Chinese operations.

At the end of the day, in fact, the whole trade war against China has little to do with trade, but a lot to do with crony capitalist cry-babies lobbying Washington to act as their unpaid deal agent in China, or their patent protection attorney on the taxpayers' dime.

For instance, consider the White House screed against China written apparently by Peter Navarro and released earlier this year called "How China's Economic Aggression Threatens the Technologies and Intellectual Property of the United States and the World."

That unhinged exercise in anti-Chinese bellicosity was testimony to sheer economic ignorance and a nasty form of Big Government nationalism — not any valid issues about bilateral trade with China.

For instance, Navarro whined about "reverse engineering" as if this staple of business life from time immemorial were some insidious new trick invented by the Chicoms:

"..... reverse engineering in China is widespread and entails the process of disassembling (products). . . . for the purpose of cloning something similar without authorization from the rights holder. . . . . (which) is illegal when the unauthorized production is of technology under patent or other protection. "

Goodness me. Illegal patent infringement is exactly why more than 7,000 patent cases are filed in the US court system each year.

Under the rules of honest capitalism, it is the job of the patent owner to protect his property rights in court — not some Trade Nanny in Washington.

The story is similar with respect to Navarro's complaint that China forces US companies doing business there to share their technologies and that getting a government license or regulatory approval can often require similar JV arrangements.

So what?

Exactly no one mandated US companies to do business in China. If the Red Suzerains of Beijing are stupid enough to enforce a "no ticky, no washy" policy on foreign capital, it's their loss, not the business of the US government.

As investors have long understood, capital goes where it is appreciated and treated nicely or at least fairly. If China wants to be hostile to foreign capital by imposing unreasonable conditions, capitalists should take the cue and go elsewhere — not run to Washington seeking redress.

Stated differently, corporate America wants to have its cake and eat it too. But for crying out loud, China is a communist country, not Texas!

So of course the government will impose onerous conditions on business — foreign and domestic, too — because that's what statist regimes do.

That's why China forces foreign patent and technology holders to accept below-market royalty rates; limits the time that a foreign patent or rights holder has exclusive control over the technology; uses security reviews to force foreign enterprises to disclose propriety information; and mandates the placement of foreign research and development facilities in China as a condition of access to its markets.

And that's why the White House's litany of grievances against Chinese controls on foreign capital is so off the mark and borderline ludicrous. Navarro actually worked himself into a boiling lather on this particular onerous requirement often placed on US companies doing business in China:

- *"(mandate)including Chinese Communist Party Committees in corporate charters and in their corporate governance"*

Hmmm. That just might be a tip-off that Xi Jinping has revived the cult of Mao Zedong for a reason.

So here's the truth of the matter. If the Donald really wants to close the $375 billion trade deficit with China, he doesn't need a trade war. He only needs to call to Jay Powell and tell him to get the Fed out of the money market and to allow interest rates to find their own honest free market levels.

To be sure, that would cause one rip-roaring recession in the US as interest rates soared in the face of the Fed's disabled printing press. It would also cause US imports to plunge immediately, and US prices, wages and costs to steadily deflate over time versus those in China.

At length, the US overall trade deficit would substantially disappear in a world of honest money.

Needless to say, the Donald is a low interest man and is not about to permit the return of sound money and honest financial asset prices to the US economy.

By the same token, the bad money system that underlies

America's $19 trillion of continuous current account deficits (current dollars of purchasing power) over the past 43 years has also reached its sell-by date.

So its ultimately a matter of choosing your poison.

And the Donald's global trade war is the very worst possible choice.

CHAPTER 12

Trump's Trade War Folly And The Red Ponzi

It's not a skirmish — that's for sure. On the scale of trade warfare we are now at DEFCON 2.

The US is taxing $250 billion of Chinese imports or nearly half the total flow; and China is taxing $110 billion of its imports from the US or **85%** of the flow.

And from the looks of things, it'll be going full monte sooner or later. So it's time to start believing that the Donald will do what he says — unhinged or not — under the trade file.

That's because he's discovered the imperial presidency can virtually raise tariffs at will by abusing the rubbery enabling acts passed decades ago by Congresses which never imagined the Red Ponzi over there, nor the Orange Swan which arose therefrom over here.

So it is likely that by sometime in 2019 roughly $650 billion of two-way trade between the two largest economies on the planet will be subject to an open-ended tariff war that is truly unprecedented. Nothing of that magnitude has been remotely dreamed of by the protectionist lobbies in the past, but in today's memory-free fantasy-land at both ends of the Acela Corridor it's being taken as just another something to gum about and then ignore.

Actually, the China Trade War is even more off the charts of known history because it is uniquely bilateral. Moreover, both combatants are delusional about their own bargaining strength and ability to withstand their mutually inflicted blows — those that are already in force and those yet to come.

As we earlier demonstrated, the full monte Trump tariffs on China will impact about $1.7 trillion of US goods consumption or 40% of the $4.3 trillion total annual PCE for durable and nondurable goods. That's because China is the overwhelming marginal supplier to the domestic market for goods, and the China Price drives the world supply curve.

So as the prices of imports from China rise by 10% now and 25% if the full monte becomes effective in 2019, prices for the 67% share of China supplied goods which comes from other foreign suppliers or residual domestic producers will rise toward the tariffed price umbrella.

To be sure, prices won't go all the way to the notional +25% price umbrella because competitors will come in just under the landed price of China goods plus the tariff, thereby taking market share. Depending upon supply elasticities, and whether we are talking about the short run or longer time periods, price increases will be lower than the full tariff percentage.

Needless to say, the lower the price increase (and the lesser the burden on US consumers), the greater the implied supply elasticity and loss of market share and volume by China producers to other foreign and domestic US producers. Even then, China suppliers — especially state owned companies that are in the social policy and jobs-support business — will have the option to cut prices to offset some or all of the tariff, and thereby slice their already razor thin profit margin even further.

But in general, we expect that the Trump tariffs will lift prices on the China end of the supply curve significantly higher, thereby whacking domestic US consumers and moving volume and profits away from current Chinese suppliers.

So who will be the winners from the massive price umbrella that the Donald is in the process of erecting?

Why, it will be low wage places like Mexico, Vietnam, Indonesia, India, Bangladesh etc. And also Taiwan and South

Korea, too, all of whom will be enabled by the Donald to steal market share from China and get a windfall gain from higher prices on their current shipments.

No wonder the new quasi-socialist government of Mexico, for example, appears not to be at all troubled by the Donald's Trade war. They are getting $16 per hour auto worker wages from their sidebar NAFTA redo with the Trump trade team and, soon, a huge gain in market share from China, too.

For instance, at the four digit product code level, China's imports to the US last year totaled $124 billion for the top two categories — cell phones/cellular network gear and computers and related peripherals. Those Chinese supplied iPhones and computers accounted for 63% of America's total $198 billion of imports in these two leading categories during 2017.

But it isn't hard to guess who was the next largest supplier. Namely, Mexico at $31 billion, and then South Korea with $6.5 billion and Taiwan with $5.5 billion. In all, the next three suppliers after China accounted for $43 billion of imports, and therefore clearly have the production base to rapidly cut into China's share.

We develop this point further below, but the fundamental flaw in the Donald's tariff strategy is blindingly obvious and can't be emphasized enough. Namely, historic protectionism generally involved high tariffs against all or most foreign suppliers, not just those of one country. For better or worse, the aim was to give domestic producers a cost advantage against all foreign producers up to the percentage level of the tariff.

The theory, of course, was that this cost advantage would enable production and jobs to migrate back home en masse.

The rejoinder of free market economists, however, has always been to point out the adverse trade-offs. That is, the higher costs to domestic consumers and the weakening of competitive pressures in the domestic supplier markets far outweigh the benefits of shifting production from foreign to domestic factories.

The Donald's Trade War Against China — A Weird Exercise In Global Philanthropy

But the Donald's Trade War is a wholly different kettle of fish. Whether he understands it or not, his China tariffs amount to a weird exercise in global philanthropy. They will tax US consumers — and especially the Red State constituencies which live hand-to-mouth at Walmart — in order to transfer jobs and incomes to, among others, Mexico and Vietnam!

Our impression was that the Donald got elected by demonizing Mexico — so the likely outcome of his tariffs are more than a little bit ironic. But at least the production which gets shifted to Vietnam has a bit of logic — America probably does owe them some war reparations.

Yet what is not going to happen from the China tariffs is a material reduction in the $800 billion US trade deficit, nor any material return of production and jobs to the US.

When it comes to in-place production capacity the US isn't even in the game and has no obvious way to get there.

On the fully loaded global cost curve, in fact, the US is stranded up near the top due to the Fed's decades of 2%+ inflation. This means essentially that the Donald will be monkey-hammering US consumers with higher prices, but the output gains and windfall profits will go to other foreign suppliers much lower down on the supply cost curve.

We'd call this the art of madness, not deal-making of the type described in the 1987 book that the Donald, alas, didn't even write, or, according to the actual author, even proof-read.

Consider, for example, the top 25 four-digit product codes, which accounted for $286 billion of imports from China last year; and which comprised about 55% of total Chinese imports in the thousands of four-digit categories.

In addition to all the Apple products made by more than 1.0 million Foxcon workers at $4 per hour or less in factories mostly in the interior of China, other leading categories include tricycles and wheeled toys, furniture, monitors and television equipment, lamps and lighting fixtures, trunks and suitcases, printing machinery, videogame consoles, electrical transformers, footwear, numerous apparel categories etc.

The key point is that these $286 billion of Chinese imports accounted for 52% of total US imports of $556 billion reported in these 25 categories. But when it comes to where the balance — the other $270 billion — of these goods came from and where they are positioned on the global labor and cost curve, the answer is again dispositive.

To wit, the next $61 billion came from Mexico!

That is to say, from supply bases that are low on the wage and cost curve, and which will be ideally positioned to grab market share from the Red Ponzi as the Donald's tariffs begin to bite.

And there something else. The slickest way to beat the Donald's tariff hammer will be for Chinese suppliers to ship — in lieu of fully assembled iPhones — an alternative package of quasi-finished kits to Mexico for final assembly, packaging and re-export to the US.

To prevent that kind of natural market circumvention, of course, the Donald's Trade Nanny operation will have to drastically expand its rules-of-origin regulatory dragnet to stop the rampant end runs that are sure to follow.

After all, consider the $556 billion of imports in these top 25 mostly labor intensive categories. Exactly $286 billion of those goods originating in China will be taxed at up to 25%, while another $270 billion of identical goods in the same categories originating from the rest of the world will be taxed at *0%*.

Can you say arbitrage?

The Donald's idiotic tariff-war-on-one-country is fixing to cause more upheaval and dislocation in global trade channels than can scarcely be imagined. But for what?

Indeed, the net of it is stunningly perverse: US consumers will get the inflation part; low-wage foreign competitors will get the re-located production and jobs; and the Red Ponzi will suffer a devastating loss of profitability on the US exports it does manage to retain.

The Massive US/China Trade Imbalance — A Freak Of Economic History

Given this baleful scenario, the question recurs: If the Donald is right about America's huge trade imbalance problem with China, how did it actually materialize and what is the rational route to its amelioration?

As it happened, US imports from China grew from $20 billion in 1993 to $530 billion at present (dark blue bars). But nothing grows by *27X* in barely two decades in the natural order of markets, and most especially not in world merchandise trade when the US export side of the equation stands at a tiny 25% of imports.

The Freakish Evolution Of The US/China Trade Imbalance

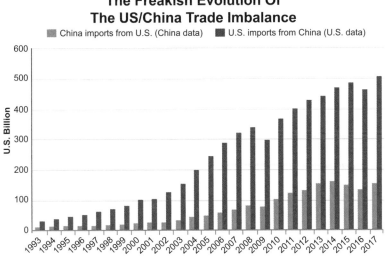

■ China imports from U.S. (China data)   ■ U.S. imports from China (U.S. data)

That is to say, there can be large trade imbalances between countries owing to comparative advantage and specialization, as well as to mercantilist trade practices.

But imbalances this freakishly large and persistent cannot

be attributed to either economics or protectionism. Instead, they are a function of money gone bad during the Fed-driven global central banking print-a-thon of the last several decades.

As shown in the chart below, the People's Printing Press of China (light blue) was a major contributor to the explosion of central bank balance sheets since the late 1990s.

More and More and More!

Aggregate balance sheet of large central banks, $tn & % of GDP

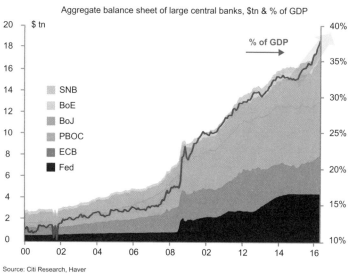

Source: Citi Research, Haver

At the essence of the matter, the Chinese radically depreciated their currency by 60% in 1994 and thereafter pegged the Yuan to the dollar (rigidly between 1995 and 2004 and loosely thereafter). The purpose was to prevent their exchange rate from soaring in the face of huge trade surpluses with the US and the rest of the world.

So doing, China acquired huge FX reserves, which went hand in hand with the massive expansion of their own domestic banking system and credit levels. That obviously happened because they had to print Yuan in order to buy-in dollars and other foreign exchange as part of their pegging operation.

The consequence, however, was not merely a massive

explosion of domestic credit, which, in fact, grew by 80X or from $500 billion to $40 trillion between 1995 and the present. By the lights of Keynesians and monetarists alike — that was supposed to be their problem, not ours.

But what it really did was totally block the natural adjustment of trade balances which would have occurred under either a gold-based sound money regime or even under an honest free-market based floating currency regime.

In the former case, the US would have lost massive amounts of gold reserves, causing the domestic banking system to contract, credit to be curtailed and domestic wages, prices and costs to decline until imports abated and exports picked-up.

And under an honest free market float, the adjustment would have occurred via massive appreciation of the Yuan exchange rate versus the dollar. That would have dramatically reduced the competitive advantage of China's cheap labor economy while opening the door to a higher level of US exports.

To be sure, China would have undoubtedly maintained a material trade surplus with the US owing to the inherent advantage of low cost labor and newly constructed manufacturing plants and related infrastructure. But it would have been nothing like the trade balance aberration shown above, which is what drove the off-shoring of American industry and the equally freakish election of Donald Trump.

That aberration, of course, was the direct result of the "dirty float" embodied in China's massive and chronic currency market intervention. But that was the outcome and symptom, not the cause of today's bad money-driven trade disaster.

But here's the thing. This all started on the US side during the Greenspan era of monetary central planning. Under a sound monetary system, the US would have experienced systematic and persistent internal *deflation* of prices, wages and costs in the face of the mobilization of the east Asian economies out of the rice paddies of subsistence agriculture.

That means, in turn, that interest rates would have been persistently high to generate larger domestic savings and efficiency-driven investment, while credit expansion to finance excess consumption would have been sharply curtailed.

In that context, there was no need for the Fed's balance sheet of $200 billion (1987) to expand at all. As it happened, of course, the Fed's balance sheet more than quadrupled during Greenspan's 19-year tenure; and then it was off to the races under his successors, who brought it to a peak of $4.5 trillion or a 23X gain in barely 27 years.

As we indicated above, excess dollar liabilities became America's #1 export — a plague on the world economy which naturally caused the statist and mercantilist governments of Asia and the EM world generally to massively intervene against the Fed's dollar tsunami in desperate efforts to hold down their own FX rates and keep their export factories humming.

Needless to say, the freakish explosion of China's FX reserves pictured below is exhibit #1.

The Red Ponzi: 20-Years of Massive Currency Manipulation is Coming Unwound

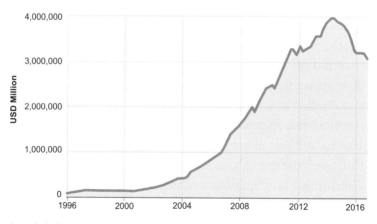

Source: Trading Economics

Greenspan's Greatest Export — Mercantilism And Central Bank Printing Presses Everywhere

Not surprisingly, the massive and chronic FX interventions of China and the EM economies linked to it ending up fueling out-of-this-world credit growth in their domestic economies.

For instance, between the year 2000 and the present, credit outstanding in the non-government, non-financial sector of the Chinese economy grew from 10 trillion Yuan to 180 trillion ($26 trillion).

18X Explosion Of Business Credit Growth In The Red Ponzi

— Total credit to private non-financial sector, adjusted for breaks, for China

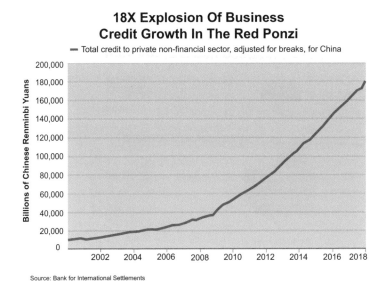

Source: Bank for International Settlements

That's an *18X* growth in 18 years, and is what makes Red Ponzi sui generis. That is to say, a debt-fueled economic mad houses that only resembles a stable capitalist economy because the Red Suzerains of Beijing are pleased to keep up the pretense; and because Wall Street long ago lost its capacity to assess reality.

Yet this is the house of cards that the Donald's trade war is now frontally attacking. The potential earth-shattering consequences of toppling it are difficult to even imagine, but below is a reminder of why the Red Ponzi is a trainwreck waiting to happen.

Given China's insane 80X credit growth since the mid-1990s, it is no wonder that the Red Ponzi consumed more cement during three years (2011-2013) than did the US during the entire twentieth century.

Enabled by an endless $40 trillion flow of credit from its state controlled banking apparatus and its shadow banking affiliates, China went berserk building factories, warehouses, ports, office towers, malls, apartments, roads, airports, train stations, high speed railways, stadiums, monumental public buildings and much more.

China Used More Cement in the Last Three Years Than the U.S. Used in the Entire 20th Century

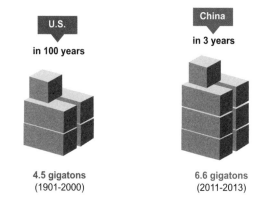

U.S.	China
in 100 years	in 3 years
4.5 gigatons	6.6 gigatons
(1901-2000)	(2011-2013)

Sources: USGS, Cement Statistics 1900-2012; USGS, Mineral Industry of China 1990-1913

If you want an analogy, 6.6 gigatons of cement is 14.5 trillion pounds. The Hoover dam used about 1.8 billion pounds of cement. So in 3 years China consumed enough cement to build the Hoover dam 8,000 times over — 160 of them for every state in the union!

The New Middle Kingdom Of Concrete

In effect, the Middle Kingdom has been reborn in towers of preformed concrete. They now rise in their tens of thousands in every direction on the horizon. They are connected with ribbons of highways, which are scalloped and molded to wind through endless forests of concrete verticals.

Some of them are occupied, a lot of them are not. In fact, there are upwards of 60 million empty apartment units in China, most of them never occupied. They stand as a tribute to the insane notion that rent-less real estate is a wonderful investment because it never stops appreciating and the government will never let prices fall — even if the implied rental yields are unaffordable to the overwhelming share of the population.

The "before" and "after" contrast of Shanghai's famous Pudong waterfront is illustrative of the illusion.

The first picture on the next page is from about 1990 at a time before Mr. Deng discovered the printing press in the basement of the People's Bank of China and proclaimed that it is glorious to be rich; and that if you were 18 and still in full possession of your digital dexterity and visual acuity it was even more glorious to work 12 hours per day 6 days per week in an export factory for 35 cents per hour.

We don't know if the first picture is accurate as to its exact vintage. But by all accounts the glitzy skyscrapers of today's

Pudong waterfront did ascend during the last 25 years from a rundown, dimly lit area of muddy streets on the east side of Huangpu River. The pictured area was apparently shunned by all except the most destitute of Mao's proletariat.

But the second picture we can vouch for. It's what you see from the Bund on the other side of the Huangpu River.

Today's Pudong district does look spectacular — presumably a 21st century rendition of the glory of the Qing, the Ming, the Soong, the Tang and the Han.

But to conclude that would be to be deceived. The apparent prosperity is not that of a sustainable economic miracle; its the front street of the greatest Potemkin Village in world history.

The heart of the matter is that output measured by

TRUMP'S TRADE WAR FOLLY AND THE RED PONZI

Keynesian GDP accounting — especially China's blatantly massaged variety — isn't sustainable wealth if it is not rooted in real savings, efficient capital allocation and future productivity growth. Nor does construction and investment which does not earn back its cost of capital over time contribute to the accumulation of real wealth.

Needless to say, China's construction and "investment" binge manifestly does not meet these criteria in the slightest. It was funded with credit manufactured by state controlled banks and their shadow affiliates, not real savings.

It was driven by state initiated growth plans and GDP targets. These were cascaded from the top down to the province, county and local government levels — an economic process which is the opposite of entrepreneurial at-risk assessments of future market based demand and profits.

China's own GDP statistics are the smoking gun. During the last 18 years fixed asset investment — in private business, state companies, households and the "public sector" combined — has averaged 45-50% of GDP. That's per se crazy.

Even in the heyday of its 1960s and 1970s boom, Japan's fixed asset investment never reached more than 30% of GDP. Moreover, even that was not sustained year in and year out (they had three recessions), and Japan had at least a semblance of market pricing and capital allocation — unlike China's virtual command and control economy.

The reason that Wall Street analysts and fellow-traveling Keynesian economists miss the latter point entirely is because China's state-driven economy works through credit allocation rather than by tonnage toting commissars.

The gosplan is implemented by the banking system and, increasingly, through China's mushrooming and metastasizing shadow banking sector. The latter amounts to trillions of credit potted in entities which have sprung up to evade the belated growth controls that the regulators have imposed on the formal banking system.

Malinvestment At Biblical Scale

For example, Beijing tried to cool down the residential real estate boom by requiring 30% down payments on first mortgages and by virtually eliminating mortgage finance on second homes and investment properties. So between 2013 and the present more than 2,500 on-line peer-to-peer lending outfits (P2P) materialized — mostly funded or sponsored by the banking system — and these entities have advanced more than $2 trillion of new credit.

The overwhelming share went into meeting "downpayments" and other real estate speculations. On the one hand, that reignited the real estate bubble — especially in the Tier I cities were prices have risen by 20% to 60% during the last two years.

At the same time, this P2P eruption in the shadow banking system has encouraged the construction of even more excess housing stock in an economy that is already saddled with the aforementioned 60 million empty units.

In short, China has become a credit-driven economic madhouse. The 40%-50% of GDP attributable to fixed asset investment actually constitutes the most spectacular spree of malinvestment and waste in recorded history. It is the footprint of a future depression, not evidence of sustainable growth and prosperity.

Consider a boundary case analogy. With enough fiat credit during the last three years, the US could have built the aforementioned 160 Hoover dams on dry land in each state.

That would have elicited one hellacious boom in the jobs market, gravel pits, cement truck assembly plants, pipe and tube mills, architectural and engineering offices etc. The profits and wages from that dam building boom, in turn, would have generated a secondary cascade of even more phony "growth."

But at some point, the credit expansion would stop. The

demand for construction materials, labor, machinery and support services would dry-up; the negative multiplier on incomes, spending and investment would kick-in; and the depression phase of a crack-up boom would exact its drastic revenge.

The fact is, China has been in a crack-up boom for the last two decades, and one which transcends anything that the classic liberal economists ever imagined. As we mentioned above, since 1995 credit outstanding has grown from $500 billion to upwards of $40 trillion, and that's only counting what's visible.

But the very idea of a *80X* expansion of credit in hardly two decades in the context of top-down allocation system suffused with phony data and endless bureaucratic corruption defies economic rationality and common sense.

Stated differently, China is not simply a little over-done. And it's not in some Keynesian transition from exports and investment led growth to domestic services and consumption.

Instead, China's fantastically over-built industry and public infrastructure embodies monumental economic waste equivalent to the construction of pyramids with shovels and spoons or giant dams on dry land.

Accordingly, when the credit pyramid finally collapses or simply stops growing, the pace of construction will decline dramatically, leaving the Red Ponzi riddled with economic air pockets and negative spending multipliers.

Take the simple case of the abandoned cement mixer plant pictured below. The high wages paid in that abandoned plant are now gone; the owners have undoubtedly fled and their high living extravagance is no more. Nor is this factory's demand still extant for steel sheets and plates, freight services, electric power, waste hauling, equipment replacement parts and so forth on down the food chain.

And, no, a wise autocracy in Beijing will not be able to off-set the giant deflationary forces now assailing the construction and industrial heartland of China's hothouse economy with massive amounts of new credit to jump start green industries and neighborhood recreation facilities. That's because China has already shot is its credit wad, meaning that every new surge in its banking system threatens to trigger even more capital outflow and expectations of FX depreciation.

Moreover, any increase in fiscal spending not funded by credit expansion will only rearrange the deck chairs on the titanic.

Indeed, whatever borrowing headroom Beijing has left will be needed to fund the bailouts of its banking and credit system. Without massive outlays for the purpose of propping-up and stabilizing China's vast credit Ponzi, there will be economic and social chaos as the tide of defaults and abandonments swells.

Empty factories like the above — and China is crawling with them — are a screaming marker of an economic doomsday machine. They bespeak an inherently unsustainable and unstable simulacrum of capitalism where the purpose of credit has been to fund state mandated GDP quotas, not finance efficient investments with calculable risks and returns.

The relentless growth of China's aluminum production is just one more example. When China's construction and investment binge finally stops, there will be a huge decline in

this industry's wages, profits and supply chain activity.

But the mother of all malinvestments sprang up in China's steel industry. From about 70 million tons of production in the early 1990s, it exploded to 875 million tons in 2017. Beyond that, it is the capacity build-out behind the chart below which tells the full story.

To wit, Beijing's tsunami of cheap credit enabled China's state-owned steel companies to build new capacity at an even more fevered pace than the breakneck growth of annual production. Consequently, annual crude steel capacity now stands at nearly 1.4 billion tons, and nearly all of that capacity — about

60% of the world total — was built in the last ten years.

Needless to say, it's a sheer impossibility to expand efficiently the heaviest of heavy industries by 17X in a quarter century.

What actually happened is that China's aberrationally massive steel industry expansion created a significant one-time increment of demand for its own products; it effectively padded its own order book.

That is, pell mell steel industry expansion generated an enormous demand for plate, structural and other steel shapes that go into blast furnaces, BOF works, rolling mills, fabrication plants and iron ore loading and storage facilities. It also fueled soaring orders for plate and other steel products for shipyards where new bulk carriers were built to carry the iron ore and coking coal to the new steel works; and it also generated demand for steel to fabricate the massive equipment and infrastructure used at the iron ore mines and ports.

That is to say, the Chinese steel industry has been chasing its own tail, but the merry-go-round has now stopped.

And that's where the pyramid building nature of China's insane steel industry investment comes in. The industry is not remotely capable of "rationalization" in the DM economy historical sense. Even Beijing's much ballyhooed 100-150 million ton plant closure target is a drop in the bucket —

China's Explosion Of Aluminum Production Capacity Now Dwarfs The US Industry

A surge in Chinese aluminum production has all but crushed U.S. smelters

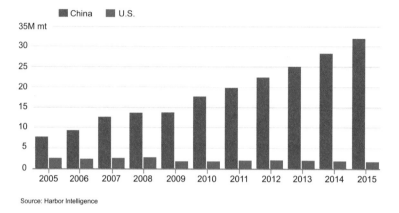

Source: Harbor Intelligence

and its not scheduled to be completed until 2020 anyway.

To wit, China will be lucky to have 400 million tons of true sell-through demand — that is, on-going domestic demand for sheet steel to go into cars and appliances and for rebar and structural steel to be used in replacement construction once the current one-time building binge finally expires.

For instance, China's construction and shipbuilding industries consumed about 500 million tons per year at the crest of the building boom. But shipyards are already going radio silent and the end of China's manic eruption of concrete, rebar and I-beams is not far behind. Use of steel for these purposes could easily drop to 200 million tons on a steady state basis.

But contrast, China's vaunted auto industry uses only 45 million tons of steel per year, and consumer appliances consume less than 12 million tons. In most developed economies autos and white goods demand accounts for about 20% of total steel use.

Likewise, much of the current 200 million tons of steel which goes into machinery and equipment including

Madcap Explosion of Chinese Steel Production

massive production of mining and construction machines, rails cars etc. is of a one-time nature and could easily drop to 100 million tons on a steady state replacement basis. So its difficult to see how China will ever have recurring demand for even 400 million tons annually, yet that's just 30% of its massive capacity investment.

In short, we are talking about wholesale abandonment of a half billion tons of steel capacity or more. That is, the destruction of steel industry capacity greater than that of Japan, the EC and the US combined.

Needless to say, that thunderous liquidation will generate a massive loss of labor income and profits and devastating contraction of the steel industry's massive and lengthy supply chain. And that's to say nothing of the labor market disorder and social dislocation when China is hit by the equivalent of dozens of burned-out Youngstowns and Pittsburgs.

Needless to say, China was always destined to suffer the greatest post-boom depression in recorded history. Now, thanks to the Donald's unhinged Trade War, that cataclysm will come sooner rather than later.

291

And its repercussions will violently cascade throughout the warp and woof of the global economy and financial system.

PART 3

America First: Existential Threat To The Empire

CHAPTER 13

America First And The Failed Promise Of Helsinki

The major — perhaps only — redeeming virtue of the Donald's ersatz campaign platform was his clear intent to seek a rapprochement with Russia, revamp America's commitments to NATO and other cold war relics and to discard "Regime Change" as the core tenant of foreign policy.

In essence, "America First" was to become the new route to domestic security and safety.

Those eminently sensible notions struck the Deep State's raison d'etre to the quick during the campaign; and by hook or crook, the Donald's rapid fire actions toward these objectives since spring of 2018 have induced a palpable shock in the Imperial City.

Clearly he means to withdraw America's *29,000* military hostages now stationed in South Korea in return for some sort of peace treaty, economic normalization and denuclearization arrangement with Kim Jong-un.

Likewise, he has sensibly suggested that demonizing Russia and Putin has accomplished nothing, and that they should be invited back into the old G-8. And as soon as Robert Mueller finishes his RussiaGate farce, Trump can get rid of the present asinine sanctions on various Russian officials and Putin cronies, too.

We also now know — owing to the sullen reporting of

the **Washington Post** — that Trump has been hounding the national security bureaucracy about another utterly ridiculous artifact of the Empire.

Namely, the fact that 73 years after Hitler descended into Hades from his bunker and 27 years after the Soviet Union slithered off the pages of history, there are still 35,000 US troops in Germany. So Trump has tasked the Pentagon to review the cost and impact of a large-scale withdrawal or transfer of American troops:

"The effort follows Trump's expression of interest in removing the troops, made during a meeting earlier this year with White House and military aides, U. S. officials said. Trump was said to have been taken aback by the size of the US presence, which includes about 35,000 active-duty troops, and complained that other countries were not contributing fairly to joint security or paying enough to NATO.

"Word of the assessment has alarmed European officials, who are scrambling ..."

Scrambling?

We doubt whether real Europeans are scrambling at all — the **Post** is surely just quoting from the NATO echo chamber.

Then again, the latter is absolutely the most useless, obsolete, wasteful and dangerous multilateral institution in the present world. But like the proverbial clothes-less emperor, NATO doesn't dare risk having the purportedly "uninformed" amatuer in the Oval Office pointing out its buck naked behind.

So the NATO subservient think tanks and establishment policy apparatchiks are harrumphing up a storm, but for crying out loud most of Europe's elected politicians are in on the joke. They are fiscally swamped paying for their Welfare States and are not about to squeeze their budgets or taxpayers to fund military muscle against a non-existent threat.

As Justin Raimondo aptly notes,

Finally an American president has woken up to the fact

that World War II, not to mention the cold war, is over: there's no need for US troops to occupy Germany.

Vladimir Putin isn't going to march into Berlin in a reenactment of the Red Army taking the Fuehrer-bunker – but even if he were so inclined, why won't Germany defend itself?

Exactly. If their history proves anything, Germans are not a nation of pacifists, meekly willing to bend-over in the face of real aggressors. Yet they spent the paltry sum of $43 billion on defense during 2017, or barely 1.1% of Germany's $3.8 trillion GDP, which happens to be roughly three times bigger than Russia's.

In short, the policy action of the German government tells you they don't think Putin is about to invade the Rhineland or retake the Brandenburg Gate. And this live action testimonial also trumps, as it were, all of the risible alarums emanating from the beltway think tanks and the 4,000 NATO bureaucrats talking their own book in behalf of plush Brussels sinecures.

The Helsinki Summit: Trump Blurts Out The Truth, Beltway Firestorm Follows

In this context, the Donald's trip to Helsinki to make peace with Vlad Putin could have been the beginning of re-normalization of US relations with Russia.

In one-fell swoop they could have reached an agreement to get the US military out of Syria; normalize the return of Crimea and Moscow's historic naval base at Sevastopol to the Russian motherland; stop the civil war in Ukraine via a mutually agreed de facto partition; stand-down from the incipient military clashes from the Baltic to the Black Sea; and pave the way for lifting of the absurd sanctions on Russian businessmen and citizens.

But it was not to be because at his post-meeting press conference, the Donald blurted out the truth. To wit, after

16-months in office and access to the deepest secrets of the
nation's entire $75 billion Intelligence Community, no one had
presented to him any compelling proof of Russian meddling in
the 2016 election.

So, of course, he couldn't reject Putin's assurances that Russia
didn't attempt to defeat Hillary Clinton, as the collaborationist
US press demanded.

That's because Putin didn't do it: The whole Russian
collusion story is just a tissue of Deep State lies designed to
thwart the Donald's honest desire for rapprochement with
Russia; and one which has been desperately seized upon by
distraught partisan Dems stung by America's rebuke at the polls
in November 2016.

Needless to say, the firestorm after Helsinki has put a fuse
on American First. Every hour that the Donald wastes tweeting
insults, bloviating about his beloved Mexican wall, sabotaging
American exports and jobs and watching Fox & Friends reruns
is just more opportunity for the vast apparatus of the Deep State
(and most of his own top officials) to deep-six Trump's emerging
and thoroughly welcome attempt to rein in the Empire.

For instance, the same Washington Post article cited above
is laced with not for attribution quotes from officials determined
to maintain the NATO status quo and therefore continuing,
needless provocation of Russia.

*Several officials suggested that Pentagon policymakers may
have moved ahead with the assessment to prove the worth of the
current basing arrangement and dissuade Trump from carrying
the thought of withdrawal any further.*

*Pentagon spokesman Eric Pahon dismissed any suggestion of
a full or partial withdrawal from Germany and described such
analysis as routine.*

Overcoming the self-interested inertial forces of the Deep
State and its vast syndicate of contractors, weapons suppliers,
military pork barrels and think tank supplicants, of course, is

its own monumental challenge. Yet the Donald's pathway to America First is further obstructed by the fact that the Dems are way off-sides for purely partisan reasons.

The New Handmaids Of The Warfare State

That is to say, Democratic politicians — including most of the so-called liberals and progressives — have turned themselves into handmaids of the Warfare State owing to their inconsolable grief and anger over losing the 2016 election to the very worst candidate the GOP has fielded in modern times, including Barry Goldwater in 1964.

Consequently, they are virtually incapable of thinking rationally about Russia — or of even thinking at all. In effect, they have become beltway saboteurs — witting or otherwise — who will stop at nothing to keep the current utterly unnecessary and pointless cold war revival cranking at full steam.

Nor does the motivation of the Dems really matter. That is, that their Russian vendetta is driven by raw partisanship, not foreign policy substance.

After all, to paraphrase the great Randolph Bourne, the Russian ogre is the health of the military/industrial/intelligence/think tank complex. So even a rapprochement — to say nothing of peace — with Russia is an existential threat to the Deep State; it would necessarily pull the fiscal pins right out from under the hideous $800 billion per year defense, intelligence and foreign aid apparatus.

As it has happened, even his own government has been doing its best to sabotage the brief moment of goodwill which emanated from the Helsinki summit. Indeed, the very prosperity of the Imperial City depends upon continued demonization of Putin and Russia.

As Justin Raimondo observed even before the Donald's ill-fated presser with Putin:

..... *Trump campaigned on making peace with Russia: he has a mandate to do so. That, however, matters little to the "intelligence community" and their media camarilla, which is up in arms at the very prospect of a Russo-American partnership for peace. The national security bureaucracy and the laptop bombardiers who inhabit ThinktankWorld have a vested interest in maintaining a cold war status quo that should've ended when the Berlin Wall fell. They are horrified by Trump's "America First" foreign policy views, and they are out to stop him by any means necessary – because his victory meant the end of their worldview and their careers.*

In the grand sweep of history, the significance of the post-Helsinki firestorm of attacks on Trump cannot be over-stated. Had Trump been allowed to succeed, it would have been proof positive that America faces no large state-based enemy.

That is to say, it would have mightily illuminated the hidden fact that neither Russia nor China (for that matter) even remotely possess the intent or the means to threaten the American homeland.

Likewise, a potential US withdrawal from Syria and incipient agreement with Russia to de-escalate tensions in the middle east would remind America that Regime Change has been an utter failure.

Yet without an imperial foreign policy that is implicitly designed to either bully or remove recalcitrant lesser governments anywhere on the planet — whether or not they have the intent or capacity to harm the US homeland — there would be no case at all for Washington's huge expeditionary forces. That is, 11 carrier battle groups, massive air and sealift capacity and a far flung string of bases and occupations spread among more than 100 countries around the planet.

So, all of this was riding in the balance at Helsinki — including the possibility that a strong success could have opened the door to a real, far more systematic and intellectually cogent America First policy over the longer haul.

Unfortunately, it was not to be. Still, we propose to dig

deeper — to tease out the full possibilities of an America First foreign policy given that the Donald nearly succeeded in saddling his ample belly right up close to the bar.

If nothing else, an explication of a more sophisticated and thorough-going version of America First can help explain why the Deep State and its collaborators in the Imperial City will go to any lengths to extinguish the Donald's presidency and incipient lurch in that direction.

The Profoundly Correct Taftian Roots Of America First

In the first place it needs be observed that lurking not far below the surface of the Donald's "America First" slogan is the ghost of Senator Robert Taft's profoundly correct case for non-intervention.

Back in the 1950s, the great statesman from Ohio fully understood that free enterprise prosperity, minimal government and maximum personal liberty were incompatible with a permanent, fiscally debilitating Warfare State leviathan designed to function as the world's boots-&-suits-on-the-ground hegemon.

Consequently, Taft strongly opposed a big peacetime navy, a large standing army with forward stationing and rapid global deployment capacities and the proliferation of foreign treaties and aid commitments.

To the contrary, he reasoned that in the nuclear age a US-based bomber and missile force of unquestioned striking capacity would more than adequately protect the homeland from foreign military aggression; and that it could do so at a fraction of the cost of what amounted to permanent imperial legions assigned to patrolling the fairest part of the planet.

Today Taft's vision of a homeland defense would be more apt than ever. It would constitute an even cheaper and more efficacious guarantor of the safety and security of the American people than in his time. That's because there are now no rival super-powers with even a fraction of the military and economic might relative to the US that was possessed by the former Soviet Union.

Moreover, missile technology has become so advanced that a relative handful of submarines and hardened domestic launch sites can deter any conceivable foreign threat, which is inherently a nuclear one, to America's homeland security.

That is, in this day and age there is absolutely *no conventional military threat* to the safety and liberty of citizens in Omaha NE, Spokane WA or Springfield MA.

That's because there is no nation on earth that could mount a giant naval and air armada sufficient to invade the American homeland. Or, if it were foolish enough to try, could it survive the guided missile blitz that would send its forces to Davy Jones' locker long before they crossed the blue waters which surround the North American continent.

Stated differently, nuclear deterrence, the great ocean moats and a territorial military defense is all that it would take to keep America secure in today's world.

There is no need for Pax Americana, even if it could succeed, which manifestly it has not; and even if it could be afforded, which clearly it can't be.

To be sure, the Donald is too full of egotistical bluster and too infatuated with militarist trappings to go the full Taft nonintervention route, but given a fair chance he might have at least shimmied policy in that direction. Clearly a rapprochement with Russia would enable a de-escalation of Washington's imperial presence in the middle east and avoid a dangerous build-up of military tensions and expense in eastern Europe.

In any event, as crude and bombastic as Trump's articulation of the America First proposition sometimes sounds, it does amount to a frontal attack on the intellectual superstructure which keeps the Fifth Fleet in the Persian Gulf, 35,000 troops in Germany, 29,000 of America's military personal in harm's way on the Korean peninsula, 11 carrier battle groups on the oceans, a continued expeditionary force of 100,000 troops, dependents and support personnel in Japan and military operations and economic and military aid in more than 100 other nations around the planet.

The Bogus Predicate For Empire: America As The Indispensable Nation

Underneath this vast Empire, of course, lays the utterly bogus notion that America is the Indispensable Nation and that Washington Leadership is always and everywhere the sine quo non of stability, order and peace all around the planet.

Ironically, therefore, the very obnoxious nature of the Donald's personality and modus operandi has done much to tarnish the idea of Washington Leadership; and that is a considerable step toward global peace in its own right.

That's because the best way to stop more American wars is for no one to come next time Washington puts out the call, and for the so-called Coalition of the Willing to shrink to a quorum of none.

That prospect has surely terrified the foreign policy establishment. Even though to date the Donald has been throttled at nearly every turn by the War Party in his discombobulated and amateurish pursuit of America First, that has not stopped its leading spokesman and institutions from lambasting him for allegedly sullying Washington's self-assigned "leadership" role in the world.

In that respect there are few grand poobahs of the War Party who better embody the arrogant pretensions of the American Imperium than the odious president of the Council on Foreign Relations, Richard Hass.

According to the latter, the trouble with Trump is that after 22 months in office he still didn't get it; he's turned his back on

the core predicate that animates the Imperial City:
"Trump is the first post-WWII president to view the burdens of world leadership as outweighing the benefits. The United States has changed from the principal preserver of order to a principal disrupter. "

Exactly what hay wagon does he think we fell off from?

How did the war in Vietnam, the First Gulf War to save the Emir of Kuwait's oil wealth, the futile 17-year occupation of Afghanistan, the destruction of Iraq, the double-cross of Khadafy after he gave up his nukes, the obliteration of much of civil society and economic life in Syria, the US-supplied Saudi genocide in Yemen and the Washington sponsored coup and civil war on Russia's doorstep in Ukraine, to name just a few instances of Washington's putative "world leadership", have anything to do with preserving "order" on the planet?

And exactly how did the "benefits" of these serial instigations of mayhem outweigh the "burdens" to America's taxpayers — to say nothing of the terminal costs to the dead and maimed citizens in their millions who had the misfortune to be domiciled in these traumatized lands?

Likewise, have the refugees who have been flushed out of Syria, Libya, Yemen, Iraq and elsewhere in the middle east by Washington's wars done anything for the peace and stability of Europe, where Washington's victims have desperately fled in their millions?

Yet, there would have been no long-lasting civil war in Syria without the billions of cash and weapons supplied to the so-called rebels and the outright jihadis by Washington and its Persian Gulf vassals; nor would Yemen by sinking into famine and cholera plagues without the American bombs, missiles and drones dispatched by the Saudi pilots essentially functioning as hired Pentagon mercenaries.

Indeed, the smoldering ruins of Mosul, Aleppo, Fallujah, Benghazi and lesser places in their thousands hardly speak to a beneficent hegemony.

Yet had Washington never brought its fleets and occupying forces to the Middle East after 1970 and had the region not come under the heavy boot of the Central Command and Washington's assorted proconsuls and plenipotentiaries, the plague of radical Sunni jidhadism would never have arisen. Nor is it likely that the ancient rift between the Sunni and Shiite confessions of Islam would have erupted into today's lethal armed conflicts.

Washington's Regime Change Folly — Cradle of Jihadi Terrorism

It is well to note that during peacetime before 1970, no American soldiers were killed in the middle east. After 1990, however, virtually all US serviceman who were killed or wounded in combat were stationed in the greater middle east.

It is also worth noting that the Persian Gulf is not an American lake and that the answer to high oil prices is high prices, not the Fifth Fleet.

In fact, global oil production today has doubled since 1973 owing to price, technology and the worldwide quest for profits by state and private oil companies alike — even as constant dollar prices per barrel stand far below prior peaks.

So the entire three-decade long US occupation of the Middle East has been a complete folly. There never was any economic imperative whatsoever to bring the American armada into the region, and self-evidently none of the squabbling nations which occupy the region are any military threat whatsoever to the American homeland.

So when candidate Trump said the Iraq invasion was a stupid mistake, that Hillary's war on Khadafy was misbegotten, that he would like to cooperate with Putin on pacifying Syria and that NATO was obsolete, he was actually calling into question the fundamental predicates of the American Imperium.

The War Party's Risible Demonization Of Putin

And that gets us to the Russian threat bogeyman, the War Party's risible demonization of Vladimir Putin and the cocked-up narrative about the Kremlin's meddling in the 2016 election — all of which the Helsinki summit could have knocked into a cocked hat had the Imperial City not erupted into a ferocious 24/7 attack mode on the Donald for blurting out the truth.

Yet the latter was par for the course. When Trump captured the GOP nomination against all odds and expectations in the spring of 2016, the War Party went into hyper-drive and it has not desisted since then in its efforts first to derail his candidacy; and then, after the fact, to delegitimize and imperil his presidency.

In the case of the election meddling meme, there are few more hypocritical instances of the cat-calling-the-kettle-black than this one.

To wit, the total US intelligence community (IC) budget is upwards of $75 billion — 25% more than Russia's entire military budget including ships, planes, tanks, ammo, fuel, rations, operations, maintenance and even spare boots — and a

Real Oil Prices

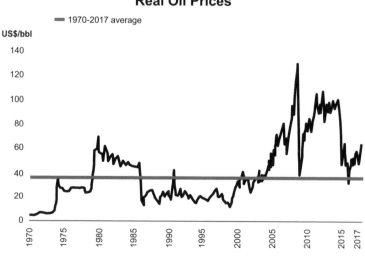

big part of that giant IC spend goes to, well, meddling, hacking and sabotage of foreign nations!

The recently renamed Tailored Access Operations (TAO) unit inside NSA alone has a multi-billion budget. It funds thousands of in-house and contractor personnel who spend day and night hacking the communications channels of virtually every government in the world, friend, foe and enemy alike.

It goes without saying, of course, that the very purpose of these intrusions is to interfere with the domestic politics and governance of most of the planet's population, and in some cases to actually sabotage perfectly appropriate operations, such as the Natanz uranium centrifuges in Iran which were destroyed by the Washington's stuxnet virus.

Thus, if you are not caught up in the War party's self-serving group think, it seems entirely plausible that in the face of these massive Washington cyber-assaults that targeted nations might indeed seek to counterattack, as apparently the Russian security services have done

After all, what the whole Russian meddling meme boils down to is an assertion that Kremlin operatives have been attacking America in plain sight. That is, they hacked the DNC's gossip and intrigue-ridden computers and breached the content of Podesta's password protected political skullduggery.

But airing intra-party dirty laundry is neither a national security matter nor does its disclosure jeopardize American democracy in the slightest.

The very idea that these two alleged hacks — the DNC and Podesta emails — amount to some grand assault on American democracy is just plain laughable; and it surely does not take a dozen congressional investigations and the rogue Mueller witch-hunt to preclude any future recurrence.

All it would really require is a handshake agreement between Trump and Putin because it is plainly obvious that Russia got nothing out of the St Petersburg troll farm or any of the other related allegations of "meddling."

At the end of the day, we are supposed to believe that a country with a puny $1.5 trillion GDP, which is just 7% of the United States' $20.0 trillion GDP, and which consists largely of aged hydrocarbon provinces, endless wheat fields, modest industrial capacities and a shrinking Vodka-favoring workforce, is actually a threat to America's security.

And we are also supposed to fear the military capacity of a country that has no blue water Navy to speak of and no conventional air-lift and air-attack capacity which could remotely threaten the New Jersey shores? Or one that spends less in a full year than the Pentagon consumes every 35 days?

Oh, yes, and this midget military is run with an apparent iron-hand by the Cool Hand Luke of the modern world. Yet as was readily apparent to the unwashed American masses from his demeanor at Helsinki, the last thing Putin is going to do is commit Russian national suicide by launching a nuclear attack on America.

Yet that's all he's got: To wit, a non-existent military threat and a justifiable desire to protect the Russian-speaking populations on his doorstep in Crimea and the Donbas from the depredations of the civil war that Washington itself instigated.

Were it to be given half a chance, an America First foreign policy would illuminate this and much more, as we essay in the chapters which follow.

CHAPTER 14

Why The Empire Never Sleeps —
The Indispensable Nation Folly

Like the case of Rome before it, the Empire is bankrupting America. The true fiscal cost is upwards of *$1.0 trillion* per year (counting $200 billion for veterans and debt service for past wars), but there is no way to pay for it.

That's because the 78-million strong Baby Boom is in the driver's seat of American politics. It plainly will not permit the $3 trillion per year retirement and health care entitlements-driven Welfare State to be curtailed.

Trump and the congressional GOP have already sealed that deal by refusing to reform Social Security and Medicare and by proving to be utterly incapable of laying a glove politically on Obamacare/Medicaid. At the same time, boomers keep voting for the GOP's anti-tax allergy, thereby refusing to tax themselves to close Washington's yawning deficits.

More important, the generation which marched on the Pentagon in 1968 against the insanity and barbarism of LBJ's Vietnam War has long since abandoned the cause of peace. So doing, boomers have acquiesced in the final ascendancy of the Warfare State, which grew like topsy once the US became the world's sole superpower after the Soviet Union shuffled off the pages of history in 1991.

Why There Was No Peace On Earth When The 77-Years War Finally Ended In 1991

Yet there is a reason why the end of the 77-years world war which incepted with the "guns of August" did not enable the world to resume the pre-1914 status quo ante of relative peace and capitalism-fueled global prosperity.

To wit, the hoary ideology of American exceptionalism and the Indispensable Nation was also, ironically, liberated from the constraints of cold war realism when the iron curtain came tumbling down.

Consequently, Washington burst into a quest for unadulterated global hegemony. In short order (under Bush the Elder and the Clintons) it morphed into the Imperial City, and became a beehive not only of militarism, but of an endless complex of think-tanks, NGOs, advisories and consultancies, "law firms", lobbies and racketeers.

The unspeakable prosperity of Washington flows from that Imperial beehive. And it is the Indispensable Nation meme that provides the political adhesive that binds the Imperial City to the works of Empire and to provisioning the massive fiscal appetites of the Warfare State.

Needless to say, Empire is a terrible thing because it is the health of the state and the profound enemy of capitalist prosperity and constitutional liberty.

It thrives and metastasizes by abandoning the republican verities of non-intervention abroad and peaceful commerce with all the nations of the world in favor of the self-appointed role of global policeman. Rather than homeland defense, the policy of Empire is that of international busybody, military hegemon and brutal enforcer of Washington's writs, sanctions, red lines and outlawed regimes.

There is nothing more emblematic of that betrayal of republican non-interventionism than the sundry hot spots which dog the Empire today. These include the Ukraine/Crimea confrontation with Russia, the regime change fiasco in Syria, the US sponsored genocide in Yemen, the failed, bloody 17-year occupation of Afghanistan, the meddling of the US Seventh Fleet in the South China Sea, and, most especially, the swiftly intensifying contretemps in Iran.

As to the latter, there is absolutely no reason for the Empire's attack on Iran. The proverbial Martian, in fact, would be sorely perplexed about why Washington is marching toward war with its puritanical and authoritarian but relatively powerless religious rulers.

After all, Iran hasn't violated the nuke deal (JPAOC) by the lights of any credible authority — or by even less than credible ones like the CIA. Nor by the same consensus of authorities has it even had a research program for nuclear weaponization since 2003.

Likewise, its modest GDP of $430 billion is equal to just eight days of US output, thereby hardly constituting an industrial platform from which its theocratic rulers could plausibly menace America's homeland.

Nor could its tiny $14 billion defense budget — which amounts to just seven days worth of DOD outlays — inflict any military harm on American citizens.

In fact, Iran has no blue water navy that could effectively operate outside of the Persian Gulf; its longest range warplanes can barely get to Rome without refueling; and its array of mainly defensive medium and intermediate range missiles are limited to 1200 miles by order of the Ayatollah and cannot strike most of NATO, to say nothing of the North American continent.

The answer to the Martian's question, of course, is that Iran is no threat whatsoever to the safety and security of the US homeland, but it has run badly afoul of the dictates of the American Empire.

That is to say, it has presumed to have an independent foreign policy involving Washington proscribed alliances with the sovereign state of Syria, the leading political party of Lebanon (Hezbollah), the ruling authorities in Baghdad and the reining power in the Yemen capital of Sana'a (the Houthis).

All these regimes except the puppet state of Iraq are deemed by Washington to be sources of unsanctioned "regional instability" and Iran's alliances with them have been capriciously labeled as acts of state sponsored terrorism.

The same goes for Washington's demarche against Iran's modest array of short, medium and intermediate range ballistic missiles. These weapons are palpably instruments of self-defense, but Imperial Washington insists their purpose is aggression — unlike the case of practically every other nation which offers its custom to American arms merchants for like and similar weapons.

For example, Iran's arch-rival across the Persian Gulf, Saudi Arabia, has more advanced NATO supplied ballistic missiles with even greater range (1,600 mile range). So does Israel, Pakistan, India and a half-dozen other nations, which are either Washington allies or have been given a hall-pass in order to bolster US arms exports.

In short, Washington's escalating war on Iran is an exercise in global hegemony, not territorial self-defense. It is a testament to the manner in which the historic notion of national defense has morphed into Washington's arrogant claim that it constitutes the "Indispensable Nation" which purportedly stands as mankind's bulwark against global disorder and chaos among nations.

Needless to say, Iran is just the case de jure of the Indispensable Nation in action. Yet the other hot spots of the moment are no less exercises in the hegemonic aggression which inexorably flows from it.

Washington's Ukrainian Folly

Thus, Washington started the Ukrainian confrontation by sponsoring, funding and instantly recognizing the February 2014 coup that overthrew a Russia-friendly government, replacing it with one that is militantly nationalistic and bitterly antagonistic to Russia. And it did so for the most superficial and historically ignorant reason imaginable.

Namely, it objected to the decision of Ukraine's prior government in late 2013 to align itself economically and politically with its historic hegemon in Moscow rather than the EU and NATO. Yet the fairly elected and constitutionally legitimate government of Ukraine then led by Viktor Yanukovych had gone that route mainly because it got a better deal from Moscow than was being demanded by the fiscal torture artists of the IMF.

Needless to say, the ensuing US sponsored putsch arising from the mobs on the street of Kiev re-opened deep national wounds. As we have seen, Ukraine's bitter divide between Russian-speakers in the east and Ukrainian nationalists elsewhere dates back to Stalin's brutal rein in Ukraine during the 1930s and Ukrainian collusion with Hitler's Wehrmacht on its way to Stalingrad and back during the 1940s.

It was the memory of the latter nightmare, in fact, which triggered the fear-driven outbreak of Russian separatism in the Donbas and the 96% referendum vote in Crimea to formally re-affiliate with mother Russia.

In this context, even a passing familiarity with Russian history and geography would remind that Ukraine and Crimea are Moscow's business, not Washington's.

In the first place, there is nothing at stake in the Ukraine that matters. During the last 700 years it has been a meandering set of borders in search of a country.

In fact, the intervals in which the Ukraine existed as an independent nation have been few and far between. Invariably, its rulers, petty potentates and corrupt politicians made deals with or surrendered to every outside power that came along. These included the Lithuanians, Turks, Poles, Austrians, Muscovites and Czars, among others. Indeed, in modern times Ukraine largely functioned as an integral part of Mother Russia, serving as its breadbasket and iron and steel crucible under czars and commissars alike. Given this history, the idea that Ukraine should be actively and aggressively induced to join NATO was just plain nuts.

As we have also seen, the allegedly "occupied" territory of Crimea, in fact, was actually purchased from the Ottomans by Catherine the Great in 1783, thereby satisfying the longstanding quest of the Russian Czars for a warm-water port. Over the ages Sevastopol then emerged as a great naval base at the strategic tip of the Crimean peninsula, where it became home to the mighty Black Sea Fleet of the Czars and then the Soviet Union, too.

For the next 171 years Crimea was an integral part of Russia (until 1954). That span exceeds the 170 years that have elapsed since California was annexed by an aggressive thrust of "Manifest Destiny" on this continent, thereby providing, incidentally, the United States Navy with its own warm-water port in San Diego.

While no foreign forces subsequently invaded the California coasts, it was most definitely not Ukrainian and Polish rifles, artillery and blood which famously annihilated The Charge Of The Light Brigade at the Crimean city of Balaclava in 1854; they were Russians defending the homeland from invaders —Turks, French and Brits.

And the portrait of the Russian "hero" hanging in Putin's office is that of Czar Nicholas I — whose brutal 30-year reign brought the Russian Empire to its historical zenith. Yet despite his cruelty, Nicholas I is revered in Russian hagiography as the defender of Crimea, even as he lost the 1850s war to the Ottomans and Europeans.

Washington Is Actually Enforcing The Dead Hand Of The Soviet Presidium In Crimea

At the end of the day, security of its historic port in Crimea is Russia's Red Line, not Washington's. Unlike today's feather-headed Washington pols, even the enfeebled Franklin Roosevelt at least knew that he was in Soviet **Russia** when he made port in the Crimean city of Yalta in February 1945.

Maneuvering to cement his control of the Kremlin in the intrigue-ridden struggle for succession after Stalin's death a few years later, Nikita Khrushchev allegedly spent 15 minutes reviewing his "gift" of Crimea to his subalterns in Kiev.

As it happened, therefore, Crimea became part of the Ukraine only by writ of one of the most vicious and reprehensible states in human history — the former Soviet Union:

On April 26, 1954. The decree of the Presidium of the USSR Supreme Soviet transferring the Crimea Oblast from the Russian SFSR to the Ukrainian SSR..... Taking into account the integral character of the economy, the territorial proximity and the close economic and cultural ties between the Crimea Province and the Ukrainian SSR....

That's right. Washington's hypocritical and tendentious accusations against Russia's re-absorption of Crimea imply that the dead-hand of the Soviet presidium must be defended at all costs — as if the security of North Dakota depended upon it!

In fact, the brouhaha about "returning" Crimea is a naked case of the hegemonic arrogance that has overtaken Imperial Washington since the 1991 Soviet demise.

After all, during the long decades of the Cold War, the West did nothing to liberate the "captive nation" of Ukraine — with or without the Crimean appendage bestowed upon it in 1954. Nor did it draw any red lines in the mid-1990's when a financially desperate Ukraine rented back Sevastopol and the strategic redoubts of the Crimea to an equally pauperized Russia.

In short, in the era before we got our Pacific port in 1848, and even during the 170-year interval since then, America's national security has depended not one whit on the status of Russian-speaking Crimea. That the local population has now chosen fealty to the Grand Thief in Moscow over the ruffians and rabble who have seized Kiev amounts to a giant: So what!

The truth is, when it comes to Ukraine there really isn't that much there, there. Its boundaries have been morphing for centuries among the quarreling tribes, peoples, potentates, Patriarchs and pretenders of a small region that is none of Washington's damn business.

Still, it was this final aggressive drive of Washington and NATO into the internal affairs of Russia's historic neighbor and vassal, Ukraine, that largely accounts for the demonization of Putin. Likewise, it is virtually the entire source of the false claim that Russia has aggressive, expansionist designs on the former Warsaw Pact states in the Baltics, Poland and beyond.

The latter is a nonsensical fabrication. In fact, it was the neocon meddlers from Washington who crushed Ukraine's last semblance of civil governance when they enabled ultra-nationalists and crypto-Nazis to gain government positions after the February 2014 putsch.

As we indicated above, in one fell swoop that inexcusable stupidity reopened Ukraine's blood-soaked modern history. The latter incepted with Stalin's re-population of the eastern Donbas region with "reliable" Russian workers after his genocidal liquidation of the kulaks in the early 1930s.

It was subsequently exacerbated by the large-scale collaboration by Ukrainian nationalists in the west with the Nazi Wehrmacht as it laid waste to Poles, Jews, gypsies and other "undesirables" on its way to Stalingrad in 1942-43. Thereafter followed an equal and opposite spree of barbaric revenge as the victorious Red Army marched back through Ukraine on its way to Berlin.

So it may be fairly asked. What beltway lame brains did not chance to understand that Washington's triggering of "regime change" in Kiev would reopen this entire bloody history of sectarian and political strife?

Moreover, once they had opened Pandora's box, why was it so hard to see that an outright partition of Ukraine with autonomy for the Donbas and Crimea, or even accession to the Russian state from which these communities had originated, would have been a perfectly reasonable resolution?

Certainly that would have been far preferable to dragging all of Europe into the lunacy of the current anti-Putin sanctions and embroiling the Ukrainian factions in a suicidal civil war. The alleged Russian threat to Europe, therefore, was manufactured in Imperial Washington, not the Kremlin.

China's Sand Castles In The South China Sea — So What!

Even more hideous is the rhetorical provocations and Seventh Fleet maneuvers ordered by Washington with respect to China's comical sand castle building in the South China Sea. Whatever they are doing on these man-made islets, it is not threatening to the security of America — nor is there any plausible reason to believe that it is a threat to global commerce, either.

After all, it is the mercantilist economies of China and East Asian that would collapse almost instantly if Beijing attempted to interrupt world trade. That is, any theoretical red military shoe would first fall on the Red Suzerains of Beijing themselves because it is the hard currency earnings from its export machine that keep the Red Ponzi from collapsing and the Chinese people enthrall to their communist overlords.

Needless to say, none of these kinds of interventions were even imaginable in the sleepy town of Washington DC just

317

100-years ago. But it's baleful evolution from the capital of an economically focused Republic to seat of power in a globally mobilized Empire ultimately sprung from the Indispensable Nation heresy.

So in the next chapter we intend to delve into the historic roots of that conceit because it not only guarantees unending calamities abroad, but also an eventual fiscal and financial horror show at home.

Indeed, so long as Imperial Washington is stretched about the planet in its sundry self-appointed missions of stabilization, peacekeeping, punishment, attack, occupation, sanctions and other hegemonic maneuvers — there is zero chance that America's collapsing fiscal accounts can be salvaged.

The Indispensable Nation folly thus hangs over the rotten edifice of Bubble Finance (Part 2) like a modern day Sword of Damocles.

But Empire is a corrosive disease upon democratic governance. It eventually metastasizes into imperial arrogance, over-reach and high-handedness. Ultimately, like at present, it falls prey to the rule of bellicose war-mongers and thugs like John Bolton and Mike Pompeo.

Washington's Economic Sanctions — Acts of War By Any Other Name

In the present instance, it is they who exploited Trump's abysmal ignorance on the Iranian nuke deal; it is their specious imperial beef with Iran's legitimate right as a sovereign nation to its own foreign policy which gave him cover to withdraw and to re-impose of maximum sanctions, thereby effectively bracing Tehran with an act of war by any other name.

Yes, the feinschmeckers of the foreign policy establishment consider economic sanctions to be some kind of benign instrument of enlightened diplomacy — the carrot that preempts resort to the stick. But that is just sanctimonious prattle.

When you hound the deep water ports of the planet attempting to block Iran's oil sales, which are its principal and vital source of foreign exchange, or cut-off access by its central bank to the global money clearance system known as SWIFT or pressure friend and foe alike to stop all investment and trade — that's an act of aggression every bit as menacing and damaging as a cruise missile attack.

Or at least it was once understood that way. Even as recently as 1960 the great Dwight Eisenhower (very) reluctantly agreed to lie about Gary Power's U-2 plane when the Soviets shot it down and captured its CIA pilot alive.

But Ike did so because he was old-fashioned enough to believe that even penetrating the air space of a foe without permission was an act of war. And that he did not intend — the CIA's surveillance program notwithstanding.

Today, by contrast, Washington invades the *economic space* of dozens of foreign nations with alacrity. In fact, the US Treasury Department's Office of Foreign Asset Control (OFAC) proudly lists 30 different sanctions programs including ones on Belarus, Burundi, Cuba, Congo, Libya, Somalia, Sudan, Venezuela, Yemen and Zimbabwe — along with the more visible programs against the alleged malefactors of Iran, Russia and North Korea.

These, too, are the footprints of Empire, not measures of a homeland defense befitting a peace-seeking Republic. As we demonstrate in chapter 18, the latter would cost around $250 billion per year, and would rely on an already built and paid for triad nuclear capacity for deterrence, and a modest Navy and Air Force for protection of the nation's shorelines and air space.

The $500 billion excess in today's Trump-bloated national security budget of $750 billion is the cost of Empire; it's the crushing fiscal burden that flows from the Indispensable Nation folly and its calamitously wrong assumption that the planet would descend into chaos without the good offices of the American Empire.

Needless to say, we do not believe that the planet is chaos-prone absent Washington's ministrations. After all, the historic record from Vietnam through Afghanistan, Iraq, Libya, Syria and Iran suggests exactly the opposite.

CHAPTER 15

Woodrow Wilson And The Myth
Of The Indispensable Nation

The Indispensable Nation meme originates not in the universal condition of mankind and the nation-states into which it has been partitioned. Instead, it stems from an erroneous take on the one-time, flukish and historically aberrant circumstances of the 20th century that gave raise to giant totalitarian states in Hitler's Germany and Stalin's Russia, and the resulting mass murder and oppressions which resulted therefrom.

What we mean is that Stalinist Russia and Nazi Germany were not coded into the DNA of humanity; they were not an incipient horror always waiting to happen the moment more righteous nations let down their guard.

To the contrary, they were effectively born and bred in April 1917 when the US entered what was then called the Great War. And though it did so for absolutely no reason of homeland security or any principle consistent with the legitimate foreign policy of the American Republic, its entry tilted the outcome to the social chaos and Carthaginian peace of Versailles from which Stalin and Hitler sprang.

So you can put the blame for the monumental evil of 20th century totalitarianism squarely on Thomas Woodrow Wilson. This megalomaniacal madman, who was the very worst President in American history, took America into war for the worst possible reason: Namely, a vainglorious desire to have a big seat at the post-war peace table in order to remake the world as God had inspired him to redeem it.

The truth, however, was that the European war posed not an iota of threat to the safety and security of the citizens of Lincoln NE, or Worcester MA or Sacramento CA. In that respect, Wilson's putative defense of "freedom of the seas" and the rights of neutrals was an empty shibboleth; his call to make the world safe for democracy, a preposterous pipe dream.

Indeed, the shattered world extant after the bloodiest war in human history was a world about which Wilson was blatantly ignorant. And remaking it was a task for which he was temperamentally unsuited — even as his infamous 14 points were a chimera so abstractly devoid of substance as to constitute mental play dough.

Wilson's Megalomania And Its Awful Legacy

The monumentally ugly reason for America's entry into the Great War, in fact, was revealed — if inadvertently — by his alter-ego and sycophant, Colonel House. As the latter put it: Intervention in Europe's war positioned Wilson to play,

"The noblest part that has ever come to the son of man."

America thus plunged into Europe's carnage, and forevermore shed its century-long Republican tradition of anti-militarism and non-intervention in the quarrels of the Old World. From Wilson's historically erroneous turn — there arose at length the Indispensable Nation folly, which we shall catalogue in depth below.

For now, suffice it to say that there was absolutely nothing noble that came of Wilson's intervention.

It led to a peace of vengeful victors, triumphant nationalists and avaricious imperialists — when the war would have otherwise ended in a bedraggled peace of mutually exhausted bankrupts and discredited war parties on both sides.

By so altering the course of history, Wilson's war bankrupted

THE MYTH OF THE INDISPENSABLE NATION

Europe and midwifed 20th century totalitarianism in Russia
and Germany.

These developments, in turn, eventually led to the Great
Depression, the Welfare State and Keynesian economics, World
War II, the holocaust, the Cold War, the permanent Warfare
State and its military-industrial-surveillance complex.

They also spawned Nixon's 1971 destruction of sound
money, Reagan's failure to tame Big Government and
Greenspan's destructive cult of monetary central planning.

So, too, flowed the Bush dynasty's wars of intervention and
occupation, and from them a fatal blow to the failed states in
the lands of Islam foolishly created by the imperialist map-
makers at Versailles. The legacy: endless waves of blowback and
terrorism now afflicting the world.

The rise of the murderous Nazi and Stalinist totalitarian
regimes during the 1930s and the resulting conflagration of
World War II is held to be, correctly, the defining event of the
20th century. But that truism only begs the real question.

To wit, were these nightmarish scourges always latent just
below the surface of global civilization — waiting to erupt
whenever good people and nations fell asleep at the switch,
as per the standard critique of the British pacifism and US
isolationism that flourished during the late 1930s?

Or were they the equivalent of the 1000 year flood? That
is, a development so unlikely, aberrant and unrepeatable as to
merely define a horrid but one-off chapter of history, not the
ordinary and probable unfolding of affairs among the nations.

We contend that the answer depends upon whether you
start with *April 2, 1917*, when America discarded its historic
republican policy of non-intervention and joined the bloody
fray on the old continent's Western Front, or *December 7, 1941*,
when Japan's attack on Pearl Harbor allegedly awoke America
from its isolationist slumber and called it to global leadership of
the so-called American Century.

Needless to say, the Deep State's ideology of the Indispensable Nation and its projects of Empire are rooted in the Pearl Harbor narrative. That is, the claim that global affairs go to hell in a hand basket when virtuous nations let down their guard or acquiesce to even modest acts of regional aggression.

The now faded verities of republican non-intervention, by contrast, properly finger Woodrow Wilson's perfidious declaration of war on Germany as the event that changed the ordinary course of history, and paved the way for the once in a 1000 years aberration of Hitler and Stalin which ultimately ensued.

Not surprisingly, the official historical narratives of the Empire glorify America's rising to duty in World War II and after, but merely describe the events of 1917-1919 as some sort of preliminary coming of age.

As a consequence, the rich, history-defining essence of what happened during those eventful years has been lost in the fog of battles, the miserable casualty statistics of the Great War, the tales of prolonged diplomatic wrangling at Versailles and the blame-game for the failed Senate ratification of Wilson's League of Nations thereafter.

In this connection, the defeat of the League of Nations is treated as a colossal error in the mainstream narrative. It is held to constitute a crucial default by the Indispensable Nation that hurried the rise of the totalitarian nightmares, and only compounded America's task of righting the world in the 1940s and after.

In fact, however, the defeat of Wilson's treaty was the last gasp of republicanism — an echo of the stand that had kept America true to its interests and non-interventionist traditions as the calamity of the Great War unfolded.

In effect, the so-called isolationists (actually the original America Firsters) were trying to turn the clock back to April 1, 1917.

That was the day before Wilson summoned the Congress to war based on his own megalomania and the high-handed maneuvers of his State Department. After William Jennings Bryan's principled anti-war resignation in June 1915, the latter had been operating in complete cahoots with the Morgan interests (which had risked billions financing England and France) and had essentially maneuvered the messianic Wilson into war.

Stalin and Hitler Were Wilson's Progeny, Not The Fruit Of Mankind's DNA

Consequently, the powerful truths of what actually preceded the 1919 defeat of the League have been lost to standard history. In what follows, we mean to revive these crucial developments and inflection points because they clearly do demonstrate that the 1000 year flood of 20th century totalitarianism originated in the foolish decisions of Wilson and a few others, not the DNA of mankind nor a death urge of the nations.

Needless to say, that is not a matter of academic history; it makes all the difference in the world of here and now because virtually every maneuver of Imperial Washington, such as it current demented attacks on Iran, are predicated on the Hitler and Stalin syndrome. That is, the hoary belief that there is always another one of these monsters lurking in the ordinary political, economic and cultural conflicts of the nations.

To the contrary, of course, if the world actually needs no Indispensable Nation the whole predicate for Empire is invalidated. The raison d'etre of the Imperial City and all its hegemonic projects of "leadership", meddling, intervention, and occupation, in fact, belong in the dustbin of history.

Needless to say, that is also why Imperial Washington was so aghast at Donald Trump's election. By whatever cockamamie route of thinly informed reasoning he got there — he did seem to comprehend that the national security of America and the policing of a global Empire are not the same thing at all.

So herewith is a capsulized dissection of the 1000 year flood — explaining why Stalin and Hitler should have never happened. Accordingly, the hot, cold and permanent wars that followed thereafter condemn the case for Empire, not make it; and they show that Trump's America First is a far more appropriate lodestone for national security policy than Imperial Washington's specious claim that America is the Indispensable Nation.

As indicated above, the Great War had been destined to end in 1917 by mutual exhaustion, bankruptcy and withdrawal from the utterly stalemated trenches of the Western Front. In the end, upwards of *3.3 million* combatants had been killed and **8.3 million** wounded over four years for movement along blood-drenched front-lines that could be measured in mere miles and yards.

Still, had America stayed on its side of the great Atlantic moat, the ultimate outcomes everywhere would have been far different. Foremostly, the infant democracy that came to power in February 1917 in Russia would not have been so easily smothered in its crib.

There surely would have been no disastrous summer offensive by the Kerensky government to rollback Germany on the eastern front where the czarist armies had earlier been humiliated and dismembered.

In turn, an early end to the war in Russia would also have precluded the subsequent armed insurrection in Petrograd in November 1917, which enabled the flukish seizure of power by Lenin and his small band of fanatical Bolsheviks.

That is, the 20th century would not have been saddled with what inexorably morphed into the Stalinist nightmare. Nor would a garrisoned Soviet state have poisoned the peace of nations for 74 years thereafter, while causing the nuclear sword of Damocles to hang precariously over the planet.

Likewise, there would have been no abomination known as the Versailles peace treaty because it was a toxic peace of victors. But without America's billions of aid and munitions and two million fresh doughboys there would have been no Allied victors, as we demonstrate below.

Without Versailles, in turn, there would have been no "stab in the back" legends owing to the German government's forced signing of the "war guilt" clause; no continuance of England's brutal post-armistice blockade that delivered hundreds of thousands of Germany's women and children into starvation and death; and no demobilized 3-million man German army left humiliated, destitute, bitter and on a permanent political rampage of vengeance.

So, too, there would have been no acquiescence in the dismemberment of Germany at the Versailles "peace" table.

As it happened nearly one-fifth of Germany's pre-war territory and population was spread in parts and pieces to Poland (the Danzig Corridor and Upper Silesia), Czechoslovakia (the Sudetenland), Denmark (Schleswig), France (the Saar, Alsace-Lorraine and the neutralized Rhineland) and Belgium (Eupen and Malmedy).

This sweeping loss of territory also meant Germany lost 50% of its iron production capacity, 16% of it coal output and 100% of its far flung colonies in Africa and East Asia to England and France.

Needless to say, god did not create the map of Europe on the 6th day of his labors. But it is absolutely the case that it was the vast German territories and peoples "stolen" at Versailles that provided the fuel for Hitler's revanchist agitation; and it was that campaign to regain the lost territories which nourished the Nazis with patriotic public support in the rump of the fatherland.

Likewise, the France-Belgium occupation of the Ruhr in 1923 would not have happened because the justification for that invasion of German lands was that the latter had not paid its oppressive war reparations — a staggering sum that would amount to more than **$500 billion** in today's purchasing power.

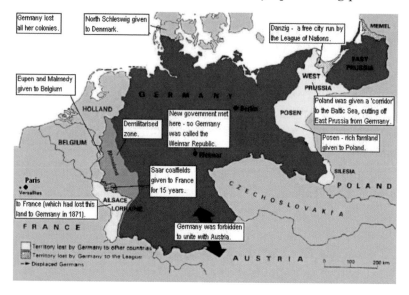

As it happened, it was the reparations crisis that led to Germany's insane printing press monetary spree and the destruction of the German middle class in the 1923 hyperinflation. And without that society-crushing development along with all of the above, the history books would have never recorded the Hitlerian ascent to power and all the evils that flowed thereupon.

Even The Younger John Maynard Keynes Got It Right

Even John Maynard Keynes, who was a British Treasury official at Versailles, could see that the Carthaginian Peace of Versailles was only sowing the seeds of economic breakdown in Germany and throughout much of warn-torn Europe.

In his famous tract, ***The Economic Consequences of the Peace***, Keynes rightly foresaw the disaster ahead:

The Treaty includes no provisions for the economic rehabilitation of Europe,– nothing to make the defeated Central Powers into good neighbors, nothing to stabilize the new states of Europe, nothing to reclaim Russia; nor does it promote in any way a compact of solidarity amongst the Allies themselves; no arrangement was reached at Paris for restoring the disordered finances of France and Italy, or to adjust the systems of the Old World and the New.

The Council of Four paid no attention to these issues, being preoccupied with others,– Clemenceau to crush the economic life of his enemy, Lloyd George to do a deal and bring home something that would pass muster for a week, the President to do nothing that was not just and right. It is an extraordinary fact that the fundamental economic problems of a Europe starving and disintegrating before their eyes, was the one question in which it was impossible to arouse the interest of the Four. Reparation was their main excursion into the economic field, and they settled it as a problem of theology, of politics, of electoral chicane, from every point of view except that of the economic future of the States whose destiny they were handling.

... Economic privation proceeds by easy stages, and so long as men suffer it patiently the outside world cares very little. Physical efficiency and resistance to disease slowly diminish, but life proceeds somehow, until the limit of human endurance is reached at last and counsels of despair and madness stir the sufferers from the lethargy which precedes the crisis. The man shakes himself, and the bonds of custom are loosed. The power of ideas is sovereign, and he listens to whatever instruction of hope, illusion, or revenge is carried to them in the air. ...

As it happened, Adolf Hitler himself later validated Keynes' prophecy in spades. Writing in *Mein Kampf,* he made absolutely clear that the unjust treaty of Versailles was the key to mobilizing the German nation:

What a use could be made of the Treaty of Versailles. . . . How each one of the points of that treaty could be branded in the minds and hearts of the German people until sixty million men and women find their souls aflame with a feeling of rage and shame;

and a torrent of fire bursts forth as from a furnace, and a will of steel is forged from it, with the common cry: "We will have arms again!"

So Woodrow Wilson has a lot to answer for because he is the father of the Carthaginian Peace that broke the world at Versailles. But the matter is far greater than just Wilson's Folly of leading the US into war in April 1917.

His reasons for doing so are all the more important. Wilson's 14 Points and his "make the world safe for democracy" slogans were essentially the original and incipient vision of the Indispensable Nation.

Ironically, therefore, the false idea that triggered the whole train of 20th century events, which then mid-wifed the American Empire, is now used to justify the continuing disorder and mayhem that it has unleashed upon the world.

Accordingly, Wilson's own "war guilt" is a mighty stain, extending to most of the wars of the 20th century. That because America's wholly unjustified entry into a war that was already over prolonged the original Old World catastrophe for decades to come.

So doing, it first fostered the 1000 year flood of totalitarianism in Germany and Russia, and from that the Indispensable Nation folly that continues to bedevil the entire world.

The Great War — Europe's Folly With Blame For All

In this context, it is essential to recall that the Great War was about nothing worth dying for and engaged no recognizable principle of human betterment; it was not the case of a short-run necessity that inadvertently gave rise to a later, greater evil.

Among the cast of characters who broke the world in the summer of 1914 there were many blackish hats, but no white ones. The onset of the Great War, in fact, was an avoidable calamity issuing from a cacophony of political incompetence, cowardice, avarice and tomfoolery.

In part, you can blame the bombastic and impetuous Kaiser Wilhelm for setting the stage with his foolish dismissal of Bismarck in 1890; his failure to renew the Russian reinsurance treaty shortly thereafter (which forced the Czar to ally with France); and his quixotic build-up of the German Navy after the turn of the century (which turned much of English opinion against Germany).

Likewise, you can blame the French for lashing themselves to a war treaty that could be triggered by the intrigues of a decadent court in St. Petersburg where the Czar still claimed divine rights and the Czarina ruled behind the scenes on the mystical advice of Rasputin.

Similarly, you can censure Russia's foreign minister Sazonov for his delusions of greater Slavic grandeur that had encouraged Serbia's provocations of Austria after Sarajevo; and you can also castigate the doddering emperor Franz Joseph for hanging onto power into his 67th year on the throne and thereby leaving his crumbling empire vulnerable to the suicidal impulses of General Conrad's war party.

So too, you can indict the duplicitous German Chancellor, Bethmann-Hollweg, for allowing the Austrians to believe that the Kaiser endorsed their declaration of war on Serbia; and pillory Winston Churchill and London's war party for failing to recognize that the Schlieffen Plan's invasion through Belgium was no threat to England, but a unavoidable German defense against a two-front war on the continent.

But after all that — you most especially can't talk about the defense of democracy, the vindication of liberalism or the thwarting of Prussian autocracy and militarism.

The British War Party led by the likes of Churchill and General Kitchener was all about the glory of empire, not the vindication of democracy.

So, too, France' principal war aim was the revanchist drive

to recover Alsace-Lorrain. The latter was mainly a German speaking territory for 600 years until it was conquered by Louis XIV in the 17th century, and then forcibly re-acquired by Germany after its humiliating defeat of the French in 1870-71.

In any event, German autocracy was already on its last leg as betokened by the arrival of universal social insurance and the election of a socialist-liberal majority in the Reichstag on the eve of the war; and the Austro-Hungarian, Balkan and Ottoman goulash of nationalities, respectively, would have erupted in interminable regional conflicts and nationalist fragmentation, regardless of who won the Great War.

In short, nothing of principle or higher morality was at stake in the outcome

No Threat Whatsoever To The Security Of The American Homeland

The war posed no national security threat whatsoever to the US. And that presumes, of course, the danger was not the Entente powers — but Germany and its allies.

From the very beginning, however, there was no chance at all that Germany and its bedraggled allies could threaten America — and that had become overwhelmingly true by April 1917 when Wilson launched America into war.

In fact, within a few weeks, after the Schlieffen Plan offensive failed on September 11, 1914, the German Army became incarcerated in a bloody, bankrupting, two-front land war. That ensured its inexorable demise and utter incapacity in terms of finances and manpower to even glance cross-eyed at America on the distant side of the Atlantic moat.

Likewise, after the battle of Jutland in May 1916, the great German surface fleet was bottled up in its homeports — an inert flotilla of steel that posed no threat to the American coast 4,000 miles away.

As for the rest of the central powers, the Ottoman and

Hapsburg empires already had an appointment with the dustbin of history. Need we even bother with any putative threat from the fourth member of the Central Powers — that is, Bulgaria?

Beyond the absence of any threat to homeland security, Wilson's pretexts for war on Germany — submarine warfare and the Zimmerman telegram — are not half what they are cracked-up to be by Warfare State historians.

As to the first item in Wilson's casus belli — the so-called freedom of the seas and neutral shipping rights — the story is blatantly simple.

In November 1914, England declared the North Sea to be a "war zone." So doing, it threatened neutral shipping with deadly sea mines; declared that anything which could conceivably be of use to the German army — directly or indirectly — to be contraband that would be seized or destroyed; and announced that the resulting blockade of German ports was designed to starve it into submission.

In retaliation a few months later, Germany announced its submarine warfare policy designed to the stem the flow of food, raw materials and armaments to England. It was the desperate antidote of a land power to England's crushing sea-borne blockade.

Accordingly, there existed a state of total warfare in the northern European waters — and the traditional "rights" of neutrals were irrelevant and disregarded by both sides.

Indeed, in arming merchantmen and stowing munitions on passenger liners, England was hypocritical and utterly cavalier about the resulting mortal danger to innocent civilians. That was exemplified tragically by the 4.3 million rifle cartridges and hundreds of tons of other munitions carried in the hull of the **Lusitania**, when it was sunk by a German submarine off the coast of Ireland in May 1915.

Likewise, German resort to so-called "unrestricted submarine warfare" in February 1917 was brutal and stupid, but came in response to massive domestic political pressure during what was known as the "turnip winter" in Germany. By then, the country was starving from the English blockade — literally.

Before he resigned on principle in June 1915, Secretary William Jennings Bryan got it right. Had he been less diplomatic he would have said never should American boys be crucified on the cross of Cunard liner state room — so that a few thousand wealthy plutocrats could exercise a putative "right" to wallow in luxury while knowingly cruising into harm's way.

As to the Zimmerman telegram, it was never delivered to Mexico at all. It was actually only an internal diplomatic communique sent from Berlin to the German ambassador in Washington, who had labored mightily to keep his country out of war with the US.

As it happened, this draft communique was intercepted by British intelligence in February 1917, which sat on it for more than a month waiting for an opportune moment to incite America into war hysteria.

Contrary to the mainstream history books, therefore, the so-called Zimmerman bombshell was actually the opposite of what it is cracked-up to be. Rather than a threatened aggression against the American homeland, it was actually an internal foreign ministry rumination about approaching the Mexican president regarding an alliance and the return of territories in the event that the US first went to war with Germany

And exactly why would such a defensive action in the face of an attack be all that surprising — let alone a valid casus belli?

After all, did not the Entente (England, France and Russia) bribe Italy into the war with promises of large chunks of Austria?

Did not the hapless Rumanians finally join the Entente when they were promised Transylvania?

Did not the Greeks bargain endlessly over the Turkish territories they were to be awarded for joining the allies?

Did not Lawrence of Arabia bribe the Sherif of Mecca

with the promise of vast Arabian lands to be extracted from the Turks?

Why, then, would the Germans — if forced into war with the USA — not promise the return of Texas?

Why The Great War Was Effectively Over When Wilson Intervened

In any event, by the end of 1916 the expected "short war" was long ago a faded delusion. What existed at that point was a guaranteed military stalemate, mutual political exhaustion and impending financial bankruptcy among all the European belligerents.

To be sure, Europe had almost gotten its "short war" when the German "Schlieffen Plan" offensive brought its armies within 30 miles of Paris during the first weeks of the war. But the offensive bogged down on the Marne River in mid-September 1914.

Within three months thereafter, the Western Front had formed and coagulated into blood and mud. It soon became a ghastly 400 mile corridor of senseless carnage, unspeakable slaughter and incessant military stupidity that stretched from the Flanders coast and then across Belgium and northern France to the Swiss frontier.

The next four years witnessed an undulating line of trenches, barbed wire entanglements, tunnels, artillery emplacements and shell-pocked scorched earth that rarely moved more than a few miles in either direction, and which ultimately claimed more than *7 million* casualties on the Allied side and nearly *5 million* on the German side.

If there was any doubt that Wilson's catastrophic intervention converted a war of attrition, stalemate and eventual mutual exhaustion into Pyrrhic victory for the allies, it was memorialized in four developments during 1916 that preceded the US declaration of war.

In the first, the Germans wagered everything on a massive offensive designed to overrun the french fortresses of Verdun. These historic defensive battlements on France's northeast border had stood since Roman times, and had been massively reinforced after the France's humiliating defeat in the Franco-Prussian War of 1870.

But notwithstanding the mobilization of 100 divisions, the greatest artillery bombardment campaign ever recorded until then, and repeated infantry offensives from February through November that resulted in upwards of 400,000 German casualties, the Verdun offensive failed.

The second event was its mirror image — the massive British and French offensive known as the Second Battle of the Somme. The latter commenced with equally destructive artillery barrages on July 1, 1916 and then for three month sent waves of infantry into the maws of German machine guns and artillery.

It too ended in colossal failure, but only after more than 600,000 English and French casualties including a quarter million dead.

In between these bloodbaths, the stalemate was reinforced by the above mentioned naval showdown at Jutland. That battle cost the British far more sunken ships and drowned sailors than the Germans, but also caused the Germans to retire their surface fleet to port and never again challenge the Royal Navy in open water combat.

Finally, by year-end 1916 the German generals who had destroyed the Russian armies in the East with only a tiny one-ninth fraction of the German army — Generals Hindenburg and Ludendorff — were given command of the entire war effort.

Presently, they radically changed Germany's war strategy by recognizing that the growing allied superiority in manpower, owing to the British homeland draft of 1916 and mobilization of forces from throughout the Commonwealth, made a German offensive breakthrough well nigh impossible.

The result was the Hindenburg Line — a military marvel of awesome defensive impregnability. It consisted of a checkerboard array of hardened pillbox machine gunners and maneuver forces rather than mass infantry on the front lines and also an intricate labyrinth of highly engineered tunnels, deep earth shelters, rail connections, heavy artillery and flexible reserves in the rear.

It was also augmented by the transfer of Germany's eastern armies to the western front in 1917 — giving it 200 divisions and 4 million men on the Hindenburg Line.

This precluded any hope of Entente victory. By 1917 there were not enough able-bodied draft age men left in France and England to overcome the Hindenburg Line, which, in turn, was designed to bleed white the Entente armies led by butchers like British General Haig and French General Joffre until their governments sued for peace.

Thus, with the Russian army's disintegration in the east and the stalemate frozen indefinitely in the west by early 1917, it was only a matter of months before mutinies among the French lines, demoralization in London, mass starvation and privation in Germany and bankruptcy all around would have led to a peace of exhaustion and a European-wide political revolt against the war-makers.

Wilson's intervention thus did turn an impossible stalemate into an unwarranted victory for the Entente. It was only a matter of time before Washington's unprecedented mobilization of men and material during the balance of 1917 flooded into the battlefields of France and turned the tide of war.

So Wilson's crusade did not remake the world, but it did radically re-channel the contours of 20th century history. That is, by giving rise to the Entente victory and the disaster of Versailles it unleashed the once in a thousand years aberration of Nazi and Stalinist totalitarianism that flowed therefrom.

CHAPTER 16

Imperial Washington — Global Menace

When the Berlin Wall fell in November 1989 and the death of the Soviet Union was confirmed two years later as Boris Yeltsin courageously stood down the red army tanks in front of Moscow's White House, a dark era in human history came to an end.

As we have seen, the world had descended into what was in effect an unbroken global war, incepting with the mobilization of the armies of old Europe in August 1914. The "77 Years War" is the appropriate name for it.

If you want to count bodies, **150 million** were killed by all the depredations which germinated in the Great War, its foolish aftermath at Versailles, and the march of history into the second world war and cold war which followed inexorably thereupon.

To wit, upwards of *8%* of the human race was wiped-out during that span. The toll encompassed the madness of trench warfare during 1914-1918; the murderous regimes of Soviet and Nazi totalitarianism that rose from the ashes of the Great War and Versailles; and then the carnage of WWII and all the lesser (unnecessary) wars and invasions of the Cold War including Korea and Vietnam.

So the seminal point cannot be gainsaid. The end of the cold war meant the chance for a new start toward world peace was finally at hand. Yet 27 years later there is still no peace because Imperial Washington confounds it.

In fact, the War Party entrenched in the nation's capital

is dedicated to economic interests and ideological perversions that guarantee perpetual war. They ensure endless waste on armaments and the inestimable death and human suffering that stems from 21st century high tech warfare; and the reciprocal mayhem and terrorist blowback it inherently generates among those upon whom the War Party inflicts its violent hegemony.

In short, there was a virulent threat to peace still lurking on the Potomac after the 77 Years War ended. The great general and president, Dwight Eisenhower, had called it the "military-industrial complex" in his farewell address. But that memorable phrase had been abbreviated by his speechwriters, who deleted the word "congressional" in a gesture of comity to the legislative branch.

So restore Ike's deleted reference to the legislative pork barrels and Sunday afternoon warriors of Capitol Hill and toss in the legions of beltway busybodies that constituted the civilian branches of the cold war armada (CIA, State, AID, NED etc.) and the circle would have been complete. It constituted the most awesome machine of warfare and imperial hegemony since the Roman legions bestrode most of the civilized world.

The Real Threat To Peace Circa 1991 — Pax Americana

In a word, the real threat to world peace circa 1991 was that *Pax Americana* would not go away quietly into the good night.

In fact, during the past 27 years Imperial Washington has lost all memory that peace was ever possible at the end of the cold war. Today it is as feckless, misguided and bloodthirsty as were Berlin, Paris, St. Petersburg, Vienna and London in August 1914.

Back then, a few months after the slaughter of the Great War had been unleashed, soldiers along the western front broke into spontaneous truces of Christmas celebration, singing and even exchange of gifts. For a brief moment they wondered why they were juxtaposed in lethal combat along the jaws of hell.

As we have seen, the truthful answer is that there was no good reason. The world had stumbled into war based on false narratives, petty short-term political and diplomatic maneuvers and the institutional imperatives of military mobilization plans, alliances and treaties — arrayed into what amounted to a doomsday machine. And so the Christmas trucers were ordered back into a killing mode on the pain of firing squads on both sides of the trenches.

Yet as pointless as the Great War was, it took more than three-quarters of a century for all the consequential impacts and derivative evils to be purged from the life of the planet.

Sadly, the peace that was lost last time (Christmas 1914) has not been regained this time — and for the same reasons. Indeed, since the casus belli of 1914 were criminally trivial in light of all that metastisized thereafter, it might do well to name the institutions and false narratives that block the return of peace today.

The fact is, these impediments are even more contemptible than the forces that crushed the Christmas truces one century ago.

There is no peace on earth today for reasons mainly rooted in Imperial Washington — not Moscow, Beijing, Pyongyang, Tehran, Damascus, Mosul or Raqqah. The former has become a global menace owing to what didn't happen in 1991.

What needed to happen was for Bush the Elder to declare "mission accomplished" and slash the Pentagon budget from $600 billion to $250 billion.

So doing he should have demobilized the military-industrial complex by putting a moratorium on all new weapons development, procurement and export sales; dissolved NATO and dismantled the far-flung network of US military bases; slashed the US standing armed forces from 1.5 million to a few hundred thousand; and organized and led a world disarmament and peace campaign, as did his Republican predecessors during the 1920s.

Unfortunately, George H. W. Bush was not a man of peace, vision or even mediocre intelligence. He was the malleable tool of the War Party, and it was he who single-handedly blew the peace when he plunged America into a petty arguement between the impetuous dictator of Iraq and the greedy Emir of Kuwait that was none of our business.

By contrast, even though liberal historians have reviled Warren G. Harding as some kind of dumbkopf politician, he well understood that the Great War had been for naught, and that to insure it never happened again the nations of the world needed to rid themselves of their huge navies and standing armies.

To that end, he achieved the largest global disarmament agreement ever made during the Washington Naval conference of 1921, which halted the construction of new battleships for more than a decade.

And while he was at it, President Harding also pardoned Eugene Debs. He thereby gave witness to the truth that the intrepid socialist candidate for president and vehement anti-war protestor, who Wilson had thrown in prison for exercising his first amendment right to speak against US entry into a pointless European war, had been right all along.

In short, Warren G. Harding knew the war was over, and the folly of Wilson's 1917 plunge into Europe's bloodbath should not be repeated at all hazards.

The Unforgiveable Sins
Of George H. W. Bush

Not George H. W. Bush. The man should never be forgiven for enabling the likes of Dick Cheney, Paul Wolfowitz, Robert Gates and their neocon pack of jackals to come to power — even if he did denounce them in his bumbling old age.

Even more to the point, by opting not for peace but for war

and oil in the Persian Gulf in 1991 he opened the gates to an unnecessary confrontation with Islam. In turn, that nurtured the rise of jihadist terrorism that would not haunt the world today — save for forces unleashed by George H. W. Bush's petulant quarrel with Saddam Hussein.

We will address more fully below the 45-year old error that holds the Persian Gulf is an American Lake and that energy security requires it be patrolled by the Fifth Fleet. As we previously indicated, the real answer to high oil prices everywhere and always is high oil prices and the wonders they work to rebalance the global energy market.

But first it is well to remember that there was no plausible threat anywhere on the planet to the safety and security of the citizens of Springfield MA, Lincoln NE or Spokane WA when the cold war ended.

The Warsaw Pact had dissolved into more than a dozen woebegone sovereign statelets; the Soviet Union was now unscrambled into 15 independent and far-flung republics from Belarus to Tajikistan; and the Russian motherland would soon plunge into an economic depression that would leave it with a GDP about the size of the Philadelphia SMSA.

Likewise, China's GDP was even smaller and more primitive than Russia's. Even as Mr. Deng was discovering the PBOC printing press that would enable it to become a great mercantilist exporter, an incipient Chinese threat to national security was never in the cards.

After all, it was 4,000 Wal-Marts in America upon which the prosperity of the new red capitalism inextricably depended and upon which the rule of the communist oligarchs in Beijing was ultimately anchored. They were not about to militarily attack their golden goose.

In 1990 there was no global Islamic threat or jihadi terrorist menace at all. What existed under those headings were sundry fragments and deposits of middle eastern religious, ethnic and tribal history that were of moment in their immediate region, but no threat to America whatsoever. The Shiite/Sunni divide had co-existed since 671 AD, but its episodic eruptions into battles and wars over the centuries had rarely extended beyond the region, and certainly had no reason to fester into open conflict in 1990.

Inside the artificial state of Iraq, which had been drawn on a map by historically ignorant European diplomats in 1916, for instance, the Shiite and Sunni got along tolerably well. That's because the nation was ruled by Saddam Hussein's Baathist brand of secular Arab nationalism.

The latter championed law and order, state driven economic development and politically apportioned distribution from the spoils of the extensive government controlled oil sector. To be sure, Baathist socialism didn't bring much prosperity to the well-endowed lands of Mesopotamia, but Hussein did have a Christian foreign minister and no sympathy for religious extremism or violent pursuit of sectarian causes.

As it happened, the bloody Shiite/Sunni strife that plagues Iraq — and the greater middle east — today and functions as a hatchery for angry young jihadi terrorists in their thousands was unleashed only after Saddam Hussein had been driven from Kuwait and the CIA had instigated an armed uprising in the Shiite heartland around Basra. That revolt was brutally suppressed by Hussein's republican guards, but it left an undertow of resentment and revenge boiling below the surface.

Needless to say, Bush the Younger and his cabal of neocon warmongers could not leave well enough alone. When they foolishly destroyed Saddam Hussein and his entire regime in the pursuit of nonexistent WMDs and ties with al-Qaeda, they literally opened the gates of hell, leaving Iraq as a lawless failed state where both recent and ancient religious and tribal animosities are given unlimited violent vent.

The Myth Of Iranian Aggression

Likewise, the Shiite theocracy ensconced in Tehran was an unfortunate albatross on the Persian people, but it was no threat to America's safety and security. The very idea that Tehran is an expansionist power bent on exporting terrorism to the rest of the world is a giant fiction and tissue of lies invented by the Washington War Party and its Bibi Netanyahu branch in order to win political support for their confrontationist policies.

Indeed, the three decade long demonization of Iran has served one over-arching purpose. Namely, it enabled both branches of the War Party to conjure up a fearsome enemy, thereby justifying aggressive policies that call for a constant state of war and military mobilization.

When the cold-war officially ended in 1991, in fact, the Cheney/neocon cabal feared the kind of drastic demobilization of the US military-industrial complex that was warranted by the suddenly more pacific strategic environment. In response, they developed an anti-Iranian doctrine that was explicitly described as a way of keeping defense spending at high cold war levels.

And the narrative they developed to this end is one of the more egregious Big Lies ever to come out of the beltway. It puts you in mind of the young boy who killed his parents, and then threw himself on the mercy of the courts on the grounds that he was an orphan!

To wit, during the 1980s the neocons in the Reagan Administration issued their own fatwa again the Islamic Republic of Iran based on its rhetorical hostility to America. Yet that enmity was grounded in Washington's 25-year support for the tyrannical and illegitimate regime of the Shah, and constituted a founding narrative of the Islamic Republic that was not much different than America's revolutionary castigation of King George.

That the Iranians had a case is beyond doubt. The open US archives now prove that the CIA overthrew Iran's democratically elected government in 1953 and put the utterly unsuited and

344

megalomaniacal Mohammad Reza Shah on the peacock throne to rule as a puppet in behalf of US security and oil interests.

During the subsequent decades the Shah not only massively and baldly plundered the wealth of the Persian nation. With the help of the CIA and US military, he also created a brutal secret police force known as the Savak, which made the East German Stasi look civilized by comparison.

All elements of Iranian society including universities, labor unions, businesses, civic organizations, peasant farmers and many more were subjected to intense surveillance by the Savak agents and paid informants. As one critic described it:

Over the years, Savak became a law unto itself, having legal authority to arrest, detain, brutally interrogate and torture suspected people indefinitely. Savak operated its own prisons in Tehran, such as Qezel-Qalaeh and Evin facilities and many suspected places throughout the country as well.

Ironically, among his many grandiose follies, the Shah embarked on a massive civilian nuclear power campaign in the 1970s, which envisioned literally paving the Iranian landscape with dozens of nuclear power plants.

He would use Iran's surging oil revenues after 1973 to buy all the equipment required from Western companies — and also fuel cycle support services such as uranium enrichment — in order to provide his kingdom with cheap power for centuries.

At the time of the Revolution, the first of these plants at Bushehr was nearly complete, but the whole grandiose project was put on hold amidst the turmoil of the new regime and the onset of Saddam Hussein's war against Iran in September 1980. As a consequence, a $2 billion deposit languished at the French nuclear agency that had originally obtained it from the Shah to fund a ramp-up of its enrichment capacity to supply his planned battery of reactors.

Indeed, in this very context the new Iranian regime proved

345

quite dramatically that it was not hell bent on obtaining nuclear bombs or any other weapons of mass destruction. In the midst of Iraq's unprovoked invasion of Iran in the early 1980s the Ayatollah Khomeini issued a fatwa against biological and chemical weapons.

Yet at that very time, Saddam was dropping these horrific weapons on Iranian battle forces — some of them barely armed teenage boys — with the spotting help of CIA tracking satellites and the concurrence of Washington. So from the very beginning, the Iranian posture was wholly contrary to the War Party's endless blizzard of false charges about its quest for nukes.

However benighted and medieval its religious views, the theocracy which rules Iran does not consist of demented war mongers. In the heat of battle they were willing to sacrifice their own forces rather than violate their religious scruples to counter Saddam's chemical weapons.

Then in 1983 the new Iranian regime decided to complete the Bushehr power plant and some additional elements of the Shah's grand plan. But when they attempted to reactivate the French enrichment services contract and buy necessary power plant equipment from the original German suppliers they were stopped cold by Washington. And when the tried to get their $2 billion deposit back, they were curtly denied that, too.

To make a long story short, the entire subsequent history of off again/on again efforts by the Iranians to purchase dual use equipment and components on the international market, often from black market sources like Pakistan, was in response to Washington's relentless efforts to block its legitimate rights as a signatory to the Nuclear Nonproliferation Treaty (NPT) to complete some parts of the Shah's civilian nuclear project.

Needless to say, it did not take much effort by the neocon "regime change" fanatics which inhabited the national security machinery, especially after the 2000 election, to spin every attempt by Iran to purchase even a lowly pump or pipe fitting as evidence of a secret campaign to get the bomb.

The exaggerations, lies, distortions and fear-mongering which came out of this neocon campaign are downright despicable. Yet they incepted way back in the early 1990s when George H. W. Bush actually did reach out to the newly elected government of Hashemi Rafsanjani to bury the hatchet after it had cooperated in obtaining the release of American prisoners being held in Lebanon in 1989.

Rafsanjani was self-evidently a pragmatist who did not want conflict with the United States and the West; and after the devastation of the eight year war with Iraq was wholly focused on economic reconstruction and even free market reforms of Iran's faltering economy.

It is one of the great tragedies of history that the neocons managed to squelch even George Bush's better instincts with respect to rapprochement with Tehran.

The Neocon Big Lie About Iranian Nukes And Terrorism

So the prisoner release opening was short-lived — especially after the top post at the CIA was assumed in 1991 by Robert Gates. As one of the very worst of the unreconstructed cold war apparatchiks, it can be well and truly said that Gates looked peace in the eye and then elected to pervert John Quincy Adams' wise maxim by searching the globe for monsters to fabricate.

In this case the motivation was especially loathsome. Gates had been Bill Casey's right hand man during the latter's rogue tenure at the CIA in the Reagan administration. Among the many untoward projects that Gates shepherded was the Iran-Contra affair that nearly destroyed his career when it blew-up, and for which he blamed the Iranians for its public disclosure.

From his post as deputy national security director in 1989 and then as CIA head Gates pulled out all the stops to get even. Almost single-handedly he killed-off the White House goodwill from the prisoner release, and launched the blatant myth that Iran was both sponsoring terrorism and seeking to obtain nuclear weapons.

Indeed, it was Gates who was the architect of the demonization of Iran that became a staple of War Party propaganda after 1991. In time that morphed into the utterly false claim that Iran is an aggressive wanna be hegemon that is a fount of terrorism and is dedicated to the destruction of the state of Israel, among other treacherous purposes.

That giant lie was almost single-handedly fashioned by the neocons and Bibi Netanyahu's coterie of power-hungry henchman after the mid-1990s. Indeed, the false claim that Iran posses an "existential threat" to Israel is a product of the pure red meat domestic Israeli politics that have kept Bibi in power for much of the last two decades.

But the truth is Iran has only a tiny fraction of Israel's conventional military capability. And compared to the latter's 100 odd nukes, Iran has never had a nuclear weaponization program after a small scale research program was ended in 2003.

That is not merely our opinion. It's been the sober assessment of the nation's top 17 intelligence agencies in the official National Intelligence Estimates ever since 2007. And now in conjunction with a further study undertaken pursuant to the 2015 nuke deal, the IAEA has also concluded the Iran had no secret program after 2003.

On the political and foreign policy front, Iran is no better or worse than any of the other major powers in the Middle East. In many ways it is far less of a threat to regional peace and stability than the military butchers who now run Egypt on $1.5 billion per year of US aid.

And it is surely no worse than the royal family tyrants who squander the massive oil resources of Saudi Arabia in pursuit of unspeakable opulence and decadence to the detriment of the 30 million citizens which are not part of the regime, and who one day may well reach the point of revolt.

When it comes to the support of terrorism, the Saudis have funded more jihadists and terrorists throughout the region than Iran ever even imagined.

Myth Of The Shiite Crescent

In this context, the War Party's bloviation about Iran's leadership of the so-called Shiite Crescent is another component of Imperial Washington's 27-year long roadblock to peace. Iran wasn't a threat to American security in 1991, and it has never since then organized a hostile coalition of terrorists that require Washington's intervention.

Start with Iran's long-standing support of Bashir Assad's government in Syria. That alliance that goes back to his father's era and is rooted in the historic confessional politics of the Islamic world.

The Assad regime is Alawite, a branch of the Shiite, and despite the regime's brutality, it has been a bulwark of protection for all of Syria's minority sects, including Christians, against a majority-Sunni ethnic cleansing. The latter would surely have occurred if the Saudi (and Washington) supported rebels, led by the Nusra Front and ISIS, had succeeded in taking power.

Likewise, the fact that the Bagdhad government of the broken state of Iraq — that is, the artificial 1916 concoction of two stripped pants European diplomats (Messrs. Sykes and Picot of the British and French foreign offices, respectively) — is now aligned with Iran is also a result of confessional politics and geo-economic propinquity.

For all practical purposes the old Iraq is no more. The Kurds of the northeast have declared their independence and seized their own oil. At the same time, the Sunni lands of the Upper Euphrates, which were temporarily lost to the short-lived ISIS caliphate, are now a no man's land of rubble and broken communities.

That is, after first being brutally conquered by ISIS with American weapons dropped in place by the hapless $25 billion Iraqi army minted by Washington's departing proconsuls, they have been physically and economically destroyed yet again — this time while being "liberated" by a new round of American bombs and high tech warfare.

Accordingly, what is left of the rump of the Iraqi state is a population that is overwhelmingly Shiite, and which nurses bitter resentments after two decades of violent conflict with the Sunni forces. Why in the world, therefore, would they not ally with their Shiite neighbor?

Likewise, the claim that Iran is now trying to annex Yemen is pure claptrap. The ancient territory of Yemen has been racked by civil war off and on since the early 1970s. And a major driving force of that conflict has been confessional differences between the Sunni south and the Shiite north.

In more recent times, Washington's blatant drone war inside Yemen against alleged terrorists and its domination and financing of Yemen's governments eventually produced the same old outcome. That is, another failed state and an illegitimate government which fled at the 11th hour, leaving another vast cache of American arms and equipment behind.

Accordingly, the Houthis forces now in control of substantial parts of the country are not some kind of advanced guard sent in during the dead of night by Tehran. They are indigenous partisans who share loosely defined confessional tie with Iran, but which have actually been armed (inadvertently) by the US.

Moreover, the real invaders in this destructive civil war are the Saudis. Their vicious bombing campaign against civilian populations — which have killed more than 10,000 and left millions to face starvation and cholera — are outright war crimes if the word has any meaning at all.

Finally, there is the fourth element of the purported Iranian axis — the Hezbollah controlled Shiite communities of southern Lebanon and the Bekaa Valley. Like everything else in the Middle East, Hezbollah is a product of historical European imperialism, Islamic confessional politics and the chronically misguided and counterproductive security policies of Israel.

In the first place, Lebanon was not any more a real country than Iraq was when Sykes and Picot laid their straight-edged rulers on a map. The result was a stew of religious and ethnic divisions — Maronite Catholics, Greek Orthodox, Copts, Druse, Sunnis, Shiites, Alawites, Kurds, Armenians, Jews and countless more — that made the fashioning of a viable state virtually impossible.

At length, an alliance of Christians and Sunnis gained control of the country, leaving the 30% Shiite population disenfranchised and economically disadvantaged. But it was the inflow of Palestinian refugees in the 1960s and 1970s that eventually upset the balance of sectarian forces and triggered a civil war that essentially lasted from 1975 until 1990.

It also triggered a catastrophically wrong-headed Israeli invasion of southern Lebanon in 1982, and a subsequent brutal occupation of mostly Shiite territories for the next eighteen years. The alleged purpose of this invasion was to chase the PLO and Yassir Arafat out of the enclave in southern Lebanon that they had established after being driven out of Jordan in 1970.

Eventually Israel succeeded in sending Arafat packing to north Africa, but in the process created a militant, Shiite-based resistance movement that did not even exist in 1982, and which in due course became the strongest single force in Lebanon's fractured domestic political arrangements.

After Israel withdrew from Lebanon in 2000, the then Christian President of the county made abundantly clear that Hezbollah had become a legitimate and respected force within the Lebanese polity, not merely some subversive agent of

Tehran:

"For us Lebanese, and I can tell you the majority of Lebanese, Hezbollah is a national resistance movement. If it wasn't for them, we couldn't have liberated our land. And because of that, we have big esteem for the Hezbollah movement. "

So, yes, Hezbollah is an integral component of the so-called Shiite Crescent and its confessional and political alignment with Tehran is entirely plausible. But that arrangement — however uncomfortable for Israel — does not represent unprovoked Iranian aggression on Israel's northern border.

Instead, it's actually the blowback from the stubborn refusal of Israeli governments — especially the rightwing Likud governments of modern times — to deal constructively with the Palestinian question.

In lieu of a two-state solution in the territory of Palestine, therefore, Israeli policy has produced a chronic state of war with the large majority of the population of southern Lebanon represented by Hezbollah.

The latter is surely no agency of peaceful governance and has committed its share of atrocities. But the point at hand is that given the last 35 years of history and Israeli policy, Hezbollah would exist as a menacing force on its northern border even if the theocracy didn't exist and the Shah or his heir was still on the Peacock Throne.

In short, there is no alliance of terrorism in the Shiite Crescent that threatens American security. That proposition is simply one of the Big Lies that was promulgated by the War Party after 1991; and which has been happily embraced by Imperial Washington since then in order to keep the military/ industrial/security complex alive, and to justify its self-appointed role as policeman of the world.

Washington's Erroneous View That The Persian Gulf Should Be An American Lake — The Root Of Sunni Jihaddism

Likewise, the terrorist threat that has arisen from the Sunni side of the Islamic divide is largely of Washington's own making; and it is being nurtured by endless US meddling in the region's politics and by the bombing and droning campaigns against Washington's self-created enemies.

At the root of Sunni based terrorism is the long-standing Washington error that America's security and economic well-being depends upon keeping an armada in the Persian Gulf in order to protect the surrounding oilfields and the flow of tankers through the straits of Hormuz.

That doctrine has been wrong from the day it was officially enunciated by one of America's great economic ignoramuses, Henry Kissinger, at the time of the original oil crisis in 1973. The 45 years since then have proven in spades that its doesn't matter who controls the oilfields, and that the only effective cure for high oil prices is the free market.

Every tin pot dictatorship — from Libya's Muammar Gaddafi to Hugo Chavez in Venezuela to Saddam Hussein, to the bloody-minded chieftains of Nigeria, to the purportedly medieval Mullahs and fanatical Revolutionary Guards of Iran — has produced oil. And usually all the oil they could because almost always they desperately needed the revenue.

For crying out loud, even the barbaric thugs of ISIS milked every possible drop of petroleum from the tiny, wheezing oilfields scattered around their backwater domain before they were finally driven out. So there is no economic case whatsoever for Imperial Washington's massive military presence in the middle east, and most especially for its long-time alliance with the benighted regime of Saudi Arabia.

The truth is, there is no such thing as an OPEC cartel — virtually every member produces all they can and cheats whenever possible. The only thing that resembles production control in the global oil market is the fact that the Saudi princes treat their oil reserves not much differently than Exxon.

That is, they attempt to maximize the present value of their 270 billion barrels of reserves. Yet ultimately they are no more clairvoyant at calibrating the best oil price to accomplish that objective at any given time than are the economists employed by Exxon, the DOE or the International Energy Agency.

For instance, during the run-up to the late 2014 collapse of the world oil price, the Saudis over-estimated the staying power of China's temporarily surging call on global supply.

At the same time, they badly under-estimated how rapidly and extensively the $100 per barrel marker reached in early 2008 would trigger a flow of investment, technology and cheap debt into alternative sources of supply. That is, the US shale patch, the Canadian tar sands, the tired petroleum provinces of Russia, the deep offshore of Brazil, etc. — to say nothing of solar, wind and all the other government subsidized alternative source of BTUs.

Way back when Jimmy Carter was telling us to turn down the thermostats and put on our cardigan sweaters, those of us on the free market side of the so-called energy shortage debate said high oil prices are their own best cure. Now we know for sure.

To wit, the Fifth Fleet and its overt and covert auxiliaries should never have been in the Persian Gulf and it environs. And we mean from the very beginning — going all the way back to the CIA's coup against Iranian democracy in 1953 that was aimed at protecting the oilfields from nationalization.

But having turned Iran into an enemy, Imperial Washington was just getting started when 1990 rolled around. Once again in the name of "oil security" it plunged the American war machine into the politics and religious fissures of the Persian Gulf; and did so on account of a local small beans conflict between Iraq and Kuwait that had no bearing whatsoever on the safety and security of American citizens.

As US ambassador Glaspie rightly told Saddam Hussein on the eve of his Kuwait invasion, America had no dog in that hunt. After all, Kuwait wasn't even a proper country: It was merely a bank account sitting on a swath of oilfields surrounding an ancient trading city that had been abandoned by Ibn Saud in the early 20th century.

That's because the illiterate Bedouin founder of the House of Saud didn't know what oil was or that it was there; and, in any event, Kuwait had been made a separate protectorate by the British in 1913 for reasons that are lost in the fog of British diplomatic history.

The Folly Of The Bush Clan's Persian Gulf Wars

As it happened, Iraq's contentious dispute with Kuwait was over its claim that the Emir of Kuwait was "slant drilling" across his own border and into Iraq's Rumaila field. Yet it was a wholly elastic boundary of no significance whatsoever.

In fact, the dispute over the Rumaila field started in 1960 when an Arab League declaration arbitrarily marked the Iraq–Kuwait border two miles north of the southernmost tip of the Rumaila field.

And that newly defined boundary, in turn, had come only 44 years after the English and French diplomats had carved up their winnings from the Ottoman Empire's. As we described above, they had done so by laying a straight edged ruler on the map. So doing, they had confected the artificial country of Iraq from the historically independent and hostile Mesopotamian provinces of the Shiite in the south, the Sunni in the west and the Kurds in the north.

In short, both of the combatants in the 1990 Iraq/Kuwait

war were recently minted artifacts of late-stage European imperialism. That Bush the Elder choose to throw American treasure and blood into the breach is, accordingly, one of the stupidest crimes every committed from the Oval Office.

The truth is, it didn't matter who controlled the southern tip of the Rumaila field — the brutal dictator of Baghdad or the opulent Emir of Kuwait. Not the price of oil, nor the peace of America nor the security of Europe nor the peace of the world depended upon it.

But once again Bush the Elder got persuaded to take the path of war. This time it was by Henry Kissinger's economically illiterate protégés at the national security council and his Texas oilman Secretary of State. They falsely claimed that the will-o-wisp of "oil security" was at stake, and that 500,000 American troops needed to be planted in the sands of Arabia.

That was a catastrophic error, and not only because the presence of crusader boots on the purportedly sacred soil of Arabia offended the CIA-trained Mujahedeen of Afghanistan, who had become unemployed when the Soviet Union collapsed.

The 1991 CNN-glorified war games conducted in the Gulf by Bush the Elder also further empowered another group of unemployed crusaders. Namely, the neocon national security fanatics who had mislead Ronald Reagan into a massive military build-up to thwart what they had claimed to be an ascendant Soviet Union bent on nuclear war winning capabilities and global conquest.

All things being equal, the sight of Boris Yeltsin, Vodka flask in hand, facing down the Red Army a few months later should have sent these neocon charlatans into the permanent repudiation and obscurity they so richly deserved. But Dick Cheney and Paul Wolfowitz managed to extract from Washington's pyric victory in Kuwait a whole new lease on life for Imperial Washington.

Right then and there came the second erroneous predicate. To wit, that "regime change" among the assorted tyrannies of the middle east was in America's national interest. More fatally, the neocons now insisted that the Gulf War proved it could be achieved through a sweeping interventionist menu of coalition diplomacy, security assistance, arms shipments, covert action and open military attack and occupation.

What the neocon doctrine of regime change actually did, of course, was to foster the Frankenstein that ultimately became ISIS. In fact, the only real terrorists in the world which threaten normal civilian life in the West are the rogue offspring of Imperial Washington's post-1990 machinations in the middle east.

Sunni Jihaddism — Washington's Frankenstein

The CIA trained and armed Mujahedeen of Afghanistan mutated into al-Qaeda not because Bin Laden suddenly had a religious epiphany that his Washington benefactors were actually the Great Satan owing to America's freedom and liberty.

His murderous crusade was inspired by the Wahhabi fundamentalism loose in Saudi Arabia. This benighted religious fanaticism became agitated to a fever pitch by Imperial Washington's violent plunge into Persian Gulf political and religious quarrels, the stationing of troops in Saudi Arabia, and the decade long barrage of sanctions, embargoes, no-fly zones, covert actions and open hostility against the nominally Sunni regime in Bagdad after 1991.

Yes, Bin Laden would have amputated Saddam's secularist head if Washington hadn't done it first, but that's just the point. The two were bitter enemies, not natural allies — so the attempt at regime change in March 2003 was one of the most foolish acts of state in American history.

Bush the Younger's neocon advisers had no clue about the sectarian animosities and historical grievances that Hussein had bottled-up by parsing the oil loot and wielding the sword under the banner of Baathist nationalism. But Shock and Awe blew the lid and the de-baathification campaign unleashed the furies.

Indeed, no sooner had George W. Bush pranced around on the deck of the Abraham Lincoln declaring "mission accomplished" than Abu Musab al-Zarqawi, a CIA recruit to the Afghan war a decade earlier and small-time specialist in hostage-taking and poisons, fled his no count redoubt in Kurdistan to emerge as a flamboyant agitator in the now dispossessed Sunni heartland.

The founder of ISIS succeeded in Fallujah and Anbar province just like the long list of other terrorist leaders Washington claims to have exterminated. That is, Zarqawi gained his following and notoriety among the region's population of deprived, brutalized and humiliated young men by dint of being more brutal than their occupiers.

Indeed, even as Washington was crowing about its eventual liquidation of Zarqawi, the remnants of the Baathist regime and the hundreds of thousands of demobilized Republican Guards were coalescing into al-Qaeda in Iraq. Their future leaders were actually being incubated in a monstrous nearby detention center called Camp Bucca that contained more than 26,000 prisoners.

As one former US Army officer, Mitchell Gray, later described it,"

You never see hatred like you saw on the faces of these detainees," Gray remembers of his 2008 tour. "When I say they hated us, I mean they looked like they would have killed us in a heartbeat if given the chance. I turned to the warrant officer I was with and I said, 'If they could, they would rip our heads off and drink our blood.'"

What Gray didn't know — but might have expected — was that he was not merely looking at the United States' former enemies, but its future ones as well. According to intelligence experts and Department of Defense records, the vast majority of the leadership of what later became known as ISIS, including its leader, Abu Bakr al-Baghdadi, did time at Camp Bucca.

And not only did the US feed, clothe and house these jihadists, it also played a vital, if unwitting, role in facilitating their transformation into the most formidable terrorist force in modern history.

The point is, regime change and nation building can never be accomplished by the lethal violence of 21st century armed forces; and they were an especially preposterous assignment in the context of a land rent with 13 century-old religious fissures and animosities.

In fact, the wobbly, synthetic state of Iraq was doomed the minute Cheney and his bloody gang decided to liberate it from the brutal, but serviceable and secular tyranny of Saddam's Baathist regime. That's because the process of elections and majority rule necessarily imposed by Washington was guaranteed to elect a government beholden to the Shiite majority.

After decades of mistreatment and Saddam's brutal suppression of their 1991 uprising, did the latter have revenge on their minds and in their communal DNA? Did the Kurds have dreams of an independent Kurdistan that had been denied their 30 million strong tribe — going way back to Versailles and ever since?

Why, yes, they did. So the $25 billion spent on training and equipping the putative armed forces of post-liberation Iraq was bound to end up in the hands of sectarian militias, not a cohesive national army.

In fact, when the Shiite commanders fled Sunni-dominated Mosul in June 2014 they transformed the ISIS uprising against the government in Baghdad into a vicious fledgling state in one fell swoop. It wasn't by beheadings and fiery jihadist sermons that it quickly enslaved dozens of towns and several million people in western Iraq and the eastern Euphrates Valley of Syria.

The new Islamic State's instruments of terror and occupation were the best weapons that the American taxpayers could buy. That included 2,300 Humvees and tens of thousands of automatic weapons, as well as vast stores of ammunition, trucks, rockets, artillery pieces and even tanks and helicopters.

The Syrian Regime Change Fiasco

And that wasn't the half of it. The newly proclaimed Islamic State also filled the power vacuum in Syria created by its so-called "civil war." But in truth that bloody carnage was the offspring of still another exercise in Washington inspired and financed regime change — this one undertaken in connivance with Qatar and Saudi Arabia.

The latter were surely not interested in expelling the tyranny next door; they are the living embodiment of it.

Instead, the rebellion was about removing Bashir Assad's, Iran's Alawite/Shiite ally, from power in Damascus and laying gas pipelines across the upper Euphrates Valley to take Qatar's abundant natural gas to Europe.

In any event, ISIS soon had troves of additional American weapons. Some of them were supplied to Sunni radicals by way of Qatar and Saudi Arabia. More came up the so-called "ratline" from Gaddafi's former arsenals in Benghazi through Turkey.

And still more came through Jordan from the "moderate" opposition trained there by the CIA, which more often than not sold them or defected to the other side.

That the Islamic State was Washington's Frankenstein monster became evident from the moment it rushed upon the scene in the summer of 2014. But even then the Washington War Party could not resist adding fuel to the fire, whooping up another round of Islamophobia among the American public and forcing the Obama White House into a futile bombing campaign for the third time in a quarter century.

The rationale for the bombing campaign, of course, was that

it would quickly pound the fledgling Islamic State into a heap of sand and gravel. But as shown by the dark-shaded areas of the map below, that's all it ever was anyway!

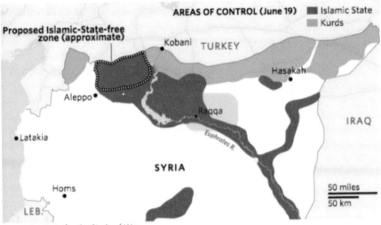

Source: Institute for the Study of War

The dusty, broken, impoverished towns and villages along the margins of the Euphrates River and in the bombed out precincts of Anbar province did not attract thousands of wannabe jihadists from the failed states of the middle east and the alienated Muslim townships of Europe because the caliphate offered prosperity, salvation or any particular future at all.

What recruited them was a meager paycheck and a mountain of outrage at the bombs and drones being dropped on Sunni communities by the US air force; and by the cruise missiles launched from the bowels of the Mediterranean, which ripped apart homes, shops, offices and mosques containing as many innocent civilians as ISIS terrorists.

The map above shows the Islamic State at its maximum extent several year ago (dark shaded areas), and reminds that even absent the tender mercies of the US Air Force, it was always destined for a short half-life.

It was contained by the Kurds in the north and east (green)

and by Turkey with NATO's second largest army and air force in the northwest. And it was surrounded by the Shiite crescent in the populated, economically viable regions of lower Syria and Iraq.

So absent Washington's misbegotten campaign to unseat Assad in Damascus and demonize his confession-based Iranian ally, there would have been nowhere for the murderous fanatics who pitched a makeshift capital in Raqqa to go.

As subsequent history has proven, ISIS was destined to run out of money, recruits, momentum and public acquiesce to their horrific rule in due course.

But with the US Air Force functioning as their recruiting arm and France's anti-Assad foreign policy helping to foment a final spasm of anarchy in Syria, the gates of hell were temporarily opened wide.

What had been puked out, however, was not an organized war on Western civilization as so hysterically proclaimed by neocon propagandists; it was just blowback carried out by that infinitesimally small salient of mentally deformed young men who can be persuaded to strap on a suicide belt.

Needless to say, bombing didn't stop them; it just made more of them.

Ironically, what in the end did stop them was the Assad government and the allies it had every right to enlist as a sovereign nation. That is, the air support of Russia and the ground forces of Hezbollah and Iran's Islamic Revolutionary Guard Corps.

But Imperial Washington was so caught up in its myths, lies and hegemonic stupidity that it could not see the obvious.

And that is why a quarter century after the cold war ended peace still hasn't been given a chance; and it's also the reason that even the American homeland is needlessly subjected to so-called terrorist "inspired" attacks from time to time like those a few years back in San Bernardino and Orlando.

The truth is, these terrible attacks emerge episodically

because the terror that Washington's bombs, drones and missiles visits upon Muslim lands is what actually inspires them.

After all, whatever the Koran has to say about purging the infidel, it inspired no attacks on US soil for all the decades of America's existence up until 1990.

That is, until Imperial Washington went into the regime change and military intervention business in the middle east. It was, in fact, the War Party which brought the threat of terrorism to the American homeland.

CHAPTER 17

You Can See "Russia" From Here

We are here speaking of our view from the 19th floor of our apartment above the East River in New York City, and it's the honest truth. We can see more GDP from our balcony than the IMF can tabulate for the whole of Russia.

The fearsome bogeyman at the center of Imperial Washington's war palpitations, therefore, is a complete chimera.

Russia is actually an economic and industrial midget transformed beyond recognition by relentless Warfare State propaganda. It is actually no more threatening to America's homeland security than the Siberian land mass that Sarah Palin once espied from her front porch in Alaska.

GDP Of Russia In USD

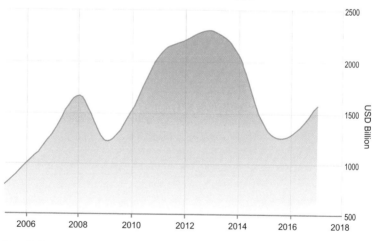

Source: Tradingeconomics.com | World Bank

After all, how could it be? The the GDP of the New York City metro area is about $1.7 trillion, which is well more than Russia's 2017 GDP of $1.5 trillion. And that, in turn, is just 7% of America's $20 trillion GDP.

Russia's Shrinking Work Force

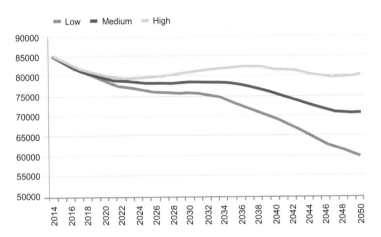

Moreover, Russia' dwarf economy is composed largely of a vast oil and gas patch; a multitude of nickel, copper, bauxite and vanadium mines; and some very large swatches of wheat fields. That's not exactly the kind of high tech industrial platform on which a war machine capable of threatening the good folks in Lincoln NE or Worcester MA is likely to be erected.

And especially not when the Russian economy has been heading sharply south in dollar purchasing terms for several years running.

Indeed, in terms of manufacturing output, the comparison is just as stark. Russia's annual manufacturing value added is currently about *$200 billion* compared to *$2.2 trillion* for the US economy.

And that's not the half of it. Not only are Russia's vast hydrocarbon deposits and mines likely to give out in the years ahead, but so are the livers of its Vodka-chugging work force.

That's a problem because according to a recent Brookings study, Russia's working age population — even supplemented by substantial in-migration and guest worker programs — is heading south as far into the future as the eye can see.

Even in the Brookings medium case projection shown below, Russia's working age population will be nearly 20% smaller than today by 2050. Yet today's figure of about 85 million is already just a fraction of the US working age population of 255 million.

Russia's Punk Defense Budget Equals 32 Days Of Pentagon Spending

Not surprisingly, Russia's pint-sized economy can not support a military establishment anywhere near to that of Imperial Washington. To wit, its $61 billion of military outlays in 2017 amounted to less than *35 days* of Washington's current $720 billion of expenditures for defense.

Indeed, it might well be asked how Russia could remotely threaten homeland security in America short of what would be a suicidal nuclear first strike. Recall the remnant of the Soviet strategic weapons arsenal at Putin's disposal today amounts to 4,500 operational nuclear warheads, of which under two-fifths are actually deployed. That compares to 4,600 nuclear weapons in the US arsenal with a similar fraction actually deployed.

Accordingly, what exists on the nuclear front is a state of mutual deterrence (MAD) — the arrangement by which we we got through 45-years of cold war when the Kremlin was run by a totalitarian oligarchy committed to a hostile ideology; and during which time it had been armed to the teeth via a forced-draft allocation of upwards of 40% of the GDP of the Soviet empire to the military.

By comparison, the Russian defense budget currently amounts to less than 4% of the country's anemic present day economy — one shorn of the vast territories and populations of Belarus, Ukraine, Georgia, Uzbekistan, Kazakhstan and all the Asian "stans" among others. Yet given those realities we are supposed to believe that the self-evidently calculating and cautious kleptomaniac who runs the Kremlin is going to go mad, defy MAD and trigger a nuclear Armageddon?

Indeed, the idea that Russia presents a national security threat to America is laughable. Not only would Putin never risk nuclear suicide, but even that fantasy is the extent of what he's got. That is, Russia's conventional capacity to project force to

the North American continent is nonexistent — or at best, lies somewhere between nichts and nothing.

For example, in today's world you do not invade any foreign continent without massive sea power projection capacity in the form of aircraft carrier strike groups. These units consist of an armada of lethal escort ships, a fleet of aircraft, massive suites of electronics warfare capability and the ability to launch hundreds of cruise missiles and other smart weapons.

Each US aircraft carrier based strike group, in fact, is composed of roughly 7,500 personnel, at least one cruiser, a squadron of destroyers and/or frigates, and a carrier air wing of 65 to 70 aircraft. A carrier strike group also sometimes includes submarines and attached logistics ships.

The US has *eleven* such carrier strike groups. Russia has *zero* modern carrier strike groups and one beat-up, smoky old (diesel) aircraft carrier that the Israeli paper, Haaretz, described as follows when it recently entered the Mediterranean:

Russia's only aircraft carrier, a leftover from the days of Soviet power, carries a long history of mishaps, at sea and in port, and diesel engines which were built for Russia's cold waters – as shown by the column of black smoke raising above it. It needs frequent refueling and resupplies and has never been operationally tested.

For want of doubt, just compare the image of the Admiral Kuznetsov belching smoke in the Mediterranean with that of the Gerald R. Ford CVN 48 below it.

The latter is the US Navy's new $13 billion aircraft carrier and is the most technologically advanced warship ever built.

The contrast serves as a proxy for the vastly inferior capability of the limited number of ships and planes in Russia's conventional force. Where it does have numerical superiority in is tanks — but alas they are not amphibious nor ocean-capable!

Likewise, nobody invades anybody without massive airpower and the ability to project it across thousands of miles of oceans via vast logistics and air-refueling capabilities.

On that score, the US has 6,100 helicopters to Russia's 1,200 and 6,000 fixed wing fighter and attack aircraft versus Russia's 2,100. More important, the US has 5,700 transport and airlift aircraft compared to just 1,100 for Russia.

In short, the idea that Russia is a military threat to the US homeland is ludicrous. Russia is essentially a land-locked military shadow of the former Soviet war machine. Indeed, for the world's only globe-spanning imperial power to remonstrate about an aggressive threat from Moscow is a prime facie case of the cat calling the kettle black.

Moreover, the canard that Washington's massive conventional armada is needed to defend Europe is risible nonsense. Europe can and should take care of its own security and relationship with its neighbor on the Eurasian continent.

After all, the GDP of NATO Europe is $17 trillion or 12X greater than that of Russia, and the current military budgets of European NATO members total about $280 billion or 4X more than that of Russia.

More important, the European nations and people really do not have any quarrel with Putin's Russia, nor is their security and safety threatened by the latter. All of the tensions that do exist and have come to a head since the illegal coup in Kiev in February 2014 were fomented by Imperial Washington and its European subalterns in the NATO machinery.

In fact, the current fight with Russia and Washington's mickey-mouse "sanctions" against some of Putin's ministers and business associates are about nothing more than the endless search of an obsolete institution — NATO — for a mission and justification for its fiscally burdensome costs.

Washington Promised Not An Inch And Took A MileAs we previously indicated,

George H. W. Bush and his Secretary of State, James Baker, were correct back in 1989 when they promised Gorbachev that NATO's then 15 members would not expand "by a single inch" of territory eastward in return for his acquiesce to the reunification of Germany and the effective end of the Warsaw Pact.

But rather than declaring cold war victory and dismantling its NATO machinery once the 50,000 Soviet tanks on the central front were effectively melted down for scrap, virtually the opposite happened. NATO has been expanded to 29 countries including such powers as Slovenia, Slovakia, Bulgaria, Romania and now the statelet of Montenegro that has a military half the size of the police force of Philadelphia.

In the context of this relentless and pointless NATO expansion to the very borders of the shrunken Russian state, Washington not only sponsored and funded the overthrow of Ukraine's constitutionally elected government in February 2014. But once it had unleashed a devastating civil war, it relentlessly blocked the obvious alternative to the bloodshed that has claimed 10,000 civilian and military casualties.

To wit, Ukraine could have been partitioned with autonomy for the Russian-speaking Donbas provinces — or even accession to the Russian state from which these communities had essentially originated.

After all, the artificial country of Czechoslovakia, created on a political whim at Versailles, was peacefully and inconsequentially devolved into its separate Czech and Slovakian nations a few years ago. The same is true of Yugoslavia — a polyglot federation that has now devolved into six nations.

In that instance, the partition was partially owing to American bombers that forcibly separated Kosovo from its Serbian parent. And even then, this Washington-sanctioned partition ended up in the hands of a criminal mafia in Kosovo that makes Putin appear sainted by comparison.

The plain fact is, Russia is not an expansionist nation and the troubles on its borders result from the provocations of

NATO and Washington.

Likewise, why all the hysteria about Russian hacking and interference in the US political process — if the alleged source is a pint-sized economy that harbors no military threat to American or European security?

The short answer, of course, is that is rooted in pure partisan politics and something even more dangerous. Namely, the shock and fear of the ruling elites that their long-running reign is in danger of being ended by Donald J. Trump.

The fact is, hacking is a universal feature of the internet age and the US government is by far the world's most intrusive and unhinged state operator in the business of stealing or corrupting data and networks that belong to foreign governments, corporations and private citizens.

As indicated above, the operation called TAO (Tailored Access Operations), which is lodged deep in the bowels of NSA and is an integral component of Washington $75 billion per year surveillance and spying operation, has thousands of civilians and military personal at work 24/7 hacking foreign governments, political parties, elections and much more.

The TAO is now known to the world public thanks to Edward Snowden's disclosures including a mission statement that makes a complete mockery of all the establishment harrumphing about alleged Russian hacker groups coded with such comical names as "Fancy Bear" and "Cozy Bear".

The latter are actually just a self-promoting invention of the cyber-security start-up venture firm and DNC contractor called CrowdStrike mentioned above. By contrast, here's what the real hackers, intelligence analysts, targeting specialists and engineers of all types do at Ft. Meade and four other NSA installations under TAO's succinct motto :

"Your data is our data, your equipment is our equipment - anytime, any place, by any legal (?) means. "

Washington's Kiev Coup — When Meddling Is Just Brokering

In fact, when it comes to meddling, Moscow cannot hold even a tiny candle compared to Washington.

It should never be forgotten that the coup which overthrew the constitutionally elected government in Kiev was a $5 billion all-hands Washington undertaking. It was organized and financed by the US State department along with the National Endowment for Democracy, the CIA and a raft of so-called NGOs (non-government organizations) indirectly funded by Washington and NATO.

Moreover, this was an altogether different kind of "meddling" and "interference" compared to the thousands of Podesta emails — mostly about campaign trivia — that were leaked during the 2016 US election.

Ukraine had already held own its election by the time of the Maidan putsch in February 2014 and four years earlier had installed the winner, Viktor Yanukovych, as President. But Washington didn't merely leak the man's emails to make him look bad to voters — it cancelled the election long after the fact and sent him fleeing for his life.

As it happened, Washington nullified Ukraine's 2010 election — even though Yanukovych got 49% of the vote compared to 45% for the runner-up — on the grounds that its duly elected President had disobeyed certain apparatchiks in the State Department and NATO. That is, he rejected an aid and affiliation deal with the EU/NATO in late 2013 for a better deal with Ukraine's historic hegemon in Moscow.

Needless to say, nullification of a country's election — backed by the stick of NATO's military might and the carrot of billions from a Washington/EU/IMF consortium — is big league meddling. It makes the ballyhooed hacking of the emails of Washington fixer and Clinton campaign chairman, John Podesta, look like a schoolyard prank by comparison.

As former president Obama told CNN at the time, Washington was just going about its "indispensable nation" business. It had helpfully encouraged another "flowering of democracy" and to that end had,

". . . . . . brokered a deal to transition power in Ukraine. "

That's right. Washington wasn't interfering in the governance of an independent nation; it was just "brokering" a few more pieces on Imperial Washington's global chessboard.

Never mind that Washington's massive political and financial support for the Maidan uprising on the streets of Kiev, and then nearly instantaneous recognition of the resulting putsch as the official government of the Ukraine was a frontal assault on the nation's sovereignty.

What added insult to injury was that Victoria Nuland, the US assistant Secretary for Europe, didn't merely tell some undercover operatives to buy ads on Ukrainian social media. She actually picked Yanokovych's successor and cabinet. And we know this from a hacked phone call between Nuland and the US ambassador in Kiev.

In discussing who should lead the Washington-installed government, Nuland made clear who the next prime minister would be and who he should be talking to for advice.

Nuland: I think Yats (Arseniy Yatseniuk) is the guy who's got the economic experience, the governing experience. . . . what he needs is Klitsch and Tyahnybok on the outside. He needs to be talking to them four times a week, you know.

As it turned our, the putsch leaders followed Nuland's advice to the letter, installing "Yats" as the new prime minister. But it also filled four cabinet posts out of eleven with rabid anti-Russian crypto-Nazis.

Indeed, at the heart of the putsch were Ukrainian organizations called *Svoboda* (national socialist party of Ukraine) and Right Sector. Their national hero was one Stepan Bandera — a collaborator with Hitler who led the liquidation of thousands of Poles, Jews and other minorities as the Nazi Wehrmacht made it way through Ukraine toward Stalingrad in 1942-1943.

As shown below, there could be little doubt where one of the founders of Svoboda and a principal leader of the Maidan coup, Oleh **Tyahnybok**, was coming from. The leaked transcript cited above also shows that Viceroy Nuland had no problem telling the new prime minister that he needed to talk to this self-avowed Nazi "four times a week."

In fact, another founder and leader of Svoboda, Andriy Parubiy, was given a portfolio which included the Ministry of Defense, the Armed Forces, Law Enforcement, National Security and Intelligence. That the Kremlin was alarmed by these developments and that the Russian-speaking populations of Crimea and the Donbas feared an ethnic cleansing led by the new Ukrainian nationalist government in Kiev — given the bloody history described above — is hardly surprising.

In any event, that's what real foreign "meddling" looks like, and it is exactly what Imperial Washington does over and over again.

Indeed, the real truth of the matter is that Imperial Washington is now reaping the whirlwind it sowed over decades by massive interference in the internal politics and governance process of countries all over the world — of which the vignette above about the Ukrainian coup is only the latest example.

Contrary to the bombast, jingoism, and shrill moralizing

flowing from Washington and the mainstream media, America had absolutely no national security interest in the spat between Putin and the coup that unconstitutionally took over Kiev in February 2014.

As we detailed earlier, for several centuries the Crimea has been Russian; for even longer, the Ukraine has been a cauldron of ethnic and tribal conflict, rarely an organized, independent state, and always a meandering set of borders looking for a redrawn map.

Like everything reviewed above, the source of the current calamity-howling about Russia is the Warfare State. That is, the existence of vast machinery of military, diplomatic and economic maneuver that is ever on the prowl for missions and mandates and that can mobilize a massive propaganda campaign on the slightest excitement.

The post-1991 absurdity of bolstering NATO and extending it into eastern Europe, rather than liquidating it after attaining "mission accomplished", is just another manifestation of its baleful impact.

In truth, the expansion of NATO is the underlying causes of America's needless tension with Russia and Putin's paranoia about his borders and neighbors.

Indeed, it needs be asked: Precisely what juvenile minds bivouacked in the Warfare State beehive actually determined that America needs a military alliance with Slovenia, Slovakia, Bulgaria, Romania, Montenegro and now possibly the mini-state of Macedonia!

So the resounding clatter for action against Russia emanating from Washington and its house-trained media is not even a semi-rational response to the facts at hand; its just another destructive spasm of the nation's Warfare State and its beltway machinery of diplomatic meddling, economic warfare and military intervention.

CHAPTER 18

How To Drain The Swamp —
Homeland Defense, Not Empire

When the Cold War officially ended in 1991 Washington could have pivoted back to the pre-1914 status quo ante. That is, to a national security policy of America First because there was literally no significant military threat left on the planet.

Post-Soviet Russia was an economic basket case that couldn't even meet its military payroll and was melting down and selling the Red Army's tanks and artillery for scrap. China was just emerging from the Great Helmsman's economic, political and cultural depredations and had embraced Deng Xiaoping proclamation that "to get rich is glorious."

The implications of the Red Army's fiscal demise and China's electing the path of Soviet export mercantilism and Red Capitalism were profound.

Russia couldn't invade the American homeland in a million years and China chose the route of flooding America with shoes, sheets, shirts, toys and electronics. So doing, it made the rule of the communist elites in Beijing dependent upon keeping the custom of 4,000 Wal-Marts in America, not bombing them out of existence.

In a word, god's original gift to America — the great moats of the Atlantic and Pacific oceans — had again become the essence of its national security.

After 1991, therefore, there was no nation on the planet

that had the remotest capability to mount a conventional military assault on the U. S. homeland; or that would not have bankrupted itself attempting to create the requisite air and sea-based power projection capabilities — a resource drain that would be vastly larger than even the $720 billion the US currently spends on its own global armada.

Indeed, in the post-cold war world the only thing the US needed was a modest conventional capacity to defend the shorelines and airspace against any possible rogue assault and a reliable nuclear deterrent against any state foolish enough to attempt nuclear blackmail.

Needless to say, those capacities had already been bought and paid for during the cold war. The triad of minutemen ICBMs, Trident SLBMs (submarines launched nuclear missiles) and long-range stealth bombers cost only a few ten billions annually for operations and maintenance and were more than adequate for the task of nuclear deterrence.

Likewise, conventional defense of the U. S. shoreline and airspace against rogues would not require a fraction of today's 1.3 million active uniformed force — to say nothing of the 800,000 additional reserves and national guard forces and the 765,000 DOD civilians on top of that.

Rather than funding 2.9 million personnel, the whole job of national security under a homeland-based America First concept could be done with less than 500,000 military and civilian payrollers.

In fact, much of the 475,000 US army could be eliminated and most of the Navy's carrier strike groups and power projection capabilities could be mothballed. So, too, the Air Force's homeland defense missions could be accomplished for well less than $50 billion per annum compared to its current $145 billion budget.

Overall, the constant dollar defense budget (2017$) was $550 billion in 1989 when the cold war ended and the Soviet

Union subsequently disappeared from the face of the earth. Had Washington pivoted to an America First national security policy at the time, defense spending could have been downsized to perhaps $250 billion per year.

Instead, the Imperial City went in the opposite direction and ended up embracing a de facto policy of *Empire First*. The latter will cost $720 billion during the current year and is heading for $900 billion annually a few years down the road.

Empire First — The Reason For An Extra Half Trillion For Defense

In a word, *Empire First* easily consumes one-half trillion dollars more in annual budgetary resources than would *America First*. And that giant barrel of weapons contracts, consulting and support jobs, lobbying booty and Congressional pork explains everything you need to know about why the Swamp is so deep and intractable.

Obviously, it's also why Imperial Washington has appointed itself global policeman. Functioning as the gendarme of the planet is the only possible justification for the extra $500 billion per year cost of Empire First.

For example, why does the US still deploy 100,000 US forces and their dependents in Japan and Okinawa and 29,000 in South Korea?

These two counties have a combined GDP of $7 trillion — or 235X more than North Korea and they are light-years ahead of the latter in technology and military capability. Also, they don't go around the world engaging in regime change, thereby spooking fear on the north side of the DMZ.

Accordingly, Japan and South Korea could more than provide for their own national security in a manner they see fit without any help whatsoever from Imperial Washington. That's especially the case because North Korea would seek a rapprochement and economic help, and their relationship with

China is based on business, not military confrontation.

Indeed, sixty-five years after the unnecessary war in Korea ended, there is only one reason why the Kim family is still in power in Pyongyang and why they have (until the recent Singapore Summit) noisily brandished their incipient nuclear weapons and missiles. To wit, it's because the Empire still occupies the Korean peninsula and surrounds its waters with more lethal firepower than was brought to bear against the industrial might of Nazi Germany during the whole of WWII.

And speaking of Germany, why is it that its modest $41 Billion defense budget amounts to only 1.1% of GDP if Russia is really some kind of expansionist military threat?

The Germans clearly don't believe it and see Russia as a vital market for exports and as a source of supply for natural gas, other natural resources and food stuffs. Besides, with a GDP of $3.8 trillion or nearly 3X Russia's $1.5 trillion GDP, Germany could more than handle its own defenses if Russia should ever become foolish enough to threaten it.

From there you get to the even more preposterous case for the Empire's NATO outposts in eastern Europe. As recounted above, the history books are absolutely clear that in 1989 George H. W. Bush promised Gorbachev that NATO would not be expanded by a "single inch" in return for his acquiescence to German unification.

The Obsolete Folly Of NATO's Article 5 Mutual Defense Obligations

At the time, NATO had 15 member nations bound by the Article 5 obligation of mutual defense, but when the Soviet Union and the Red Army perished, there was nothing left to defend against. NATO should have declared "mission accomplished" and dissolved itself.

Instead, it has become a political jackhammer for Empire

First policies by expanding to 29 nations — many of them on Russia's doorstep.

Yet if your perception is not distorted by Washington's self-justifying imperial beer-goggles, the question is obvious. Exactly what is gained for the safety and security of the citizens of Lincoln NE or Springfield MA by obtaining the defense services of the pint-sized militaries of Latvia (6,000), Croatia (14,500), Estonia (6,400), Slovenia (7,300) or Montenegro (1,950)?

Indeed, the whole post-1991 NATO expansion is so preposterous as a matter of national security that its true function as a fig-leaf for Empire First fairly screams outloud. Not one of these pint-sized nations would matter for US security if they decided to have a cozier relationship with Russia — voluntarily or not so voluntarily.

But the point is, there is no threat to America in eastern Europe unless such as Montenegro, Slovenia, or Latvia were to become Putin's invasion route to effect the Russian occupation of Germany, France, the Benelux and England.

And that's just plain silly-ass crazy!

Yet aside from that utterly far-fetched and economically and militarily impossible scenario, there is no reason whatsoever for the US to be in a mutual defense pact with any of the new, and, for that matter, old NATO members.

And that gets us to most ridiculous NATO fig leaf of all. The patently bogus claim that Russia's self-evidently defensive actions in Crimea and the Donbas (eastern Ukraine) prove that it is an aggressive expansionist. But on that score, Washington's imperial beer goggles are utterly blind to history and geopolitical logic.

As we indicated above, Sevastopol in Crimea has been the homeport of the Russian Naval Fleet under czars and commissars alike and was purchased from the Ottoman's for good money by Catherine the Great in 1783. It is the site of one of Russia greatest patriotic events — the defeat of the English invaders in 1854 made famous by Tennyson's Charge of the Light Brigade — and is 80% Russian speaking.

After 171 years as an integral part of the Russian Motherland, it only technically became part of Ukraine during a Kruschev inspired shuffle in 1954.

The fact is, only **10%** of the Crimean population is Ukrainian speaking, and it was the coup on the streets of Kiev in February 2014 by extremist anti-Russian Ukrainian nationalists and proto-fascists that caused the Russian-speaking majority in Crimea to panic and Moscow to become alarmed about the status of its historic naval base, for which it still had a lease running to the 2040s.

In a word, **83%** of eligible Crimeans turned out to vote and **97%** of those approved cancelling the aforementioned 1954 edict of the Soviet Presidium and rejoining mother Russia during the March 2014 referendum. There is absolutely no evidence that the *80%* of Crimeans who thus voted to sever their historically short-lived affiliation with Ukraine were threatened or coerced by Moscow.

Indeed, what they actually feared were the anti-Russian edicts coming out of Kiev in the Damascus aftermath of the Washington funded, supported and instantly recognized overthrow of the legally elected government. And exactly the same thing is true of the overwhelmingly Russian-speaking populations of the Donbas.

After all, the good folks of that industrial heartland of the former Soviet Union had always been an integral part of its iron, steel, chemical and munitions industries, and, indeed, their grandparents had been put there by Stalin because most native Ukrainians had not cottoned to his bloody rule.

By the same token, Uncle Joe's 1930s Russian transplants forever hated the Ukrainian nationalist collaborators, who rampaged though their towns, farms, factories and homes in the

Donbas side-by-side with Hitler's Wehrmacht on the way to Stalingrad.

So the appalling truth of the matter is this: By Washington's edict the grandsons and granddaughters of Stalin's industrial army in the Donbas are to be ruled by the grandsons and granddaughters of Hitler's collaborators in Kiev, whether they like it or not.

But we repeat and for good reason: You simply can't make up $500 billion worth of phony reasons for an Empire First national security policy without going off the deep-end. You have to invent missions, mandates and threats that are just plain stupid (like the purported Russian "occupation" of Crimea) or flat out lies (like Saddam's alleged WMDs).

Indeed, you must invent, nourish and enforce an entire universal narrative based on completely implausible and invalid propositions, such as the "Indispensable Nation" meme and the claim that global peace and stability depend overwhelmingly on Washington's leadership.

Yet, is there not a more cruel joke than that?

Was the Washington inflicted carnage and genocide in Vietnam a case of "American leadership" and making the world more peaceful or stable?

Did the two wars against Iraq accomplish anything except destroy the tenuous peace between the Sunni, Shiite and Kurds, thereby opening up the gates of hell and the bloody rampages of ISIS?

Did the billions Washington illegally channeled into the rebel and jihadist forces in Syria do anything except destroy the country, create millions of refugees and force the Assad regime to engage in tit-for-tat brutalities, as well as call-in aid from his Iranian, Russian and Hezbollah allies?

In a word, Imperial Washington's over-arching narratives and the instances of its specific interventions alike rest on a threadbare and implausible foundation; and more often than not, they consist of arrogant fabrications and claims that are an insult to the intelligence of anyone paying even loose attention to the facts.

When You Are An Empire, You Create Your Own Reality

Then again, Imperial Washington no longer cares about facts, logic, history or truth. At the time of the Bush War on Saddam's WMD's, Karl Rove explained the Empire's New Creed without pulling any punches.

"That's not the way the world really works anymore. We're an **empire now,** *and when we act, we* **create our own reality.** *And while you're studying that reality — judiciously, as you will — we'll act again,* **creating other new realities,** *which you can study too, and that's how things will sort out. We're history's actors ... and you, all of you, will be left to just study what we do. "*

There you have it. And Rove is no out-of-the-way academic scribbler inventing some high-flutin' rationalization for American global hegemony. To the contrary, he's a lifetime Swamp creature, leading beltway racketeer and the strategic brain trust of the GOP establishment.

Needless to say, Washington continues to create its "own reality" almost weekly, for instance, as during last spring's hideously unjustified bombing attack on Syria.

This was purportedly in retaliation for Assad's alleged use of chemical weapons against his own people, but within hours it became evident that no gas attack actually occurred and that the event was staged by desperate jihadis holed up in the suburb of Douma before it fell to government forces.

In that instance the machinery of state literally took our impulsive President captive by exploiting his macho delusions, thereby decreeing that no one — not even the Donald — may brook with the War Party's narrative.

Yet the case for launching a spanking attack on Assad was so threadbare that it might as well have been derived from a

Washington claim of full spectrum dominance over planet Earth. Or as one astute observer noted: *(Those who have) been*

properly following the situation in Syria for the last few years will know the truth, which is that the US and its allies have been arming, funding and supporting Islamist terrorists, and using them as proxies to topple the Syrian Government. Not "moderate rebels", as the dutiful stenographers in the Mainstream Media have been telling you, but fanatical head-choppers who want to see Syria turned into a Wahhabi state replete with Sharia Law.

Now even the OPCW has weighed in with its firm conclusion that it found no evidence that nerve agents were used in the area of the attacks. Instead, it was most surely a false flag attack staged by the rebels.

After all, the "evidence" for the alleged gas attack came entirely from unverified social media accounts, the White Helmets and the Syrian American Medical Society (SAMS).

The latter is a tool of the Sunni Muslim Brotherhood, which for better or worse had been banned from Syria by Assad's father way back in the early 1980's owing to its opposition to the secularist rule of the Alawite-based coalition of nationalists, socialists, Christians and other non-Sunni minorities.

Not surprisingly, SAMS has only operated in jihadist and rebel occupied territories — just as has been the case with the vaunted  White Helmets, which have been repeatedly caught in the act of staging and fabricating false flag attacks.

We are aware, in fact, of solid documentation for more than 20 of such staged attacks, but here are three which give the flavor. In the first one above, the boy depicted in the side-by-side photos was not named Lazarus, and neither was he ever dead.

The second one, of White Helmets, speaks for itself. And  in the last example, it is obvious that the lazy shills in the mainstream media, which played this image over and over, were duped by chicken blood!

Nor was Douma attack a case of dueling liars. Why would you believe the White Helmets, but not Halil Ajiji, a medical student who

385

worked at the only functioning hospital in Douma? He described the origin of the chemical victims being desperately sprayed in a hospital as follows:

On April 8, a bomb hit a building. The upper floors were damaged and a fire broke at the lower floors. Victims of that bombing were brought to us. People from the upper floors had smoke poisoning. We treated them, based on their suffocation. "

Ajij said that a man unknown to him came and said there was a chemical attack and panic ensued. "Relatives of the victims started dousing each other with water. Other people, who didn't seem to have medical training, started administering anti-asthma medicine to children. We didn't see any patient with symptoms of a chemical weapons poisoning," he said.

The point is, before Washington turned loose the cruise missiles and bombers, it could have sent a delegation to Douma with the blessing of Putin and Assad, and interviewed Ajij and several thousand more to find out what actually happened.

What was different about the Douma incident compared to all of the past "gas attack" incidents, however, is this one happened in what is now safe government controlled territory. Accordingly, any Washington delegation of investigators could have inspected the site until their hearts content and with Assad's blessing. They could have even been accompanied by CNN's own Baghdad Bob — that is, Wolf Blitzer himself.

Perhaps the latter would have ascertained whether the protection gear pictured above and found in an abandoned rebel site was used for handling chemical weapons; and also whether or not the rooms full of rockets and components also pictured above were used by the jihadist terrorists strictly for killing people with good old fashioned shrapnel and percussion effects rather than chlorine gas.

Likewise, maybe Washington could have demanded that the chief paint and plastics engineer at the Barzeh research center give international investigators who were arriving from the OPCW the next morning a tour of every room in that largely empty facility before they blew it to smithereens with 71 missiles.

After all, the man stood on the rubble within an hour or two of the attack and was not overcome with any kind of toxic agent chemical release. Thus said, Mr. Said Said,

The building had three storeys: a basement, ground floor, and second floor," said Said Said, an engineer who identified himself as head of the centre's paint and plastics department.

"If there were chemical weapons, we would not be able to stand here. I've been here since 5:30 am in full health — I'm not coughing," he added.

Said said the Organisation for the Prohibition of Chemical Weapons had visited the site in Barzeh in recent years and had declared it free of any toxic weapons.

"The OPCW used to stay in the two upper rooms, and use the labs, and we would cooperate with them completely," he said.

"The OPCW has proven in two reports that this building and the centre as a whole are empty and do not produce any chemical weapons."

We leave it to the French, however, to spill the beans. Their proof was surmise, and social media pictures!

On the basis of this overall assessment and on the intelligence collected by our services, and in the absence to date of chemical samples analysed by our own laboratories, France therefore considers (i) that, beyond possible doubt, a chemical attack was carried out against civilians at Douma on 7 April 2018; and (ii) that there is no plausible scenario other than that of an attack by Syrian armed forces as part of a wider offensive in the Eastern Ghouta enclave.

The French services analysed the testimonies, photos and videos that spontaneously appeared on specialized websites, in the press and on social media in the hours and days following the attack.

After examining the videos and images of victims published

387

online, they were able to conclude with a high degree of confidence that the vast majority are recent and not fabricated. . . . Lastly, some of the entities that published this information are generally considered reliable.

Say again?

"Some of the entities" that were the basis for attacking a country that has never harmed France, England or the US are "generally considered reliable."

Goodness gracious!

Fortunately, General Mattis talked the Donald into attacking several nothing-burger sites. Perhaps that was the cruelest insult of all to Imperial Washington.

And perhaps the absolute bunkum of these repeated video-game bombing missions will finally alert America to the fraud that is Empire First.

CHAPTER 19

The Iranian File: The Donald Undone, America First Crushed

The Donald's action to terminate the Iranian nuclear deal was a complete triumph for the War Party. It gutted the very idea of *America First* because Washington's renewed round of sanctions constitute economic aggression against a country that is no threat to the U. S. homeland whatsoever.

Indeed, Trump's reckless, unwarranted and essentially irrational action will pull Washington ever deeper into an incendiary middle eastern vortex of political and religious conflict that has absolutely nothing to do with the safety and security of the America people.

To the contrary, Iran did not violate any term of the nuke deal, and as we demonstrate below, scrupulously adhered to the letter of it. So the real reasons for Trump's abandonment of the nuke deal have everything to do with the kind of Imperial interventionism that is the antithesis of America First.

Trump's action, in fact, is predicated on the decades long neocon-inspired Big Lie that Iran is an aggressive expansionist and terrorism-supporting rogue state which threatens the security of not just the region, but America too.

But that's flat out poppycock. As we documented in chapter 16, the claim that Iran is the expansionist leader of the Shiite Crescent is based on nothing more than the fact that Tehran has an independent foreign policy based on its own interests and confessional affiliations — legitimate relationships that are demonized by virtue of not being approved by Washington.

Likewise, the official charge that Iran is the leading state sponsor of terrorism is not remotely warranted by the facts: The listing is essentially a State Department favor to the Netanyahu branch of the War Party.

The fact is, the Iranian regime with its piddling $14 billion military budget has no means to attack America militarily and has never threatened to do so. Nor has it invaded any other country in the region where it was not invited by a sovereign government host.

Even Iran's minor skirmishes with American forces in recent years have been owing to the happenstance of Washington's far-flung imperial ventures.

As we detailed in chapter 16, for instance, Washington destroyed Saddam's Sunni/secular government in Iraq and installed a Shiite regime in Baghdad, thereby leaving the Sunni lands of western Iraq in chaos.

That's why even the successor puppet regime in Baghdad, which is Shiite, felt compelled to invite their co-religionists from Iran to help excise the scourge of ISIS — a barbaric mutant that actually formed from the remnants of Saddam's army and government.

As we have also seen, Washington and its allies sent thousands of jihadist warriors and billions of aid and supplies into Syria to topple its dully elected government. Again, that's why the Alawite (Shiite) Assad regime invited help from its confessional compatriots in Tehran.

Iran's Sin Against Washington — Its Own Foreign Policy

And you can't find any more ludicrous example of the cat calling the kettle black than the Donald's claim that Iran is a terrorist state because it is aligned with the Shiite population of

Lebanon represented by Hezbollah.

But for crying out loud, after the country's first legislative elections in nine years in May 2018, Hezbollah has emerged as a leading force in the so-called "March 8" coalition, which is comprised of Hezbollah, the Amal Shi'a party, the Free Patriotic Movement (FPM) of Maronite Christians and some smaller Druze and Sunni factions. This coalition won 68 out of 128 seats in the Lebanese parliament, and is positioned to control Lebanon's unique confession-based system of representation and office-holding.

That is to say, Hezbollah's power derives from the ballot box, not roadside IEDs and suicide bombers. And that fact alone puts the lie to the War Party's deceptions and hypocrisy.

To wit, Washington has reduced much of the middle east into rubble and barbarism — allegedly for its own good. That is, in order to spread democracy to these bedraggled nations — whether they wanted it or not, and whether they were ready for it or not.

But Lebanon is already a serviceable, if fractured, democracy. Hezbollah and its Christian allies — including certain Sunni factions — now have the power to name the Prime Minister (who must be a Sunni) and the Speaker of the Parliament (who must be a Shiite). Both are pledged to work with the country's president (who must be a Christian), and who, in fact, is Michele Aoun, the founder of Hezbollah's major coalition partner (FPM) and the elder Christian statesman of Lebanon.

That particular outcome of democracy, of course, the War Party obviously couldn't abide. But it fairly violates the English language itself to call Hezbollah's pivotal role in Lebanese governance the fruit of Iran's state sponsored terrorism.

In a similar vein, the Houthi tribes — who profess a variant of Shiite Islam — have dominated much of northern and western Yemen for centuries. They generally ruled North Yemen during the long expanse after it was established in 1918 until the two Yemen's were reunified in 1990.

So when a Washington installed government in Sana'a was overthrown and Yemen disintegrated into warring religious factions, the Houthi took power in northern Yemen, while Sunni tribes aligned with the Muslim Brotherhood and al-Qaeda held sway in the south.

Needless to say, the Houthis have no Navy, Air Force or regular Army. So they are no threat whatsoever to Saudi Arabia, bristling with $250 billion of advanced weapon bought from America over recent decades.

In fact, the entire GDP of the war-torn and impoverished nation of Yemen is just $27 billion, and much of that lies outside of areas controlled by the Houthis government in Sana'a.

By contrast, Saudi Arabia has the third largest defense budget in the world at $69 billion or 2.5X the entire economy of Yemen, and it is a lethal modern military force trained and equipped with the Pentagon's best.

In a word, the Houthis are being brutally bombed and droned by Saudi Arabia in what amounts to a genocidal proxy attack on its Iranian rival across the Persian Gulf. So it is the Houthis who are the victims of a vicious aggression that has left more than 10,000 civilians dead and the land plagued with famine, cholera, rubble and economic collapse.

There is no telling which faction in Yemen's fratricidal civil war is the more barbaric, but the modest aid provided by Iran to its Shiite kinsman in northern Yemen is absolutely not a case of state sponsored terrorism.

In a word, the Donald has fallen hook, line and sinker for the War Party's lie and propaganda filled demonization of the Iranian regime. We debunk this false history further below, but suffice to say here that it boils down to two very imperialistic propositions.

First, Washington is essentially decreeing that Iran is not entitled to have its own foreign policy via alliances with Iraq,

Syria, the dominant party of Lebanon or the official government in Sana'a, Yemen .

Why? Because both the Washington and Israeli branches of the War Party say so.

Likewise, to hear Washington tell it, Iran should also be forbidden to build or test intermediate and medium range missiles to defend itself— even though they can't reach either the US or most of Europe. And that writ stands despite the fact that over the past several decades Washington has armed its far wealthier Saudi rival with upwards of $250 billion of America's most advanced warplanes, attack helicopters, missiles, drones and sundry other accoutrements of war.

If these considerations weren't enough, it appears that even Iran's tiny residual capacity under the JCPA (Joint Comprehensive Plan of Action) to enrich uranium to 3.5% purity (compared to 90% weapons grade) for its civilian power reactors is more than the War Party can abide.

That's right. Under the nuke deal, all that Iran has left from more than 20,000 centrifuges is a few thousand of its oldest and slowest spinning machines. Still, unlike 15 other signatories to the Nuclear Non-Proliferation Treaty which operate civilian enrichment facilities, Iran is apparently guilty of sinister intentions by that fact alone.

In short, demonization has supplanted facts, logic and analysis when it comes to Iran. And foremost among these deleted facts is the aforementioned certification by all 17 US intelligence agencies in an official NIE (national intelligence estimate) in 2007 and again in 2011 that Iran only had a small weaponization research program between 1999 and 2003, which was then abandoned and never restarted.

That is, it never had a anything that looked remotely like the nefarious quest for nuclear weapons which the War Party repeats endlessly as if it were the gospel truth.

Moreover, the documentary proof of that was thoroughly

investigated by the IAEA after the 2015 nuke deal, which then re-validated that the Iranian weapons program was indeed disbanded in 2003.

In short, the Donald has fallen for a pack of lies and distortions that are plausible — only if the real aim is to find enemies and territories around the planet to police, occupy or otherwise hegemonize. And to thereby keep the Warfare State in business, its $800 billion budget funded, and the Imperial City's vast beehive of think-tanks, contractors, NGOs, lobbyists and racketeers in financial clover.

So the Donald did not simply make an isolated error in withdrawing from the JCPA. What has really happened is that the Deep State's invincible grip on power has now been completely reaffirmed.

And that's a full-on tragedy because, as we have demonstrated, the Donald's inchoate notion of America First was an incipient challenge to its power.

Indeed, the only challenge it has faced since the end of the cold war — and that, too, has now been largely defenestrated.

Demonization of the Unwilling

This brings us to the broader context. To again paraphrase the great Randolph Bourne: Demonization of the Unwilling is the Health of the Deep State.

At least that much the Donald has now, regrettably, confirmed with his endless sophomoric attacks on Iran and the re-imposition of sanctions-based economic war on its people.

The fact is, there was virtually nothing in the substance of the JCPA deal for the War Party to attack. So the neocon campaign against the nuke deal amounted to desperately hurtling the axis-of-evil narrative at the agreement, claiming that the Iranian regime is so untrustworthy, diabolical and existentially dangerous that no product of mere diplomacy is valid.

Stated differently, according to the neocon narrative the Iranians are by axiom hell-bent on evil and no mere "scrap of paper" will stop them.

As we have seen, however, the three-decade long axis-of-evil narrative was never remotely true. And if the truth be told, the War Party has never been required to defend this spurious fabric of lies thanks in large part to a lazy, gullible mainstream press that has been as negligent on the Iranian evil meme as they were on Saddam's weapons of mass destruction.

As will be demonstrated below, the evil Iran narrative rests on repetition and political bombast, not historical fact. Iran was turned into a pariah state not owing to its own deeds and actions, but because it served the domestic political needs of the War Party.

That is, Bibi Netanyahu's Israeli branch used it to win elections by mobilizing the right-wing and extremist religious parties against a purported external peril; and Washington's neo-cons used it to rescue the Pentagon's war machine and the military industrial complex after the cold war ended its reason for being.

The Iranian Nuke Deal Was A Stride For Peace, Not A Modern Munich

While the whole axis-of-evil narrative is bogus, the War Party has repaired to it in flat-out hysterical tones because it has nowhere else to go. Indeed, at the time the nuke deal was announced, it did not take long for a shrill demagogue like GOP Senator Mark Kirk to play the Hitler card:

"I would say that Neville Chamberlain got a lot more out of Hitler than (U. S. negotiator) Wendy Sherman got out of Iran."

No, Senator, what Hitler got out of Munich was the annexation of the Sudetenland which was 85% German; had been part of various German-speaking predecessor states from the Middle Ages until Versailles; and had voted by referendum overwhelmingly to return to the fatherland.

Whether the greater foolishness occurred in Paris in 1919, when the Sudetenland was handed to the Czech politicians as war spoils, or in Munich in 1938, when Chamberlain badly misjudged his interlocutor, is a topic which will keep the historians busy debating for centuries.

But Munich has absolutely nothing to do with the matter at hand because Iran is not remotely comparable to Nazi Germany. In fact, Iran is a nearly bankrupt country that has no capability whatsoever to threaten the security and safety of the citizens of Spokane WA, Peoria IL or anywhere else in the USA.

Its $430 billion GDP is the size of Indiana's and its 68,000 man military is only slightly larger than the national guard of Texas.

It is a land of severe mountains and daunting swamps that are not all that conducive to rapid economic progress and advanced industrialization. It has no blue water navy, no missiles with more than a few hundred miles of range, and, we must repeat again, has had no nuclear weapons program for more than a decade.

And unlike Hitler at Munich who got most of what he wanted, the Iranians at Lausanne where the JCPA was signed gave up almost all of what they had. That is, they made huge concessions on nearly every issue that made a difference.

That included deep concessions on the number of permitted centrifuges at Natanz; the dismantlement of the Fordow and Arak nuclear operations; the virtually complete liquidation of its enriched uranium stockpiles; the intrusiveness and scope of the inspections regime; and the provisions with respect to Iran's so-called "breakout" capacity.

For instance, while every signatory of the non-proliferation treaty has the right to civilian enrichment, Iran agreed to reduce the number of centrifuges by 70% from 20,000 to 6,000.

And its effective spinning capacity was reduced by

significantly more. That's because the permitted Natanz centrifuges now consist exclusively of its most rudimentary, outdated equipment — first-generation IR-1 knockoffs of 1970s European models.

Not only was Iran not be allowed to build or develop newer models, but even those remaining were permitted to enrich uranium to a limit of only 3.75% purity. That is to say, to the generation of fissile material that is not remotely capable of reaching bomb grade concentrations of 90%.

Equally importantly, pursuant to the agreement Iran has eliminated enrichment activity entirely at its Fordow plant — a facility that had been Iran's one truly advanced, hardened site that could withstand an onslaught of Israeli or US bunker busters.

Instead, Fordow has become a small time underground science lab devoted to medical isotope research and crawling with international inspectors. In effectively decommissioning Fordow and thereby eliminating any capacity to cheat from a secure facility — what Iran got in return was at best a fig leave of salve for its national pride.

The disposition of the reactor at Arak has been even more dispositive. For years, the War Party has falsely waved the bloody shirt of "plutonium" because the civilian nuclear reactor being built there was of Canadian "heavy water" design rather than GE or Westinghouse "light water" design; and, accordingly, when finished it would have generated plutonium as a waste product rather than conventional spent nuclear fuel rods.

In truth, the Iranians couldn't have bombed a beehive with the Arak plutonium because you need a reprocessing plant to convert it into bomb grade material. Needless to say, Iran never had such a plant — nor any plans to build one, and no prospect for getting the requisite technology and equipment.

But now even that bogeyman no longer exists. Iran removed and destroyed the reactor core of its existing Arak plant in

2016 and filled it with cement, as attested to by international inspectors under the JCPA.

As to its already existing enriched stock piles, including some 20% medical-grade material, 97% has been eliminated as per the agreement. That is, Iran now holds only 300 kilograms of its 10,000 kilogram stockpile in useable or recoverable form. Senator Kirk could store what is left in his wine cellar.

But where the framework agreement decisively shut down the War Party was with respect to its provision for a robust, comprehensive and even prophylactic inspections regime. All of the major provision itemized above are being enforced by continuous IAEA access to existing facilities including its main centrifuge complex at Natanz — along with Fordow, Arak and a half dozen other sites.

Indeed, the real break-through in the JCPA lies in Iran's agreement to what amounts to a cradle-to-grave inspection regime. It encompasses the entire nuclear fuel chain.

That means international inspectors can visit Iran's uranium mines and milling and fuel preparation operations. This encompasses even its enrichment equipment manufacturing and fabrication plants, including centrifuge rotor and bellows production and storage facilities.

Beyond that, Iran has also been subject to a robust program of IAEA inspections to prevent smuggling of materials into the country to illicit sites outside of the named facilities under the agreement. This encompasses imports of nuclear fuel cycle equipment and materials, including so-called "dual use" items which are essentially civilian imports that can be repurposed to nuclear uses, even peaceful domestic power generation.

In short, not even a Houdini could secretly break-out of the control box established by the JCPA and confront the world with some kind of fait accompli threat to use the bomb.

That's because what it would take to do so is absurdly implausible. That is, Iran would need to secretly divert thousands of tons of domestically produced or imported uranium and then illicitly mill and upgrade such material at secret fuel preparation plants.

It would also need to secretly construct new, hidden enrichment operations of such massive scale that they could house more than 10,000 new centrifuges. Moreover, they would need to build these massive spinning arrays from millions of component parts smuggled into the country and transported to remote enrichment operations — all undetected by the massive complex of spy satellites overhead and covert US ands Israeli intelligence agency operatives on the ground in Iran.

Finally, it would require the activation from scratch of a weaponization program which has been dormant according to the National Intelligence Estimates (NIEs) for more than a decade. And then, that the Iranian regime — after cobbling together one or two bombs without testing them or their launch vehicles — would nevertheless be willing to threaten to use them sight unseen.

So just stop it!

You need to be a raging, certifiable paranoid boob to believe that the Iranians can break out of this framework box based on a secret new capacity to enrich the requisite fissile material and make a bomb.

In the alternative scenario, you have to be a willful know-nothing to think that if it publicly repudiates the agreement, Iran could get a bomb overnight before the international community could take action.

To get enough nuclear material to make a bomb from the output of the 6,000 "old and slow" centrifuges remaining at Natanz would take years, not months. And if subject to an embargo on imported components, as it would be after a unilateral Iranian repudiation of the JCPA, it could not rebuild its now dismantled enrichment capacity rapidly, either.

At the end of the day, in fact, what you really have to believe is that Iran is run by absolutely irrational, suicidal madmen. After all, even if they managed to defy the immensely prohibitive constraints described above and get one or a even a few nuclear bombs, what in the world would they do with them?

Drop them on Tel Aviv? That would absolutely insure Israel's navy and air force would unleash its 100-plus nukes and thereby incinerate the entire industrial base and major population centers of Iran.

Indeed, the very idea that deterrence would fail even if a future Iranian regime were to defy all the odds, and also defy the fatwa against nuclear weapons issued by their Supreme Leader, amounts to one of the most preposterous Big Lies ever concocted.

There is no plausible or rational basis for believing it outside of the axis-of-evil narrative. So what's really behind Trump's withdrawal from the JCPA is nothing more than the immense tissue of lies and unwarranted demonization of Iran that the War Party has fabricated over the last three decades.

Iran Never Wanted The Bomb

At bottom, all the hysteria about the mullahs getting the bomb was based on the wholly theoretically supposition that they wanted civilian enrichment only as a stepping stone to the bomb. Yet the entirety of the US intelligence complex as well as the attestation of George W. Bush himself say it isn't so.

As we have indicated, the blinding truth of that proposition first came in the National Intelligence Estimates of 2007. These NIEs represent a consensus of all 17 US intelligence agencies on salient issues each year, and on the matter of Iran's nuclear weapons program they could not have been more unequivocal:

"We judge with high confidence that in fall 2003, Tehran halted its nuclear weapons program; we also assess with moderate-to-high confidence that Tehran at a minimum is keeping open the

option to develop nuclear weapons. … We assess with moderate confidence Tehran had not restarted its nuclear weapons program as of mid-2007, but we do not know whether it currently intends to develop nuclear weapons. …

"Our assessment that Iran halted the program in 2003 primarily in response to international pressure indicates Tehran's decisions are guided by a cost-benefit approach rather than a rush to a weapon irrespective of the political, economic and military costs."

Moreover, as former CIA analyst Ray McGovern noted recently, the NIE's have not changed since then.

An equally important fact ignored by the mainstream media is that the key judgments of that NIE have been revalidated by the intelligence community several times since then.

More crucially, there is the matter of "Dubya's" memoirs. Near the end of his term in office he was under immense pressure to authorize a bombing campaign against Iran's civilian nuclear facilities.

But once the 2007 NIEs came out, even the "mission accomplished" President in the bomber jacket was caught up short. As McGovern further notes,

Bush lets it all hang out in his memoir, *Decision Points.* Most revealingly, he complains bitterly that the NIE "tied my hands on the military side" and called its findings "eye-popping."

A disgruntled Bush writes, *"The backlash was immediate. . . . . . "I don't know why the NIE was written the way it was. … Whatever the explanation, the NIE had a big impact — and not a good one."*

Spelling out how the Estimate had tied his hands "on the military side," Bush included this (apparently unedited) kicker: *"But after the NIE, how could I possibly explain using the military to destroy the nuclear facilities of a country the intelligence community said had no active nuclear weapons program?"*

So there you have it. How is it possible to believe that the

Iranian's were hell-bent on a nuclear holocaust when they didn't even have a nuclear weapons program?

What they do have, of course, is something altogether different and not at all sinister. To wit, they do have is a regional political program — some of it accompanied by rhetoric which is bombastic and often unsavory.

The substance of it, however, amounts to the ordinary business of statecraft, which has been twisted and contorted by the War Party into an utterly false claim that Iran is out to conquer and even destroy its neighbors. Yet as we have seen, the evidence for that does not exist and the flimsy arguments which are proffered amount to a giant so what!

The truth, in fact, is that Washington is the relentless aggressor in the region, not Iran. After more than a decade of US military interventions and occupations, political manipulation and conduct of arms supply and deadly droning campaigns against mainly civilian populations, the middle east is littered with failed states and economic hell holes. Iraq, Syria, Libya and Yemen are catastrophes made in Washington, not Tehran.

Even in the ballyhooed case of Lebanon, it was not Iran which invaded southern part of the country and gave rise to Hezbollah. More than three decades ago it was Ronald Reagan who mistakenly inserted US forces into Beirut in 1983.

But Reagan did learn from the tragedy of 241 dead Marines and promptly got US forces out of harm's way. That is to say, he quickly grasped that Lebanon's sectarian conflicts are none of Washington's business, nor are they within its capacity to resolve.

Yet that painful lesson was lost on the Israelis. Twice they have invaded Lebanon with Washington's acquiescence. So doing they have inflicted massive destruction, death and undying animosity on the preponderant Shiite population of southern Lebanon.

Thanks to Israel's imperial arrogance, therefore, Hezbollah has been preternaturally empowered, thereby becoming the protector of the Shiite population and a powerful political party in the Lebanese government.

That Iran chooses to ally with and transfer modest economic aid to its Shiite brethren is certainly not conducive to normalizing relations between Lebanon and Israel. But it is hardly evidence of some grand design of conquest — nor does it constitute an "existential threat" to a state that has vastly superior economic and military capabilities.

And that gets to the heart of the issue. Other than for a few brief months during his first term in office in the late 1990s, Bibi Netanyahu has brazenly, cynically and unremittingly demonized Iran in furtherance of his own brobdingnagian will to political power and absurd pretension that he is some latter day Winston Churchill.

The reason for his hysterical opposition to the Iranian nuke deal is therefore readily apparent. To wit, no demonic state of the kind Netanyahu has castigated for two decades could possibly embrace the giant step toward peace which came out of Lausanne negotiations.

Obama's nuke deal simply called out his epic Big Lie and was on the way to thoroughly repudiating it. But now the gullibility of Donald Trump and the servility of his Bibi-worshipping son-in-law, Jared Kushner, have given Netanyahu's lies a new lease on life.

So too with the domestic neocons. The historical record of the early post cold war years makes absolutely clear that the Iranian regime was designated as the Soviet successor threat in order to keep the nation's massive war machine in tact. Cheney, Wolfowitz and Robert Gates were all there at the founding — as Gareth Porter has so brilliantly documented in his indispensable book called "Manufactured Crisis."

Indeed, there could be no more appropriate metaphor than

"manufactured" for the War Party's shrill opposition to the nuke deal. It is a manufactured case against a manufactured enemy.

Had it not been snuffed in its infancy by an unhinged Donald Trump, the JCPA could have changed the course of history by relieving 75 million long-suffering Iranians of the punishing impact of sanctions. That could have, in turn, fostered further moderation of the Iranian regime and the return of a proud country which, unlike Washington, has invaded no one for more than a century, to the community of nations.

Now all bets are off. Brutal US sanction are back on, the moderates around President Rouhani have been put on their back-foot and the risk of drastic escalation and military confrontation in the Persian Gulf is higher than ever before.

And that's exactly how both branches of the War Party have wanted it all along.

CHAPTER 20

Singapore! It Didn't Take A Village Of Deep Staters

The village idiots of Imperial Washington had conniption fits about the Singapore summit. That's because after 65 years of lobbing military threats and diplomatic poison pens at Pyongyang, the Donald showed the way to resolving the North Korean file in just six hours.

In the case of the Korean peninsula, like the rest of the world, Washington's real job to safeguard the American homeland, not to pass judgment on the merits and morality of foreign leaders and regimes.

That's the essence of the Donald's triumph in Singapore.

By not listening to the Washington

U.S. MILITARY IN THE WEST PACIFIC

■ With active U.S. bases   • Naval bases   ▲ Air Force bases

SOUTH KOREA
Deployment: 25,374*
Navy
CFA Chinhae
Air Force
Osan
Kunsan

*Numbers are overall total which includes Army, Navy, Air Force and Marine Corps

Beijing
Tokyo

CHINA
Shanghai

PACIFIC OCEAN

PHILIPPINES
117
Subic Bay Naval Station was handed over to the Philippine government in 1992
An increase in the number of U.S. forces visiting the Philippines is possible, but there is no plans for permanent U.S. bases, the Philippine government says

TAIWAN

Manila
Spratly Islands
MALAYSIA

JAPAN
35,598*
Navy   Air Force
NAF Misawa   Kadena
NAF Atsugi   Misawa
CFA Yokosuka Yokota
CFA Sasebo
CFA Okinawa

GUAM
2,982
Joint Region Marianas

SINGAPORE
122
Navy Region Center Singapore

INDONESIA
INDIAN OCEAN

PAPUA NEW GUINEA

AUSTRALIA
U.S. military eyes Cocos Islands as a future surveillance aircraft base

200 Darwin
Expected to grow in size over time to become a 2,500-person Task Force

129
• Pine Gap

NAF: Naval Air Facility, CFA: Commander Fleet Activities
Sources: Military Balance 2011, Commander Navy Installations, Pacific Air Forces REUTERS

poobahs of failure and perpetual war, Trump ended in one grand photo op the senseless demonization, isolation and ostracization of a regime that has maintained its brutal rule owing to one over-riding factor: Namely, the omnipresent hostility implicit in Washington's military occupation of the peninsula's southern half and in the lethal armadas it maintains in the seas and airspace all around it, as dramatized by the map above.

The encirclement of North Korea by Washington's war machine was never remotely justified, however, because the former did not and does not present a threat to the American homeland. How could it with a per capita income of barely $1,200 and a miniscule, impoverished, technologically-stillborn economy whose annual production amounts to *12 hours* of US GDP?

Yes, in recent years North Korea has embarked on a quest for nuclear weapons. But its understandable need for deterrence should be evident to any simpleton not schooled in the hypocrisy of Imperial Washington.

To wit, its ruling family did not wish to become another experiment in "regime change" and thereby end up hanging from an American gallows like Saddam Hussein or being dragged from the back of a Jeep and brutally sodomized like Moammar Khadafy.

And that's why the Kim regime was going for ICBMs and nukes. Full stop.

In fact, the picture below tells you all you need to know. Perhaps somewhere in the deep clutter of his purportedly uninformed mind, the Donald recalled that Nixon took tea with Mao in Beijing and Ronald Reagan visited Gorbachev at the

Kremlin.

So Trump resolved to fly to Singapore to see if he could talk sense to the Little Rocket Man. And at least judging by the Korean press on both sides of the DMZ, he came, he spoke and he did.

Indeed, the heartening breakthrough in Singapore was a much needed reminder of why our vote for the Donald in November 2016 wasn't entirely wasted after all.

Admittedly, the image below is not pleasant to see. But it's surely a facsimile of what Imperial Washington had in store for Kim Jong-un had the Great Disrupter not landed in the Oval Office.

When Hillary Clinton infamously said about Khadafy that "we came, we saw, he died", she apparently omitted the "savagely" part.

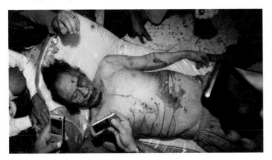

Then again, Washington's own special brand of terror mainly produces pushback from the regimes its targets and blowback from the peoples it bombs, drones and incinerates — not enhanced safety and security for the citizens of Lincoln NE and Springfield MA,

To be sure, the Singapore Summit was only an epochal reset of relations, not a treaty to de-nuclearize, de-militarize and delegate the future of the Korean peninsula to the Koreans.

But that can come — in the fits and starts of diplomacy and, hopefully by the Donald's art-of-the-deal modus operandi. That is, if this breakthrough for peace is not first asphyxiated at the hands of virtually the entire national security team of Deep State servitors around him.

In this instance, at least, there is a modicum of hope that America First will out. Kim would like 50 years of prosperous rule; America is tired of war and the debilitating costs of Empire; and the Donald desperately wants to grasp the mantle of peacemaker and prove his rabid mainstream critics wrong.

Needless to say, if the Donald can pull off a settlement with North Korea, it would have implications far beyond the peninsula. It would discredit Imperial Washington's false, decades-old narrative — repeated endlessly by Deep State apparatchiks and their stenographers in the MSM — that denuclearization is bafflingly complex and that the North Koreans have persistently cheated upon and subverted past deals.

To the contrary, a settlement would expose that proposition for the tissue of lies and misdirection that it actually is, and open the door to a reexamination of the entire edifice of falsehoods which comprise the raison d'etre for the American Imperium.

Why The "Agreed Framework" Failed

In the present instance, the failure of the so-called *Agreed Framework* negotiated by the Clinton Administration in 1994 has been continuously waved like a bloody shirt by Washington hawks and neocons. Yet the real history overwhelming proves that it was Washington, not Pyongyang, which reneged.

The purpose of the 1994 deal was to terminate North Korea's plutonium route to a nuclear bomb. According to US intelligence at the time, Pyongyang otherwise would have had enough nuclear material to build upwards of 75 bombs by the beginning of the next decade.

The Agreed Framework was designed to end that threat by having North Korea dismantle its two plutonium reactor facilities in return for four things:

- Two new light-water reactors to be built in North Korea by 2003 by a US-led consortium to compensate for the loss of plutonium based power;

- An interim supply of 500,000 tons per year of heavy fuel oil to generate electrical power;
- The lifting of US economic sanctions, removal of North Korea from Washington's list of state sponsors of terrorism and supplanting of the 1953 armistice with a formal peace treaty; and
- "formal assurances" from the US against the threat or use of nuclear weapons.

Initially, developments unfolded according to the Framework and by 1998 US officials involved in the implementation testified to Congress that both Washington and the International Atomic Energy Agency (IAEA) were satisfied that there had been "no fundamental violation of any aspect of the Framework Agreement" by North Korea.

For all practical purposes, North Korea's plutonium facilities became unusable and un-restorable.

What didn't happen, however, was the implementation of most of Washington's end of the bargain.

Most importantly, the light-water reactors were never built because the US consortium tasked with constructing them was in severe debt; and because the whole project became a partisan football on Capitol Hill, which blocked the necessary funding.

Likewise, the heavy fuel oil shipments were often delayed or missed, and North Korea was not removed from the list of state sponsors of terror until 2008, even though it had long met the criteria for removal.

At the same time, a limited number of economic sanctions were eased, but not until 2000. That was six years later than pledged in the Agreed Framework and was owing to continuous political attacks on the deal from hawkish quarters on Capitol Hill — especially from partisan Republicans accusing the Clinton Administation of selling out to America's purported enemies.

Finally, no action was ever taken to formally end the Korean War and "formal assurances" that the US would not attack North Korea were only provided years after they were to have been made.

In short, throughout the 1990s Congressional politicians and their Deep State allies played the North Korea card against the Clinton White House, thereby strangling the 1994 deal in a twilight zone of inconsistency, failed deliverables and bad faith.

Even then, South Korea persisted and its government formally launched an opening to the north called the Sunshine Policy in the late 1990s.

But as explained below that too came under unremitting attack by the neocons in the Bush Administration; and when the Pyongyang regime was foolishly identified as a link in the "axis of evil" in Bush's 2002 State of the Union address, it was all over except the shouting.

The truth is, Washington had no reason to be on the Korean peninsula or to threaten the Kim regime with devastating military force in the first place; and most especially not after the cold war ended in 1991 and the purported "dominoes" of communist world conquest had slithered off the pages of history.

The so-called North Korean reneging since 1991, in fact, has simply been the by-product of rear-guard action by the unrepentant hawks, neocons and military/industrial complex supplicants who dominate the Washington policy machinery.

They made it their purpose to insure that the Empire would never vacate the Korean peninsula, thereby also insuring that denuclearization and normalization among the Korean peoples would never happen and that the US Warfare State would never go wanting for enemies and funding.

You would never know this, of course, from listening to the infinitely lazy, uninformed and group think addled chatter of the mainstream media. Still, the realized truth of modern history is crystal clear.

410

Washington Never Had Reason To Be On The Korean Peninsula

Going all the way back to the beginning, Washington had no business intervening in a quarrel between two no-count wanna be dictators (Syngman Rhee and Kim il Sung) on the Korean peninsula in June 1950; and surely has no business still stationing 29,000 American soldiers there 68 years later.

For sure, it was never about strategic real estate. After 40 years of brutal and predatory Japanese occupation, post-war Korea was an economic backwater with the GDP of perhaps Cleveland, Ohio, and had been temporarily divided at the 38th parallel by Truman and Stalin as an afterthought at Potsdam (July 1945).

Far from any intent to create separate nations on a peninsula that had been ethnically and politically unified for centuries, the line of division was only meant to facilitate staging of forces for the final attack on Japan that Stalin had committed to aid. In fact, Washington's suave original cold warrior, Dean Acheson, had described the Potsdam demarcation as a mere "surveyors line."

But as US/Soviet tensions heated up in the late 1940's, the U. S. occupation forces in the south encouraged the puppet government they had established under ex-pat and Washington dandy, Syngman Rhee, to cleanse the country of left-wing influences and to prepare to eventually rule the entire peninsula.

So when hostilities broke out between the two Korean sides in June 1950, Washington instantly transformed it into a proxy war against the Soviet Union and its fledgling ally in China, which had just fallen under Mao's control the previous year.

What we know today, of course, and what staunch non-interventionists like Senator Robert Taft and Congressman Howard Buffett (R-Nebraska and Warren's father) knew even then, is that 1950s style communism could take care of its own

411

self-destruction.

America only needed to militarily secure the homeland, and then wait out the eventual demise of the wretched states that had temporarily fallen victim to communist misrule.

That is to say, a vastly different foreign policy would have emerged if it had been rooted in an understanding of the inherent superiority of free market capitalism and the inexorable certainty that centralized socialism would fail.

Such a policy would never have been duped into the folly of a proxy war on this economically and strategically irrelevant Asian littoral.

As it happened, the Soviet Union did destroy itself from within in a matter of decades. And just in the nick of time, Mr. Deng discovered that Mao had nearly destroyed China on the false belief that it could be collectivized from the barrel of a gun.

Instead, Deng not only rescued Mao's calamity by turning from firing squads to a hyperactive printing press, but spawned the greatest Ponzi scheme of borrowing, building, speculation and malinvestment in human history.

It is surely a false and unsustainable prosperity, but for the moment it rings out a great irony.

Rather than a threat to America's security, Mr. Deng's great Red Ponzi is considered by Wall Street to be the very engine of "growth" in the modern world — even as the suzerains of Beijing are held to be the very model of unfailing prosperity managers which never fail to provide economic "stimulus" if, as and when needed.

That begs the question, of course, as to what would have happened when the Chinese army poured across the Yalu River in November 1950 if it had not been impeded by American GIs.

After all, had Korea ended up as #8 among China's "autonomous and special" administrative units exactly why would that imperil the safety and security of the American homeland any more than does the current Chinese rule over Guangxi, Inner Mongolia, Tibet, Ningxia, Xinjiang or even Hong Kong and Macau?

So if there would be no threat now, why then? Why ever?

The fact is, the seven decade confrontation on the 38th parallel is an artifact of empire, not a necessity of homeland security. It is the handiwork of a Warfare State served by a permanent political class that derives its power, purpose and resources from the faithful pursuit and stewardship of an American Imperium.

Imperial Washington, like Rome, needs purportedly imperiled frontiers to justify its rule and heavy draft of military and economic resources.

The History Of Missed Opportunities For Washington To Vacate The Peninsula

Indeed, after 1960 when the tyrannical Syngman Rhee was driven from office by his own people, there were numerous times that Washington could have vacated the peninsula, but one imperial project after another prevented the return of the Korean peninsula to the Koreans to settle their differences as they saw fit.

In the 1960s and early 1970s it was the folly of the Vietnam invasion that kept the fear of falling "dominoes" alive in the Imperial City and American forces bivouacked on the 38th parallel in order to keep the two Koreas divided.

Likewise, during the 1980s the giant and unnecessary Reagan defense build-up was predicated on the myth of a globally resurgent "Evil Empire" in Moscow, meaning that the South Korean frontier required military reinforcement, not the rational course of abandonment.

Indeed, we recall well that the predicate for the massive squandering of resources in the Reagan defense build-up was that America needed the capacity to fight two-and-one-half wars simultaneously — the "half" war part being on the Korean peninsula.

Yes, China had just been enfeebled by Mao's famines and the madness of the cultural revolution and the Soviet economy was lapsing into the entropic decay of over-centralization and militarization. So the two-and-one-half war fighters never did say who it was that would occupy the Korean peninsula other than some variant of the Korean people.

Then came the demise of the Soviet Union in 1991 and Mr. Deng's massive shift to export-mercantilism a few years later to save China from an economic and civil collapse that would have ended the rule of the communist party. At that point, there was zero chance of a renewed proxy war.

So surely that was the very time to bring 29,000 American servicemen and women home, thereby enabling the former Hermit Kingdom to work-out a 21st century arrangement for either the reunification of all Koreans or at least their co-existence in autonomous zones of self-governance.

But that didn't happen, either. And the reason is not hard to resurrect from the history of the 1990s.

Bill and Hillary were far more intent on gaining a second term in the White House than in carrying out the assigned mandate of their 1960s generation. That is, to dismantle the American Empire and bring the possibility of general peace to the world for the first time since August 1914.

So they temporized and equivocated and chickened out when the Agreed Framework was attacked by the GOP, thereby precluding a readily available peace settlement in Korea.

After that chance was blown, the South Koreans themselves attempted to normalize the peninsula and pave the way for an end to the American occupation.

As indicated above, between 1998 and 2006 they diligently pursued what they called the "sunshine policy." And it did begin to thaw the tensions between north and south for the first time in 50 years — including humanitarian aid from the south, family reunifications and the beginnings of cross-DMZ flows of trade and investment.

At length, the policy failed, but there should be no confusion as to why. The blood-thirsty neocons of the George W. Bush administration killed it in the cradle by naming North Korea to the axis of evil, when, in fact, it was an accident of history long past its sell-by date.

Rarely has there been a stupider act of foreign policy than the hideous refrain inserted into Bush's 2002 State of the Union address by a speechwriting twit named David Frum, who apparently invented the "axis of evil" from wholecloth.

So if anything, the bellicose hostility from Pyongyang since then is as much the responsibility of Frum and his fellow neocon belligerents as anything else.

Still, after all those blown chances to roll-back what is really an illicit forward frontier of Imperial Washington, there is still no reason for any American presence at all on the Korean peninsula.

And that's to say nothing of the massive 350,000 soldier war game rehearsals for an invasion of North Korea that are staged annually by U. S. and South Korean forces.

And that get's us to the bottom line. To wit, as impetuous, egomaniacal and uninformed as he may be — even Donald Trump could see the pointlessness of America's imperial misadventure in Korea.

And so he has frozen these insanely provocative war games in return for Kim Jong-un's commitment to freeze any further testing of ICBMs and nuclear bombs.

What remains, therefore, is to keep the Singapore window open and to allow the Koreans on both sides of the DMZ to find — as they are now actively pursuing — their own modus vivendi that will eventually rid this hapless peninsula of both the nukes and the yanks.

For that possibility alone the Donald's election (but hopefully not re-election) will prove to have been worth the price.

CHAPTER 21

The Vlad And Donald Show — A Fleeting Blow For Peace

The Vlad and Donald show in Helsinki last summer was simply brilliant and breathtaking — we'd say even a beautiful thing to behold.

Between them, they left CNN's nattering nabobs of neocon nonsense sounding like the shrieking monkeys they actually are. And that's to say nothing of the fools they made out of the newly minted liberal and progressive war-mongers on the Dem side of the aisle in Washington or the so-called journalists who fill 90% of the space in the mainstream media with endless pro-war propaganda.

But most of all it was the single greatest blow to the War Party since it turned Imperial Washington into a global hegemony-seeking menace after the Soviet Union disappeared from the pages of history in 1991.

As we have demonstrated, Putin and Russia have been demonized because the Warfare State desperately needs an "enemy" to justify its *$800 billion* annual mugging of America's taxpayers. So for the moment anyway, the spontaneous chorus by the two leaders in behalf of détente, dialogue and diplomacy put the kibosh on that Big Lie more completely than could 100 dovish Ted Talks or a year's worth of pro-peace op eds in the Washington Post.

We also have no doubt that Flyover America had no trouble

417

seeing the good of the Helsinki Summit. Trump and Putin just killed it on every topic where the War Party and its shills in the press wanted to drive a wedge.

That encompassed cooperation on Syria, arms control, terrorism, North Korea and Ukraine; friendly competition on supplying natural gas to Europe; Putin's invitation to Mueller to send his legal sleuths to Russia to interrogate the 12 GRU ham sandwiches named in the indictment; and best of all, a reciprocal notion that Russian prosecutors come here to question Deep State operatives about how they helped one of the greatest swindlers of modern times, Bill Browder, abscond from Russia with almost $1.5 billion skimmed from its people and on which he and his posse paid zero taxes both there and here.

Indeed, the debunking of the false mainstream narrative about Russia's nefarious intentions and doings was so complete that the Deep State apparatchiks were reduced to sputtering hysterically. For instance, here is the bile issued by the central architect of the Russian collusion lie, former CIA director John Brennan:

Donald Trump's press conference performance in Helsinki rises to & exceeds the threshold of "high crimes & misdemeanors." It was nothing short of treasonous. Not only were Trump's comments imbecilic, he is wholly in the pocket of Putin. Republican Patriots: Where are you???

Then again, when you actually read the transcript of the joint press conference, you will find the very words, phrases and tonalities that were uttered four decades ago by statesman of that era urging that peace be given a chance. We are referring, of course, to the courageous efforts of liberal democrats like Senators George McGovern and Frank Church and even President Jimmy Carter to promote diplomacy and detente during the height of the Cold War confrontation when each side had 9,000 nuclear warheads on hair-trigger alert.

And exactly what was John Brennan doing circa 1976?

Why, back then he was voting for the communist candidate for President, Gus Hall, because he thought Jimmy Carter was too much of a cold warrior!

In other words, the man subsequently sold his soul to the Warfare State in pursuit of position, power and pelf as he

Former CIA Director John Brennan

shimmied up the ranks during a 25 year career in the CIA that began in 1980. Unlike the pro-peace statesman who risked their careers back then, Brennan ended up a partisan hack and enemy of peace.

But beyond our joy in hearing the gaskets popping all over the Imperial City we can say this: In the course of that Helsinki press conference the Donald threw down the gauntlet to the Deep State in a manner so explicit and unequivocal that there is now no turning back: Either they will take him out or he will finally turn the tide against Empire First.

Stated differently, either the Donald will rally the undoubtedly dazed GOP troops on Capitol Hill and his Flyover America base in behalf of rapprochement with Russia and an end to Washington's arrogant Imperial hegemony — or they will indeed put him on the Dick Nixon Memorial Helicopter for a final ride to Gonesville.

At this point we are at a loss — 50 years of studying the Imperial City notwithstanding — to know which way it will go.

But there was never any doubt as to what would transpire next. The Deep State and its shills, assigns and nomenklatura throughout the Imperial City have escalated their war against the Donald to red hot intensity.

The signal for that was embodied in the very first words that came off Anderson Cooper's viperous tongue the instant the press conference was finished:

"You have been watching perhaps one of the most disgraceful performances by an American president at a summit in front of a Russian leader, that I have ever seen."

But just call it fever pitch on steroids. The Helsinki press conference, in fact, came after CNN, NBC and most of the MSM had already spent a full weekend of near-hysterical gumming about Robert Mueller's latest ham sandwich indictment.

Mueller's Deep State Sabotage Maneuver

We are referring, of course, to his pre-summit indictment of 12 alleged election meddlers slathered in Russian dressing. Mueller's move was a deliberate, nefarious attack on America's very constitutional order and you simply cannot overstate its danger.

To wit, his purpose was flat-out to sabotage the Helsinki summit, thereby executing another Deep State anti-Trump "insurance policy" maneuver — and one cloaked again in sanctimonious blather about upholding the rule of law and safeguarding the national security.

Otherwise, why did these indictments come down on Friday afternoon July 13?

Did Mueller and Rosenstein need to hurry-up their indictments and make lightening perp-walk style arrests so that their targets wouldn't flee the country in the dead of night?

Not at all. The 12 indictees were already long gone. In fact, these particular Russians were never here, if they actually exist at all.

The truth is, Mueller is a card-carrying apparatchik of the Deep State and his Friday afternoon action was a brazen shot across Donald Trump's bow the likes of which we have never before seen. It raised deeply troubling questions about whether even the veneer of democratic self-government has much shelf-life left in America.

After all, the entire RussiaGate witch hunt and Mueller's pre-summit theatrics amount to a frontal attempt to nullify the 2016 election for a self-evident reason: If the Donald said anything about his agenda during the 2016 campaign that was remotely coherent (besides building the Mexican Wall) it was that he would seek a rapprochement deal with Putin — a proposition that made him an existential threat to the Warfare State.

Indeed, the War Party's risible demonization of Putin is literally its principal authorization to continue squandering $800 billion per year on "national security", which, in turn, is the very life-blood of Imperial Washington's malodorous prosperity.

In any event, Mueller's attempted sabotage of the Helsinki summit via his indictment of 12 ham sandwiches from the GRU (Russian military security agency) had nothing to do with justice or genuine national security.

As to the former, there will never be any arrests, let alone a trial or conviction. That's because the source of Mueller's purported "evidence", memorialized in the indictment's 29 pages of spurious exactitude, is presumably classified.

So there can never be a legitimate trial — not with empty defendants' chairs and no admissible evidence that the government is willing to present in a public proceeding.

At the time, in fact, the despicable Rod Rosenstein made absolutely clear that those indictments were going directly into the dead letter file, with nary a passing swipe by Robert Mueller's vaunted prosecutors:

"The special counsel's investigation is ongoing and there will be no comments by the special counsel at this time ... we intend to transition responsibility for this indictment to the Justice Department's National Security Division (NSD) while we await the apprehension of the defendants."

Really?

To be sure, it would be hard to top that for rank cynicism, but that only begs the larger question. Namely, why in the world would anyone with honest intent risk blowing up a summit between the leaders of the world's principle nuclear powers in order to issue an indictment that was already buried in the round file before it was even issued?

Either the DOJ is fixing to send Seal Team Six into Moscow to snatch the 12 GRU operatives or it expects the Kremlin to dispatch them to Washington handcuffed to their seats on a Russian air force jet at the very next opportunity.

As it happened, fortunately, the Donald and Vlad put the fork in even that absurdly improbable prospect during their post-meeting presser.

That is, Putin referenced a 1999 cooperation agreement between the two countries on criminal matters and welcomed Mueller's grand inquisitors to come to Moscow to participate in an interrogation of the defendants; and the Donald welcomed it as a creative approach on the matter.

Needless to say, absolutely nothing has come of that offer in the months since because there never was any intent to bring the GRU 12 to justice.

Mueller's purpose, instead, was to countermand the decision of the US president to pursue the very objective of rapprochement with Russia that he promised the American electorate. Indeed, since Brennan and his Deep State ilk did not hesitate to bring up the "treason" word, Justin Raimondo's rejoinder at the time cannot be improved upon:

Yet the brazenness of this borderline treason is what makes it so ineffective. The American people aren't stupid: to the extent that they're paying attention to this Beltway comic opera they can figure out the motives and meaning of Mueller's accusations without too much difficulty.

The indictment reads like a fourth-rate spy thriller: we are treated to alleged "real time" transcripts of Boris and Natasha in action, draining the DNC's email system as well as our precious bodily fluids. This material, perhaps supplied by the National Security Agency, contains no evidence that links either Russia or the named individuals to the actions depicted in the transcripts. We just have to take Mueller's word for it.

Needless to say, the post-press conference hail of calumny at the Donald by a endless line of Dem pols made perfectly clear that the alleged Russian election meddling is a sideshow. In fact, the Dems are so distraught and unreconciled to their loss to surely the weakest presidential candidate ever fielded by the GOP (including Alf Landon and Barry Goldwater) that they have subordinated rationality itself to their pursuit of vendetta.

So doing, they have made the Democratic party the new handmaids of the Warfare State, as Justin Raimondo further aptly observed:

The disgusting – and depressing – response of the Democrats to the Helsinki summit has been a concerted campaign to ... cancel it. Yes, that's how myopic and in thrall to the Deep State these flunkies are: world peace, who cares? Never mind that we're still on hair-trigger alert, with our nukes aimed at their cities and their nukes targeting ours. The slightest anomaly could spark a nuclear exchange – the end of the world, the extinction of human life, and probably of most life, for quite some time to come.

And yet — what does the survival of the human race matter next to the question of how and why Hillary Clinton was denied her rightful place in history? I mean, really!

At the end of the day, the entire post-Helsinki contretemps in the Imperial City and across the MSM was not about a national security threat in any way, shape or form because Russia isn't one.

Time For A NATO Mercy Killing

And that brings us to another immense opportunity for peace that was implicit in the spirit of Helsinki. Had not the Donald been stopped cold by the hail of hysteria which emanated from the War Party and their dutiful stenographers in the main stream media, the next step would have been to take up where H. W. Bush faltered in 1991.

That is, on the dismantlement and interment of NATO and the re-opening of Europe to peaceful commerce among all the nation's that had been artificially separated by the now long departed Iron Curtain.

The fact is, Washington doesn't need its budget-busting *$720 billion* defense budget to defend Europe from Russia, nor

Expenditure of Nato Countries in 2016

Military spending of Nato countries and estimated share of GDP in 2016 (in millions of U.S. dollars)

Country	Spending	% of GDP
United States	664,058	3.6
United Kingdom	60,347	2.2
France	43,620	1.8
Germany	40,663	1.2
Italy	21,878	1.1
Canada	15,395	1.0
Turkey	11,573	1.6
Spain	11,064	0.9
Poland	9,349	2.0
Netherlands	9,016	1.2
Norway	5,936	1.5
Greece	4,550	2.4
Belgium	4,023	0.9
Denmark	3,474	1.2
Portugal	2,783	1.4
Romania	2,766	1.5
Czech Republic	1,930	1.0
Hungary	1,243	1.0
Slovak Republic	1.024	1.2
Bulgaria	663	1.4
Lithuania	630	1.5
Croatia	607	1.2
Estonia	497	2.2
Latvia	400	1.5
Slovenia	400	0.9
Luxembourg	263	0.4
Albania	144	1.2

should it be endlessly haranguing those nations to waste more of their own money on defense than they already are.

That's because there is absolutely no reason to believe that Russia wants to attack Germany or any other country in Europe. Indeed, the very idea is just plain madness.

As shown by the table above the NATO-28 (excluding the US) are now actually spending *$250 billion* per year on defense (2017). That's *4X* Russia's entire military budget of *$61 billion*.

Likewise, the GDP of Russia is but $1.5 trillion compared to $18 trillion for the NATO-28. So is Cool Hand Vlad so completely foolish and reckless as to think that he could invade and occupy territories that have an economy 13X bigger than that of Russia?

Actually, it's far more ludicrous than that. As we mentioned above, Russia is a giant hydrocarbon province attached to some wheat fields, timber lands and mineral deposits — all dependent upon an aging work force afflicted with an undue fondness for Vodka etc.

What that means is that Russia must export its commodities big time or die. In fact, during 2017 Russian exports totaled $357 billion or 26% of its GDP. And 55% of that went to Europe!

Moreover, when you breakdown Russian exports it is plain to see that the industrial maw of Europe is the port of first call for its vast tonnages of exported commodities. These included $173 billion of oil and gas and $60 billion of iron, steel, aluminum, precious metals, forest products, fertilizers, grains and copper, among others.

Finally, the table on defense spending by country below speaks for itself as to the purported Russian threat. If the German government really feared that Russian tanks would be soon rolling through the Brandenburg Gates, it would have more than 20 operational tanks, and it would spend far more than $40.6 billion or *1.2%* of GDP to defend itself.

And the same is even more true of the former Warsaw pact countries that are located cheek-by-jowl on Russia's border. Yet Romania spends the tiny sum of *$2.8 billion* or *1.2%* of GDP on its military.

Likewise, the figure for Hungary, which learned all about Soviet-style invasion in 1956, spends only $1.2 billion or barely 1.0% of GDP. And besides that, its intrepid leader, Viktor Orban, doesn't even support NATO's ridiculous sanctions on Putin's cronies and allies.

And as for the allegedly threatened Baltic states, their combined defense budgets are less than $1.5 billion, representing a miniscule 1.7% of combined GDP; and Bulgaria, fast upon the Russian Lake called the Black Sea, spends only $660 million or 1.4% of its GDP.

In short, European policy action on the defense spending front trumps all the hot air that wafts from NATO's spanking new Brussels headquarters. Their governments and parliaments positively do not think they are threatened by the Russian Bear because they aren't.

What would help alot, therefore, is for the Great Disrupter to forget about his unfortunate infatuation with the idea that bigger is always better, and do what no other American politician in thrall to the Warfare State has been unable to do since 1991 when the Soviet Union vanished.

That is, declare "mission accomplished" with respect to NATO and disband it forthwith.

You could call it a Mercy Killing, and yet a couple more NATO summits like the 2018 event, and the Europeans themselves may well start begging for exactly that.

NSA's Tailored Access Operations — The Typhoid Mary Of The Global Internet

Let us again observe that even in its current state of alleged disrepair and under-spending that the NATO-29 (including the

US) have a combined GDP of *$36 trillion* and military budget of *$1 trillion*.

Those figures are **24X** Russia's GDP of $1.5 trillion and **16X** its military budget of $61 billion. Accordingly, there is not a snow balls' chance in the hot place that the perfectly rational leader of what is actually a pint-sized nation, who stood alongside the Donald at the Helsinki press conference, has any illusions (or intentions) whatsoever about military aggression.

But now that he has thrown the gauntlet at the Deep State, we can hope that the Donald will reclaim his powers as the dully elected President of the United States and order an examination of the DNC computer that has been AWOL during this entire witch-hunt; and, even more to the point, declassify every single NSA intercept on which this comic book indictment was based — as well as all other classified material relating the Mueller witch-hunt.

We are perfectly willing to believe that operatives of the GRU went spear-phishing at the DNCC and DNC. And that like millions of everyday folks who fall for these gambits daily on a global internet that is rampant with hackers — some naïve or stupid DNC staffers, as the case may be, opened their digital kimono's to the intruders.

But so what?

None of the shenanigans and skull-doggery inside the Dem apparatus that were revealed to the American electorate were untrue. So how did the truth of the matter undermine America's democratic process of selecting a leader?

The only thing the Mueller indictment proves — even if it is accurate to the chapter and verse cited — is that if you live in a glass house, don't start throwing stones.

As we have previously mentioned, the US spends *$75 billion* per year on a colossal globe-spanning surveillance, hacking and internet intruding operation that makes the indictment's alleged GRU tom foolery look trite by comparison.

The recently renamed TAO (tailored access operations) alone consists of a dozen sprawling buildings in Maryland, Texas, Hawaii, Georgia and Colorado chock-a-block with a veritable army of military and civilian computer hackers, intelligence analysts, targeting specialists, computer hardware and software designers, and electrical engineers.

And their job is to do a thousand times over to foreign governments, elections and political processes exactly what the Mueller indictment charges against the GRU.

Indeed, TAO is the Typhoid Mary of the global internet, infecting systems of friend and foe alike with a continuous tsunami of implanted malware. While originally chartered as an eavesdropping agency, the NSA has embraced hacking as an especially nifty way to spy on foreign targets.

The intelligence collection is often automated with malware implants — computer code designed to find material of interest — left sitting on the targeted system for months or even years, sending files back to the NSA

According to the diligent 2013 investigation published by a leading German news site, Hamburg based Spiegel ONLINE, and based on leaked NSA documents, the US engages in massive malware implanting activities which are far more menacing than the primitive "phishing" operations described by Mueller's latest comic book:

One of the hackers' key tasks is the offensive infiltration of target computers with so-called implants or with large numbers of Trojans. They've bestowed their spying tools with illustrious monikers like "ANGRY NEIGHBOR," "HOWLERMONKEY" or "WATERWITCH." These names may sound cute, but the tools they describe are both aggressive and effective.

According to details in Washington's current budget plan for the US intelligence services, around 85,000 computers worldwide are projected to be infiltrated by the NSA specialists by the end of this year. By far the majority of these "implants" are conducted by

TAO teams via the Internet.

Nevertheless, TAO has dramatically improved the tools at its disposal. It maintains a sophisticated toolbox known internally by the name "QUANTUMTHEORY." "Certain QUANTUM missions have a success rate of as high as 80%, where spam is less than 1%," one internal NSA presentation states.

A comprehensive internal presentation titled "QUANTUM CAPABILITIES," which SPIEGEL has viewed, lists virtually every popular Internet service provider as a target, including Facebook, Yahoo, Twitter and YouTube.

Finally, why do we think these indictments were an utterly desperate move by Mueller?

Because the indictments go out of their way to deny that any Americans — especially dissident employees in the DNC — had any involvement in these "hacking events" at all; and to slam the door on the obvious probability that the DNC and Podesta emails were down-loaded on a memory stick and "leaked" to the outside world without any help from the Russians at all.

To that extent, Mueller succeeded in spades: From day one the wolf-pack was out howling — dripping with blood in tooth and claw — and since then has steadily smothered the chance for peace which came out of Helsinki.

Indeed, barely four months later at the Buenos Aires G-20, the Donald was railroaded into declining to even meet with Putin owing to the obvious attempt by the Ukrainians to provoke a crisis in the Kerch Strait. Yes, they deliberately sent war boats right into the shallow Russian territorial waters beneath the new $6 billion bridge that connects Crimea to the Russian mainland, — and that was enough to extinguish the spirit of Helsinki.

Still, we never thought we'd see the occasion when the Donald was actually lyrical, but alas back in July he rose to the occasion.

Said the Donald,

I would rather take a political risk in pursuit of peace than risk peace in pursuit of politics.

Truer words were never spoken.

So shame on Imperial Washington for its shrill attacks on a President who was actually seeking peace with a rival who has done no harm to America.

Apparently, the Deep State has won again.

PART 4

Deep State Debunked: Why RussiaGate Is Even Worse Than A Hoax

CHAPTER 22

Deep State Classified: Hey, Donald, Tear Down That Wall Of Secrecy

When the Donald promised to "drain the swamp" during the 2016 election campaign — it did sound vaguely like an attack on Big Government, and at least a directional desire to shrink the state and let free market capitalism breathe.

After 24 months in office, however, the truth is patently obvious: The only Swamp that Donald Trump wants to drain is one filled with his political enemies and policy adversaries at any given moment in time. Even then, you have to consult his tweetstorm ledger to know who the swamp creature de jour actually are.

Still, the Donald's daily Twitter assaults on the Deep State are a wondrous thing. They surely do undermine public confidence in rogue institutions like the FBI, CIA and NSA, which profoundly threaten America's constitutional liberties and fiscal solvency.

Likewise, his frequently unhinged tweets also lather their congressional sponsors and beltway poo-bahs with well-deserved mud and opprobrium. And the Donald's increasingly acrimonious public feuding with Deep State criminals like James Comey and John Brennan is just what the doctor ordered.

The Deep State thrives and milks the public treasury so successfully in large part because the Imperial City's corps of permanent policy apparatchiks like Comey and Brennan (and thousands more) pretend to be performing god's work. So doing, they preen sanctimoniously to the adoration of their sycophants in the mainstream media, claiming to be above any governance or sanction from the unwashed electorate.

Attacking this rotten perversion of democracy, therefore, is the Donald's real calling. While he lacks both the temperament and ideas to solve the nation's metastasizing economic and social challenges and has no hope whatsoever to make MAGA, he is more than suited for his "Great Disrupter" mission.

That is, the existing order needs to be discredited and brought down first, and on that score his primitive economic populism will more than do its part. As we have seen in Parts 1 and 2, Trump's deadly combination of Fiscal Debauchery, Protectionism and Easy Money will eventually blow the nation's debt and bubble-ridden economy sky-high.

Likewise, as we saw in Part 3, his crude rendition of America First is not a blueprint for rebooting America's national security policy, but it is an existential threat to Empire First and the Deep State's usurpation of constitutional government. And even as the Donald lurches to and fro on Russia, Korea, the Middle East, NATO, globalism and so-called allies, the main job is getting done. That is, the War Party's self-appointed role as global policeman and the Indispensable Nation is getting thoroughly discredited in Flyover America.

In terms of the Donald's great mission of wrecking the Deep State, we would only take issue with him to this extent: Why in the world does he not understand that he is actually President and has a far more powerful weapon at his disposal than his Twitter account — 44 million followers to the contrary notwithstanding?

To wit, he has the unquestioned constitutional power to both appoint and fire his own cabinet, sub-cabinet and upwards of 3,000 Schedule C policy jobs; and also to declassify anything lurking behind the Deep State's massive wall of unjustified secrecy if he deems it in the public interest.

Accordingly, Trump could have and should have fired Jeff Sessions long before he did and Rod Rosenstein even before that. After all, it is the spinelessness of the former and the Deep State treachery of the latter, that launched the hideous Mueller witch-hunt in the first place and that keeps it going from one absurdity to the next ridiculous over-reach.

Can there be anything more pitiful after 17 months of nothingburgers on the phony Russian collusion file than Mueller's list of indictments. These include:

- 13 Russian twenty-somethings for essentially practicing English as a third language at a St Petersburg troll farm for $4 per hour;
- 12 Russian intelligence operatives who might as well have been picked from the GRU phonebook;
- Baby George Papadopoulos for mis-recalling an irrelevant date by two weeks;
- Paul Manafort for standard Washington lobbyist crimes committed long before he met Trump;
- Michael Cohen for shirking taxes and running Trump's bimbo silencing operation;
- Michael Flynn for doing his job talking to the Russian Ambassador and confusing the confusable Mike Pence on what he said and didn't say about Obama's idiotic 11th hour Russian sanctions;
- Rick Gates for helping Manafort shakedown the Ukrainian government and other oily Washington supplicants.;
- Sam Patten, another Manafort operative who forget to register correctly as a foreign agent;
- Richard Pinedo, a grifter who never met Trump and got caught selling forged bank accounts on-line to Russians for a couple bucks each;

- Alex van der Zwaan, a Dutch lawyers who wrote a report for Manafort in 2012 and misreported to the FBI what he told Gates about it.

That's all she wrote and it's about as pathetic as it gets. If nothing else, the fact that Mueller hasn't been guffawed out of town on account of this tommyrot is a measure of the degree to which the Imperial City has fallen prey to the Trump Derangement Syndrome.

The Brennan Report — The Foundational Document of the RussiaGate Witch-Hunt

Still, we have to wonder why Trump doesn't get the joke. Long ago he could have declassified everything related to the foundational RussiaGate document. That is, the January 6, 2017 report entitled, "Assessing Russian Activities And Intentions in Recent US Elections."

The report was nothing of the kind, of course, and is now well-understood to have been written by outgoing CIA director John Brennan and a hand-picked posse of politicized analysts from the CIA, FBI and NSA. It was essentially a political screed thinly disguised as the product of the professional intelligence community and was designed to discredit and sabotage the Trump presidency.

As presented to the President-elect and released to the public in declassified form, it is all gussied-up with caveats, implying that the real dirt is in the "highly classified" version of the report. Except that's just the typical Deep State hide-the-ball trick: When it can't prove its assessments and judgments, it claims the evidence is top secret.

In the current case, the Imperial City is so red hot with Trump antipathy that any undisclosed smoking guns in the highly classified version would have leaked long ago. So the truth is, there is nothing more to the allegedly sinister Russian "influencing campaign" than the superficial blarney in the public version of the document.

And the latter boils down to ten pages of sweeping insinuations and airballs — plus a loony 9-page appendix which proves the totally public RT America cable TV network doesn't think much of the Washington's global meddling!

Indeed, we second the motion. In fact, when we first read this ballyhooed report our thought was that someone at the Onion had pilfered the CIA logo and published a side-splitting satire.

The 9-pager on RT America, which is presented as evidence of "Kremlin messaging", is so sophomoric and hackneyed that it could have been written by a summer intern at the CIA. It consists entirely of a sloppy catalogue of leftist and libertarian based dissent from mainstream policy that has been aired on RT America on such subversive topics as Occupy Wall Street, anti-fracking, police brutality, foreign interventionism and civil liberties.

Actually, your author has appeared dozens of times on RT America and advocated nearly every position cited by the CIA as evidence of nefarious Russian propaganda. And we thought it up all by ourselves!

So, yes, we do think US intervention in Syria was wrong; that Georgia was the aggressor when it invaded South Ossetia; that the American people have been disenfranchised and need to "take this government back"; that Washington runs a "surveillance state" where civil liberties are being ridden roughshod upon; that Wall Street is riven with "greed" and the "US national debt" is out of control; that the two-party system is a "sham "and that it doesn't represent the views of "one-third of the population" (at least!); and that most especially after killing millions in unnecessary wars Washington has "no moral right to teach the rest of the world."

So there you have it: Policy views on various topics that are embraced in some instances by both your libertarian author as well as the left-wing *Nation* magazine are held to be examples of Russian messaging, and alarming evidence of nefarious meddling in our electoral process at that.

Moreover, it turns out that RT America is not even in the top 95 cable channels according to published rankings, and may have an audience of less than 30,000 viewers per day according to even the rabidly anti-Putin *Daily Beast*. Still, by the lights of John Brennan and his coterie of CIA hacks, that's apparently 30,000 too many citizens being exposed to anti-establishment opinion.

In that regard, we especially got a yuck from the following example of RT's nefarious attempt to influence American voters. Not only have we uttered these very same thoughts on RT America, but we also conveyed them on the Fox Business network and didn't even get censored!

Some of RT's hosts have compared the United States to Imperial Rome and have predicted that government corruption and 'corporate greed' will lead to US financial collapse."

Needless to say, if this is an example of the work being done by the US intelligence community with its $75 billion annual budget, they are giving the idea of pouring money down a rathole an altogether new definition.

In fact, does the juvenile fool who penned this drivel think Washington is purer than Caesar's wife? The report whines and slobbers about RT America's indirect support from the Russian government and an alleged $190 million subsidy from the Russian state.

Yet Washington spends upwards of $800 million per year on the U.S. Agency for Global Media, which is the parent organization of its own international propaganda arms: Voice of America, Radio Free Europe/Radio Liberty, Radio y Television Marti, Radio Free Asia and the Middle East Broadcast Networks.

And that's just the tip of the iceberg. It doesn't count,

for example, the $170 million per year spent by the National Endowment for Democracy (NED) to subvert governments Washington doesn't like. Indeed, the two sub-agencies of NED (one for the Dems and one for the GOP) were chaired by two of Washington's most blood-thirsty regime changers — Madeleine Albright and the late Senator John McWar of Arizona.

Unlike RT America, of course, these two cats caused the deaths of hundreds of thousands of innocent civilians who happened to be domiciled in places they deemed in need of that very special kind of "influencing" that is delivered from the business end of a Tomahawk cruise missile.

Beyond that, there is billions more of "agit prop" and NGO funding that is channeled through the CIA, DOD, the State Department, the Agency for International Development and many more — all designed to "influence opinion" in dozens of foreign countries where the people need to be advised of the correct line from Washington.

Yet the report's mendacious attack on the utterly irrelevant RT America is the stronger part of the document!

The main body of the document consists of 10 pages of bloviation which amount to this: The very distinct probability that Vlad Putin strongly dislikes Hillary Clinton, who did liken him to Adolph Hitler; and preferred Donald Trump, who was a wet-behind-the-ears real estate gambler from New York City, thereby still in possession of sufficient common sense to see that Russia is no threat to America and that rapprochement with Putin was in order.

Actually, it gets a lot richer. The US government did spend tens of millions covertly supporting the so-called "color revolutions" on Russia's doorstep, including the Rose Revolution in Georgia, the Orange Revolution in Ukraine, the Tulip Revolution in Kyrgyzstan, the Jeans Revolution in Belarus, the Grape Revolution in Moldova and, most especially, the so-called pro-democracy protests in Russia during 2011-2013 that were aimed at vilifying and discrediting Vladimir Putin.

Yet Imperial Washington wears absolute blinders with respect to this kind of bald-faced meddling in the internal politics of other sovereign nations. There is not an iota of connection between the safety and security of the American people domiciled between their ocean moats and whatever some two-bit dictator is doing in Belarus or the intrigues of the communist party in Moldova.

Soft Power Aggression — How The Imperial City Makes a Living

The explanation for this kind of soft-power aggression, therefore, is not national security: It's what Imperial Washington does for a living. That is, the billions of taxpayer money being pumped through the foreign policy agencies, NGOs, think tanks, advocacy organizations and sleazy lobbying operations like those of the Podesta brothers and Paul Manafort finance there own raison d'etre.

Needless to say, it does not occur to the busy-bodies of the imperial city beehive that their meddling and interventions are not welcome or that the big sacks of walking around money they dispense end up being plundered arbitrarily by whichever faction of local bandits gets Washington's ear first.

In short, Washington's hands are so deep in the meddling business that blowback and political resentment abroad are absolutely certain to happen. In the case at hand, Putin has become deeply miffed about Washington's claim of a divine right to meddle in the political processes of any country it deems in need of being straightened out or uplifted, and especially when they form a ring around his own territory.

Still, the Brennan/CIA report not only takes Russia's legitimate pushback against Imperial Washington's machinations on its borders (and within, too) as proof of Putin's bad intentions; it actually leaps to the conclusion that Russia has retaliated in kind — with all the proof hidden behind a top secret classification stamp.

Putin most likely wanted to discredit Secretary Clinton because he has publicly blamed her since 2011 for inciting mass protests against his regime in the late 2011 and early 2012, and because he holds a grudge for comments he almost certainly saw as disparaging him"

And well he should, but so what?

Exactly, how does that prove the intent and fact of a secret nefarious plot to meddle in America's 2016 election? Besides, you didn't need any heavy lifting spooks on the ground in Moscow or internet hackers at NSA to understand Putin's minimum regard for Hillary Clinton; you could find chapter and verse about it on Google.

Likewise, does anyone with a pulse need a phalanx of CIA spooks and analysts to dig up the following remarkable insight, and why does such roundhouse philosophizing matter, anyway?

"...the Kremlin sought to advance its longstanding desire to undermine the US-led liberal order, the promotion of which Putin and other senior Russian leaders view as a threat to Russia and Putin's regime."

But here's the meat of the matter. The Deep State is so insular and intolerant of policy dissent when it comes to the projects of Empire that it apparently viewed Trump's far more rational views on Syria and Ukraine as a reason for suspecting that Putin was trying to throw the electoral college vote Trump's way:

"...Putin publicly indicated a preference for President-elect Trump's stated policy to work with Russia, and pro-Kremlin figures spoke highly about what they saw as his Russia-friendly positions on Syria and Ukraine. Putin publicly contrasted the President-elect's approach to Russia with Secretary Clinton's 'aggressive rhetoric."

Again, are we supposed to believe that Putin's fully logical public views are evidence that he plotted secretly to influence and alter the on-the-ground reality during America's election?

In fact, the single proposition in the entire ten-pages of political opinionating that relates to an actual Russian intrusion (other than the hideous St. Petersburg troll farm which we debunk in chapter 25) in the American electoral process is the completely discredited notion that the Russian GRU hacked the DNC emails and handed them off to Wikileaks:

"We assess with high confidence that the GRU used the Guccifer 2.0 persona, DCLeaks.com, and Wikileaks to release US victim data obtained in cyber operations......We assess with high confidence the GRU relayed material it acquired from the DNC and senior Democratic officials to Wikileaks...."

No, not at all.

As we detail below, William Binney, who is the father of modern NSA internet spying technologies, says that the DNC emails were **_leaked_** on a thumb-drive and couldn't have been **_hacked_** as a technical matter; and equally competent analysts have shown that Guccifer 2.0 is almost surely a NSA contrived fiction based on the oldest trick in the police precinct station house — planting evidence, in this case telltale Cyrillic letters and the name of a notorious head of the Soviet secret police.

Yet that's all they've got. To wit, an "assessment" that the Russian state caused some Democrat political skullduggery to get into the public domain based on "classified" evidence that they are not sharing, but if made public would easily disprove the charge.

And that get's us to the meat of the matter. If the Donald had had the experience and good sense to understand that this foundational report — that was thrown in his face on the eve of his inauguration — was a political attack document, not an intelligence community product, he would have released the classified version in its entirety on January 21, 2017.

That would have been the end of RussiaGate then and there because, as we will see in the balance of Part 4, there is absolutely no there, there; and that the entire collusion hoax embodied in the Brennan Report is really nothing more than a dim-witted attempt to conjure up a Russian assault on American democracy that absolutely did not happen.

And, to be clear, we are referring not just narrowly to the question of collusion by the Trump campaign or the Donald himself, but to the whole cock-and-bull story that there was some kind of sweeping, sinister and efficacious Russian influence operation during the 2016 election that impacted voters and reflected a hostile intent by Putin to "undermine the US-led democratic order."

Alas, the scam only got worse after the January 6th launch of the Deep State sabotage campaign. The Donald didn't get the joke then — so they just kept piling on, building the whole RussiaGate narrative on an insidious (and ludicrous) game of hide the ball behind a veil of classified secrets.

For crying out loud, the whole modus operandi of the Deep State in disenfranchising the open processes of American democracy is to hide everything from Congress and the American public behind a wall of secrecy. Thus, it was recently revealed that DOJ had classified a document which disclosed the *$70,000* cost of a new conference table for former FBI deputy director, Andrew McCabe; and when it was forced to turn-over the document under Congressional pressure, DOJ actually redacted the $70k cost on national security grounds!

Indeed, the absurdity of the whole secrecy wall behind which Deep State operatives hide is stunningly evident in the very mandate from Rod Rosenstein, which established the Special Counsel and gave Mueller his marching orders, charter, remit etc. To wit, parts of the damn thing (the August 3, 2017 addendum) are classified as "secret"!

That's right.

Supposedly, American democracy itself was imperiled by traitorous acts of Donald Trump and his campaign via collusion with Russia to rig the outcome of the 2016 election. Consequently, it was alleged that the extraordinary step of a Special Counsel investigation was necessary to protect the integrity and transparency of US elections, and that Mueller was to be the people's tribune charged with uncovering the corruption and treason.

Yet "the people" cannot even read the terms of Mueller's charter. And, indeed, a Federal judge presiding over the Manafort trial in Virginia had to literally pound the table to get his own private access to the document.

So the Deep State just keeps playing rope-a-dope with the Donald, attempting to nullify his election based on Fake Evidence hidden behind a wall of official secrecy. And yet he continues to eschew using the unquestioned powers of his office to *declassify* the whole shooting match.

In this context, consider two items that point to the absurdity of the secrecy wall Washington is throwing in the Donald's face.

First, the only thing that even remotely qualifies as "influencing" the 2016 election was the release of the highly compromising emails from the DNC and Hillary Clinton's campaign chairman, John Podesta.

But if the Russians did it — from a troll farm in St. Petersburg or the Kremlin itself — the fingerprints from any remote hacking operation would be all over the computers involved. Moreover, the National Security Agency (NSA) would have a record of the breach stored at one of its server farms because it does capture and store everything that comes into the US over the internet.

Said record, of course, would amount to the Smoking Intercept. So the only think the Donald really needs to do is call the head of NSA to the carpet and tell him to put up or shut-up. That is to say, if Russia did hack the DNC — then declassify and publish the NSA intercept.

In the alternative, if NSA has no such record, confiscate the DNC computers — which have never even been inspected by the FBI let alone taken into custody — and determine whether William Binney is right.

The latter is a 30-year NSA veteran and actually the father of much of today's NSA internet spying capability. Binney says that the recorded download speed of the DNC emails could only have been done by plugging a thumb-drive into the machines on site. That is, nothing downloads across 5,000 miles of digital expanse at the recorded 22.7 megabytes per second.

So figuratively speaking, the Donald only needs to dial-up Vlad on the red phone and offer him a chance to prove that Russia didn't do it. All that would be required is for him to give Putin the DNC's IP address and invite him to run a test to see if the Kremlin's hackers can sprint at 22.7 megabytes per second.

How simple is that!

And failing this kind of bold theatrics, just have some reliable and competent people test the DNC servers. If the Russians hacked them, the evidence is all there in the hard drives; and if they didn't, the entire RussiaGate hoax could be shutdown once and for all.

Cyber Garbage From The St. Petersburg Troll Farm

After all, the only other part of the meddling narrative that remotely qualifies is the pitiful efforts of the Russian troll farm called the Internet Research Agency (IRA). The latter is work place of the 13 ham sandwiches that Mueller wasted the taxpayers' dollars indicting. **(See chapter 25)**.

The pure grandstanding nature of this blow against the purported election meddling of the nefarious Russians is more than evident in the 3,000 ads IRA bought on Facebook for about $100,000 — many of which were posted after the election.

These ads have now been released by the Congressional investigators. So here's a typical example of how the Russians stormed into America's sacred election space — even if according to Facebook this particular ad got less than 10,000 "impressions" and the mighty sum of 160 "shares."

For crying out loud, it didn't take any nefarious Russian intelligence agent to post this kind of cartoonish Islamophobia. There are millions of American xenophobes more than happy to do it with their own dime, time and bile.

Still, the fact that these Facebook ads and the St Petersburg troll farm are taken seriously shows how insidious the Deep State's RussiaGate campaign has been. In order to prove that their writ and rule will not be denied by the American electorate, they have cynically fostered a mindless public hysteria that makes the work of Joe McCarthy appear benign by comparison.

Yet the Donald can't seem to target his arrows where they belong. When these ads were released earlier this spring, the White House coms operation should have been all over them like a wet blanket, burying them in ridicule and derision — enlightening the American public to the utter farce of the whole notion that $100k

worth of stupid Facebook ads had any impact whatsoever on an election campaign in which more than *$20 billion* was spent one way or another.

And during a period, by the way, when the 80,000 Facebook posts attributable to IRA were up against the 33 trillion messages posted on that fetid network by its billions of users.

Indeed, talk about shooting fish in a barrel. Even Keeping Up With The Kardashians voters would get a pretty good yuck from the example displayed below.

A post called "Power to the people!" was typed out by some troll farm operative in St Petersburg, whose $4 per hour pay probably was not worth the effort: It was shared by the grand some of *20* people, who might well have been algos, anyway!

The fact is, the "evidence" for Russian meddling is nonsense, and if there was no "meddling", how could there have been "collusion" to accomplish something which didn't happen?

What we are saying is that the Trump White House has been totally asleep at the switch. The public release of these ludicrous Facebook posts should have been accompanied by the wholesale *declassification* of the trove of evidence held by agencies of the Deep State with respect to the Russian troll farm.

It would have shown how Brennan & Co literally manufactured the RussiaGate narrative from wholecloth; illegally and abusively used the nation's intelligence apparatus to meddle in a domestic election campaign; and then leaked to the press like a sieve to thwart Trump's election before November 8 and savage his legitimacy afterwards.

To be sure, Trump is undoubtedly bombarded constantly with the old canard that declassification would jeopardize "methods and sources." But every U.S. friend, foe, enemy and fake ally on the planet knows that the massive *$75 billion* intelligence agency complex intercepts and captures everything which moves and everything which stands still on the entire worldwide web.

So virtually everything which is captured electronically could be declassified with no harm done — except to reveal the nightmarish insanity of what the 17 intelligence agencies do day in and day out.

Williams&Kalvin
Sponsored ·

Like Page

Power to the People! We have to grow up, we have to wise up.
We don't have any other choice this time but boycott the election.
This time we choose between two racists. No one represents Black people.
Don't go to vote. Only this way we can change the way of things....
See More

108 Reactions 32 Comments 20 Shares

Like   Comment   Share

Likewise, virtually any and all internal government communications which are now hiding behind a "Secret" stamp — such as the Obama White House's "unmasking " requests in the run-up to the election and after — could and should also be declassified.

After all, you can't have a workable democracy and rule by the people if the permanent ruling class in the Imperial City can hide behind a massive and impenetrable wall of secret documents, communications, projects and procedures.

In fact, other than in the utmost special circumstances, no intergovernmental communications should ever be classified as "Secret." Full stop.

That gets us, of course, to the ballyhooed issue of protecting HUMINT (human intelligence) and the purportedly courageous CIA operatives spread around the world conducting good old fashioned spycraft and skullduggery.

Needless to say, if Washington didn't pretend to be the global hegemon and seat of the Indispensable Nation there are precious few places that it would actually need clandestine spies. The Islamic State is no more, for instance, and Syria, Iraq and Yemen are none of Washington's business.

Apparently, we do have a few spies on the ground in Iran,

but what good are they? Washington had no clue whatsoever in 2013 that the middle of the road statesman, Hassan Rouhani, was going to win the presidential election.

Likewise, a peace deal with Putin would do far more for American security than whatever dozens of spooks Washington now has running around the fleshpots of Moscow.

And the same goes for China. Open sources on the ground, satellites in the sky and NSA's internet dragnet tell Washington all it needs to know about the Red Ponzi's tottering tower of debt — the very survival of which requires that its economy keeps shipping $500 billion per year of exports to America.

By contrast, attacking 4,000 US Wal-Marts and their surrounds would be suicidal for Beijing's communist ruling party, and at least that much about economics even the Red suzerains of Beijing surely know.

The Stefan Halper Caper — Same Old, Same Old

Anyway, consider the cause celebre of a few months ago — professor Stefan Halper, who apparently befriended some low level Trump campaign flunkies (Carter Page and George Papadopoulos) at the behest of the CIA. This man both literally and figuratively would be hard to hide — since he has been an open source CIA asset since at least the late 1970s.

Stefan Halper

Even after all Halper's dirty laundry came out, the Deep State handmaids at CNN refused to speak his name on the air for fear of what — jeopardizing his life and safety?

C'mon. During the last several years alone, Halper has harvested *$1 million* in consulting contracts from a nasty little

DOD operation called the "Office of Net Assessment."

But these utterly wasteful contracts — which came in $250,000 installments — are published in a government register of contract awards. That is, Halper is a publicly disclosed parasite, not a valuable secret "asset" doing heroic work in behalf of homeland security.

Indeed, this man is hiding nowhere and is a secret to exactly nobody. And as to his 40 years of open air service as an asset of the Deep State, we can attest from personal experience.

Our entry into the cabinet of Ronald Reagan as a young Michigan congressman way back in 1980 was a fluke happenstance owing to having been chosen to play the role of Jimmy Carter during a week of mock debate rehearsals with the Gipper.

And we, apparently, came across during those practice sessions as a stand-out in the eyes of the soon to be president of the United States. But mainly, as it happened, because we had the advantage of preparing for the rehearsals with a stolen copy of Jimmy Carter's debate briefing book!

And, yes, we mention this because the pilfering act that landed Carter's briefing book on our doorstep in Georgetown was the fruit of a Reagan campaign operation populated with CIA types and run by, well, Stefan Halper!

Moreover, when we subsequently got the job as director of OMB and needed a deputy director for national security programs we tried to recruit Halper, who was the son-in-law of a legendary CIA operative at the time named Ray Cline.

Alas, even then the Deep State functioned as an old boys network, and the latter did not trust the egomaniacal incoming Secretary of State, Al Haig.

So it told us, no dice on Halper and, instead, sent him over to the State Department to man a post where he could keep a close eye on General Haig.

In any event, the Donald is being flummoxed and then some in his true mission as the Great Disrupter because he fails to use the tools that would make a difference. That is, he should be firing the Deep State operatives and their patsies who are systematically undermining his presidency and declassifying their nefarious doings, which are now hidden behind the phony veil marked "Secret."

CHAPTER 23

The Donald Undone: Tilting At The Swamp, Succumbing To The Empire

You can't build the Empire and drain the Swamp at the same time. That's because the Swamp is largely the fruit of Empire. And it's also the reason that the Donald is being rapidly undone.

Indeed, it is the Empire's *$800 billion* national security budget which feeds Washington's vast complex of weapons suppliers, intelligence contractors, national security bureaucrats, NGOs, think tanks, K-street lobbies, so-called "law" firms and all-purpose racketeers. It's what accounts for the Imperial City's unseemly and ill-gotten prosperity.

It goes without saying that the number one priority of these denizens of Empire is to keep the gravy train rolling. That is accomplished by inventing and exaggerating threats to America's homeland security and by formulating far-flung and misbegotten missions designed to extend and reinforce Washington's global hegemony.

As we demonstrated in Chapter 18, a true homeland security defense budget would consist of the strategic nuclear triad and modest conventional forces to defend the nation's shoreline and air space; it would cost about *$250 billion* per year plus a few $10 billion more for a State Department which minded its own business.

So the *$500 billion* difference is the fiscal cost of Empire, which is pushing the US toward an immense generational fiscal crisis. But it's also a measure of the giant larder that fills the Swamp with the projects and busywork of Washington's global hegemony.

In fact, it is the vasty deep of that $500 billion larder which gives rise to the forces that not only thwart the Donald's desire to drain the Swamp, but actually enlist him the cause of deepening its brackish waters.

Moreover, these missions encompass far more than direct military occupations, such as in Afghanistan and Iraq; or indirect aggressions, such as in Washington's arming of anti-government terrorists in Syria and facilitating and supplying Saudi Arabia's genocidal bombing campaign in Yemen; or even the kind of rank provocation implicit in the 29,000 troops Washington still bivouacs on the Korean peninsula 65 years after the war there ended and the thousands of US and NATO forces which conduct virtually constant maneuvers and war games on the very borders of Russia.

OFAC And Washington's Economic Sanctions Strike Force

Beyond the Empire's purely military dimension lies a vast stratum of economic and financial warfare. The US currently has sanctions — trade, financial and proscribed nationals — on more than 30 countries including highly visible alleged malefactors like Russia, Iran and North Korea — but also Lebanon, Liberia, Libya, Somalia, Sudan and Syria, to name a few.

These sanctions are enforced by an office in the US Treasury Department, which is aptly named the Office of Foreign Asset Control (OFAC). Being openly in the business of controlling the assets of foreign countries, in fact, its name speaks volumes about the daily purposes of the Imperial City.

In addition to enforcement actions against the above named three dozen countries, OFAC's global reach has been fantastically expanded by the so-called war on terror, and the mechanism of sanctioning "Specially Designated Nationals" or SDNs.

We are here talking about individual citizens and officers of foreign countries, one at a time. It so happens that the OFAC periodically publishes a list of SDNs and the latest one (May 24, 2018) is a staggering *1,132 pages* long. By our reckoning it lists in excess of *500,000* foreign evil doers of one type or another.

The fact that it takes *221 pages* just to get through the "A's" in its alphabetical listing — owing to the prevalence of Ali's, Abdul's, and Ahmed's — is perhaps indicative of the nature and scope of Washington's SDN dragnet.

Needless to say, sanctioning 500,000 foreigners generates endless make-work for the denizens of the Swamp and the phalanx of national security agencies and private contractors which employ them. But it's all in a day's work in the Empire because this list exists only by virtue of Washington's self-appointed role of global policeman and hegemon of global order.

Moreover, the list now encompasses far more than the Abdul's and Ahmed's arising from the Imperial City's misbegotten "war on terror." In truth, the latter has actually been a hatchery of terror in the form of blowback and vengeful retaliation for Washington's military devastation of the Middle East and elsewhere.

Nevertheless, there are also thousands of Russian, Iranian and Chinese names on this list owing to Washington's putting a hex on certain disapproved behaviors and policies of these nations. And many tens of thousands more names appear for the sin of not compliantly observing Washington's sanctions on third-parties with which they had wished to do business.

That is, OFAC is now into a higher level of sanctioning those who fail to sanction the sanctioned.

Here's the thing. Almost none of this busywork of Empire has anything to do with the safety and security of the American homeland.

It is the fruit of middle eastern interventions and occupations which should never have happened — going all the way back to the first Gulf War and all that followed.

Indeed, it goes back even further in time to Washington's siding with Saddam Hussein during the 1980s Iran/Iraq War and to the so-called Charlie Wilson's War during which the CIA recruited and armed the mujahedeen in Afghanistan against the Soviets after the latter's misbegotten invasion of the "graveyard of empires" in 1979.

It is also the fruit of a needless demonization of Russia and Putin, which , as we have seen, comprise no threat to the American homeland whatsoever; and also, increasingly, the designation of alleged Chinese malefactors for failure to enforce Washington's foreign policy.

Imperial Arrogance: Sanctioning China For Not Enforcing Washington's Economic War On Iran

The Trump Administration's recent attempt — purposeful or not — to destroy China's second largest telecom supplier (ZTE) is an hideous case in point. Once upon a time that would have been considered an act of war, but under the aegis of Empire the shoe goes on the other foot: It's China's fault, apparently, that ZTE failed to comply with Washington's hex on Iran.

In effect, the Donald is getting sucked into functioning as another handmaid of Empire rather than actually performing the noble work of draining the Swamp. After all, the essence of draining the Swamp boils down to shrinking the state and unleashing the energies of free market capitalism — including generation of more export to the rest of the world.

But in the ZTE case, Trump and his neocon and warhawk advisors were doing just the opposite. They had slapped an edict on US telecom component and software suppliers like Qualcomm, prohibiting them from engaging in acts of trade with China's #2 telecom equipment manufacturer and the #4 mobile phone provider in the world.

That is, they were about the business of pumping the Swamp full with even more busybody regulation and bloat — and once again bamboozling the Donald with phony threats to national security.

In this case, ZTE apparently violated "sanctions" put upon Iran and North Korea by the Empire in its self-appointed role of global policeman.

That's right. There have been no charges that ZTE has "stolen" American technology or subsidized exports to the harm of American cell phone factories — because, well, there are none left.

The Chinese state-owned company's only alleged offense, in fact, was not functioning as a complaint enforcement arm of Washington's foreign sanctions strike force.

But threatening to bring daily production at ZTE to a halt because it cannot (in the short-run) make cell phones without those designed-in Qualcomm parts, the Donald was also in danger of putting the kibosh on American production, jobs and leadership in the high technology components end of ZTE's business.

Since ZTE sits on a giant mountain of debt, however, the Chinese had no choice in the near term except to bend over and request Washington's bar of soap. To that end, in fact, they are now negotiating the complete housecleaning of the company's board and top executives and replacing them with names satisfactory to Washington.

Indeed, when this compromise settlement with China was announced a few months ago, we learned that the Donald had told his "friend" President Xi Jinping that in return for letting ZTE off the sanctions hook, Washington would be happy to collect a $1.3 billion fine and take control of company's board and management!

But here's the thing. ZTE is not only a state-owned company; it's also a core national technology champion in the

Red Ponzi's statist scheme of economic management.

So the idea that Washington should control ZTE is flat-out idiotic, yet it stems 100% from the Empire's hex on Iran and North Korea — a futile, destructive exercise in the sanctions game which never should have happened in the first place.

As we explained in Part 3, Iran should be free to conduct a foreign policy of its own choosing in its own middle eastern neighborhood; and that if we got the machinery of war and empire out of the way, the Koreans — north and south — would readily find a way to denuclearize, demilitarize and economically reunite.

And yet that's not the half of it. The Donald's doddering Secretary of Commerce and former crony capitalist thief, Wilbur Ross, explained to bubble vision at the time of the July deal that "compliance" would be assured by placing an entire squadron of Washington operatives inside the company on a permanent basis to makes sure it does not again violate Washington's sanctions and other edicts.

That's right. Wilbur proposes to run China's giant state telecom company from the Commerce Department Building on *Constitution Avenue*.

That's draining the swamp?

Well, at least there is some irony — surely not intended — in proposing to control a communist state industrial behemoth from Constitution Avenue.

Then again, through the largesse of the state and the Fed's Bubble Finance, Wilbur Ross became a self-proclaimed billionaire, like his boss.

So how would either have a clue about draining the real statist Swamp?

China Trade Deal — Recipe For A Big Washington Trade Nanny

And that get's us to the Donald utterly wrong-headed pursuit of an overall "trade deal" with China — a prospect that has the far-flung agencies and contractors in the Imperial City giddy with anticipation. It would simply mean a whole new regime of economic meddling, trade management, bureaucratic enforcement and sanctions for not measuring up.

It would also have the meters running overtime at Washington's law firms and consultancies, which would be over-run with demand from Chinese companies and state agencies seeking help with "compliance."

The fact is, America doesn't need no stinkin' trade deal with China.

Yes, as we have seen, we did import *$526 billion* last year from China compared to just *$130 billion* of exports. But that *$396 billion* deficit is due to factors that trade negotiators and enforcement bureaucrats could not fix in a month of Sundays. As we have shown, it's an artifact of bad money and the machinations of central bankers, starting with the Fed.

So even though China doesn't import much, it's not mainly owing to its high tariffs or its labyrinth of non-tariff barriers. Instead, it results from the fact that Beijing has run the People Printing Press overtime for the last 25 years and has thereby buried its economy in *$40 trillion* of unsustainable and unrepayable debt — debts that will eventually grind its economy to a halt or trigger the mother of all financial implosions.

In the interim, however, it won't import much because most foreign suppliers — and most especially the US — cannot compete with a state controlled economy temporarily blessed with spanking new, debt-financed capital equipment, essentially proletarian labor in a red economy and a minimal welfare state burden on businesses owing (temporarily) to favorable demographics and the stingy benefit policies of its allegedly socialist rulers in Beijing.

Thus, even if the Donald should succeed in strong-arming Beijing into tripling its current *$15 billion* of agricultural imports from the US and doubling its *$20 billion* of energy imports, the resulting *$50 billion* uptick in combined exports from these sectors wouldn't make a dent in the trade deficit.

And even if they do cut their tariffs on auto imports as promised, that's not going to amount to a hill of beans, either. That because a long time ago all high volume US auto producers — GM, Ford and Chrysler — recognized that taking coals to Newcastle was the better part of wisdom.

That is, they all moved their assembly plants and their parts suppliers to China where they face capital and labor costs that are only a fraction of those in the US. Accordingly, there is not a snowball's chance in the hot place that US based production — other than perhaps in the case of tiny volumes of niche or prestige vehicles — can compete in China's 30 million unit auto market.

Even when it comes to the heavy capital equipment made by Caterpillar or the advanced commercial aircraft supplied by Boeing — -these US suppliers are doing a increasing share of their production and valued added in their own or JV plants in China, not Peoria and Seattle.

And as to most consumer goods, fuggetaboutit!

On the other hand, the Donald doesn't have a clue about the other side of the equation — the *$526 billion* of annual US imports from China. That baleful fact, however, is the legacy of 30 years of monetary central planning by the Fed, not cheating by the Chinese.

The essence of the Fed's false prosperity trick was to enable American households to live beyond their means by raising their debts by nearly *6X* to $15.6 trillion during the last three decades — even as wage and salary incomes grew by only *3.7X*.

The difference essentially reflected unearned consumption borrowed from the economic future, but also on the margin was supplied by goods emanating from the far lower cost factories of the Red Ponzi.

At the same time, as we have seen, the Fed's insensible pursuit of *2.00%* inflation essentially inflated the cost-price-wage structure of the US economy, and at the very worst time imaginable: That is, after Mr. Deng's early 1990's pronouncement that it is "glorious to be rich" and its adoption of mercantilist, credit fueled, state-driven economic development model.

Compensation to Employees

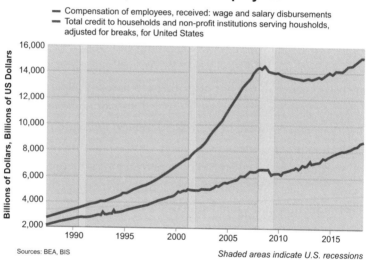

— Compensation of employees, received: wage and salary disbursements
— Total credit to households and non-profit institutions serving housholds, adjusted for breaks, for United States

Sources: BEA, BIS

Shaded areas indicate U.S. recessions

In a word, China was draining its rice paddies of cheap industrial labor, thereby driving the global labor cost curve downward — at the very time that the geniuses in the Eccles Building did their level best to inflate the nominal wage levels of US factories in the opposite direction. The result was that the borrowed consumption of the American household sector got supplied by the peasantry-turned-factory worker in the Red Ponz1.

So, is some kind of Imperial City fostered "trade deal" going to alter these deeply embedded historical legacies?

No, they will not — that is, at least not until sound money policies are once again replanted in the Eccles Building.

The arrival of Janet Yellen in tie and trousers at the helm of the Fed, however, means that the one chance the Donald had to do something meaningful about the China trade gap has been blown.

That's not only owing to the appointment of Jerome Powell, who is a Keynesian Imperial City lifer, but also due to the constant drumbeat of suggestion from the White House that the Donald is a "low interest man" and would prefer to keep the monetary status quo in place; or more recently, has even demanded that the Fed cut an interest rate target that is still negative in real terms..

So why is the Donald wasting his time and fueling growth of Imperial Washington via his "art of the deal" dueling with President Xi?

In part, of course, that's because the Donald has been a life-long dyed-in-the-wool protectionist — a virtual paragon of 18th century mercantilism.

Needless to say, protectionism and mercantilism are the health of the Swamp because they rest on government-to-government deals, not the enlightened self-interest and mutual benefits of capitalist commerce.

Accordingly, the central pillar of the Donald's economic policy — new bilateral "trade deals" — is inherently designed to fill the Swamp, not drain it.

In the first place, if the Red Suzerains are economically benighted enough to figuratively throw rocks into their own harbors to repel imports and to subsidize exports with cheap credit, repressed wages and other state subventions, guess what?

It's their wealth being penalized, not America's. The Red Ponzi is effectively sending foreign aid to America!

Technology Protectionism — Trojan Horse Of The Warfare State

And it is here where the Imperial City has taken the Donald by the short orange ones. The Warfare State sees trade as just another venue of battle — -and in this case based on the completely spurious notion that China's alleged theft of US intellectual property is a threat to national security.

That just patent nonsense because nearly every technology in today's world is dual use. So if you start with the false premise that China has the will and capability to threaten America militarily — either now or in the relevant future — you are automatically embarking down the road of state control of the economy and an ever deeper Swamp in the Imperial City.

The fact is, the Red Ponzi is a giant house of cards that cannot survive in the long-run, and in the mid-term is completely dependent of US markets to earn the dollar surpluses that it needs to keep its $40 trillion tower of debt from having a crash landing.

So the truth is, it doesn't matter what technologies the Chinese have — they are almost definitionally not a threat to the American homeland. Nevertheless, the Donald's glandular protectionism plays right into the hands of the Washington hegemonists.

They now have him busily attempting to administer a trade spanking to China because purportedly it does not buy enough American soybeans, LNG and Ford Explorers.

But the Deep State has something far bigger in mind. Namely, the complete control of trade in the name of national security in the new age of advanced information technology — and on that front the Donald is turning out to be a battering ram beyond their wildest dreams.

For instance, here is what a true Swamp creature has to say about the matter. Mr. Paul Rosenzweig is apparently a Republican but actually a certified denizen of the Imperial City.

"I knew what was critical in 1958 — tanks, airplanes, avionics. Now, truthfully, everything is information. The world is about information, not about things," said Paul Rosenzweig, who worked with CFIUS while at the Department of Homeland Security during President George W. Bush's second term. "And that means everything is critical infrastructure. That, in some sense, means CFIUS really should be managing all global trade."

Needless to say, the misbegotten China Trade Deal is only one of the avenues by which the Empire has enlisted the Donald in the business of deepening the Swamp, not draining it.

CHAPTER 24

The Actual 2016 Election Meddling Plot — The Deep State's Assault On Donald Trump

There was a sinister plot to meddle in the 2016 election, after all. But it was not orchestrated from the Kremlin; it was an entirely homegrown affair conducted from the inner sanctums of the Imperial City — the White House, DOJ, the Hoover Building and Langley.

Likewise, the perpetrators didn't speak Russian or write in the Cyrillic script. In fact, they were lifetime beltway insiders occupying the highest positions of power in the US government.

Here are the names and rank of the principal conspirators: John Brennan, CIA director; Susan Rice, National Security Advisor; Samantha Power, UN Ambassador; James Clapper, Director of National Intelligence; James Comey, FBI director; Andrew McCabe, Deputy FBI director; Sally Yates, deputy Attorney General, Bruce Ohr, associate deputy AG; Peter Strzok, deputy assistant director of FBI counterintelligence; Lisa Page, FBI lawyer; and countless other lesser and greater poobahs of Washington power, including President Obama himself.

To a person, the participants in this illicit cabal shared the core trait that made Obama such a blight on the nation's well-being. To wit, he never held an honest job outside the halls of government in his entire adult life; and as a careerist agent of the state and practitioner of its purported goods works, he exuded a sanctimonious disdain for everyday citizens who make their living along the capitalist highways and by-ways of America.

The above cast of election-meddlers, of course, comes from the same mold. If Wikipedia is roughly correct, just these ten named perpetrators have collectively punched in about 300 years of post-graduate employment — and 260 of those years (87%) were on government payrolls or in the employ of government contractors.

As to whether they shared Obama's political class arrogance, Peter Strzok left nothing to the imagination in his now celebrated texts to his gal-pal, Lisa Page:

"Just went to a southern Virginia Walmart. I could SMELL the Trump support......I LOATHE congress....And F Trump."

You really didn't need the ALL CAPS to get the gist.

In a word, the anti-Trump cabal is comprised of thoroughly statist denizens of the Swamp.

Their now obvious effort to alter the outcome of the 2016 election was nothing less than the Imperial City's immune system attacking an alien threat, which embodied the very opposite trait: That is, the Donald had never spent one moment on the state's payroll, had been elected to no government office and displayed a spirited contempt for the groupthink and verities of officialdom in the Imperial City.

But it is the vehemence and flagrant transparency of this conspiracy to first prevent Trump's ascension to the Oval Office and then discredit and disable his Presidency that reveals the profound threat to capitalism and democracy posed by the Deep State and its prosperous elites and fellow travelers domiciled in the Imperial City.

That is to say, Donald Trump was no kind of anti-statist and only a skin-deep economic populist, at best. Even his signature anti-immigrant meme was apparently discovered by accident when in the early days of the campaign he went off on Mexican thugs, rapists and murderers — only to find that it resonated strongly among a certain element of the GOP grass roots.

But a harsh line on immigrants, refugees and Muslims would not have incited the Deep State into an attempted coup d'état. It wouldn't have mobilized so overtly against Ted Cruz, for example, whose positions on the ballyhooed terrorist/ immigrant threat were not much different than Trump's.

Why The Donald Incited Apoplexy In The Imperial City

No, what sent the Imperial City establishment into a fit of apoplexy was exactly two things that struck at the core of its raison d' etre.

First was Trump's stated intentions to seek rapprochement with Putin's Russia and his sensible embrace of a non-interventionist "America First" view of Washington's role in the world. And secondly, and even more importantly, was his very persona.

That is to say, the role of today's president is to function as the suave, reliable maître d' of the Imperial City and the lead spokesman for Washington's purported good works at home and abroad. And for that role the slovenly, loud-mouthed, narcissistic, bombastic, ill-informed and crudely-mannered Donald Trump was utterly unqualified.

Stated differently, welfare statism and warfare statism is the secular religion of the Imperial City and its collaborators in the mainstream media; and the Oval Office is the bully pulpit from which its catechisms, bromides and self-justifications are propagandized to the unwashed masses — the tax-and-debt-slaves of Flyover America who bear the burden of its continuation.

Needless to say, the Never Trumpers were eminently correct in their worry that Trump would sully, degrade and weaken the Imperial Presidency. That he has done in spades with his endless tweet storms that consist mainly of petty score settling, self-justification, unseemly boasting and shrill partisanship; and on top of that you can pile his impetuous attacks on friend, foe and bystanders (e.g. NFL kneelers) alike.

Yet that is exactly what has the Deep State and its media collaborators running scared. To wit, Trump's entire modus operandi is not about governing or a serious policy agenda — and most certainly not about Making America's Economy Great Again. (MAEGA)

As we have seen, by appointing a passel of Keynesian monetary central planners to the Fed and launching an orgy of fiscal recklessness via his massive defense spending and tax-cutting initiatives, the Donald has more than sealed his own doom: There will unavoidably be a massive financial and economic crisis in the years just ahead and the rulers of the Imperial City will most certainly heap the blame upon him with malice aforethought.

In the interim, however, what the Donald is actually doing is sharply polarizing the country and using the Bully Pulpit for the very opposite function assigned to it by Washington's permanent political class. Namely, to discredit and vilify the ruling elites of government and the media and thereby undermine the docility and acquiescence of the unwashed masses upon which the Imperial City's rule and hideous prosperity depend.

It is no wonder, then, that the inner circle of the Obama Administration plotted an "insurance policy." They saw it coming. That is, Trump would be an offensive rogue disrupter who was soft on Russia, to boot — and out of that alarm the entire hoax of RussiaGate was born.

When The RussiaGate Hoax Was Born — August 15, 2016

As is now well known from the dump of thousands of Strzok/Gates text messages, there occurred on August 15, 2016 a meeting in the office of FBI Deputy Director Andrew

McCabe to kick off the RussiaGate campaign. As Strzok later wrote to Page, who was also at the meeting:

"I want to believe the path you threw out for consideration in Andy's office — that there's no way he gets elected — but I'm afraid we can't take that risk......It's like an insurance policy in the unlikely event that you die before you're 40."

They have tried to spin this money quote seven-ways to Sunday, but in the context of everything else now known there is only one possible meaning: The national security and law enforcement machinery of the Imperial City was being activated then and there in behalf of Hillary Clinton's campaign.

Indeed, the trail of proof is quite clear. At the very time of this August 2016 meeting, the FBI was already being fed the initial elements of the Steele dossier, and the latter had nothing to do with any kind of national security investigation.

For crying out loud, it was plain old "oppo research" paid for by the Clinton campaign and the DNC. The only way that it bore on Russian involvement in the US election, ironically, was in the form of its very own footprints: Virtually all of the salacious material about the Donald and the false narratives about Trump emissaries meeting with high level Russian officials was disinformation *sourced* in Moscow, and was completely untrue.

At the same time, there is no real public evidence based on hard NSA intercepts that prove Russian government agents were behind the only two acts — the leaks of the DNC emails and the Podesta emails — that were of even minimal import to the outcome of the 2016 presidential campaign. As we showed in chapter 22, the blather in Mueller's indictment about the GRU 12 is completely suspect. Besides, if true, the intercepts proving it would have leaked long ago.

As to the veracity of the dossier, the raving anti-Trumper and former CIA interim chief, Michael Morrell, settled the matter. If you are paying ex-Russian intelligence agents for information from the back streets of Moscow, the more you pay, the more "information" you will get:

Then I asked myself, why did these guys provide this information, what was their motivation? And I subsequently learned that he paid them. That the intermediaries paid the sources and the intermediaries got the money from Chris. And that kind of worries me a little bit because if you're paying somebody, particularly former [Russian Federal Security Service] officers, they are going to tell you truth and innuendo and rumor, and they're going to call you up and say, 'Hey, let's have another meeting, I have more information for you,' because they want to get paid some more,' Morrell said.

Far from being "verified," the dossier is best described as a pack of lies, gossip, innuendo and irrelevancies. Take, for example, the dossier's claim that Trump's ex-lawyer Michael Cohen (and now turncoat) met with Russian Federation Council foreign affairs head Konstantin Kosachev in Prague during August 2016.

That claim was verifiably false as proven by Cohen's own passport at the time. But now that Cohen is singing and composing, "Summertime in Prague" is apparently not among his courthouse hits.

Likewise, the dossier's claim that Carter Page was offered a giant bribe by the head of Rosneft, the Russian state energy company, in return for lifting the sanctions is downright laughable. That's because Carter Page never had any serious role in the Trump campaign and was one of hundreds of unpaid informal advisors who hung around the basket hoping for some role in a future Trump government.

Carter Page: The Nobody Who Got Wire-Tapped

Like the hapless George Papadopoulos, in fact, Carter Page was an absolute nobody in Trump world. He apparently never even met DonaldTrump, had no foreign policy credentials and had been drafted onto the campaign's so-called foreign policy advisory committee out of sheer desperation.

That is, because the mainstream GOP foreign policy establishment had so completely boycotted the Trump campaign, the latter was forced to fill its advisory committee essentially from the phone book; and that desperation move in March 2016, in turn, had been undertaken in order to damp-down the media uproar over the Donald's assertion that he got his foreign policy advise from....well, watching TV!

That's how no-counts like 29-year old George Papadopoulos (indicted for allegedly lying to the FBI about the date of an irrelevant meeting) and Carter Page got on the foreign policy advisory committee — a phony campaign operation that held a single meeting, which was essentially a photo op.

And that's why Page has been able to keep repeating — without being indicted for perjury — what he said on an ABC interview awhile back:

"I never spoke with him (Trump) any time in my life," Page said on Good morning America this morning. Stephanopoulos followed up, asking, "no e-mail, no text, nothing like that?"

Page replied: *"never."*

Surely that's also the reason why his appointment to the advisory committee back in March 2016 elicited a "who-he?" harrumph from the MSM:

Carter Page was one of the five members of then-candidate Donald Trump's foreign policy advisory team that he named to The Washington Post editorial board on March 21, 2016. The announcement initially drew attention because Page, who owns (and is the sole employee of) the energy consulting firm Global Energy Capital, was a relative unknown....

Well, of course he was an unknown no count. That's all Trump's seat of the pants campaign could recruit for the photo op on short notice.

The truth of the matter is that Page had been a stock analyst in the Merrill Lynch Moscow office between 2002 and 2007, and thereafter set out to peddle himself as an international energy expert and the proprietor of a two-bit international energy advisory firm (of which he was the only employee).

In that capacity he bounced around various international energy conferences in New York, London and St Petersburg and undoubtedly attempted to burnish his credentials by touting his contracts in Moscow. At one point he even bragged about serving as an unpaid energy advisor to the Kremlin:

"Over the past half year, I have had the privilege to serve as an informal advisor to the staff of the Kremlin in preparation for their Presidency of the G-20 Summit next month, where energy issues will be a prominent point on the agenda," the letter reads.

For crying out loud: the man was spinning his resume to land work. That's why he had signed on, again, as an unpaid adviser to the Trump campaign, and had gotten their approval to attend another international conference in Moscow during July 2016, but on his own dime.

In fact, not only did he have no mandate to represent the Trump campaign; he was actually instructed to represent himself in Moscow as a private citizen. And in that modality, it turns out that his "meeting" with Rosneft actually consisted of drinks with an old buddy from his broker days who had become head of investor relations at Rosneft.

Yes, Carter Page did try to puff up his tail-feathers at the time via an email to colleagues on the Trump campaign claiming that he had met Russian Deputy Prime Minister Arkady Dvorkovich and learned that Putin was keen on Trump's openness to rapprochement with Russia.

Aside from the fact that there would be absolutely nothing illicit about either the meeting or the idea of rapprochement, it turns out that the encounter with Dvorkovich was actually a handshake at a cocktail party held during the conference at which they both spoke; and that Page's insights about the

Russian governments view of Trump came from listening to Dvorkovich's speech in an auditorium attended by about 1,000 others!

Yes, and it's also true that several years earlier (2013) Carter Page had apparently been the target of a recruitment effort by Russian intelligence operatives. In fact, a national security investigation worthy of the name could have determined that in a day or two by simply reading the newspaper and consulting the FBI closed case on the unwitting and harmless contacts he had had with Russian government personal during the 2012-2015 period.

As FBI Special Agent Gregory Monaghan noted in an originally sealed complaint against several alleged Russian spies, Page never took the bait and was even ridiculed by his would be handlers as not one of the sharpest tools in the shed.

In the complaint, Monaghan attested to how Page was the target of efforts by Russian Foreign Intelligence Service (SVR) agents Igor Sporyshev and Victor Podobnyy to recruit sources in New York City. According to the documents, Page and Podobnyy first met at an energy symposium in New York in January 2013. At this conference, Podobnyy gave his contact information to Page, who subsequently followed up with the Russian both by email and in-person to talk about energy policy. Page transferred unspecified "documents" to Podobnyy "about the energy business," but Monaghan did not recommend that any charges be levied against Page.

In fact, the section of the document discussing Page never characterizes him as a conscious spy or security risk, instead framing him as a victim of Sporyshev and Podobnyy, who expressly denied that Page knew about their status as intelligence agents.

Agent Monaghan followed this up by also detailing how Page cooperated with FBI officials in telling them about his contact with Podobnyy during their subsequent interview with him. And that was the extent of Carter Page's alleged clandestine Russia connections: A brief encounter with some sketchy Russian operatives, and on that brief incident the FBI itself gave him a clean bill of health.

So when you cut through all the sinister spin that Deep State operatives and their stenographers in the MSM have put on the raw facts of the case, it is pretty evident that the Steele dossier's tale about Page's alleged bribery scheme was completely bogus. Yet the dossier was the overwhelming basis for the FISA warrant that resulted in wiretaps on Carter Page and other officials in Trump Tower during October 2016 and for nine months thereafter.

And that's crucial. There is nothing more insidious than intervention by the intelligence and law enforcement apparatus of the state in the most important process of American democracy — the election of the President.

Indeed, if a Presidential campaign were ever to be wiretapped by the FBI at all, it would needs be triggered by the gravest and most compelling evidence of treason at the very highest level of the campaign: That is, the probable fact of a Manchurian candidate at the top of the ticket.

By contrast, if the suspicion concerned a mere campaign official or lesser staffer, the appropriate recourse for law enforcement would be to go to the candidate himself to disclose the compromising information and seek some mutually agreed course of action.

But did the FBI or John Brennan consider for even one single moment going to the Republican presidential candidate with their suspicions about a non-entity whom Trump would have surely (and honestly) referred to as "Carter who?"

No, they went to the FISA court instead with a dossier of dubious hearsay and gossip that had been paid for by the Clinton campaign, and for the explicit purpose of getting an order to wiretap the Trump headquarters.

Accordingly, there is no way to describe the Obama Administration's course of action other than as a monumentally corrupt act of bad faith. That is, a knowing and deliberate abuse of the most sensitive tool in the national security tool kit — a FISA warrant — for the purpose of undermining the Republican candidate for President.

Needless to say, in the scale of abuse of state power, there is not a cardinal sin which ranks any higher than that.

So that's the essence of the DOJ "insurance policy" at work: The Deep State and its allies in the Obama administration were desperately looking for dirt with which to crucify the Donald, and thereby insure that the establishment's anointed candidate would not fail at the polls.

That is to say, that the state's candidate, not the people's choice, would win the presidential election.

Indeed, the most chilling thing about the Carter Page FISA application is right at the top of the document. It essentially says that if you talk to any foreign government not approved by Washington about any civilian topic, such as energy policy, you can be accused of being a foreign agent, wire-tapped and charged with a crime:

......The target of this application is Carter W. Page, a U.S. person, and <u>an agent of a foreign power</u>, described in detail below."

That assertion is just flat-out preposterous. What is actually described in the FISA application is all about Page's doings in international energy policy meetings and forums, which is not surprising because that was his academic and business field of endeavor.

By contrast, there is not a single word about real espionage: That is, about the theft or compromise of ***military secrets***, which is the only possible justification for governments to spy on their own citizens.

So let's cut to the chase. Since Carter Page self-evidently had nothing to do with military secrets, officials of the Obama

Administration had no excuse whatsoever for wire-tapping him
— even if he had been a paid energy advisor on Vlad Putin's
personal payroll.

By wantonly infringing upon Carter Page's constitutional
right to free speech at home and abroad, therefore, Obama
officials committed the gravest possible assault on American
democracy: They misused the vast machinery of national
security to meddle in a presidential election for partisan
advantage — an heinous action which cuts right to the quick of
democracy's survival in America.

Indeed, the FSA application — slathered in blackout ink as
it is — proves that the real meddlers in the 2016 election are the
signers of the application. That is, the very top tier of Obama's
national security team including John Brennan, Susan Rice,
James Clapper and the secretaries of Defense and State.

Their downright criminality, in fact, has now been
established by the Mueller witch-hunt itself. That is, after 17
months of the most abusive prosecutorial tactics on record they
have not found a single thing upon which to indict Carter Page!

Yet that is not a all surprising because the case against
Carter Page was bogus from day one — meaning that their true
purpose for the wire-tap all along was to set up a *listening post*
in the Trump campaign. The aim of the latter, of course, was
to spy on other higher-up advisors and possibly even Trump
himself — and for the ultimate purpose of disrupting his
campaign and defeating his candidacy.

If that smacks of a preventative Deep State coup — it was.

Likewise, by any reasonable reading of the evidence Russia
was an uncooperative adversary of US foreign policy. But it was
not a mortal enemy or existential threat to the homeland by
any stretch of the imagination — and therefore one that would
justify extra-ordinary intervention in the election process by the
national security machinery of the state.

So we must underscore again: Trump's sin, apparently,

was to openly advocate an abandonment of Obama's rapidly escalating Russian confrontation policy in favor of an attempt at rapprochement with Putin based on the Donald's brimming confidence in his own prowess at the Art of the Deal.

Undoubtedly, the latter was misplaced. But elections are supposed to be about teeing up policy alternatives for the voters to consider. So doing, however, it landed the Trump campaign right in the Deep State's line of fire.

The Steele Dossier Is All They Had

So the question recurs: Even if the Obama inner circle had determined to rig the election, why did the conspirators resort to the outlandish and even cartoonish disinformation contained in the Steele dossier in order to get their wiretap?

The answer to that question cuts to the quick of the entire RussiaGate hoax. To wit, that's all they had!

As we have seen, notwithstanding the massive surveillance machinery and communications vacuum cleaners operated by the $75 billion US intelligence communities and its vaunted 17 agencies, there are still no digital intercepts proving that Russian state operatives hacked the DNC and Podesta emails.

Yet when it comes to anything that even remotely smacks of "meddling" in the US election campaign, that's all she wrote. In essence, the Clinton campaign with the aid of its corrupt advisor — CrowdStrike — instantaneously decreed that these embarrassing disclosures of its internal dirty laundry were the work of the Russian state, and on that basis enlisted the US law enforcement apparatus to prosecute the Trump campaign.

There is nothing else of moment, and most especially not the alleged GRU phishing expeditions directed at 20 or so state election boards. Most of these have been discredited, denied by local officials or were simply the work of everyday hackers looking for voter registration lists that could be sold.

The patently obvious point here is that in America there

is no on-line network of voting machines on either an intra-state or interstate basis. And that fact renders the whole election machinery hacking meme null and void. Not even the treacherous Russkies are stupid enough to waste their time trying to hack that which is unhackable.

In that vein, the Facebook ad buying scheme is even more ridiculous. In the context of an election campaign in which upwards of *$7 billion* of spending was reported by candidates and their committees to the FEC, and during which easily double that amount was spent by independent committees and issue campaigns, the notion that just *$44,000* of Facebook ads made any difference to anything is not worthy of adult thought.

And, yes, out of the ballyhooed $100,000 of Facebook ads, the majority occurred *after* the election was over and none of them named candidates, anyway. The ads consisted of issue messages that reflected all points on the political spectrum from pro-choice to anti-gun control.

And even this so-called effort at "polarizing" the American electorate was "discovered" only after Facebook failed to find any "Russian-linked" ads during its first two searches. Instead, this complete drivel was detected when the Senate's modern day Joe McCarthy, Sen. Mark Warner, who is the vice chairman of the Senate Intelligence Committee and a leading legislator on Internet regulation, showed up on Mark Zuckerberg's doorstep at Facebook's headquarters.

At that point, apparently, baby billionaire Zuck figuratively browned his diapers and came up with the aforementioned $100,000 worth of crudely written click bait from a St. Petersburg troll farm that actually didn't amount to a hill of beans, as we document in chapter 25.

So the real meaning of the Strzok/Gates "insurance policy" text message is straight foreword. There was a conspiracy to prevent Trump's election, and then after the shocking results of

November 8, this campaign morphed into an intensified effort to discredit the winner.

For instance, Susan Rice got Obama to lower the classification level of the information obtained from the Trump campaign intercepts and other dirt-gathering actions by the Intelligence Community (IC) — so that it could be disseminated more readily to all Washington intelligence agencies.

In short order, of course, the IC was leaking like a sieve, thereby paving the way for the post-election hysteria and the implication that any contact with a Russian — even one living in Brooklyn — must be collusion. And that this presumption of nefarious purpose even included calls to the Russian ambassador by the president-elect's own national security advisor-designate.

Should there by any surprise, therefore, that it turns out that Andrew McCabe bushwhacked General Flynn on January 24 when he called to say that FBI agents were on the way to the White House for what Flynn presumed to be more security clearance work with his incipient staff.

No at all. The FBI team was there to interrogate Flynn about the transcripts of his perfectly appropriate and legal conversations with Ambassador Kislyak about two matters of state — the UN resolution on Israel and the spiteful new sanctions on certain Russian citizens that Obama announced on December 29 in a fit of pique over the Dems election loss.

Indeed, the latter point can't be emphasized enough. What responsible departing President would provoke the other major nuclear armed nation of the world 22 days before leaving office over the thin gruel about Russian election meddling that Obama actually possessed at the time?

The fact is, the Russian sanctions of December 29 were actually the product a petulant Obama hissy fit. They never should have been issued at all, yet now General Flynn — who is a bit of a whack job himself — was threatened with time in

U.S. MILITARY PERSONNEL DEPLOYMENTS BY COUNTRY
Nearly 200,000 troops are currently deployed overseas in 177 countries

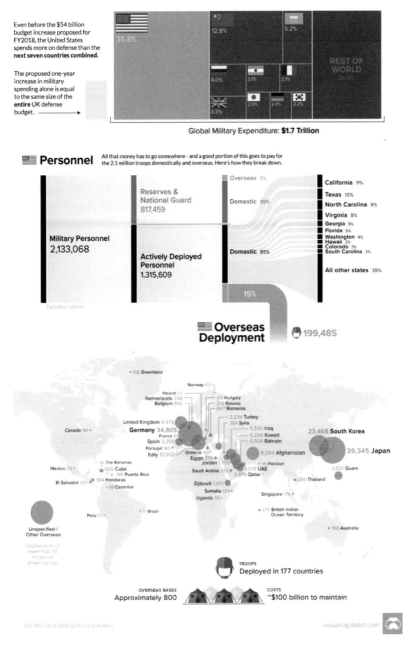

Even before the $54 billion budget increase proposed for FY2018, the United States spends more on defense than the **next seven countries combined.**

The proposed one-year increase in military spending alone is equal to the same size of the **entire** UK defense budget.

35.8% 12.9% 5.2%
REST OF WORLD 25.6%
4.0% 3.1% 3.1%
2.5% 2.4% 2.2%
3.3%

Global Military Expenditure: **$1.7 Trillion**

Personnel
All that money has to go somewhere - and a good portion of this goes to pay for the 2.1 million troops domestically and overseas. Here's how they break down.

Military Personnel 2,133,068

Reserves & National Guard 817,459

Actively Deployed Personnel 1,315,609

Overseas 5%
Domestic 95%
Domestic 85%
15%

California 11%
Texas 10%
North Carolina 9%
Virginia 8%
Georgia 5%
Florida 5%
Washington 4%
Hawaii 3%
Colorado 3%
South Carolina 3%
All other states 39%

Excludes civilians

Overseas Deployment
199,485

158 Greenland
Norway 83
Poland 51
Netherlands 398
Belgium 842
20 Hungary
278 Kosovo
667 Romania
2,234 Turkey
264 Syria
United Kingdom 8,479
Germany 34,805
France 57
Spain 3,250
Portugal 195
Italy 12,102
5,540 Iraq
6,296 Kuwait
6,504 Bahrain
9,294 Afghanistan
66 The Bahamas
806 Cuba
145 Puerto Rico
Greece 407
Egypt 375
Jordan 1,759
185 Pakistan
Saudi Arabia 352
1,079 UAE
2,976 Qatar
23,468 South Korea
39,345 Japan
3,831 Guam
Canada 141
Mexico 93
El Salvador 197
384 Honduras
68 Colombia
Djibouti 1,961
Somalia 134
Uganda 56
Singapore 178
289 Thailand
Peru 51
51 Brazil
275 British Indian Ocean Territory
188 Australia

Unspecified / Other Overseas

Deployments of fewer than 50 troops not shown on map

TROOPS
Deployed in 177 countries

OVERSEAS BASES
Approximately 800

COSTS
~$100 billion to maintain

SOURCE: DoD, SIPRI (2015 data), Politico

visualcapitalist.com

Uncle Sam's hospitality center for the crime of trying to function as the adult in the room during his phone call with Kislyak.

Moreover, the insidious team of FBI gotcha cops who set-up General Flynn for this screaming injustice was led by none other than......Peter Strzok!

The Great Disrupter — The Gift That Never Stops Giving

When it comes to the imperative task of exposing and disabling the Deep State, the Great Disrupter is the gift that never stops giving. He is bringing the Deep State out of hiding and into open assault on what remains of American democracy.

There is no telling the outcome, of course, but there was no stopping the Deep State, either, until the Donald stumbled into battle with the real ruling forces of the Imperial City.

Indeed, owing to honest but naïve utterances during the campaign about deal-making with Putin, the obsolesence of NATO and the stupidity of trying to fight both ISIS and Assad in Syria at the same time, the Donald brought down upon his head the wrath of the Deep State like no other time in American history.

Those single-sentence campaign talking points — along with a quaint rhetorical flourish about America First — were not rooted in any profound or consistent diagnosis of Washington's failing global imperium. Yet by happenstance or otherwise they did cut to the quick of it.

After all, if like candidate Trump you eschew regime change in the middle east, recognize that Crimea was an integral part of Russia for 171 years and none of Washington's business and that Putin is not evil incarnate but just the autocratic head of a pipsqueak state that is no threat whatsoever to the American homeland, you puncture the very raison d'etre for Washington's vast $800 billion war machine and its above-depicted far-flung Imperial deployments and outposts all around the globe.

And that the Deep State cannot abide. The truth is, the $800 billion Warfare State has no reason for existence, and, in present circumstances, for bleeding the nation dry fiscally. That's because America has no heavily militarized industrial state enemies left on the planet.

To repeat: Russia is a glorified hydrocarbon province with a few nickel mines, 100 million acres of wheat fields, an aging, shrinking, Vodka-favoring work force and a pint-sized GDP the size of the New York metro area.

Its capacity to launch an invasion of the New Jersey shores depends upon a single 45 year-old smoke-belching aircraft carrier now bottled up in the Mediterranean Sea by the US naval and missile armada.

And its 1,000-odd deployable nuclear warheads are pinned down by a US retaliatory nuclear force that literally would turn every Russian city into a parking lot. Besides, Putin is the Cool Hand Luke of today's international arena, not a suicidal maniac.

Likewise, China is a vast house of cards swollen by a $40 trillion explosion of state credit that has created the most unstable and unsustainable Ponzi in recorded history. The red rulers of Beijing do not need the 7th Fleet to keep them contained within the borders of the Middle Kingdom; they are stuck like a tar baby to a mutant domestic economy that will ultimately implode upon the heads of a regime that thinks building sand bars in the South China Sea is a sign of military vigor.

And self-evidently, Washington's imperial adventures cannot end jihadist terrorism. In fact, its destructive interventions created, enabled and armed ISIS and its offspring in the first place. The way to stop terrorist blowback is to stop bombing, droning, invading and occupying the already demolished cities and towns of the Middle East — many of which have been "liberated" by Washington more than once (e.g. Mosul).

In short, whether out of guile, naiveté or inordinate

confidence in his own deal-making powers, the Donald threatened to expose that the Empire was naked. In turn, that elicited from the Deep State a blatant effort to stop his candidacy before November 8 and destroy his Presidency thereafter.

The Empire's War Machine

With all this at stake, it is not surprising that the Deep State has concocted the threadbare and outlandish memes of the RussiaGate madness which is now loose upon the land. They were desperate and had no compunction at all about deploying the whole Russia meddling/collusion narrative — as preposterous as it is — to undermine the nation's duly elected President.

But, alas, there is a silver lining. Based on what is known already and what is sure to come, the whole RussiaGate hoax will end up making a laughingstock of the so-called Intelligence Community (IC), and that is the necessary first step in liberating America's democracy from the deadly grip of Empire.

Recall from chapter 22 that the foundational document of the RussiaGate hoax, the January 2017 Brennan report, wasn't even vetted by the 17 agencies and reads like a C- term paper written for government 101 at Clear Creek Baptist Bible College.

As we have seen, in fact, there was no intelligence content in the report at all with respect to the Kremlin's alleged nefarious meddling in America's governance — just a dimwitted screed against RT America and a claim of "high confidence" that the Russkies did it.

By your way, at least when the US intelligence agencies concluded with "high confidence" that Iraq was "expanding its chemical, biological, nuclear and missile programs" in 2002 it was an official report of the IC, not the scribblings of a hand-picked tag-team like the Brennan/Comey posse.

Needless to say, back then the IC was rewarded for its acuity with a resource explosion which now amounts to a *$75 billion* annual budget and more than a million workers directly or through contractors.

That's right. Washington's IC budget is nearly 25% larger than the *$61 billion* Putin spends on his entire military — including fuel, spare parts, soldier pay, R&D, weapons procurement, operational maintenance and military boots and gloves, too. The Deep State puts more resources into cyber-hackers than Russia spends on military attackers.

And yet notwithstanding this massive apparatus of spying and surveillance, neither the FBI nor any of the other gaggle of IC agencies has ever even examined the DNC computers which were allegedly hacked.

The Dog Which Didn't Bark — The Missing NSA Intercepts

Indeed, this is a story of the dog which didn't bark if there ever was one. If either the DNC or Podesta emails were hacked as alleged, NSA would have the digital logs because its bulk collection operations scoop up everything that passes through the global internet — even the work of hackers and cyber-terrorists.

So if the evidence exists, NSA is sitting on it. And the excuse that these digital logs have not been transcribed and released to the American public on the grounds that "sources and methods" might be compromised is just rank nonsense.

NSA's digital gumshoes can't be captured or shot for espionage by our alleged enemies. That's because they are silicon, not carbon, based units.

The only theoretical risk to the latter — that is, to HUMINT (human intelligence) assets — has nothing to do with this matter.

After all, no one has alleged that some modern-day Russian

equivalent of Elizabeth and Phillip of the "Americans" broke into Podesta's computer in the wee hours of the night on the sage guess that his password was "password"; and that the US spooks who were tailing them might have their identities disclosed if the evidence were to be made public.

In fact, the only plausible source of evidence on the supposed Russian hackers — NSA's bulk collection of every email and cell phone call and message — has been known to the entire world after Edward Snowden's disclosures of June 2013.

So absolutely nothing is being safeguarded by the IC's failure to declassify the evidence and pony-up the proof; it's just a ruse to distract attention from the fact that there isn't any proof at all that it was the Russians.

To the contrary, according to former British ambassador and now Julian Assange associate, Craig Murray, the DNC's gossip and skullduggery file was handed-off to him not via an encrypted transmission surreptitiously snatched from the DNC servers, but in what amounted to an envelope containing a thumb drive delivered by a guy reading a newspaper on a DC park bench!

And that's where it gets curiouser and curiouser. As we indicated above, the DNC computers have never been examined by the FBI. The whole investigation was outsourced to an outfit known as "CrowdStrike." The latter had a $200,000 per year contract with the DNC and is a "burn-baby" (i.e. unprofitable) start-up funded by the Deep State's chief collaborators — that is, the always honest folks at Google.

A Daniel Lazare reported in Consortium News, here is what actually happened. It is a striking case of the incestuous, money-driven corruption which is riff within the Empire's $75 billion intelligence and surveillance monster and merits full elaboration:

When DNC officials discovered that their computers had been compromised, they did what anyone in such a situation would do:

they called their lawyer, in this case a former federal prosecutor and cybercrime specialist named Michael Sussmann.

Sussman, in turn, called an old friend named Shawn Henry, former head of the FBI's cyber division and now president of an Irvine, California, cyber-security firm known as CrowdStrike. Henry contacted his chief technical officer, Russian-born Dimitri Alperovitch, who sent over a team of investigators. Within the day, the CrowdStrike team concluded that the intruders were Russian government operatives.

Like any enterprise, CrowdStrike is in the business of convincing potential customers to purchase its services. Hence it had an incentive to blame the email loss on a dark and spooky Kremlin conspiracy rather than something more mundane such as an internal leak.

As an ex-Soviet who emigrated to America as a teenager, moreover, Alperovitch was particularly inclined to blame Russia first. As he once told a reporter: "A lot of people who are born here don't appreciate the freedoms we have, the opportunities we have, because they've never had it any other way. I have."

Since then, Alperovitch has joined forces with the Atlantic Council, a hawkish Washington think tank funded by the U.S. State Department, NATO, Ukrainian exiles, Persian Gulf oil exporters, and U.S. arms manufacturers, all with interests hostile to a sensible and constructive approach to U.S.-Russian relations.

Indeed, the Atlantic Council has been a spark-plug powering the New Cold War with Russia and maintains close ties with Clinton and her supporters. In 2013, it gave her its "distinguished leadership award," and in 2015 it recruited her to give a major address kicking off its "Latin American women's leadership initiative."

The Atlantic Council also chose ex-Secretary of State Madeleine Albright, a major Clinton ally, to head a Mideast study group that echoed Clinton's call for a Syrian "no-fly zone, "a proposal that would almost certainly lead to a direct U.S.-Russian military clash.

So the Russophobic Clinton camp hired Russophobic Dimitri Alperovitch, both linked via the Russophobic Atlantic Council, to find out who hacked the DNC. To absolutely no one's surprise, they decided that Russia was it.

You can't make this stuff up. The Atlantic Council is a truly unhinged collection of retired Deep State operatives, warmongers, militarists, neocons and plain old whack-jobs. Yet it has worked check-by-jowl with high Washington officials to shape and promulgate the Russian meddling and collusion hoax.

Not only is the whole DNC/Podesta hacking story essentially a glorified piece of opposition research peddled by the DNC and its contractors like CrowdStrike and bag-carriers in the mainstream media, but whatever odds and sots of forensic evidence that may exist were most probably manufactured by the Deep State itself.

Vault 7 And The Planted Evidence Factor

That's right. Owing to some Wikileaks disclosures of March 2017 via a trove of leaked CIA documents called "Vault 7", it now appears that various dubious IC's claims and "assessments" about Russian hacking can be readily debunked.

That is, Vault 7 suggests the US intelligence community has the ability to manufacture and deposit electronic trails to "misdirect attribution" by leaving false cyber fingerprints. Using a library of foreign malware and hacking tools, the CIA can plant Russian, Chinese, Iranian or other hackers' fingerprints to make the internet security breaches appear to be from one of those countries — even as they do the job from the comfort of their offices in Langley, VA.

Needless to say, that well explains how the alleged Russian hackers, who CrowdStrike described as ultra-sophisticated and diabolical, could be so "clumsy" as to leave obvious and damning fingerprints on their work, such as the underlying Cyrillic letters, the Russian email addresses and even an alias name that was the founder of the Soviet intelligence service 100 years ago .

So it is probable that the Russians were "clumsy" because they weren't actually "Russians." They might well have been CIA operatives from the Center for Cyber Intelligence who had been charged with planting the evidence.

Indeed, as one independent cyber-security expert, Jeffrey Carr, put it with respect to these apparently planted tell-tale signs, such as the reference to Felix E. Dzerzhinsky, founder of the Soviet Cheka,

OK. Raise your hand if you think that a GRU or FSB officer would add Iron Felix's name to the metadata of a stolen document before he released it to the world while pretending to be a Romanian hacker. Someone clearly had a wicked sense of humor."

A Last Chance To Restore Democratic Sovereignty In America

That gets us to the heart of the matter. To wit, the Donald's utterly improbable election victory and his subsequent impetuous, undisciplined, impulsive tweeting has set the Deep State on its heels, and has opened up fissures and conflicts within the IC that will eventually come oozing and erupting to the daylight of public knowledge.

The resulting beltway brawl will result in absolute paralysis and dysfunction in Washington soon — if it has not arrived already. And the new factor in the equation is that the continuing exposure of the RussiaGate hoax has finally alerted the GOP to the monster security state that it helped erect — especially after 9/11 — and the awful potential for partisan abuse that always lurked within.

In this regard, Senator Rand Paul hit the nail on the head at the time it was revealed that Obama's top national security advisor, Susan Rice, had ordered the unmasking of the NSA intercepts collected at Trump Tower. He called it a "smoking gun" and well it was.

But we would go him one further. It's actually a thundering body blow to the Deep State's massive apparatus of surveillance and secrecy that long ago usurped national security policy from the people's elected representatives on Capitol Hill; and which has now, apparently, launched the very diabolical attack on our democratic processes that civil libertarians have long warned about.

What we are saying is that the Donald was right when he said that Trump Tower was being "wire tapped." As we have seen, the Deep State and its handmaids in the Obama Administration had been moving heaven and earth to prevent Trump's election and then afterwards to discredit his Presidency before he was even given the keys to the Oval Office.

But in that bald-faced equivalent of an attempted coup d'etat, it failed to make the kill. Now it is faced with what will be a rambunctious partisan warfare in the Imperial City, and the opening of a new front in the "election meddling" narrative.

Stated differently, the mainstream GOP politicians have been awakened not because they had a civil liberties epiphany, but because their political ox was being gored.

To wit, when the Dems said the meddler was *Vlad*, the GOP steadily came to learn that it was *Barry*. In turn, that opens up a partisan debate about whether the real threat to American democracy comes from a pint-sized economy 12,000 miles away or a $75 billion surveillance state that suffuses the warp and woof of the Imperial City itself.

As a result of these alternative election meddling narratives, it's no longer only the Donald on the warpath. Now the bulk of the GOP rank and file and the movement-oriented conservative media have joined the counter-attack on the Deep State and its Democratic servitors, as well.

It goes without saying that movement conservatives and their Sean Hannity media megaphones already hated Barack Obama with a passion. But now they realize it was even worse than they thought — that his administration facilitated and orchestrated a constitution-jeopardizing smear attack on the GOP's very candidate for President.

For instance, the shrilly partisan Daily Caller was all over the case when the Obama White House's unmasking spree was disclosed with even more inflammatory detail sourced from a former US Attorney and two White House NSC veterans:

Former President Barack Obama's national security adviser Susan Rice ordered U.S. spy agencies to produce "detailed spreadsheets" of legal phone calls involving Donald Trump and his aides when he wawas running for president, according to former U.S. Attorney Joseph diGenova.

"What was produced by the intelligence community at the request of Ms. Rice were detailed spreadsheets of intercepted phone calls with unmasked Trump associates in perfectly legal conversations with individuals," diGenova told The Daily Caller News Foundation Investigative Group Monday.

"The overheard conversations involved no illegal activity by anybody of the Trump associates, or anyone they were speaking with," diGenova said. "In short, the only apparent illegal activity was the unmasking of the people in the calls."

Col. (Ret.) James Waurishuk, an NSC veteran and former deputy director for intelligence at the U.S. Central Command, told TheDCNF that many hands had to be involved throughout the Obama administration to launch such a political spying program.

"We're looking at a potential constitutional crisis from the standpoint that we used an extremely strong capability that's supposed to be used to safeguard and protect the country," he said. "And we used it for political purposes by a sitting president. That takes on a new precedent."

Michael Doran, former NSC senior director, told TheDCNF Monday that "somebody blew a hole in the wall between national security secrets and partisan politics." This "was a stream of information that was supposed to be hermetically sealed from politics and the Obama administration found a way to blow a hole in that wall," he said.

So partisan warfare over the true 2016 election meddling attack is now in full stride and will result in the relentless unmasking, leaking and exposing of the massive resources and far-flung machinations of the Deep State. That expurgation could not come soon enough, of course, and represents the kind of inadvertent blow to statism that is the essence of the Great Disrupter's historic mission.

The irony is that the neocon-dominated GOP has been the great enabler of the Deep State — -especially after the bloodthirsty cabal in the George Bush White House worked the nation into a fever of unwarranted hysteria after 9/11. But the monster they created turned on the GOP, and now suddenly the scales are beginning to fall from its collective eyes.

To be sure, the unreconstructed neocons and War Party hands of Imperial Washington like the late Senator McWar (R-AZ) and the low-IQ Chairman of the Senate Intelligence Committee, Richard Burr, continue to pursue rear-guard "bipartisan" maneuvers from their privileged national security committees. Their purpose, of course, is to shield the intelligence community from exposure and to defend the Russian meddling story.

But now that Obama's fingerprints are all over the Deep State's 2016 election intrusions, there is an opening for junior, un-coopted GOP legislators to follow Senator Rand Paul's brilliant lead.

In pouncing on the Susan Rice smoking gun he has managed to meld a partisan attack on Team Obama with a spirited and cogent defense of constitutional liberties under the 4th Amendment; and to pull the Deep State apparatus out from the shadows of 9/11 hysteria and to expose the frightening potential for abuse of power that lies in its current legal authorities and modus operandi.

At the moment, the pro-establishment spinners and hair-splitters on CNN and the mainstream editorial pages are trying desperately to parse the case they can no longer deny.

That is to say, yes, Susan Rice — and probably CIA Director Brennan, DNI Clapper, deputy national security director Ben Rhodes and others — did "unmask" the names of Trump associates. But it was all done, these Deep State apologist maintain, in the pursuit of their duties to acquire "foreign intelligence information" and was in no way improper.

It's not gonna wash. There can be little doubt that the whole Russian hacking narrative was invented by the Deep State, and then massaged and leaked by top Obama officials including Rice, Rhodes, Brennan, Clapper and numerous others for one purpose alone that had nothing to do with national security. To wit, to prevent the election of an impetuous, strong-willed, anti-globalist that the establishment deeply disapproved and then to re-litigate the election once the unthinkable happened on November 8th.

Indeed, if the Donald has the courage of his convictions, he will authorize the DOJ to unleash one or more ambitious US Attorneys against Susan Rice, Brennan, Rhodes and others. Owing to their massive leaking campaign from the illicit Trump surveillance operation, they are all surely felons.

But we also expect that the dueling narratives about the election meddling of *Vlad versus Barry*" will expose the soft underbelly of the Deep State and the toxic anti-constitutional essence of its operations.

We are speaking of NSA's bulk collection of all the email, voice and data bits which pass through the internet and communications arteries of the nation. What the Obama "unmasking" revelations are really about is the utter impossibility of erecting and enforcing safeguards on entry into the great digital warehouse pictured below.

It's the "mother of all data centers" operated by NSA in

Bluffdale, Utah. Every single hour it collects and stores data equivalent to *36 times* the entire digital collection of the Library of Congress. That's the equivalent of 690 million books every single hour!

A recent investigation gives additional color with respect to this surveillance monster:

The Utah Data Center covers more than 1 million square feet. It houses its own water-treatment facilities, 60 huge diesel-fueled emergency standby electric generators and an undisclosed number of computers and servers with unimaginable amounts of storage and analysis capacity. The center uses more than 1.5 million gallons of water daily and consumes enough electricity to power a community of 6,000.

The heavily fortified center's stated purpose is to store vast swaths of the world's communications that have been intercepted from the underground and undersea cables of international, foreign and domestic networks, or turned over by commercial telephone companies or internet social media, data storage or communications servers.

Coursing through thousands of servers and many miles of wiring and routers is the boundless capacity to store all forms of communication. That includes the complete contents of private emails and cell phone calls — replete with their associated metadata — as well as Google searches and so-called "personal data trails" linked to parking receipts, travel itineraries, bookstore purchases and other "pocket litter."

NSA sleuths do not directly process any data at the Utah facility. Instead, the center functions purely for data storage — a digital "cloud" that stores seemingly endless amounts of digital ones and zeros.

If that appears to be an utterly unglamorous use for such an expensive facility, it's also a testament to the fact that America's premier spy-gathering apparatus is drowning in metadata: In a single hour, the agency collects and stores data equivalent to 36 times the entire digital collection of the Library of Congress, according to Matthew M. Aid, an NSA expert and visiting fellow at the National Security Archive at George Washington University, who obtained that statistic from knowledgeable sources. (The Library of Congress has archived an estimated 690 terabytes — equivalent to the contents of about 690 million books — of data, adding an average of 5 terabytes per month.)

Needless to say, there is a simple alternative to this collection and storage monster, and that is to abolish the process of bulk collection entirely.

That way there would be no "incidental" surveillance in the first place; no need for the "unmasking" of the names and communications of American citizens in violation of their clear-cut constitutional rights; and no possibility that another incumbent Administration could attempt to sabotage American democracy in the manner undertaken by the highest officials of the Obama Administration in 2016.

If there are true threats to national security in today's world — and Angela's Merkel's cell phone and Putin's security operatives are not among them — Washington need only go back to the constitutionally established process of obtaining case-by-case, court approved warrants based on probable cause.

And it might happen. What is different this time is that

an aggrieved GOP has come to understand that the Great Warehouse of all that is spoken and written residing in NSA's monumental cloud was used by the Obama Administration to nearly steal the 2016 election.

CHAPTER 25

Mueller's Comic Book Indictment: How To Prosecute A Great Big Nothingburger

We have always heard that a determined government prosecutor can indict a ham sandwich, and now we know it's true. After 38 years in the prosecution racket, Robert Mueller made his biggest score ever last winter — that is, he nailed a great big Nothingburger.

But he also did a lot more than that. Mueller's 37-page comic book indictment actually unmasks — inadvertently to be sure — the distinctly un-terrifying nature of the whole Russian meddling narrative. In fact, the crude social media emissions (ads and posts) of the so-called St. Petersburg troll farm were generally lame, often laughable and sometimes downright ludicrous as per this gem cited by Mueller:

On or about October 16, 2016, Defendants and their co-conspirators used the ORGANIZATION-controlled Instagram account "Woke Blacks" to post the following message: "[A] particular hype and hatred for Trump is misleading the people and forcing Blacks to vote Killary. We cannot resort to the lesser of two devils. Then we'd surely be better off without voting AT ALL."

Notwithstanding the grave nomenclature of BLOCK CAPITALS, endless sinister "on or about" events and 99 numbered paragraphs of particulars, the true bill (charging document) is actually just a random catalogue of social media trivia like the above "Woke Blacks" post.

Most of the cited gleanings amounted to crude word bombs, often in broken English, that presumably even Kim Kardashian's 59 million Twitter followers could see through.

"Hillary is a Satan, and her crimes and lies had proved just how evil she is"

The lion's share of these postings and ads probably disappeared into cyberspace like the sound of a falling tree in an empty forest. According to Facebook itself, the seemingly ubiquitous social media ad campaign depicted in the indictment was nothing of the kind. It actually amounted to just **3,000** placements at a cost of **$100,000** — more than half of which were purchased after the election, and *25%* of which ended-up in its dead letter office (unread).

Likewise, the handful of efforts to actually stimulate pro-Trump rallies in Florida and elsewhere were abject failures. As we document below, the Russians had absolutely no "ground game" in the US and any third-rate campaign consultant will tell you that ads alone do not produce crowds. In fact, there is virtually no evidence that anyone showed up at the rallies cited by Mueller.

Besides, the overwhelming share of the pro-Trump social media postings uncovered by Mueller's sleuths amounted to "copy and paste" relays of current partisan talking points. Thus, the indictment cites such slogans as:

"Vote Republican, vote Trump, and support the Second Amendment!"

"Trump is our only hope for a better future!"

"Donald wants to defeat terrorism, Hillary wants to sponsor it"

Really?

It took a clandestine nest of Russkie imposters and subversives to pollute the social media with this kind of tripe?

In fact, the RNC, Fox News and the Trump campaign

were already saturating the internet with this kind of stupid messaging, anyway — along with millions of pro-Trump social media activists. The 80 Russian operatives cited by Mueller didn't add one damn bit to the massive social media messaging that was already out there.

Yevgeny Prigozhin's Hobby Farm

So here's the joker in the whole deck. It seems that the nefarious"troll farm" in St. Petersburg that comprises nearly the totality of Mueller's case is not a Russian intelligence agency operation at all.

Instead, it's the relatively harmless Hobby Farm of a fanatical Russian oligarch and ultra-nationalist, Yevgeny Prigozhin, who has a great big beef against Imperial Washington's demonization of Russia and Vlad Putin. Apparently, the farm *was* (it's apparently being disbanded) the vehicle through which he gave Washington the middle finger and buttered up his patron.

Prigozhin is otherwise known as "Putin's Cook" because he made his fortune in St. Petersburg restaurants that Putin favored and via state funded food service operations at Russian schools and military installations.

Like most Russian oligarchs not in jail, he apparently tithes in gratitude to the Kremlin: In this case, by bankrolling the rinky-dink operation at 55 Savushkina Street in St Petersburg that was the object of Mueller's pretentious foray into the flotsam and jetsam of social media low life.

Prigozhin's trolling farm was grandly called the Internet Research Agency (IRA), but what it actually did was hire (apparently) unemployed 20-somethings at $4-8 per hour to pound out ham-handed political messaging on social media sites like Facebook, Instagram, Twitter, YouTube etc. They banged away twelve hours at a shift on a quota-driven paint-by-the-internet-numbers basis where their output was rated for

engagements, likes, retweets etc.

Whatever these keyboard drones might have been, they were not professional Russian intel operators. And the collection of broken English postings strewn throughout the indictment are not one bit scary.

Indeed, the utterly stupid naiveté of the whole St. Petersburg operation is crystalized by this episode when the farm purportedly garnered some startling political insight from an unwitting Trump campaign official in Texas:

On or about August 19, 2016, Defendants and their co-conspirators used the false U.S. persona "Matt Skiber" account to write to the real U.S. person affiliated with a Texas-based grassroots organization who previously had advised the false persona to focus on "purple states like Colorado, Virginia & Florida." Defendants and their co-conspirators told that U.S. person, "We were thinking about your recommendation to focus on purple states and this is what we're organizing in FL."

Jez Louise and goodness gracious, too. Who coulda thunk as early as August that Colorado, Virginia and Florida would be swing states!

In any event, even Mueller's indictment proves that the farm was strictly amateurville. None of the other 12 Russians charged had an intelligence background, either.

Thus, the CEO was a retired St. Petersburg police officer. The executive director was a 31-year old website developer and internet PR promoter who previously had garnered small beans contracts ($4k-20k each) from St. Petersburg agencies to publish municipal newspapers, make video reports about their activities or promote local programs such as one on "tolerance and prevention of drug addiction."

Likewise, two more of the operatives were graduates students in IT and advertising at St. Petersburg universities.

Then there is the husband/wife duo, Maria and Robert Bovda, who were the original heads of the US focused "translator project." Both were recent graduates in psychology from local universities, where Robert's 2011 thesis had been on "The Effects of Social-Support Conditions On Loneliness As Experienced By the Elderly."

We can't help but think they had not yet become hardened spies when the joined IRA in November 2013 and apparently left in October 2014. Whatever they did during their tenure at the farm, cooking up ways to help Donald Trump's not yet announced campaign was surely not among them, but still apparently enough to help fill out Mueller's indictment roster.

Meet Maria And Robert Bovda — Real Scary Russian Spies

Another was Dzheykhun Aslanov, who was head of IRA's

"American department" and had graduated in 2012 from the Russian State Hydrometeorological University in St. Petersburg. He had studied economics and wildlife management!

Likewise, nowhere in the entire 37 pages is there even a clause linking Prigozhin's Hobby Farm to the SVR (foreign intelligence service), the FSB (counter-intelligence and anti-terrorism), the GRU (military intelligence service), any other agency of the Russian State — or even some purported Kremlin back channel to Putin.

Yet there is every reason to believe that the entire Russian meddling narrative cooked up by the partisan hacks in Obama's inner circle — John Brennan, Susan Rice and Ben Rhodes — was based on the amateurish machinations originating in the nondescript building pictured above.

As we will show, the Hobby Farm was no Russian state secret or clandestine vehicle of its intelligence community. To the contrary, it had been fully covered in the Russian press for years as one of numerous such oligarch funded projects designed to glorify the Putin regime and vilify the Russian internal opposition.

It had also been the subject of a lengthy expose in *The Guardian* of London, as well as other western media. Even Radio Free Europe had done a lengthy profile.

All of this had happened long before Prigozhin's Hobby Farm had turned its attentions to US politics. Indeed, the IRA's pivot to the US in April 2014 occurred well before Trump's candidacy was gleam in anyone's eye except his own, but after a seminal event had occurred which Mueller's comic book narrative completely ignores.

Why Prigozhin Got Pissed

To wit, what apparently riled up Prigozhin was Washington's heavy-handed meddling in the politics of Ukraine during the US funded and enabled coup on the streets of Kiev in February 2014.

As we documented in Part 3, never mind that the incumbent pro-Russian government had come to power in an honest election and had chosen to take a more attractive economic deal from Moscow than was being offered by the West. Also ignore that fact that Ukraine was Russia's next door neighbor and had been an essential element of Greater Russia — sometimes a full fledged constituent state — for more than 700 years.

Likewise, when Crimea elected by 97% referendum vote to "rejoin" Russia, it didn't happen at gunpoint. Crimea is 80% Russian and had been an integral part of the Russian state ever since it was purchased from the Turks by Catherine the Great for good money in 1783.

Thereafter, its major port city of Sevastopol had functioned as the homeport for Russia's Black Sea fleet under Czars and Commissars alike. To repeat, the only real reason it needed to "rejoin" Russia in March 2014 was because the Ukrainian tyrant who ruled the Soviet Union in the 1950s, Nikita Khrushchev, had gifted it to his Ukrainian compatriots during a drunken celebration of his victory over two deadly rivals who also claimed Stalin's succession.

As we indicated previously, at the time of the coup in February 2014 Obama's neocon Assistant Secretary for European Affairs, Victoria Nuland, was caught telling the American ambassador in Kiev that "Yats is the guy" with respect to the new Washington designated leader of the post-coup government. When she then joined a chorus of Washington-based vilification of Putin and the Russian government, the die was cast.

Russian nationalists like Prigozhin were not going to take it lying down. As we document below, then and there he began to shift some of the activities of his Russia-focused trolling farm toward the US.

It amounted to a tit-for-tat response to the anti-Russian propaganda emanating from the Washington funded NGOs in Kiev; and also from outright government agencies like the National Endowment for Democracy and Radio Free Europe, as well as the Deep State subservient operations at CNN and its print media imitators.

That shift of focus at IRA was described as the "translator project" by Mueller's historically ignorant lawyers. The implication was that out of sheer aggression the Kremlin had unilaterally decided to attack America's democratic process through the IRA.

In fact, the overwhelming likelihood is that an arriviste Russian billionaire got a bee in his bonnet after Washington's Ukrainian coup — and then went to town on America with his trolling farm exactly as he and many others had been doing in internal Russian politics for years.

From the point of view of US/Russian relations and world peace, however, the re-direction of activity at Prigozhin's Hobby Farm could not have come at a worse time. Its wholly open and widely known operations permitted Obama's hatchet-squad to quickly seize on the IRA's new theatre of focus as evidence of a massive Russian attack on America's election process, thereby turning a molehill into a mountain.

At length, the partisan leaders of Obama's national security team, led by the detestable John Brennan at the CIA, selectively coopted and abused the resources and credibility of the vast US intelligence apparatus to put the imprimatur of a national security threat upon what was in fact a scary bedtime story of no real significance. That effort culminated in the aforementioned phony intelligence assessment published by the CIA, FBI and NSA in January 2017 based on the work of Brennan's "hand-picked" accomplices.

In what is surely a fabulous irony, therefore, the Internet Research Agency amounts to a reverse Potemkin Village. It wasn't much to look at and was nothing at all to worry about until Obama's national security posse falsely embellished it's innocuous façade into a mortal threat to American democracy and national security.

And then Robert Mueller brought in his gang of copywriters and illustrators to turn this entire tall tale into CNN-ready "news."

We will demonstrate below that what happened in this building was a complete farce and posed no threat to the security and liberty of the American people whatsoever. Nor did it even remotely impact the 2016 election process.

But with his comic book indictment, Robert Mueller actually made himself a mortal threat to America's democracy and national security. That's because his indictment unleashed a rabid anti-Russian mania in the Democratic party and turned flaming liberals and left-wing progressives, who used to form the backbone of the peace party in America, into outright war-mongers.

At the time of the February 2018 indictment of the troll farm, the Donald tweeted about Moscow "laughing its ass off" about the Mueller fairy tale, but we think he missed the mark. It was the Deep State on the banks of the Potomac that was bursting with glee — literally licking its collective chops — about the endless budget boondoggles now assured to be coming its way.

The neocons and military/industrial complex had already taken control of the GOP lock, stock and barrel. Then, his campaign rhetoric about "America First" notwithstanding, Trump abdicated to his empire-minded generals in order to concentrate on his Twitter account.

Finally, in the wake of the RussiaGate hysteria being given a powerful new boost from Mueller's comic book, the Dems too were lining up to say we will see your $720 billion DOD budget and crank it up still higher from there.

So in the great scheme of things, Mueller has now used Prigozhin's pathetic little Hobby Farm to crank-up anti-Russian hysteria in the Imperial City, which, in turn, has poured kerosene on the fires of a flaming fiscal crisis that was already engulfing the nation's finances.

With Warfare State budget soaring and the Welfare State untouched, upwards of $20 trillion of new deficits are now built-in for the next decade. And they come at the very time when the Fed has shut down is massive bond-buying experiment and the Baby Boom is hitting the social security and medicare rolls in droves.

Absent the RussiaGate hoax and the Dems descent into mindless, anti-Putin hysteria, there would have been a moment of maximum danger for the Deep State's hideously inflated military, intelligence and surveillance operations. In the impending battle against fiscal collapse, they might well have been on the fiscal chopping block like at no time since the aftermath of Vietnam in the 1970s.

But rescue is now at hand. The Dems have been shell-shocked ever since the evening of November 8, 2016, and have worked themselves into deliriums about how it was all a big mistake enabled by Russian meddling and collusion with the Trump campaign.

To a substantial degree, however, those narratives were waning until the Mueller indictment came along. For anyone who took the trouble to read it, of course, it was just a potpourri of nonsense, marginalia and irrelevance.

How Yevgeny's Little Troll Farm Got Hyped Into A Monster

But the Dems had already gone brain dead on the RussiaGate matter — so they quickly greeted Mueller's comic book as a "blockbuster", as did — on cue — the talking heads of CNN and the mainstream media. Consequently, the drivel that came out of the building pictured below was taken as evidence of a far-reaching attack on America that even rivals Pearl Harbor. As Pat Buchanan noted:

This Russian troll farm is "the equivalent (of) Pearl Harbor," says Cong. Jerrold Nadler, who would head up the House Judiciary Committee, handling any impeachment, if Democrats retake the House.

When MSNBC's Chris Hayes pressed, Nadler doubled down: The Russians "are destroying our democratic process." While the Russian trolling may not equal Pearl Harbor in its violence, said Nadler, in its "seriousness, it is very much on a par" with Japan's surprise attack.

That's right. But unlike the vast Japanese naval armada that stealthily steamed toward Hawaii in early December 1941, the Facebook cyber-missiles that allegedly hit America in 2016 came out of this little joint hiding in plain sight:

The St. Petersburg Troll Farm — An Existential Threat To America!

So let's return to the fact that Prigozhin's troll farm doesn't really look much different than countless others oligarch-sponsored troll farms which dot the Russian internet landscape, and which mushroomed after 2011 in support of the Putin-ified Russian state and the crony capitalist economy it shepherds.

A *New Yorker* piece published by journalist Adrian Chen, no fan of Donald Trump, in late July 2016 explains about as well as any where the Internet Research Agency came from:

The (Internet Research Agency) has been widely reported in Russian media to be the brainchild of Evgeny Prigozhin, an oligarch and ally of Vladimir Putin. At the time, it employed hundreds of Russians in a nondescript office building in St. Petersburg, where they produced blog posts, comments, infographics, and viral videos that pushed the Kremlin's narrative on both the Russian and English Internet.

The agency is what is known in Russia as a "troll farm," a nickname given to outfits that operate armies of sock-puppet social-media accounts, in order to create the illusion of a rabid grass-roots movement. Trolling has become a key tool in a comprehensive effort by Russian authorities to rein in a previously freewheeling Internet culture, after huge anti-Putin protests in 2011 were organized largely over social media.... wherever politics are discussed online, one can expect a flood of comments from paid trolls.

The real effect, the Russian activists told me, was not to brainwash readers but to overwhelm social media with a flood of fake content, seeding doubt and paranoia, and destroying the possibility of using the Internet as a democratic space...... The agency was a well-funded but often hapless operation — it created a cartoon character that was a giant buttocks to spread anti-Obama propaganda, for example — and this seemed like another of its far-fetched schemes to poison the Internet.

In fact, it was. How it became a fearsome Russian intel operation was entirely due to what happened in Washington DC, not St. Petersburg or the Kremlin, for that matter.

That is, in the summer of 2016, when the Obama inner circle and the Deep State national security establishment alike suddenly were confronted with the theretofore unthinkable prospect that Donald Trump might actually be elected US President, they literally transformed the Hobby Farm of a second tier Russian oligarch into monumental threat to American democracy.

And that took some doing because Prigozhin was essentially a nobody in the great scheme of national security. Unlike Putin, who cut his eyeteeth in the old Soviet era KGB, Prigozhin had fancied himself a ski racer as a privileged young man in a Soviet boarding school. Failing to make the grade on the slopes, however, he had subsequently pursued various petty criminal schemes that landed him nine years in a Soviet prison during the latter's dying days.

But timing is everything — so when he opened a hot dog stand from his mother's kitchen in newly liberated St. Petersburg in the early 1990s his entrepreneurial talents in the culinary field self-evidently flourished. Soon he branched into convenience stores and then in 1996 into a swank restaurant (Staraya Tamozhnya or "The Old Customs House") that catered to newly monied Russians who were looking for "more than cutlets with Vodka."

At length, a strategic $400,000 investment in a rusting harbor boat was turned into a floating hot spot called "The New Island Restaurant." From there flowed catering contracts for lavish state banquets after he gained the gastronomical favor of the post-Soviet St. Petersburg political operative, who became prime minister of Russia.

Putin held lavish state dinners on Prigozhin's floating emporium, where he played host to world leaders like George W. Bush and Jacques Chirac. He also apparently heaped business into Prigozhin's budding empire with a $177 million catering contract with Moscow's schools, and then the real jackpot: A two year contract in 2012 worth more than *$1.6 billion* to supply 90% of all food orders to Russian soldiers.

And that's where the troll factory came from. It opened the next year in 2013 as the kind of token of appreciation expected from oligarchs favored by the Russian state.

The Internet Research Agency — A Tweet By The Numbers Click-Bait Shop

Still, it wasn't the KGB incarnate — just a tweet-by-the-numbers body shop designed to flood Russian media and internet forums with messages extolling Russian greatness, the iniquities and hypocrisies of the morally corrupt West and the glorious works of Vlad Putin.

As indicated above, at this stage the troll farm was involved in strictly Russian business — the handiwork of an oligarch who had thrived on Russia's particular brand of crony capitalism and was more than happy to shill for his patron in the Kremlin.

Here is how the previously referenced *Guardian* article from mid-2015 described the farm before some of its modest resources were later shifted to the "American Department" in 2016:

Just after 9pm each day, a long line of workers files out of 55 Savushkina Street, a modern four-storey office complex with a small sign outside that reads "Business centre." Having spent 12 hours in the building, the workers are replaced by another large group, who will work through the night.

They painted a picture of a work environment that was humourless and draconian, with fines for being a few minutes late or not reaching the required number of posts each day. Trolls worked in rooms of about 20 people, each controlled by three editors, who would check posts and impose fines if they found the words had been cut and pasted, or were ideologically deviant.

The LiveJournal blogger, who spent two months working at the centre until mid-March, said she was paid 45,000 roubles ($790) a month, to run a number of accounts on the site.

"We had to write 'ordinary posts', about making cakes or music tracks we liked, but then every now and then throw in a political post about how the Kiev government is fascist, or that sort of thing," she said.

Scrolling through one of the LiveJournal accounts she ran, the pattern is clear. There are posts about "Europe's 20 most beautiful castles" and "signs that show you are dating the wrong girl", interspersed with political posts about Ukraine or suggesting that the Russian opposition leader Alexei Navalny is corrupt.

The desired conclusion of one reads: "The majority of experts agree that the US is deliberately trying to weaken Russia, and Ukraine is being used only as a way to achieve this goal. If the Ukrainian people had not panicked and backed a coup, the west would have found another way to pressure Russia. But our country is not going to go ahead with the US plans, and we will fight for our sovereignty on the international stage."

To add colour to their posts, websites have been set up to aid the troll army. One features thousands of pasteable images, mainly of European leaders in humiliating photoshopped incidents or with captions pointing out their weakness and stupidity, or showing Putin making hilarious wisecracks and winning the day.

When I got the job there in 2013 it was a (different) small building, I was working in the basement, and it was clear they didn't have enough space," said Andrei Soshnikov, a St Petersburg journalist who infiltrated the company two years ago and has continued to cover it. He linked the move to a much bigger office with increased online activity around the Ukraine crisis.

As we explained above, it was only after Washington massively intervened in the domestic politics of Ukraine in February 2104 that Prigozhin's Hobby Farm branched into external operations focused on Russian adversaries like the new anti-Russian Ukrainian government and the United States.

Even then, however, the main stream media headline writers, who have been intellectually lobotomized by a constant diet of anti-Russian mania, cannot seem to grasp that their hyperbolic headlines are in no way, shape or form supported by the actual written words in Mueller's indictment.

In a word, 80 twenty-somethings sitting cheek-by-jowl at banks of computer screens and banging out social media tripe in English as a (third) language did not impact anything in America, let alone the 2016 election outcome.

That is to say, what in the world is so hard to understand about the fact that the pathetic output of this group could not have amounted to 0.000001% of the content that rumbled through these social media channels during 2016?

Yet here is Mueller — writing in indictment black and white — admitting that the troll farm had deployed precious few trolls to the American department:

"spread (ing) distrust towards the candidates and the political system in general.....By approximately July 2016, more than eighty ORGANIZATION employees were assigned to the translator project."

Besides the infinitesimal volume and generally crude and unoriginal nature of the troll farm's output, this tiny 80-person contingent points to another huge flaw in the entire Mueller narrative — especially as it has been embellished and exaggerated by the main stream media. To wit, all of these posts were destined to get lost in the vast sea of cyberspace without a *ground game* in the US.

The American Ground Game That Wasn't

Yet the indictment is clear on that crucial point as well. The Russian meddlers had "no ground game" whatsoever aside from a 22-day visit in June 2014 by two operatives who were not trained spies and who had apparently never even been to America previously.

Yet they visited nine states during that brief interval and thereby "cased-out" the entirety of the American electoral scene:

Only KRYLOVA and BOGACHEVA received visas, and from approximately June 4, 2014 through June 26, 2014, KRYLOVA and BOGACHEVA traveled in and around the United States, including stops in Nevada, California, New Mexico, Colorado, Illinois, Michigan, Louisiana, Texas, and New York to gather intelligence. After the trip, KRYLOVA and BURCHIK exchanged an intelligence report regarding the trip.

The above paragraph is itself a smoking pot of borscht !

Aside from sleeping, passing through countless airports, checking into a dozen or more hotels and perhaps visiting the chamber of Commerce in Dallas or Denver, what possibly could these two travelers have done to lay the groundwork for "influencing" 133 million voters two years hence?

Mueller doesn't say and the talking heads jabber on about this trip as if it were some kind of invasion, not the pointless needle-in-the-haystack type of undertaking that it actually was.

And that gets us to the ballyhooed efforts to organize and promote Trump rallies in Florida, Washington DC, New York City and elsewhere. Once again, however, Mueller spilled large amounts of ink citing the emails and social media posts that described the aims of these long-distance media trolls. But there is not a shred of evidence presented about what actually happened on the ground.

We would be so bold as to suggest that we know why Mueller didn't document this core element of the alleged meddling campaign. Namely, because nobody came to the rallies and flash mob events called for by the keyboard jockeys in St. Petersburg.

Take the case of the "Florida Goes Trump" rallies on August 20, which the indictment dwells on at length. So doing, it purported to explain how real Trump supporters in the state were duped into cooperating, how bloggers back in Russia used social media posts to promote 13 rallies across the state of Florida and bought ads to the same end on Facebook.

In fact, compared to fleeting references with respect to similar rallies allegedly staged in Washington DC and New York City, the Florida rallies take up far more ink in the indictment and come across as exhibit #1 on Russia ground game in the US election process.

Indeed, the liberal swarm at *Politico* made the singular importance of the Florida meddling operation abundantly clear:

But the document makes clear that the operation in Florida, the nation's largest swing state, was in a class by itself. The indictment is packed with details of how Russian nationals duped Donald Trump campaign volunteers and grass-roots organizations in Florida into holding rallies they organized and helped fund with foreign cash.

Here's the problem. There seems to be scant evidence that these rallies actually happened or that anyone showed up to the ones that did occur. For instance, here is a photo of one in St. Petersburg (Florida) posted on social media at the time. We doubt whether Vlad got his money's worth on this one.

Evidence of How Russian Trolls Duped The Masses In Florida

Then there's the case of Jim Frishe of Clearwater, Florida. He was a real estate development consultant and candidate for county office, who organized a sign-waving event in response to the Russian entreaties that attracted barely a dozen people:

Frishe, 68, said he was called by someone identifying themselves as with a group called "Florida for Trump" and asked to organize a sign-waving rally. He said between 15 and 18 people showed up and that he didn't receive any signs or money or other support. He never heard from them again.

"I was going to do what I was going to do anyway. I was a Trump supporter, they didn't convince me."

Likewise, there was the "Hillary in stripes" caper allegedly promoted by the Russians. According to the indictment:

"For example, defendants and their co-conspirators asked one U.S. person to build a cage on on a flatbed truck ... and another U.S. person to wear a costume portraying Clinton in a prison uniform,"

The thing is, the main evidence for that is that the "cage"

appeared about a month later as the handiwork of a Trump supporter, Gary Howd, who did it all on his own — without any prompting, encouragement or money from the Russians.

Even the Politico account of the purported Florida invasion by the Russians let that much slip out:

The caged Clinton stunt was a hit among Trump supporters. On Sept. 23, for instance, NBC2 reported that a Cape Coral man erected a caged Clinton display in his front yard.

"I feel like I'm doing my little part at least in my little neck of the woods," homeowner Gary Howd said.

As it happened, even the *Washington Post* admits that the "Florida Goes Trump" rallies didn't amount to much.

The efforts in Florida that August day did not turn out to be particularly impressive. No people showed up to at least one of the proposed rallies, and online photos of some of the other events reveal ragtag groups with Trump signs staking out patches of grass or traffic medians.

As to the "Down With Hillary" demonstration on July 23, 2016, to take another example, here is what you get from Google on this particular element of the indictment:

No results found for "Down with Hillary" rally in New York City on July 23, 2016.

Finally, here is what a real troll farm looks like. Yet this vast suite of offices in Fort Meade, Maryland, where 20,000 SIGINT spies and technicians work for the NSA, is only the tip of the iceberg.

As indicated, the US actually spends $75 billion per year — more than Russia's entire $61 billion defense budget — spying on and meddling in the politics of virtually every nation on earth.

The outfit within NSA called Tailored Access Operations (TAO) which we previously described has a multi-billion annual budget and does nothing put troll the global internet; and it does so with highly educated, highly paid professionals, not $4 per hour keyboard jockeys.

Indeed, the cafeterias in the NSA buildings pictured below cost far more per year to operate than did Prigozhin's troll farm during it entire short lived existence (its apparently now being closed down with two of the 3.5 floors already dark).

What A Real Troll Farm Looks Like — NSA Headquarters At Ft. Meade

In that context, Charles Hugh Smith cogently reminded that the real farce in the Mueller comic book is that it is the ultimate case of the pot-calling-the-kettle black:

America's foreign policy is one of absolute entitlement to influence the domestic affairs and politics of every nation of interest, which to a truly global empire includes every nation on the planet to the degree every nation is a market and/or a potential threat to U.S. interests.

Assassination of elected leaders — no problem. Funding the emergence of new U.S.-directed political parties — just another day at the office. Inciting dissent and discord to destabilize regimes — it's what we do, folks. Funding outright propaganda — one of

our enduring specialties.

Finally, as Pat Buchanan further observed in his post on the Mueller indictment, political and election meddling is what Imperial Washington does. And now we are surprised that others aspire to the same — even if it is just the pathetic efforts of a Russian oligarch laid out in Mueller's ham sandwich indictment:

Are the CIA and National Endowment for Democracy under orders not to try to influence the outcome of elections in nations in whose ruling regimes we believe we have a stake?

"Have we ever tried to meddle in other countries' elections?" Laura Ingraham asked former CIA Director James Woolsey this weekend.

With a grin, Woolsey replied, "Oh, probably."

"We don't do that anymore though?" Ingraham interrupted. "We don't mess around in other people's elections, Jim?"

"Well," Woolsey said with a smile. "Only for a very good cause."

CHAPTER 26

Mueller Mugs America: The Case Of Baby George Papadopoulos

This is how the Deep State crushes disobedience, such as electing the wrong president, by the unwashed American public. It indicts not only ham sandwiches but, apparently, political infants in diapers too, if that's what it takes.

Hence the pathetic case of Baby George Papadopoulos, who pled guilty to "lying" about an essentially immaterial date, and ended up getting 14 days in jail — the twice the number of days (7) by which he purportedly "misled" the FBI.

Oh, and by all signs and signals that plea came after this 30 year-old novice had been wearing a wire for several months.

Here's how this noxious act of bullying by Robert Mueller's Federally-deputized thugs came down. It seems that during the early months of 2016, when Trump was winning primary after primary against all mainstream media expectations, the Donald's establishment betters began attacking his foreign policy credentials with special malice aforethought.

That was mainly owing to his sensible suggestion that it would be better to seek rapprochement with Russia rather than pursue Hillary's Cold War 2.0; and that 25 years after the disappearance of the Soviet Union from the pages of history the thought occurred to the Donald that perhaps NATO was obsolete and needed to be put out to pasture.

Since this totally plausible (and correct) viewpoint was deeply offensive to the Imperial City's group think and threatened the Warfare State's existential need for a fearsome enemy, Trump's ruminations about making a deal with Putin were roundly belittled — especially by the GOP foreign policy establishment.

Never mind that a fresh look at the realities abroad suggested to the unschooled Trump the possibility that homeland security does not require a global empire. Instead, the fault was said to lie with the candidate's lack of any pedigreed foreign policy advisors.

Indeed, when it came to the Republican-oriented foreign policy establishment — nearly all of which had joined the Never Trump cause — the Donald added insult to injury. That is, he confessed that he got his foreign policy views watching TV (like most of Washington) and that he could do a better job against terrorism than the Pentagon generals (not hard).

At length, however, the "who are your foreign policy advisors" meme got so relentless that the Donald relented. On March 21, 2016 he announced a group of five advisors that exactly no one who was anyone in the Imperial City had ever heard of, and for good reason.

The group included two recycled DOD flunkies, an anti-Muslim fanatic from the Lebanon religious wars and two kids of no accomplishment in the foreign policy field whatsoever. In a word, the foreign policy establishment's boycott of the Trump campaign at that stage was 100% effective.

Indeed, under a snarky headline the next day about how the new Trump foreign policy team "baffles GOP experts", Politico laid on the disdain good and hard:

"I don't know any of them," said Kori Schake, a research fellow at Stanford University's Hoover Institution and a former official in the George W. Bush State Department. "National security is hard to do well even with first-rate people. It's almost impossible to do well with third-rate people."

One of the five, of course, was Carter Page who, as we have

seen, had actually spent time in Moscow years earlier working as a stock broker and didn't exactly share Hillary's fulminations that Putin was Adolph Hitler incarnate.

Plucked From The Phone Book

In this context, *Politico* made short shrift of young Mr. Papadopoulos and properly so. This wholesome young man had no more qualifications to be named among the top five foreign policy advisors to the then near-presumptive GOP nominee than anyone else in the DC phone book — although at the time Baby George was called to duty he was apparently domiciled in London and perhaps listed in its phone book.

Indeed, after rounding up an ex-Pentagon bean counter, a washed-up general who had "managed" (not well) the US "occupation" of Baghdad in 2003-2004 and Walid Phares, the Lebanese war veteran who claimed that the Moslem Brotherhood had infiltrated the State Department and was fixing to spread "Sharia law" to the towns and villages of America, you almost have the impression that the Donald instructed Ivanka and Jared to check out the Mar-A-Logo sandbox for candidates to round out the roster.

That's apparently where Papadopoulos came from because he had graduated from college only in 2009, got two more degrees by 2011 in London, functioned as a junior researcher at Hudson Institute for several years and then "worked" on Ben Carson's presidential campaign for three months — if you consider that an actual job.

Per *Politico* at the time of the announcement:

... According to his LinkedIn page, he was a researcher at the conservative Hudson Institute in Washington, D.C., before joining the London Center of International Law Practice, which describes itself as dedicated to "peace and development through international law and dispute resolution."

Papadopoulos' LinkedIn page also boasts about his role at the

2012 meeting in Geneva of the Model U.N. where students debate current issues. It adds that he has "had experience lobbying foreign policy resolutions on Capitol Hill by means of coherent and concise arguments."

In a word, Baby George's "crime" came about in the process of trying to put on his Big Boy Pants and get noticed by higher-ups in the campaign. So doing, he came into contact on about March 14 with a London professor who claimed to be plugged into Russian sources with "dirt" about Hillary.

As it turned out, the London professor, one Joseph Mifsud, had credentials that were even more dubious than those of Baby George's. That is, Mifsud had formerly served in a government position in his native land of, well, Malta (as assistant to the Maltese foreign minister) and didn't know anybody in the Kremlin, either. That is, Mifsud was actually a no count talking to another no count.

Prior to his appearance on the FBI's fake stage of international intrigue, in fact, Mifsud had been what might charitably be described as an academic grifter. Moving between makeshift institutions of "higher learning" in Malta, Italy, Slovenia and finally London, he usually left behind a trail of missing money and incredulous, uneducated students.

His latest scam, apparently, was functioning as the "director" of some sort at the London Academy of Diplomacy — a place that grants degrees to young people earnestly endeavoring a career in making diplomacy, not war. By the standards of the Imperial City, it sounded like some kind of Quaker Meeting for idealistic diplomats on the road to Nowhere.

As it turned out, Mifsud never produced a promised trove of Hillary emails. Nor did Papadopoulos ever make any contact with Russian state officials or have any meetings with clandestine Putin operatives. In fact, he came up with no anti-Hillary dirt at all — despite months of trying and sending loads of essentially unanswered emails up the chain of command at Trump Tower.

Despite sending six emails volunteering his eagerness to set up a meeting between the Donald and Vlad Putin nothing happened. Even the government's charging document admits these missives were based on Papadopoulos' conversations with a "Russian National" who claimed to be Putin's niece, but wasn't; and someone who claimed to have contacts at Russia's Ministry of Foreign Affairs (MFA), but also, apparently, didn't.

As it turns out, the latter unnamed go-between was one Ivan Timofeev, a program director at a Russian government-funded think tank called the Russian International Affairs Council. The latter was actually a glorified "welcome wagon" which hosts public meetings with prominent visiting politicians and public figures from the U.S. and other countries.

Indeed, one guest speaker at the Council's forum had been none other than Obama's former US Ambassador to Russia, Michael McFaul. The latter is actually a fire-breathing Russophobe who can hardly be considered a pal of Putin's.

In any event, the government's charging document makes clear that Baby George's emails got nowhere. Indeed at one point the zealous Mr. Papadopoulos got swatted away by Paul Manafort, who replied to one such request by saying that: —

"...Trump is not doing these trips. It should be someone low-level in the campaign so as not to send any signal."

So finding no contacts, no meetings, no "collusion" or anything else validly related to Mueller's mandate, the latter's legal gunslingers came up with the usual default "crime" when a criminal investigations comes up empty. To wit, Papadopoulos allegedly perjured himself by telling the FBI that he had met the no count London professor **before** beginning his service as a Trump advisor.

And that was true enough — except by the lights of the hair-splitting Torquemadas on Team Mueller.

It seems young George met the London Professor on March 14, about a week before the Trump campaign's official announcement of its Team of Five. But in the kind of twisted gotcha that only jerks with a badge and gun can come up with, Papadopoulos stands guilty of perjury by his own (coerced) plea.

That's because at the time of the March 14 meeting he had already been recruited from the sandbox and "knew" he would be appointed to an advisory committee.

One And Done — The Donald Only Meeting Was A Photo OP

Trump apparently met with the Five only once — on March 21, 2016 — and that was for a photo op. Moreover, no one running the campaign paid much attention to this putative foreign policy advisory committee, either.

Still, Baby George's carelessness about the exact dates and sequences of utterly irrelevant and inconsequential events is enough to get him his 14 days in one of Uncle Sam's hospitality suites:

Defendant PAPADOPOULOS acknowledged that the professor had told him about the Russians possessing "dirt" on then-candidate Hillary Clinton in the forms of "thousands of emails", but stated multiple times that he learned the information prior to joining the Campaign. In truth and fact, however, defendant PAPADOPOULOS learned he would be an advisor to the campaign in early March, and met the professor on or about March 14, 2016......

That's all she wrote. This damning nugget appears on page 2 of the "Statement of Offense" and the balance of the 14 pages is a complete farcical joke. Papadopoulos' failure to get anywhere with the Russians in his digging for dirt on Hillary would make for a worthy episode starring the rascals of South Park, but that's about all.

Anyone not involved in the campaign to reverse the 2016 election and remove the Donald from office might well be forgiven for splitting a gut laughing when reading this hideous and utterly bogus case against Baby George Papadopoulos.

Needless to say, Baby George Papadopoulos was no exception. As we have seen, every single player in the cast of characters identified and indicted by Team Mueller have been charged with unrelated crimes or were so inconsequential in Trump World as to have no ability whatsoever to influence anything — let alone 139 million voters in a US election bombarded with upwards of $20 billion worth of reported and unreported campaign expenses

That, plus the mainstream media's free nonstop campaign in behalf of Hillary.

All the while the real "crime", of course, was the **$10 million** that the DNC and Clinton campaign spent on the Trump Dossier. Those scurrilous documents were actually purchased for real money on the back streets of Moscow and do cite actual, live Russian MFA sources, not the allegedly "MFA-connected" people who Baby George talked to that apparently weren't.

But that's not what has come down. The self-righteous Mueller, who turned a blind eye to the massive stench of corruption coming out of the Uranium One deal in 2009/2010 when he was FBI director, has had only one mission in mind: To mug the American electorate for its audacity in electing Donald Trump President, thereby disturbing the equanimity of the Deep State's untethered rule.

The truth of the matter, however, is nearly the opposite. Prosecuting anyone — on either side of the partisan aisle — for marginal and tangential contacts with a Russian government purportedly wishing to "influence" the US election amounts to the height of hypocrisy.

After all and we repeat: Meddling in the political life, elections and governance of virtually every nation on planet earth — enemy, foe, rival, neutral and friend, alike — is what Imperial Washington does.

It spends more than $1 billion per year on propaganda

operations by the NED and the various agencies of the Board for International Broadcasting. And that's to say nothing of the tens of billions spent by the CIA, NSA and other elements of the $75 billion per year intelligence community hacking and stealing virtually all communications that course through the worldwide web.

But all of this is lost on the beltway media brats who front for the Deep State. Here is what one of the worst of these scolds and toadies, a "journalist" named Mike Allen, had to say about the Baby George case on his pretentious Axios platform at the time of the indictment:

Be smart: There is zero doubt — and piles of new evidence — that Russia manipulated our election. This next phase will show if Trump himself was aware or involved, or has any interest in doing anything about it — and how extensively America's most powerful companies enabled the mass manipulation.

Well, let's see. If there is any evidence of Russia meddling or of hacking the Podesta and DNC emails, it lies right there in the massive NSA server farms which capture all incoming communications to the US and outgoing, too.

It is retrievable in an instant, but hasn't been because it's not there.

And we didn't need Mueller's bully boys to bushwhack Baby George Papadopoulos to find that out

CHAPTER 27

The Trump Tower Meeting

When it comes to unreality, Trump's crackpot economics is actually more than rivaled by the full retard Russophobia of the MSM, the Dems and the nomenclatura of Imperial Washington.

In fact, their groupthink mania about the alleged Russian attack on American democracy is so devoid of fact, logic, context, proportion and self-awareness as to give the Donald's tweet storms an aura of sanity by comparison.

And at the heart of the overall RussiaGate mania lies a mindless obsession — indeed, a literal brain freeze — with respect to the June 2016 Trump Tower meeting with a Russian lawyer by the name of Natalia Veselnitskaya.

Needless to say, she was not sent to New York by Vlad Putin to talk up some collusion plans. In part that's because Ms. Veselnitskaya had no ties to Putin, the Kremlin or the Russian intelligence services, but mainly because she speaks not a word of English!

Do we really need to point out that Putin is way too smart to risk having a super-sensitive discussion about meddling in the American election lost in the translation?

The Trump Tower Meeting Was An Anti-Magnitsky Act Fly-Buy

In fact, the Trump Tower meeting was a just a fly-buy. Natalia was actually in New York doing god's work, as it were, defending a Russian company, Prevezon Holdings, against hokey money-laundering charges related to the abominable Magnitsky Act and its contemptible promoter, Bill Browder.

In fact, as explained below, the whole Trump Tower meeting wasn't about the American election at all; Veselnitskaya's pitch was all about Russia's deep (and warranted) grievances at Washington's meddling in their own internal affairs, and the bellicose demonization of Russian business and government leaders that stems from its sanctimonious imposition of sanctions on upwards of 50 Russians under Magnitsky.

Astonishingly, the Prevezon case amounted to a prosecution not at all on the moral high road, but was actually a very down and dirty exercise in government greed. Namely, the US government was attempting to steal via the U.S. forfeiture laws some of the proceeds of a theft that had allegedly happened in Russia!

Defending against that money grab was why the "Russian lawyer" was in New York and ended up at Trump Tower, and why her appearance there most surely had nothing at all to do with the Trump campaign colluding with the Kremlin.

In fact, the whole foundation of the Prevezon case is so rotten that Hollywood fiction writers would be hard-pressed to top it. To wit, Prevezon's crime was that its controlling shareholder, Denis Katsyv, had allegedly defrauded the Russian government of exactly $230 million via a tax refund scheme, and then routed the money through Cyprus financial entities, where a tiny portion ($600,000) made its way into a half-dozen luxury apartments and commercial properties in New York City.

But since the NYC properties were alleged to be worth upwards of $15-20 million, they essentially amounted to the poisoned fruit of an alleged crime which happened in Russia, and therefore presented a big fat forfeiture jackpot for the U.S. government prosecutors. The excuse for the attempted seizure, of course, was that the New York City properties were being used to launder illicit Russian money.

Then again, the US government had exactly zero objective information about the Russian end of the alleged crime and had done no independent investigation whatsoever. Accordingly, it had no way of verifying whether the money was actually illicit and whether the allegedly tainted properties were actually financial laundries — and that's by the testimony of Homeland Security Special Agent Todd Hyman who had worked the case.

Except, except there was this: The Prevezon case had been brought to the headline-seeking US Attorney for the Southern District of New York (SDNY) and Senator Chuckles Schumer's former chief hatchet-man, Preet Bharara, by none other than Bill Browder; and every stich of evidence presented by the government had been exactly as dropped into Bharara's inbox by Browder without further investigation.

What's more, the alleged $230 million theft from the Russian Treasury was one and the same $230 million that is the centerpiece of Browder's cock-and-bull story about how corrupt Russian police had stole it from his firm (Hermitage Capital) in the first place back in 2005 via the aforementioned fraudulent tax refund scheme.

Stated differently, the Russian government says Browder stole the loot, not Veselnitskaya's clients; and that the case belongs in a Russian Court, not the SDNY where it was being tried.

At The Heart Of The Matter — An Epic Swindler Named William Browder

This alternative (and more likely) story, of course, is that Browder had pulled off an epic swindle during the wild west days of post-Soviet Russia, plundering billions by the unauthorized purchasing of Gazprom stock and then failing to pay the requisite Russian taxes. For the offense of not bringing Putin his expected tithe, Browder had been run him out of

Russia on a rail in the fall of 2005.

Needless to say, it doesn't really matter who stole what and who was lying about the $230 million. The relevant fact is that Prevezon Holdings and the young Mr. Katsyv (his father is a powerful Russian transportation bureaucrat) were caught up in a Kangaroo Court and had become the victims of another huge publicity stunt by serial con artist Bill Browder.

As is now well known, Browder had he turned the murky 2009 prison death of his accountant, Sergei Magnitsky, who was also charged with tax evasion, into a revenge crusade against Putin.

That resulted in a huge lobbying campaign subsidized by Browder's illicit billions and spear-headed by the Senate's most blood-thirsty trio of warmongers — Senators McCain, Graham and Cardin — to enact the 2012 Magnitsky Act, under which the aforementioned 50 Russian oligarchs, bureaucrats and Putin cronies are being sanctioned.

These sanctions, of course, are the very excrescence of Imperial Washington's arrogant meddling in the internal affairs of other countries. That is, sweeping Washington-dictated sanctions on Russians (and other foreigners) it deems complicit in Magnitsky's death in a Russian jail and for other alleged human rights violations in Russia and elsewhere.

Needless to say, imperial over-reach doesn't get any more egregious than this. Deep State apparatchiks in the US Treasury Department get to try Russian citizens in absentia and without due process for vaguely worded crimes under American law that were allegedly committed in Russia; and then to seize their property and persons if they should venture to travel abroad or involve themselves in any act of global commerce where Washington can browbeat local satrapies and "allies" into cooperation!

Only in an imperial capital steeped in a self-conferred entitlement to function as Global Hegemon would such a preposterous extra-territorial power-grab be even thinkable. After all, what happens to Russians in Russian prisons is absolutely none of Washington's business. Nor by any stretch of the imagination does it pose any threat whatsoever to America's homeland security.

So the irony of the Trump Tower nothingburger is that the alleged Russian agent in the meeting was actually there fighting against Washington's meddling in Russia's internal affairs, not hooking up with Trump's campaign to further a Kremlin plot to attack American democracy.

Indeed, the Magnitsky Act constitutes such an offensive affront to Russian sovereignty that it is not surprising that Putin and his gang are on the warpath against Bill Browder. They understandably and correctly view him as solely responsible for its enactment by dint of a relentless, well-financed anti-Putin demonization campaign.

And since the entire Prevezon case had been fabricated by Browder as just another maneuver in his fanatical campaign to vilify Russia, it is very obvious why the Russians wanted the Prevezon case defeated, and, in fact, ended up settling for a token $6 million on the eve of the trial.

In this context, the only basis for Natalia Veselnitskaya's alleged Putin ties was through Russia's Prosecutor General, Yuri Chaika.

The latter had made it a personal crusade to pursue Browder as a fugitive from Russian justice — he was convicted in absentia of tax fraud and other crimes in 2014 — and an enemy of the state.

As one report described Chaika's campaign:

Chaika's foray into American politics began in earnest in April 2016. That is when his office gave Republican congressman Dana Rohrabacher and three other US representatives a confidential letter detailing American investor Bill Browder's "illegal scheme of buying up Gazprom shares without permission of the

Government of Russia" between 1999 and 2006, one month after Rohrabacher returned from Moscow.

As it happened, Veselnitskaya had apparently brought a memo to the Trump Tower meeting that contained many of the same talking points as one written by Chaika's office two months earlier (for the Rohrabacher meeting).

There you have it. The "dirt" that Don Jr. had been promised was essentially a Trump Tower door opener so that Veselnitskaya could get in some licks against Browder and the hated Magnitsky Act.

Moreover, the dirt that she did have, as we document below, had nothing to do with the DNC and Podesta email hacks or even Hillary's 30,000 missing emails; it was still more anti-Browder stuff — a claim that certain Browder associates were then funding the Dems and the Clinton campaign with the tainted Russian money.

The Un-Smoking Gun — Veselnitskaya's Anti-Browder Talking Points

Indeed, here is the distinctly un-smoking gun — the talking points that the "Russian lawyer" brought to Trump Tower (originally in Russian). Yet there is no way that anyone in their right mind can interpret this as a pitch to meddle in America's 2016 elections.

In fact, what it reveals is the sweeping Russian antipathy to Browder and the fact that his completely fabricated and self-serving Magnitsky campaign has been a godsend to the Washington War Party by fueling irrational, anti-Russian sentiment throughout the Imperial City. That is, it was just the thing to keep the $800 billion national security pork barrel full to the brim and overflowing. The text of the memo Veselnitskaya brought to Trump Tower reads as follows:

The relationship between the United States and the Russian Federation today is tense with disagreements, the source of which

*lie in U.S. lawmakers granting international satisfaction to a
fugitive criminal accused of tax fraud in Russia, a former U.S.
citizen, William Browder, who in 1998 renounced American
citizenship for tax reasons.*

*In December 2012, after a major, three-year lobbying
campaign, the United States adopted the Sergei Magnitsky Rule
of Law Accountability Act, which laid out the in fact nonexistent
story of a "lawyer" Sergey Magnitsky who allegedly exposed
corruption crimes and embezzlement from the Russian Treasury,
for which he was arrested, tortured and beaten, leading to his
death in November 2009.*

*This law was in essence the start of a new round of the Cold
War between the United States and Russia, putting on the scales
the interests of a group of fraudsters on one side, and interstate
relations on the other.*

*....Since the end of 1999, Browder's largest client became the
company Ziff Brothers Investment, which began aggressively
buying Gazprom stock through a scheme to bypass a Russian
legislative ban on foreign companies purchasing this stock on the
internal market ... Once Browder's activities drew the attention of
the Russian law enforcement authorities, and he was not allowed
any more to visit Russia on a tourist visa, in January 2006 all the
assets controlled by the Ziff Brothers Investments were removed
from the jurisdiction of the Russian Federation.*

*According to the available information, in 2006 the American
owners of the chain of companies mentioned above gained an
income of over $800 million, including 66 million shares of
Gazprom received as dividends.*

*According to preliminary estimates, the damage to the Russian
budget in the form of unpaid taxes from these activities exceeded 1
billion rubles.*

*....According to information we have, the Ziff brothers
took part in financing both Obama election campaigns, and the
American press call them "the main sponsor of the Democrats." It*

cannot be ruled out that they took part in financing the campaign of Hillary Clinton.

Browder, realizing that sooner or later his lies would come out in a jury trial in New York (i.e. the Prevezon case), used the period of the suspension in the case to intensify his efforts to globalize his false story and strengthen his alibi. With the help of Senator Cardin, his long-time collaborator, he has the Global Magnitsky Act introduced in the Senate last December.

Browder's plan is simple: to place the global Magnitsky Act on the table of the new President of the United States, to prevent the new administration from reviewing the interstate relations between the United States and Russia, so diligently antagonized at the instigation of Browder and others interested in this.

It doesn't get any more straight forward than this. The purpose of Veselnitskaya's visit to Trump Tower in June 2016 was to share with the the Trump campaign Russia's deeply hostile attitude toward Browder and convey that his Magnitsky Act intrusion into Russia's internal affairs was deeply offensive to Moscow and a fundamental irritant to improved U.S./Russian relations.

Oh, and the simulacrum of "dirt" she had to offer, of course, was the above charge that Browder's co-fraudsters, the Ziff Brothers, were big backers of the Dems and Hillary Clinton. That is to say, the kind of "dirt" you don't need a collusion for because you can get it from your desk-top by querying the Federal Elections Commission's data base of contributors.

But what is astounding about the straight forward nature of Veselnitskaya's Trump Tower presentation, as revealed in the full text of her memo, is that the mainstream media has become so rabidly McCarthyite that they fail to see the forest for the trees.

That is, since Veselnitskaya's memo is nearly identical to the one which Prosecutor General Yuri Chaika submitted to the House committee, that supposedly proves she was in cahoots with the Kremlin and that the Trump Tower meeting had a nefarious purpose.....to collude!

For crying out loud. Being in alignment with the Russian Government's position on Browder and Magnitsky owing to her role as lead attorney for Denis Katsyv, who was a victim of both, has absolutely nothing to do with plotting to attack American Democracy.

Yet that's exactly what the New York Times has spilled buckets of ink trying to suggest via stories documenting the similarities of the Prosecutor General's pitch to Congressman Rohrabacher's subcommittee and the memo brought to Trump Tower.

Needless to say, the skunk in the woodpile doesn't smell any the better owing to the New York Times' dissembling. That is, nothing nefarious happened at the Trump Tower meeting on June 15, 2016. There was no collusion. Full stop.

As it happened, two years later at the Helsinki press conference, Putin himself reminded the Donald (and the world public) of Russia's animus against Browder in no uncertain terms, and that the meddlers, alas, reside in the Imperial City, not the Kremlin:

"Business associates of his have earned over $1.5 billion in Russia," Mr. Putin said. "They never paid any taxes. Neither in Russia nor in the United States. Yet the money escaped the country. They were transferred to the United States. They sent huge amounts of money, $400 million, as a contribution to the campaign of Hillary Clinton."

So at the heart of the Russian collusion story and its alleged pivotal meeting at Trump Tower in June 2016 is nothing more than a half-baked effort by Russians to tell their side of the Magnitsky story; and to expose the real villain in the piece — a monumentally greedy hedge fund operator who had stolen the Russian people blind and then conveniently gave up his American citizenship so that he would neither do time in a Russian jail or pay taxes in America.

The Magnitsky Act Meddling In Russian Affairs Is Merely What Imperial Washington Does

In view of these facts, you could properly call this a case of the pot calling the kettle black: Meddling is what Washington does onto others — even as it hypocritically whines about being a victim.

But Imperial Washington and its shills among the ranks of Dem politicians and the megaphones in the MSM wouldn't get the joke if it smacked them between the eyes. That's because Washington is in the business of meddling in the domestic affairs of virtually every country in the world — friend, foe and also-ran. And as we have previously documented, it's on a massive scale never before imagined in human history.

Indeed, what the hideously excessive *$75 billion* budget of the so-called 17-agency "intelligence community" (IC) buys is a backdoor into every access point and traffic exchange node on the entire global internet; and from there, the ability to hack, surveil, exfiltrate or corrupt the communications of any government, political party, business or private citizen virtually anywhere on the planet.

And, no, this isn't being done for the noble purpose of rooting-out the terrorist needles in the global haystack of communications and internet traffic. It's done because the IC has the resources to do it and because it has invested itself with endless missions of global hegemony.

These self-serving missions, in turn, justify its existence, keep the politicians of Washington well stocked in scary bedtime stories and, most importantly of all, ensure that the fiscal gravy train remains loaded to the gills and that the gilded prosperity of the beltway never falters.

Indeed, if Washington were looking for corporate pen name it would be Meddling "R" Us. And we speak here not merely of its vast and secretive spy apparatus, but also of its completely visible everyday intrusions into the affairs of other countries

via the billions that are channeled through the National
Endowment for Democracy and the vast NGO network funded
by the State Department, DOD, the CIA and other organs of
the national security complex.

As we have previously indicated, the *$800 million* per year
Board For International Broadcasting, for example, is purely in
the propaganda business; and despite the Cold War's end 27
years ago, still carries out relentless "agit prop" in Russia and
among the reincarnated states of the old Soviet Union and
Warsaw Pact via Radio Free Europe/Radio Liberty and the
Voice of America.

For example, a recent Voice of America tweet falsely
charged Russia with the occupation of the former Soviet state of
Georgia.

In fact, Russia came to the aid of the Russian-speaking
population of the breakaway province of South Ossetia in
2008; the latter felt imperiled by the grandiose pretensions
of the corrupt Saakashvili government in Tbilisi, which had
unilaterally launched an indiscriminate military assault on the
major cities of the province.

Moreover, even an EU commission investigation came to
that conclusion way back in 2009. That was shortly after the
events which the inhabitants of South Ossetia feared would lead
to a genocidal invasion by Georgia's military.

*An investigation into last year's Russia-Georgia war
delivered a damning indictment of President Mikheil Saakashvili
today, accusing Tbilisi of launching an indiscriminate artillery
barrage on the city of Tskhinvali that started the war.*

*In more than 1,000 pages of analysis, documentation and
witness statements, the most exhaustive inquiry into the five-day
conflict dismissed Georgian claims that the artillery attack was in
response to a Russian invasion......*

*The EU-commissioned report, by a fact-finding mission of
more than 20 political, military, human rights and international*

534

law experts led by the Swiss diplomat, Heidi Tagliavini, was unveiled in Brussels today after nine months of work.

Flatly dismissing Saakashvili's version, the report said: "There was no ongoing armed attack by Russia before the start of the Georgian operation ... Georgian claims of a large-scale presence of Russian armed forces in South Ossetia prior to the Georgian offensive could not be substantiated ...

The point is, whatever the rights and wrongs of the statelets and provinces attempting to sort themselves out after the fall of the Soviet Union, this was all happening on Russia's doorsteps and was none of Washington's business even at the time. But wasting taxpayer money 10 years later by siding with the revanchist claims of the Georgian government is just plain ludicrous.

It's also emblematic of why the Imperial City is so clueless about the rank hypocrisy implicit in the Russian meddling hoax. Believing that America is the Indispensable Nation and that Washington operates by its own hegemonic rules, they are now Shocked, Shocked!......to find that the victims of their blatant intrusions might actually endeavor to fight back.

Even then, the Russophobes have been frantically making a mountain out of a molehill. As we showed in chapter 25, the Russian troll farm in St. Petersburg was actually the Hobby Horse of a mid-sized Oligarch. The latter had been minding his own business trolling the Russian internet, as the oligarchs of that country are wont to do — until the US sponsored coup in Kiev in 2014 became the occasion for Washington's relentless vilification of Russia and Putin.

As we have seen, this particular Russian patriot hired a few dozen students at $4 per hour who mostly spoke English as a third-language. Operating on 12-hour shifts, they randomly trolled Facebook and other US based social media, posting crude and sometimes incoherent political messages from virtually all points on the compass — messages that were instantly lost in the great sea of social media trivia and mendacity.

Still, there is no evidence that this two-bit Hobby Farm was an instrument of Kremlin policy or that its tiny *$2 million* budget could hold a candle to the *$200 million* per year round-the-clock propaganda of Voice of America, and multiples thereof by the other Washington propaganda venues.

In any event, characterizing the Trump Tower meeting as evidence of Russian meddling and collusion actually gives the old saw about turning a molehill into a mountain an altogether new meaning. That is to say, on any given evening Anderson Cooper is still interviewing a lathered-up ex-general or ex-spook admonishing that Natalia Veselnitskaya was actually a nefarious Russian "cut out" sent by Putin to infiltrate the Trump campaign.

To the contrary, as we have seen, her mission was an innocent one of attempting to educate the Trump campaign about Washington outrageous meddling in Russia's internal affairs.

Moreover, it self evidently was no cloak-and-dagger maneuver clandestinely orchestrated by the Russian intelligence agencies. Actually, in reaching-out to the Trump campaign in behalf of her anti-Magnitsky Act agenda, she used the good offices of what appears to be the Russian Justin Bieber!

Russia's Justin Bieber Did It!

Specifically, the offer came to Don Trump Jr. via a London-based PR flack named Rob Goldstone, a music publicist who knew the Trumps through the Miss Universe pageant that was held in Moscow in 2013.

Goldstone didn't know his head from a hole in the ground when it comes to international affairs or Russian politics, but he did represent the Russian pop singer Emin Agalarov, whose father was also a Trump- style real estate mogul and had been involved in the 2013 pageant.

Said the London PR flack in an email to Don Jr:

"Emin just called and asked me to contact you with something very interesting....The Crown prosecutor of Russia met with his father Aras this morning and in their meeting offered to provide the Trump campaign with some official documents and information that would incriminate Hillary and her dealings with Russia and would be very useful to your father....(this is) "*part of Russia and its government's support for Mr. Trump.*"

And a very big so what!

For one thing, the last "Crown prosecutor of Russia" was assassinated by the Bolsheviks in 1917, suggesting Goldstone's grasp of the contemporary Russian government was well less than rudimentary.

Secondly, there is neither a crime nor national security issue involved when a campaign seeks to dig-up dirt from foreign nationals. The crime is when they pay for it, and do not report the expenditure to the Federal Elections Commission.

Of course, that's exactly what Hillary Clinton's campaign did with its multi-million funding of the Trump Dossier, generated by foreign national Christopher Steele and intermediated to the FBI and other IC agencies by Fusion GPS.

And that gets us to the mind-boggling silliness of the whole Trump Tower affair. As seen above, the promised dirt on Hillary — the Ziff Brothers money thing — was a come-on so that Veselnitskaya (through her Russian translator) could make a pitch against the Magnitsky Act; and to also point out that after 33,000 Russian babies had been adopted by Americans pre-Magnitsky — that avenue of adoption had been stopped cold when the Kremlin found it necessary to retaliate.

Don's Jr. emails to his secretary from the meeting long ago proved that he immediately recognized Natalia's bait and switch ploy and either didn't get it or was interested in the anti-Browder pitch. So he requested to be summoned to the phone so he could end the meeting.

In short, even though Veselnitskaya didn't come to conspire and Donald Jr. wasn't interested, anyway, there is still another ludicrous twist to the plot.

Its seem that Glenn Simpson, proprietor of Fusion GPS and the intermediary for the infamous Steele Dossier, was working both sides of the street in good beltway racketeering fashion.

That is, he also been hired by Veselnitskaya's Russian clients (Prevezon and Katsyv) to make a case in Washington against the Magnitsky Act, and to also dig up dirt on the scoundrel behind it: Bill Browder.

More fantastically yet, Natalia had apparently meet with Simpson both *before and after the Trump Tower meeting* apparently to be coached by him on her anti-Magnitsky pitch to the Trump campaign.

So if Ms. Veselnitskaya was part of a Trump/Russian collusion conspiracy, then so was Glenn Simpson! And at one and the same time he was midwifing the Trump Dossier which purportedly exposed said conspiracy!

It doesn't get any crazier than that — meaning that the Donald could not be more correct about this entire farce:

This is a terrible situation and Attorney General Jeff Sessions should stop this Rigged Witch Hunt right now, before it continues to stain our country any further. Bob Mueller is totally conflicted, and his 17 Angry Democrats that are doing his dirty work are a disgrace to USA!

PART 5

Border War Follies
And Bannonist Bile

CHAPTER 28

Why The Donald Is Lost — Protectionism, Nationalism And Bannonist Bile

When by Christmas Eve the S&P 500 was down nearly 600 points, or 20% from its September 2018 peak of 2940, it was reported that even the Donald was beginning to sweat the stock market averages.

Well he should have. It was (and is) his misguided agenda of Trade and Border Wars, Fiscal Debauchery and Easy Money/ Fed Bashing that is now hammering the fragile foundation he inherited — that is, faux prosperity on main street and Bubble Finance on Wall Street.

Stated differently, Trump's ersatz populism fits well with the job description for the Great Disrupter. But it never had a prayer of making MAGA.

Even though that will become ever more evident as the great Trumpian unraveling gathers momentum, it is worth dissecting why and how the Donald got so far off base.

On that score, we think last summer's departure of Steve Bannon from the White House was not only one of those true moments of good riddance, but also that Bannonism provides an illuminating window on why it's all going so wrong for the Donald.

Needless to say, the last thing America needed was a conservative/populist/statist/nativist alternative to the Welfare State/Warfare State/Bailout State status quo. Yet what

Bannonism boiled down to was essentially acquiescence to the latter — even as it drove politicization deeper into the sphere of culture, communications and commerce.

Stated differently, the heavy hand of the Imperial City in traditional domestic, foreign and financial matters was already bad enough. But Bannonism was no alternative: It just gave a thin veneer of nationalism to what was otherwise the Donald's own dogs' breakfast of protectionism, nativism, jingoism and strong-man bombast.

By the latter, of course, we mean Trump's essentially content free notion that America was falling from greatness mainly due to stupidity, corruption and a penchant for bad deals among Washington pols; and that the undeniable economic malaise, if not decline, of Flyover America was due to some kind of global grand theft from America.

That is, what rightly belonged to America was being stolen by immigrants, imports and the nefarious doings of foreign governments and globalist elites. What was needed to make America Great Again (MAGA), therefore, was a Washington-erected moat to hold back the tide of bad people and unfair foreign economic assaults and a new sheriff in the Oval Office with the "smarts" (with which he believed himself amply endowed) to start "winning" again.

In truth, the Donald had it upside down from the beginning. The unfortunate arrival of Steve Bannon to his campaign in August 2016 only served to give the Donald's disheveled basket of bromides, braggadocio and bile a rightist political edge and proto-intellectual rationalization.

The real problem, in fact, was not the evil flowing into the American homeland from abroad — whether imports, illegals or terrorists. Rather, it was the outward flow of Washington's monetary and military imperialism that was gutting capitalist prosperity domestically and generating terrorist blowback abroad.

Bannonism Never Identified The Real Culprits Behind Flyover America's Malaise

Bannonism never identified the real culprits: Namely, the Wall Street-enriching Bubble Finance policies of the Fed, which forced foreign central banks to buy dollars and trash their own currencies to keep their exports "competitive"; the military-industrial-intelligence-foreign aid complex of the Empire, which massively drained America's fiscal and moral resources; the hugely insolvent institutions of the Welfare State social insurance system (Social Security and Medicare); and the prodigious level of Federal spending on means-tested entitlements (Medicaid, food stamps EITC, etc.).

Consequently, the Bannonized agenda had no inkling, either, that fiscal catastrophe was imminent. And that the Trump administration had no real choice except the politically unpalatable path of cutting spending and/or raising taxes — or eventually getting buried by the inherited fiscal tidal wave cresting at the end of a failing (114-month-old) recovery.

Nor did it grasp that the real cause of Flyover America's distress is the Fed's multi-decade regime of financial repression and Wall Street price-keeping policies that

1. deplete the real pay of workers and send jobs abroad via the FOMC's absurd 2% inflation target;
2. savage the bank balances of savers and retirees via ZIRP;
3. gut jobs, investment and real pay in the business sector via the C-suites' strip-mining of corporate balance sheets and cash flows to fund Wall Street-pleasing stock buybacks, fatter dividends and M&A empire building; and
4. impale the bottom 80% of households on a unrepayable treadmill of (temporarily) cheap debt in order to sustain a simulacrum of middle class living standards.

At the same time, these pernicious monetary central planning policies did fuel the greatest (unsustainable) financial asset inflation in recorded history, thereby showering the top 1%

and 10% with upwards of *$35 trillion* of windfall wealth (on paper).

At bottom, the Fed's financial repression and wealth effects policies amounted to an egregious variation of the old "trickle-down" theory — sponsored and endorsed by the beltway bipartisan consensus and administered with malice aforethought.

It is no wonder, therefore, that Trump's flawed candidacy and pastiche of palliatives and pettifoggery appealed to the left-behind working classes of western Pennsylvania, Ohio, Michigan, Wisconsin and Iowa — as well as to the retirees of Florida and culturally-threatened main streeters domiciled in the small towns and countryside of Red State America.

In these precincts, the election was not especially won by Trump. Rather, the electoral college was essentially defaulted to him by a lifetime denizen of the Imperial City. Clinton had no clue that war, welfare and windfalls to the wealthy were no longer selling in Flyover America.

Then again, Bannon's raw nationalism and the Donald's walls and trademark xenophobic expostulations were not remotely up to the task of ameliorating America's economic, fiscal and financial ailments. That's because it was not bad trade deals and thieving foreigners that accounted for the post-2000 stagnation of median household incomes, huge loss of middle-income jobs and the actual decline of real net investment by the business sector.

To the contrary, the vast off-shoring of American production and breadwinner jobs was due to wage arbitrage — fueled and exacerbated by the Fed's chronic and increasingly profligate easy money policies. The latter resulted in an explosion of household borrowing that sucked in cheaper foreign goods and the continuous inflation of domestic costs, wages and prices, thereby curtailing US exports and encouraging massive import substitution.

Two figures are worth a thousands words and nullify all

the econometric equations they have stuffed away in the Eccles Building computers. To wit, since June 1987 (right before America got Greenspaned), nominal wages per hour have risen by *151%* and real wages by *1%*!

That juxtaposition is a flat-out, screaming indictment of Keynesian central banking. The academic fools who man the printing presses at the Fed and its global counterparts pretend that domestic inflation is symmetrical. That is, wages and prices all march in lock-step over any reasonable period of time to the beat of the 2.00% inflation drummer-boy at the central bank — meaning that nobody looses as the price level steadily rises.

Our PhD geniuses also seem to argue that deliberate pursuit of 2.00% inflation doesn't matter internationally. That's because either FX rates compensate (i.e. if the CPI and nominal wages goes up the dollar goes down) or it doesn't matter because the so-called savings/investment equation always balances. (i.e. if we have a huge current account deficit we get an off-setting inflow of foreign investment).

But this is all destructive poppycock. The impact of inflation domestically is anything but symmetrical. All workers face the same CPI on the cost of living side, but highly differentiated wage inflation, depending whether their employer competes with China Price for goods, the India Price for services, the Mexico Price for assembly, the Pilates Instructor Price for services or the Civil Service Price for government output.

For example, the cumulative hourly wage increase between 1987 and 2018 for all production and non-supervisory workers was 151%, as shown in the blue line below. However, the increase for manufacturing workers during that period was only 123% (orange line), while for health and education workers it was 178% (purple line).

Obviously, manufacturing workers got hammered by the China Price in world trade whereas health and education workers were more or less shielded by government monopolies

Nominal Versus Real Wage Growth Since 1987

▬ Average Hourly Earnings of Production and Nonsupervisory Employees: Total Private, Jun 1987=100
▬ Average Hourly Earnings of Production and Nonsupervisory Employees: Manufacturing, Jun 1987=100
▬ Average Hourly Earnings of Production and Nonsupervisory Employees: Education and Health Services, Jun 1987=100
▬ Employed full time: Median usual weekly real earnings: Wage and salary workers: 16 years and over: Men Q2 1987=100

Source: U.S. Bureau of Labor Statistics   *Shaded areas indicate U.S. recessions*

and provider cartels. As a consequence, the Fed's pro-inflation policy hurt manufacturing workers a lot more than health and education workers.

The Fed's 2.00% Inflation Target — Economic Crime Of The Century

But the real economic crime of the 2.00% inflation target happens in the globally traded space, which is a lot larger than is often recognized. That's because internet enabled services, such as call centers and financial processing operations, essentially face the India Price.

As we previously indicated, for example, as IBM has transitioned from a hardware company to a technology services provider its employment in India has grown from zero in 1993 to 130,000 at present. By contrast, its domestic payroll has shrunk from 150,000 to less than 90,000 during the same 25 year period.

More importantly, the supposed FX adjustment for domestic inflation only works in Keynesian textbooks and in the imagination of the late professor Milton Friedman. The latter more than anyone else convinced Nixon to trash the Bretton Woods gold exchange standard in favor of fiat money and free market based FX rates.

Transmission of the Fed's Bad Money Disease

- India / U.S. Foreign Exchange Rate, Jun 1987=100
- China / U.S. Foreign Exchange Rate, 1987-06-02=100
- Mexico / U.S. Foreign Exchange Rate, 1993-11-08=100

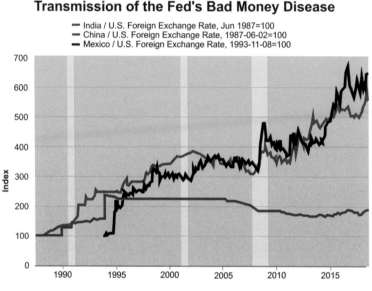

Source: U.S. Bureau of Labor Statistics   *Shaded areas indicate U.S. recessions*

Except since August 1971 there has never been a free market in currencies — just massive, nasty "dirty floats", representing central bank manipulation of exchange rates in the service of mercantilist trade policies.

Consequently, when US manufacturing wages rose by 123% in virtual lock-step with the CPI over 1987-2018, the dollar didn't drop relative to the currencies of low wage competitors like China, India and Mexico. That was supposed to happen on an honest free market in currencies, thereby nullifying some of the adverse competitive impact of the huge rise in nominal US wages.

As shown below, however, the dollar FX rate went in the opposite direction, appreciating considerably against these currencies. That is, owing to the mercantilist monetary policies of these low-wage countries, the actual FX movement completely contradicted what the text books prescribe.

Needless to say, in a Dirty Float world chronically rising nominal wages in US tradable goods and services industries just meant wage arbitrage and massive off-shoring of production. In a word, the Fed's idiotic 2.00% inflation policy is the greatest destroyer of American job and real wages every imagined.

By contrast, under a sound money regime on the free market, interest rates would have risen to premium levels after 1987. That would have triggered, in turn, a systematic deflation of domestic credit, prices, wages and costs, thereby minimizing the gap between the domestic production price and the China Price for consumer goods, the Mexican Price for assembly labor and the India Price for back-office services.

Stated differently, rather than a 123% increase in the price level since 1987, the US would have experienced a persistent but benign deflationary trend over the past quarter century — much like it did during the booming growth times of the later 19th century.

Moreover, there are some advantages to domestic production including far lower transportation and insurance costs, much simpler, speedier and more flexible supply chains and generally higher productivity per hour in the US. Accordingly, in the context of a deflating domestic economy and falling nominal wage rates (but rising purchasing power) the considerable economic costs of off-shoring would have weighed much more heavily in corporate production and sourcing decisions.

Indeed, you cannot emphasize enough the monetary cause of America's massive trade deficits and hollowed-out productive sector. As we indicated in Part 1, during the Greenspan era America's #1 export has been a tsunami of Fed created excess dollar liabilities.

In turn, this threat essentially house-trained the other central banks of the world — but especially those of the so-called emerging markets and resource economies — to run their central banks based on exchange rate targeting, not on old fashioned criteria of sound money.

In fact, in a dollar-based global monetary system, the post-1987 Fed turned the entire convoy of worldwide central banks into money printing machines by virtue of constant and heavy-handed intervention in FX markets to keep their exchange rates down and their export factories humming.

As a consequence, the ballyhooed saving/investment identify got bolloxed because foreign central banks purchased US debt at far higher prices (lower yields) than would have occurred on a free market. This meant that part of the "investment" that balanced the US current account was simply asset purchases by foreign central banks (and their private front-runners) based on fiat credits issued to buy in dollars and sequester them on their balance sheets.

Needless to say, that essentially fraudulent financing of the US current account enabled chronic US deficits to remain uncorrected. Since the last surplus in 1974, in fact, the cumulative current account deficit in 2018 dollars has been about $19 trillion — much of that financed directly or indirectly by foreign central banks.

Worse still, once the global central banking system had essentially been transformed into a beggar-thy-neighbor FX management and manipulation racket, it didn't take long for many foreign central banks to basically adopt a "see and raise" posture. That is, not only did their pegging operations aim to keep their exchange rates from appreciating against the dollar, they actually attempted to push their FX rates lower.

The chart below indexes the Mexican peso, Chinese yuan and Indian rupee to a 1987 value of 100. During the next 30 years, the US CPI rose by 123% — so according to the textbooks, one USD should have bought fewer and fewer pesos, yuan and rupee over time. That means the indexed lines in the chart should have been trending downward from a starting point of 100.

In fact, just the opposite happened. Today, the US dollar will buy 2X more yuan than in 1987, 5X more rupee and 6.4X more pesos. And, in turn, that meant more US off-shoring of jobs and production to these low-wage economies because rather than offsetting with stronger Chinese or Mexican FX rates the 151% rise in nominal US wages shown above, foreign currency depreciation actually widened the gap.

In other words, Greenspan and his heirs and assigns have unleashed a monster. They have universalized the bad money disease — essentially have made it contagious owing to the overwhelming role of the dollar in global trade and finance. So doing, they have turned Flyover America into a wasteland economically and into Trump World politically.

In short, the free trade theory of comparative advantage and universal societal welfare gains does work under a regime of hard money and free market pricing of money, debt and other capital assets. But the Fed's Bubble Finance regime of domestic inflation and subsidized debt-financed consumption simply results in the hollowing-out of the domestic economy; and also an alienated flyover electorate that, at length, apparently had no use for the nostrums of a wizened beltway lifer.

How Bannonism Begat More Welfare For The Rich

Needless to say, the Donald's lurch into unhinged protectionism and his recent morphing into the Tariff Man will only make the legacy of bad money even worse for Flyover America. As we documented earlier, if the full monte of a 25% tariff on all $526 billion of Chinese imports goes into effect — and we are confident that some time next year after negotiations breakdown completely that it will — the cost to American consumers would be $130 billion on an arithmetic basis.

But that's not how tariffs really work. Since China is overwhelmingly the low cost global supplier on most of the $526 billion of goods shipped to America, the impact of the Donald's tariff will be to erect a huge price umbrella; and not just on the actual Chinese imports, but on the entire product markets which they supply.

On average, China supplies about 31% of the goods consumed by the US economy in the product categories in which it competes. So that means essentially that upward of $1.7 trillion — or 40% — of annual goods consumption in the US economy will be subject to the Donald's brobdingnagian tariff umbrella.

In some instances, where China is the monopoly supplier at present, prices will rise by the full 25%. In other cases, where there are alternative higher-cost foreign or domestic competitors, prices will rise but not by the full 25%. In these instances, the actual rise will be dependent upon how aggressive competitors are in trying to capture market share from current Chinese suppliers.

It remains to be seen, of course, as to how Trump's insane tariff experiment works out because absolutely nothing approaching this magnitude against a single country has been effected in modern times. But if the average gain in the price level on the 25% Tariff Umbrella were to reach 15%, the cost impact to US consumers would be $250 billion per year.

That's not only not chump change — its also likely to fall heavily on the bottom 80% of US households which essentially survive pay-check to pay-check at Walmart's.

So with no action against the central bank monster which caused the problem — and, instead, loud public complaining against the tepid steps they Fed is actually taking to normalize rates and balance sheets — and also with badly counter-productive action owing to the Trade War with China and others, the Donald is essentially doing nothing to address the bread and butter grievances of Flyover America's economic left-behinds.

And that's not the half of it. The asinine Trump/GOP tax cut bill of last winter will also come back to bit the Donald hard politically.

Unlike the Bannonist part of the Donald's agenda — -protectionism and immigrant bashing — the tax bill originated with the GOP lifers on Capitol Hill. As we have seen, it was a swamp creatures' delight — conceived, written and muscled through the Congress by the lobbies, of the PACs and for the GOP donor class.

It goes without saying, however, that once the new House Dem majority gets done savaging it with hearings and investigations that show it to be a grotesque giveaway (their words) to the rich and to powerful corporations, there will be no saving grace of jobs and growth to defend it.

Indeed, it is already evident that the ballyhooed investment spree isn't happening. By Q3 2018, in fact, real business investment was up by only 2.5% on an annualized basis. And there is a powerful reason for that which was evident long before the GOP plunged into borrowing $1.7 trillion over the next decade to finance the corporate rate cut and related business reforms.

To wit, in the face of the cheapest debt and equity capital in recorded history, any project that could generate a positive rate of return was already being funded. The after-tax hurdle rate, in fact, was the lowest in modern history even before the Trump corporate rate cut.

That is to say, any company that had wished to build a factory, warehouse, grocery store or Pilates studio in America had not been stopped by the after-tax cost of capital. If it did elect foreign production, it was due to other factors such cheaper labor or better proximity to supply chains or end markets.

Accordingly, reducing the corporate tax rate from 35%

to 21% is resulting in nothing more than increased financial engineering in the C-suites and a massive recycling of corporate cash back into Wall Street — especially a massive surge in stock buybacks and debt-driven M&A.

So failing to understand the cause of America's failing economy and the artificial but dangerously intensifying mal-distribution of wealth, Bannonism has degenerated into welfare for the rich. That is, a further artificial cycling of business cash flows into stock buybacks, bloated dividends and unproductive M&A deals.

These predictable actions, of course, will add insult to injury on the wealth mal-distribution front — given that 85% of stocks and other risk assets (outside of defined benefit pension plans) are owned by the top 10% of the population and 40% are owned by the top 1%.

Nor is foreign trade and taxes the extent of the intellectually threadbare economics of Trump's Bannonism. There is likewise no case that America's GDP is lower or that there are fewer jobs available to native Americans owing to immigration — legal or otherwise. The latter neither take American jobs nor burden native taxpayers with expenditures in excess of their tax payments.

In fact, one sure route to higher aggregate growth and more tax-revenue is to have more immigrant workers. The latter could be easily regularized through a guest-worker system; and its participants could be rewarded for their contribution to American society with an earn-your-way-to-citizenship program based on cumulative taxes paid over an extended period of time, say a decade.

Rightwing Keynesian Statism

Finally, as to the matter of crime, America's colossally stupid and failed War on Drugs accounts for most of the illegal immigrant/border-crossing crime, as we show in chapter

29. By contrast, the actual settled working-class immigrant community has crime rates dramatically lower than those of the native population when adjusted for comparable age and socioeconomic status. Those are just plain facts.

So the obvious thing to do is de-criminalize drugs, put distribution in the hands of Phillip Morris rather than violent drug cartels and levy a modest nuisance (excise) tax on legalized sales from drug stores, vending machines etc. That would sure beat spending $18 billion on just the first 700 miles of the Donald's ridiculous 2,000 mile Wall on the Mexican border.

At the end of the day, when it comes to economics, Bannonism and Trum-O-Nomics amount to rightwing Keynesianism with a heavy statist flair.

That includes not only the $100 billion enlargement of the national security pork barrel and the pending vast waste on border walls and enforcement, but especially the Donald's ballyhooed infrastructure program that is apparently next in rotation.

The fact is, there is no deficiency of US highways or airports or sewer systems that cannot be solved with higher user fees, less Federal pork barrel and more local tax and spend accountability.

Washington doesn't really need to do a damn thing about it except redirect the existing Federal gas tax purely to the Interstate Highway system (as opposed to mass transit, local roads and bicycle paths). After that, Washington should activate the 10th amendment, thereby restoring Federalism and returning the infrastructure functions to the 87,000 units of state and local government extant in America.

At the end of the day, there is not a single element of Bannon's nationalist agenda that should be implemented or that would not do immense harm.

Unfortunately, while Bannon is long gone and was actually buried with malice aforethought by the Donald's subsequent rage-tweets, the damage continues unabated in what passes for the Trump agenda.

In the meanwhile, the Trumpian Fiscal Debauch continues to swell. In the short run, the tax cut bill is adding $425 billion to the baseline deficit during FY 2018 and 2019, and the GOP's February spending spree for defense, disaster relief, border control, domestic appropriations add-ons, veterans and much more added another $500 billion to the already massive built-in deficit for these two years.

Simply put, the Donald has walked into a monumental debt trap that will increasingly dominate the Washington agenda. That's especially because once the debt ceiling holiday expires in March 2019, the spectre of government shutdowns and debt ceiling showdowns is likely to once again become a chronic state of play in the Imperial City.

The resurgent Dem majority in in the U.S. House, in fact, is sure to push an expansionist fiscal program as a pre-2020 marketing campaign for its newly evolving crypto-socialist agenda. That will obviously make agreement on appropriations and debt ceiling bills well nigh impossible to achieve without shutdown showdowns.

In this context, the Donald was recently quoted as not being much concerned about the impending public debt crisis because "I won't be around when it happens."

He could not be more mistaken. Unless the stock market suffers a violent meltdown and the GOP elders decide to put him on the Tricky Dick Nixon Memorial Helicopter early, Trump is actually likely to face fiscal DEFCON 1 conditions long before he's gone.

That's because, as we have seen, the fiscally clueless White House and GOP leadership spent the last two years fiddling while the fiscal fires continued to burn. During the current fiscal year (FY 2019) alone, the Trump-GOP is now fixing to spend about $4.6 trillion (22.3% of GDP) trillion and borrow upwards of $1.2 trillion to finance it.

That huge borrowing requirement is owing to the fact that receipts will come in at only $3.4 trillion. The latter, in turn, reflects the fact that the revenue base, which was already at a historically low *17.8%* of GDP, was slashed to just *16.6%* of GDP by the Christmas Eve tax cut bill last year. It now stands at the lowest non-recession year take from national income in modern history.

Needless to say, when it comes time to raise the debt ceiling to $23 trillion or more next March, the new House majority will use the occasion to drive home the point (partially false) that the budget crisis is owing to the GOP's massive tax giveaway to the rich and the big corporations.

By then, of course, the Donald's problem will be much larger than the Fire and Fury of Bannon's apostasy. Nor will an impeachment-imperiled President be able to blame his demise on Steve Bannon — although Bannonism at the end will be the reason Trump could not actually make MAGA, and thereby retain the loyalty of his 2016 Flyover America voters.

The truth is, Trump's original campaign patter was never anything more than bile, bombast and platitudes. And Bannon's economic nationalism did nothing to make it better.

In fact, Bannonism was never more than a wrong-headed mishmash of ersatz nationalism and the skin deep intellectualism of a failed schemer and power-hungry slob who somehow stumbled into the Donald's unlikely campaign at the 11th hour.

But in short order the truth became clear: The Donald's dogs' breakfast of protectionism, nativism, jingoism and strong-man bombast was inherently a pig that couldn't be powdered — even by the ultra-glib Steve Bannon.

CHAPTER 29

The Statist Roots Of Trump's Border Walls — The Failed War On Drugs

You can't appreciate the insanity of the Donald's Border Wars without knowing one cardinal truth. To wit, virtually all of the crime and violence which he endlessly demagogues about is caused by Washington's benighted War on Drugs. By contrast, immigrants have far lower crime rates than native Americans.

Accordingly, un-conflating illegal drugs and illegal immigrants is the sine qua non for understanding that in the guise of "law and order" the Donald is really about the business of aggrandizing the state, and thereby shrinking the sphere of liberty and imperiling the nation's economic future.

Of course, the basis for the false association between immigration and crime is not hard to understand. It stems from the inherent violence and mayhem of the Mexican cartels which bring illegal drugs across the borders and the US based syndicates and gangs which distribute them throughout the land. Yet that brutal underworld of crime is not remotely a product of undocumented aliens roaming the streets of America.

Instead, it is the handiwork of the Nanny State's badges and officialdom. The latter wage a destructive, relentless and futile war against the distribution and sale of products which have a *$100 billion* annual retail value, at minimum.

The War On Drugs — A Giant Subsidy Mill For The Criminal Underworld

In fact, however,the production cost at the farm and chem lab of the four principal illegal drugs — marijuana, cocaine, heroin and meth — does not constitute much more than a few billion dollars out of the $100 billion. All the rest — $90+ billions — stems from the high cost of shielding the distribution network from law enforcement, including product lost to interdiction and seizure and the massive corruption that is endemic to the business.

For example, *$2 million* worth of cocaine coming out of Columbia is estimated to be worth *$30 million* when it leaves the major transit points in Mexico. However, by the time it reaches the streets of the US east coast it is worth upwards of *$100 million.*

Stated differently, most of that drastic *50X* inflation of the cost chain occurs *inside* the US borders. This means, in turn, that the criminal underground is flush with the economic resources needed to protect the trade from badges and thieves alike, and to generate the astounding profits that attract talented kingpins and middlemen to a life of crime and violence (or early death).

Indeed, the only thing the so-called "war on drugs" actually accomplishes is to moderately reduce the volumes that make it all the way through the supply chain, thereby driving up prices and providing funding for ever more elaborate methods of outlawry and evasion.

For instance, in its budget presentation last year, the DEA crowed that it had deprived drug distribution organizations of $25 billion in revenue during the most recent year by seizing, burning and destroying crops and processed cargos.

But we have a newsflash for our modern day prohibitionist: Destroying $25 billion of illegal drugs is an act of counter-productive futility, not something to boast about. It did not stop a single user from getting their fix — it just inflated the cost of acquiring and delivering product to satisfy market demand.

Indeed, the very interdiction and seizure efforts that led to this estimate temporarily increased product scarcity in the locales and organizations involved, thereby driving-up local street prices. In turn, these high prices incentivized and mobilized the delivery of additional supply from elsewhere.

In effect, our foolish drug warriors are in the business of systematically inflating already hideously high drug prices, thereby compensating the drug underground for product, weapons, and expense lost to, well, law enforcement.

The truth is, the law of supply and demand does will out — and especially in the face of feckless government interventions like these. Even then, the futility of the entire enterprise could not be more obvious.

As shown in the chart below, the rate of drug addiction (purple area) in the US is essentially unchanged from the time the War on Drugs was launched by Richard Nixon in the run-up to his 1972 reelection campaign. It was about 1-2% of the adult population then, and remains so almost 50 years later.

Prison Industrial Complex

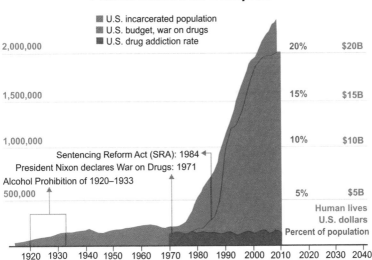

By contrast, the Federal drug war budget had soared from a cold start of *zero* in 1970 to *$20 billion* by 2010 (shown in the chart) and *$32 billion* in the most recent year (FY 2017). And the US prison population — driven directly and indirectly by the war on drugs — has exploded from *400,000* to more than *2.3 million.*

$1.5 Trillion Wasted Over The Past Half-Century

Altogether, more than *$1.5 trillion* has been wasted at all levels of government on the war on drugs over the last 48 years.

Yet notwithstanding this muscular enforcement dragnet, the principle impact of these massive expenditures have been to:

- spawn a vast network of brutal criminal enterprises to distribute the artificially inflated contraband;
- flood the nation's jails with (mainly) small time offenders, drug runners and users, where they spend 5 to 10 years in criminal training school; and
- instill in the public a false association between the 45 million law-abiding, hard-working foreign-born residents of the US, and the few tens of thousands involved in bringing illegal drugs across the borders — by land, air, sea and tunnel — and distributing them throughout the highways and byways of America.

Yes, all that societal cost and mayhem for what — a drug addiction rate that is flatter than a pancake!

And, besides, it's none of the government's business. Indeed, the aforementioned *1-2% addiction rate* does not even rank close to other public health infirmities such as alcoholism and obesity.

Then again, at least the 1920s alcohol prohibition was proven to be a cure worse than the disease, and even Washington's busy-bodies haven't yet figured out how to launch a war on fat people.

Moreover, just as the government's violent war on illegal

drugs has not lessened addiction rates, it has not reduced public use rates, either. In a survey taken every year since the 1970s, the percent of high school seniors reporting illicit drug use in the past month has always varied between *25% and 30%*.

The same is true for the drug use rate for the total total population. By 2002, it had remained steady at about *8%* after 25 years of the war on drugs; and has actually drifted slightly higher to *9.5%* in the last few years — notwithstanding record anti-drug spending and enforcement.

Percentage of Americans 12 and Older Reporting Illicit Drug Use in the Past Month

Note: Federal surveys prior to 2002 used different methodologies, so they aren't included in this chart.

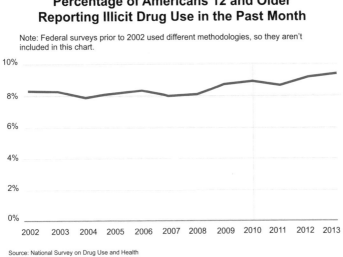

Source: National Survey on Drug Use and Health

The above flat-lining chart puts you in mind of Einstein's famous definition of insanity — doing the same thing over and over and expecting a different result. Yet that goes right to the heart of why the Washington Swamp is so impossible to drain, and why the collateral effects of a massive, pointless bureaucracy are so untoward.

Indeed, the manner in which the misbegotten war on drugs has polluted public perceptions about law and order, border security and illegal immigrants could not be more dramatic.

For instance, the incarceration rates owing to all crimes for men 18-39 years of age are actually 2-3 times higher for native born than for immigrants. Yet the widespread public view to the opposite effect — owing to the association of immigrants with drug violence — is just the tip of the iceberg of false impressions.

In this same vein, consider general arrest trends after the inception of the War on Drugs. Since 1971, the rate of police arrests for non-drug related crimes, as tracked by the FBI's Uniform Crime Reports (UCR), has declined sharply. In 1973, there were 8.7 million such arrests, equating to *5.9%* of the US population over 16.

By contrast, in 2015 non-drug related arrests had barely risen to 9.3 million, but the population over 16 years had grown from 146 million to 250 million. Accordingly, the non-drug arrest rate had dropped to *3.7%* of the adult population.

Of course, this welcome improvement did not translate into public perception of safer communities and a more pacific social order. To the contrary, it was more than nullified by the drug enforcement dragnet and the often spectacular shoot-outs, police raids and violent street level encounters it inherently engenders — and especially in the corridors and transit cities along the border.

Indeed, unlike the solidly declining arrest rate for other crimes, drug arrests have literally erupted by 5-fold in the last 45 years. Thus, at all levels of law enforcement drug-related arrests in 1973 totaled just 300,000. But by the most recent year (2015) that figure had soared to 1.5 million. Moreover, fully 84% of those arrest were for possession, not manufacturing or distribution of the proscribed substances.

As indicated above, this explosion of drug arrests has translated, in turn, into a vast swelling of the US prison population. In fact, there were only *41,000* persons in prisons or jails for drug related offenses in 1973 compared to *501,500* at present. Self-evidently, however, a 12X increase in incarceration has had no impact on drug use rates whatsoever.

Worse still, the political demoguery that has been institutionalized by the war on drugs has been a primary force behind the passage of "tough on crime" laws like minimum sentences and three-strikes and life. It has also spawned a massive increase in resources spent on border control and apprehension of undocumented immigrants on the grounds that the latter are infested with criminal elements — especially drug-related.

Not surprisingly, the number of jailed illegal aliens has also soared in response to massively stepped-up enforcement. Currently, there are 55,000 in Federal prisons and 300,000 in state and local jails compared to less than 9,000 incarcerated illegal aliens prior to 1980.

Yet the overwhelming share of this 355,000 total have been incarcerated for immigration-related violations, not general crimes against property or persons. Likewise, the overwhelming share of the undocumented population that has been caught up in the current enforcement dragnet came across the border as job or asylum seekers, not drug mules or for other criminal purposes.

So what we have had in the last 40 years is a massive increase in law enforcement against what should be non-crimes in a liberal society. That is, if people want to come here for work or asylum, they should be given papers at the border, not arrested after the get here; and if the wish to distribute, sell or consume so-called illegal drugs, it shouldn't be a crime, nor should anyone involved ever be incarcerated by the state.

That proposition, in fact, explains a lot about why the US prison population has exploded, and why US incarceration rates relative to population are literally off the charts compared to the rest of the world.

Thus, the total US jail and prison population has soared from 500,000 in 1980 to 2.3 million at present. Yet 800,000 or 45% of that 1.8 million increase is accounted for by drug offenders and illegal aliens.

Stated differently, the nation's jails are overflowing owing to state-manufactured offenses, not a surge in common crime against property and persons.

It is not surprising, therefore, that the American public fears that crime is rampant and the nation's borders over-run and imperiled by drug dealers and illegal aliens.

That something is radically amiss, however, is self-evident when you compare the prison population depicted below to rates for the rest of the world. In fact, the US hosts 25% of the world's non-military prison population but has less than 5% of the world's total population.

Consequently, the US incarceration rate of 750 per 100,000 population compares to a rate of 120 per 100,000 in Canada, and 100 and 75 per 100,000 in Europe and Japan, respectively.

Needless to say, we refuse to believe that in some mysterious way the DNA of the US population has become infected with a radical tendency toward criminality. To the contrary, the eruption in the chart below is explained by stupid laws and policies, not bad people.

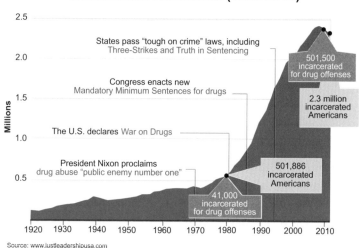

Incarcerated Americans (1920-2013)

Source: www.justleadershipusa.com

Our purpose here is not merely to lament the waste and injustice of this wrong-headed crusade against drugs (and law-abiding undocumented persons). The larger point is that it has also generated unwarranted public fears — even hysteria — about the non-issue of border security, thereby paving the way for that especially toxic brand of anti-immigrant demagoguery that has become Donald Trump's stock and trade.

To Drain The Swamp: Eliminate Inappropriate State Functions By Root And Branch

The failed war on drugs powerfully illustrates how one untoward government intervention begets another and still another — meaning that the Washington swamp can't really be drained until inappropriate functions of the state are eliminated root and branch.

Ending police meddling in citizens private decisions about their sedative, relaxant or recreational intoxicant of choice is one of those inappropriate functions. The fact is, American society functioned nicely, peacefully and prosperously for 200 years before Richard Nixon declared that the job of Washington is to protect citizens from their own personal consumption and health choices.

Early in the 2oth century, for example, before the Nanny State got up a head of steam, cannabis extracts were found on grocery store shelves, as pictured here The lack of DEA agents prowling the store aisles left the American public no worse for the choice.

Since then the prison population has soared — mainly owing to the incarceration of people who formerly had the right to calm their nerves by picking up a bottle of "Cannabis, U.S. P." from Parke, Davis & Co. Needless to say, had the company's present day owner — Pfizer — been allowed to stay in the business we doubt that its distribution methods would include assassination or lesser forms of bodily violence for failed deliveries or late payments.

Indeed, what had been a branded, store-bought product like "Mrs. Winslow's Soothing Syrup", which was cocaine based, has now been consigned to black market distribution channels and criminal underworld.

Yet every aspect of that baleful swap has been profoundly harmful to society. That is, it has vastly inflated costs to consumers; eliminated brand-based quality control enforced by retail competition and consumer litigation; and has replaced what would otherwise be everyday warehouse workers, route drivers and retail clerks with armed thugs and violent drug king-pins.

Thus, Washington's Nanny State campaign against drugs did not merely take "the mother's friend" and like products off the shelf, thereby circumscribing consumer liberties and choice; but so doing it also massively bloated the criminal justice system and its fiscal costs, while also dramatically increasing the opportunities for police abuse and corruption, as well.

In fact, the War on Drugs is the most anti-police enterprise ever invented. It creates such a yawning gap between cops' paychecks and drug-ring payoffs that it inherently fosters corruption, "dirty cops" and demoralization among the nation's men and women in blue.

Moreover, once Washington started down the slippery slope of banning illicit drugs and carrying out a related campaign for "law and order", it became infectious throughout the Imperial City.

In this context, there are few more wasteful and inappropriate Federal activities than that depicted in the chart below. To wit, at the peak of Washington's pointless "war on drugs" in 2010 the DEA funded the eradication of 11 million marijuana plants; and has caused 125 million of such "weeds" to be pulled and destroyed since 1990.

Needless to say, all the expense and associated violence and arrests were for naught. Weed is as popular as ever — perhaps measured by voter referendums in the 28 states were it is now legal for medicinal use and the 9 jurisdictions that allow recreational consumption.

Indeed, the massive machinery of drug enforcement and border interdiction has fostered a sprawling Washington bureaucratic complex that has a powerful interest in spreading fear and hysteria about the nation's purportedly imperiled borders, thereby again conflating immigration with illegal drugs.

How else in this age of advanced technology and drones, planes and fast-boats could an idea as stupid as the Donald's $30 billion border wall ever have gained currency?

If its purpose is to pose a physical barrier to the importation of illegal drugs, the idea is obviously laughable. If it were ever built, Washington would next need 2000 miles of anti-drone batteries to shoot-down all the drones which would be soon leaping over the Wall like Mexican jumping beans.

At the same time, if the idea is to stop undocumented prospective workers from crossing the border, what's the point?

As we demonstrated earlier, America does need tax-mules,

Pulling Up Less Weed

Number of indoor or outdoor plants seized and destroyed under the DEA's cannabis eradication program, in millions

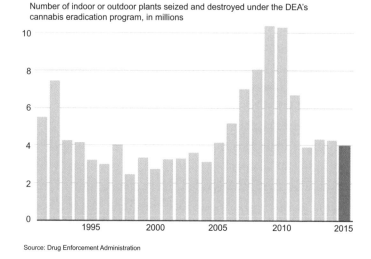

Source: Drug Enforcement Administration

so why build a wall when you can hand them guest worker papers, instead?

By the same token, why spend more than *$30 billion* per year chasing drug-mules when it is estimated that were drugs to be legalized and taxed at the same average rate across the country as alcohol and tobacco, the revenue yield would be about *$50 billion* to the positive side of the ledger.

So the question recurs as to why the nation's fiscally impaired governments collectively endure this $80 billion opportunity cost?

The Drug War Is A Huge Fiscal Racket

As we indicated previously, the War on Drugs has been an unmitigated failure, as dramatized by charts above. Yet by the year 2003 the Federal campaign against illicit drugs was already 30 years old and nearly $10 billion was being spent by Uncle Sam on domestic law enforcement, border interdiction and international drug control initiatives; and another $7 billion was being spent on treatment and prevention. But $17 billion of

Federal drug control spending was having no impact whatsoever.

But that screaming evidence of failure did not deter the beltway bandits who suckle on the taxpayers' teats. In fact, the War on Drugs has become a perpetual motion contraption that gets re-authorized and refunded year after year because special interest lobbies, inertia and log-rolling are the driving force of this enterprise just like most other functions of the domestic welfare state.

Even if some intrepid critic of the false purposes underlying these bipartisan spending silos attempts to challenge them, it is invariably for naught. Washington has become so dysfunctional and immersed in self-perpetuation that it never chooses, decides, allocates or rejects; it essentially operates by continuing resolution — last year's spending plus a little more, year after year for any program function that ever gets started and embraced by both parties.

The GOP's complicity in this horrid stalemate was evident almost from the beginning of the war on drugs. After Nixon launched it, total spending grew modestly to about *$1.7 billion per year* by the time that Ronald Reagan arrived to drain the swamp in 1981. As it happened, however, the drug control swamp got immeasurably deeper during the next 12 years of Reagan/Bush superintendence.

To wit, by FY 1993 when the man who claimed he didn't inhale — Bill Clinton — moved into the White House the so called national drug control budget was up to $12.7 billion, meaning that it had ballooned at an 18% compound annual rate during the years of GOP rule.

As it happened, your author was on the losing end of that budget breakaway. In the first Reagan budget, we had actually sharply curtailed spending for the drug control programs at the DEA, FBI and other agencies based on the above principles and the necessities of fiscal triage. Drug control falls to the bottom of the list when you are trying to actually balance the Federal budget.

Accordingly, the Federal drug control budget was pegged at less than $1 billion — representing a 41% cut; and under the original OMB budget plan was heading toward the shallow end of the swamp in the outyears.

But that didn't last long — not even one budget season. That's because the Heritage Foundation style conservatives in the Administration — and today's leading immigrant-thumpers — were able to quickly redefine the issue. No longer was it a matter of free markets, individual liberty and fiscal rectitude. Instead, it became a matter of generic "law enforcement."

Accordingly, the White House budget rollback of the war on drugs ended up DOA on Capitol Hill. It took all of three months to extinguish the challenge!

In fact, the principal advocates of Ronald Reagan's renewed and up-sized war on drugs were Attorney General William French Smith and White House domestic policy counselor, Ed Meese. Quite simply, they had the "law and order" brief and endless opinion polls which supported a crackdown on illegal drugs, and that's all it took — along with their Adam Smith ties whenever the issue was put to the President Reagan.

As we described previously the upward march of spending for the wrong-headed and failed war on drugs has not abated. During the year just ended, spending totaled *$32 billion*, representing nearly a 9% annual growth rate since the abortive challenge of 1981.

But outside the annihilation of 125 million cannabis plants and the annual arrest of 1.4 million young men — mostly black and Hispanic and mostly for simple possession and small-time dealing — this colossal waste of money has accomplished only one thing: It has visited untold drug cartel violence and mayhem on the nation's borders and inner cities, and over several decades put upwards of 20 million young citizens through crime training schools while incarcerated on drug charges.

The $32 Billion Drug War Jackpot — The Spending "Weed" Which Can't Be Exterminated

Worse still, this pointless war has insinuated itself so deeply and broadly in the Federal budget that it has actually become the "weed" which can not be exterminated. More than 50 agencies and departments share in the *$32 billion jackpot* and much of that goes for purposes that outright deny the reality that an ineradicable criminal black markets will always emerge when the state makes a commodity artificially scarce and thereby generates vast windfall margins and profits.

Nevertheless, it keeps the fear of imperiled borders and criminal immigrants alive and burning in the Imperial City.

Thus, last year $4.5 billion of the drug control budget was spend on "interdiction." This included $2.4 billion for border control and customs operations, $1.3 billion for the Coast Guard and $435 million for DOD's counterdrug programs to "detect, monitor and support the disruption of drug trafficking organizations."

So, yes, it is apparently a real war that fully validates the aforementioned Einstein's theorem about insanity. The Federal government has been doing interdictions for decades, and there has been no reduction in drug supply or use at all; just an increase in the level of violence involved in bringing it into the US at illegal crossings rather than through regular customs offices where it could be stamped and taxed.

Then another $1.6 billion was spent last year under the rubric of "international" drug control programs. Naturally, the State Department got in on that action with $380 million for its own "Bureau of International Narcotics and Law Enforcement." So did the Agency for International Development, which got $132 million to help persuade desperate farmers in drug producing third world countries not to produce the high value cash crops that the war on drugs actually enables.

Finally, the DOD got another $560 million for its

"International Counternarcotics Efforts", which comes on top of the previously itemized amounts for "interdiction."

But it is in the "Domestic Law Enforcement" component where the loot is spread far and wide, and amounts to upwards of $10 billion annually. Nearly 25 different agencies are in on the action including smalltime operations like the "Methamphetamine Enforcement and Lab Cleanup" grants which amount to $11 million per year and the Federal Law Enforcement Training Center which gets $43 million.

On the other end of the spectrum are the big bucks for "investigations", which total $3.3 billion and go to the DEA, FBI and other DOJ operations; and also Homeland Security ($540 million), Treasury ($96 million) and also lesser amounts to DO, Interior and Agriculture.

After that comes $875 million for "Prosecution" which is spread among a dozen agencies. Major amounts go to the DOJ's Organized Crime Drug Enforcement Task Force ($160 million), the US Marshals Service ($144 million), the Federal judiciary ($450 million) and lesser amounts to the DOJ criminal division, the US Attorneys and many more.

Then there is "Corrections" totaling $4.5 billion. From that particular bucket, the US Bureau of Prisons draws $3.4 billion, the Federal Judiciary gets $600 million and the US Marshals dip again for $500 million. Needless to say, not a dime of that would be needed if drugs were sold at far cheaper prices by reputable firms on the free market.

Still, "enforcement" is only part of the budgetary outpouring. There is also $1.5 billion for "prevention" which is shunted through at least 10 different programs. The latter have also failed, as evidenced by flat-lining to slightly rising use and addiction rates. But they are the archetypical sop to liberals in return for their support of the overall war on drug enterprise.

Finally, the number of Federally funded treatment and research programs — costing upwards of $13 billion annually

THE FAILED WAR ON DRUGS

— are too numerous to specify. Beyond the billions that go through Medicare and Medicaid there is also $700 million for VA treatment programs, $450 million for HSS substance abuse and mental health grants to state and local government, $700 million for NIH research, $500 million for HUD to take care of homeless addicts, $75 million for DOD health services, $92 million for drug courts, and then two more of especial salience.

The Bureau of Prisons gets $118 million to treat drug offenders while they are incarcerated (how does that work?) and then additional agencies at DOJ and HSS get another $60 million for prisoner "reentry programs" when they are released.

Then again, neither program would be needed if these guests at Uncle Sam's hospitality facilities had not been arrested in the first place.

In a word, the above catalogue of spending programs is what lies at the bottom of the beltway swamp for hundreds of like and similar Federal program silos. The above described $32 billion war on drugs silo is seemingly invulnerable to reduction owing to the bipartisan consensus as to the broad function of "law enforcement"; and because the loot has now been spread among so many agencies and congressional authorization and appropriations committees that it is virtually immune to attack.

Needless to say, the Trump administration has actually compounded the problem with its demoguery about illegal drugs pouring across the purportedly undefended border with Mexico. Not only has the Donald foolishly pledged to stop all illicit drugs at the border via his preposterous Wall, but also rid the land forthwith of the scourge of heroin addiction.

Likewise, his former attorney general, Jeff Sessions, may well have been a solid conservative on constitutional matters. But he was as bad as Ed Meese and Bill Smith rolled into one with respect to the War on Drugs.

Likewise, former Homeland Security head and then interim chief of staff, General Kelly, never saw a contraband cargo he didn't want to interdict. So under the Donald, the already vast resources of the Federal government dedicated to such futility have been enlarged still further.

So, yes, the War On Drugs is a 45-year failure that wastes vast sums of scarce fiscal resources and wreaks havoc on the nation's borders and communities.

The True Evil Of The War On Drugs — Prosecuting Drug-Mules When America Needs Tax-Mules

But its true evil is far larger. The War on Drugs is actually the lynch-pin fueling the GOP's even more damaging assault on immigration, free markets in labor and commerce and the expanding work force that can no longer be born and bred in America. Time has already run out on the demographic curve of workers versus retirees.

S0 what America really needs to do is court the tax-mules of tomorrow. Prosecuting the drug mules of today is a statist diversion.

At the end of the day, we contend that the reason for the horribly misdirected war on immigrants is the GOP's failure to understand and implement its own principles about limited government and free markets. So doing, it provides legislative votes, philosophical sanction and bipartisan political cover for beltway enterprises that eventually fill the swamp with fiscal waste and societal dysfunction.

As to the former, prevention of self-inflicted harm is never, ever a good reason for state intervention in the private lives of its citizens. The essence of liberty is that people have the right to choose for better or worse when it comes to their own health and well-being.

Moreover, while this type of "prohibition" from time immemorial has merely driven proscribed activities from the efficient, pacific venues of free market commerce into the violent, exploitive netherworld of black market distribution, in this case the societal damage amounts to a doubly whammy.

That is, the War on Drugs has fostered a massive $32 billion per year enforcement bureaucracy that has become a giant lobby and propaganda arm for border control.

The resulting counter-productive and repressive war on immigrants has not only been unjust; it also threatens the supplemental ranks of workers that America's floundering economy and shrinking native-born work force desperately needs.

CHAPTER 30

Why The Donald's Border Wars
Are The Enemy Of MAGA

If you ever needed an example of how to Not Make America Great Again (N-MAGA), consider the idiocy of the Trump Administration's big raid last year on about 100 7-Eleven convenience stores located in 17 states. Upwards of 1,000 ICE agents and support personnel were involved in storming these bottom-of-the-barrel emporiums, but what they snared was a mere 21 suspected illegals — along with gallons of digital ink heralding the Trumpian crackdown on so-called immigration "law-breakers."

Yet there is nothing more anti-free market, anti-jobs and anti-prosperity than these kinds of bully-boy raids by the law enforcement agencies of the state on private commerce.

Grass Roots Free Enterprise

The 7-Eleven chain has about 8,500 stores in the U.S., which comprise the "go to" retail outlet for hand-to-mouth America (literally). It's customer base is overwhelmingly lower income, blue collar, minority, immigrant and millennial. It's $16 average ticket at the cash register denotes customers grabbing a few urgently needed items or a Slurpee or Big Gulp (32 ounce Coke) beverage for the road.

Likewise, upwards of 75% of its units are run by franchisees — nitty-gritty immigrant entrepreneurs from Pakistan,

Afghanistan etc. who operate one or a handful of stores based on shoestring economics, sweat equity and the bottom of the labor pool. Cleaners and stockers currently make $8.60 per hour, cashiers $9.45 and store managers $12.00.

In other words, this is the free market at its best — efficiently linking together a class of businessmen, workers and customers who don't have a lot of alternatives. So what possible social ill justifies the jackboots of the state to come crashing in on these venues of voluntary commerce between consenting adults?

We don't buy the "because" argument. That is, the claim that nothing else matters because the 21 detainees from this particular raid apparently didn't have green cards and were therefore "law-breakers" needing to be administered the cat-o-nine of condign justice.

Then again, if merely breaking the law, and these cases are probably misdemeanors at that, were sufficient basis for storming 100 parking lots all at once — then half the US population should be in jail for one infraction or another of America's hideously bloated criminal statute books.

This is another way of saying that even in these law and order obsessed times, the law is actually selectively enforced based not on abstract law book infractions, but on claims of palpable harm to society and the otherwise law-abiding citizenry.

So the hue and cry about illegals living in our midst is really a claim that they are a clear and present danger, fixing to inflict injury on the innocent unless they are apprehended and deported.

The rest of the right-wing/nationalist rhetoric about sanctity of borders, the civic duty to obey the law etc. is just political window-dressing and humbug dispensed in order to add a patriotic sheen to the real reasons — pure politics — for Washington's massive crackdown on borders and immigrants.

To wit, the latter are held to be either:

- *fiscal parasites* who gobble-up welfare and unfairly burden law-abiding taxpayers;
- *job-stealers* who deprive the native born of employment or higher wage rates; or
- *incipient criminals* who threaten the security and safety of America's neighborhoods.

The purpose at hand, therefore, it to debunk these canards, myths and often deliberate lies. So doing, we expose the statist predicate behind the Donald's unhinged Border Wars and why they are actually MAGA's worst enemy.

The first of these, the welfare parasite meme, is risible nonsense. The 11 million undocumented immigrants, 2.1 million visitors on temporary visas and even most of the 13.1 million green card holders and refugees are flat-out not eligible for Federal welfare benefits. Indeed, to gain eligibility the 26 million non-citizen immigrants in these categories must be resident in the US for five years.

Moreover, this ban on welfare eligibility is sweeping in its coverage. It encompasses 31 different programs which will dispense about *$650 billion* of the **$700 billion** of projected means-tested Federal outlays in the fiscal year ahead.

These ring-fenced programs encompass Temporary Assistance for Needy Families (TANF), Food Stamps, Supplemental Security Income (SSI) and most federal health programs including non-emergency Medicaid, the Children's Health Insurance Program (CHIP), and the Medicare program.

The ban also covers Foster Care, Adoption Assistance, the Child Care and Adoption Fund and low income energy assistance. Undocumented immigrants are likewise not eligible to receive insurance subsidies under the Affordable Care Act or to participate in the ACA insurance exchanges.

The Wall We Really Need — A Washington Wall Around Federal Welfare

So there's that — the sweeping eligibility ban — but here's the even bigger newsflash: The much ballyhooed welfare abuse is not the nefarious doings of illegal immigrants, but the handiwork of Washington politicians and policy bureaucrats who have confected seven-ways-to-Sunday around these sweeping eligibility restrictions.

So there is need for a Wall alright, but rather than one made of cement and steel on the Mexican border, what is actually needed is a wall around Federal welfare that the Washington lobbies and bag-carrying pols of the Imperial City cannot vault over, tunnel under or shimmy through.

And we are not speaking just metaphorically. There is actually no better example of a cynical, loophole-ridden mockery of a putative policy rule than the immigrant welfare ban.

For instance, the school lunch and breakfast programs has been excluded from the ban; and pursuant to Federal guidelines every single state has opted to provide all immigrants — legal and otherwise — with access to the Special Supplemental Nutrition Program for Women, Infants and Children (WIC).

Similarly, short-term noncash emergency disaster assistance remains available without regard to immigration status. Also exempted from the welfare ban are other in-kind services necessary to protect life or safety, including child and adult protective services, programs addressing weather emergencies and homelessness, shelters, soup kitchens and meals-on-wheels.

Also exempted by the "life and safety" loophole are medical, public health, mental health, disability and substance abuse services — along with "emergency" Medicaid services. And the latter alone amounts to something like *$2 billion* per year of expenditures for illegal immigrant medical care.

Finally, among legal permanent resident immigrants there is a whole laundry list of categories which have been exempted

579

from the five-year eligibility rule by Congressional legislation or administrative rule-making. These include refugees, people granted asylum, Cuban/Haitian entrants, certain Amerasian immigrants, Iraqi and Afghan Special Immigrants, and survivors of human trafficking — along with qualified immigrant veterans, active duty military and their spouses and children and children who receive federal foster care delivered by US citizens.

Here's the thing. Owing to this massive labyrinth of exceptions, loopholes and emergency provisions, demagogic proponents of what might be termed the "welfare queen 2.0" thesis can cite studies showing large amounts of "welfare" going to immigrant families, thereby apparently validating the fiscal burden argument for Trumpian style cracks-downs at the border and 7-Eleven style deportation raids throughout the American interior.

For instance, one major study showed that immigrant families with three or more children received **$14,500** of welfare benefits in a recent year. But *$10,000* of this was due to the Medicaid exception for "emergency" care — a discretionary loophole that makes the underlying statutory ban on Medicaid services for routine, chronic and even non-emergency but life-threatening conditions non-operative in many, if not, most cases.

Likewise, another *$1,000* was for school lunch and WIC benefits and **$2,600** (most of the balance) was due to the Food Stamp ban's exception for children of immigrants. The latter is evident from the fact that the same study showed immigrant families with no children received only *$363* worth of food stamp assistance.

Indeed, the oft-made claim that 60% of immigrant households are on Federal welfare is essentially a statistical trick. It results from the fact the kids of undocumented households are required by law to attend public school, where they are automatically enrolled in the Federal school lunch program; and where social workers often make their parents aware of the food stamps loophole for low income immigrant children.

Moreover, the cost of school lunches and food stamps for children is only a few thousand dollars per year per recipient, and not likely to break the bank. Nor is it plausible to think that millions of working age adults bring there families to the US illegally just to get their kids on school lunches and food stamps.

Still, even that statistical reason for illegal immigrant welfare could be erased by a stroke of the pen by canceling the food stamps and school lunch loopholes. And the same is true for the other major source of welfare spending — the emergency Medicaid loophole.

Needless to say, the hard-pressed, unorganized and shadowy community of so-called illegal aliens in the US did not hire slick K-Street lobbyists to turn the immigrant welfare ban into statutory swiss cheese. The facts of high welfare costs and elevated participation rates are not their fault, and is no justification for keeping willing workers out of America or deporting the millions already here.

To the contrary, the vast loopholes described above are the product of Washington do-gooders and liberal lobbyists and legislators seeking to promote humanitarian objectives or pro-Hispanic lobbies claiming to promote equal justice.

We don't think these reasons wash and believe that every single one of these loopholes in the welfare ban should be repealed. Instead, if working families with children want to come to America, give them a work permit at the border stations and a clear explanation that until they work and pay taxes for five years they will not be eligible for a dime of Federal welfare.

In short, build a strong statutory wall around Federal welfare rather than wasting upwards of $30 billion on the Donald's useless physical wall. The former statutory wall would actually save billions per year in welfare costs and remove any semblance of incentives for immigrants to come to America for welfare rather than jobs.

Indeed, the welfare problem and citizenship issue could be handled in one fell swoop. To wit, if authorized temporary visitors and guest workers are employed for 10 years, pay full taxes and then remit a modest admission fee of say $10,000-$25,000, they should be allowed to earn American citizenship. Only then as paid-up full citizens would they be eligible for welfare — a condition that most job-seekers who come to America would gladly accept.

Indeed, this welfare queen 2.0 bogeyman points to a larger issue. Namely, the Imperial City is crawling with bureaucracies and special interest lobbies which thrive only be inciting fear about the mythical harms to the American public posed by the immigrant population. That's how they keep tens of billions of appropriations flowing for border control, homeland security and the war on drugs.

Immigrants Don't Steal American Jobs — They Add To Total Employment

In this context, the second phony argument for the Donald's Border Wars — that immigrants take American jobs — is utter nonsense. And that's true, notwithstanding the claim that millions of job-seeking immigrants causes wages to be lower than otherwise.

In fact, the US economy is assaulted by numerous wage-depressing and jobs-displacing forces. As we have demonstrated, the domestic wage-price-cost structure has been inflated by knuckleheaded Fed policy for so many decades that jobs which can be off-shored owing to the China Price for goods, the India Price for services and the Mexico Price for assembly labor, or which can be displaced by robots and automation owing to the Technology Substitution Price, will be anyway.

In these real world circumstances, any downward pressure on domestic wages at the bottom of the skill ladder owing to immigrant workers is actually a positive; it preserves tax-paying jobs on American soil that would otherwise go elsewhere. That's because downward wage pressure at least partially dilutes the payback for off-shoring or labor substituting technology investments.

Either way, thanks to the Fed's absurd 2% inflation target, America's internal prices, costs and wages have been inflated to the top of the world cost curves. And owing to the dirty float conducted by nearly every central bank in the world in response to the Fed's flood of excess dollars, the foreign exchange markets do not effectively arbitrage the difference.

As we demonstrated in chapter 28, the Fed is effectively killing jobs (via off-shoring) and crushing real wages via its 2% inflation target. The latter eats away at the modest gains in nominal wages which occur at the lower end of the labor market most exposed to off-shore competition and capital and technology substitution.

So the place to fix the jobs and real wage problem — which is real and palpable as evidenced by the heavy Trump vote among Hillary's deplorables — is not at the Mexican border or via asinine raids on 7-Elevens. The culprits dwell in the Eccles Building and could be summarily replaced if someone really wanted to address the underlying problem.

In the meanwhile, the vast machinery of the Imperial City grinds away, propagating the phony "because" reasons for denying to the American economy the giant guest worker program that it will need in order to restore historic rates of growth and avoid being fiscally crushed by the tidal wave of 100 million retirees headed for the entitlement rolls.

Unfortunately, the once and former party of fiscal austerity and free market economics has gone off the deep-end of statism and cultural chauvinism on the matter of immigration. As a result, the workingman's party built in modern times on President William McKinley's "full lunch pail" economics and the vast ranks of immigrant labor in America's Midwestern industrial belt has gone restrictionist, nativist, xenophobic and blindly intolerant.

And that GOP lapse into the dark side was only made worse by the Donald's harsh law and order demagoguery ala the campaign launch imagery of June 2015:

......They're sending people that have lots of problems, and they're bringing those problems with us. They're bringing drugs. They're bringing crime. They're rapists. And some, I assume, are good people"

The Donald's Egregious Lies About Immigrant Crime

Needless to say, there's not a shred of truth to the immigrant crime meme beyond cherry-picked anecdotes about horrendous murders and assaults by illegals, which prove exactly nothing. Even these unrepresentative anecdotes have in many instances been spun to imply the opposite of what actually happened.

For instance, the endlessly trumpeted San Francisco murder of Kate Steinle during July 2015, as tragic and insensible as it was, turns out to be a striking case of pure misdirection.

As was established by the trial, the gun did not belong to the accused illegal immigrant (Garcia Zarate) and it turns out he didn't fire it on purpose. Zarate actually found what was a semi-automatic gun under a chair on San Francisco's Pier 14, which had been stolen from the Federal BLM, wrapped in a T-shirt and abandoned on the pier.

The gun accidentally fired when Zarate picked it up, causing the bullet to travel about 15 feet where it struck the pavement, left an impact mark and was flattened — only to ricochet 100 feet or more, where it freakishly struck Steinle in the back while she was walking along the pier with her father.

As the defense attorney argued, even an expert marksman would have difficulty pulling off such a "skip shot."

The point, however, is not whether Zarate should have been convicted of manslaughter or some lesser crime given the circumstances (probably he should have been), but the fact that the freakish sequence of events established in the trial had nothing to do with his status as an illegal alien.

That is, even a native-born derelict, or a careless juvenile or even an unsuspecting upright citizen could have triggered this one-in-ten-million event. Steinle's death was the result of what amounted to lightening striking randomly, not a porous border with Mexico.

Stated differently, there is a small fraction of every sub-population which consists of thugs, criminals and misanthropes. What is is relevant in the present instance, however, is the *statistical incidence* of these anti-social behaviors, not sensationalized anecdotes.

And on that score, it is also crucial to start with a fact long known to students of crime, if not demagogic politicians. Namely, violent crimes and property theft are overwhelmingly attributable to *young men*.

So when you standardize the crime statistics for the native-born versus immigrant population for that crucial

U.S. Incarceration Rates of Men
Age 18-39, by Nativity, 1980-2010

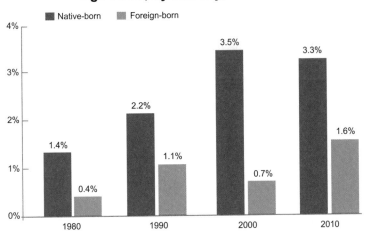

Source: Kristin F. Butcher and Anne Morrison Piehl, Why are Immigrants' Incarceration Rates so Low? (Cambridge, MA: National Bureau of Economic Research, July 2007), Table 2; 2010 ASC.

variable (men age 18-39), the data is crystal clear. Native-born young men commit crimes at ***2-3 times higher rates*** than do immigrants, as measured by incarceration rates. And that gap has not diminished during the last three decades — even as incarceration rates for both groups having risen moderately, mainly owing to the War on Drugs.

In point of fact, the only time that illegals and immigrants are statistically involved in a high incidence of "crime" is when they are engaged in the violent, law-of-the-jungle business of selling and distributing illegal drugs.

But as we showed in chapter 29, drug crime is not an imported border crasher. It is a home-grown scourge fostered by the state because "prohibition" invariably drives distribution underground and the price of the contraband (in this case illegal drugs) sky-high. The resulting massive scarcity or surplus profits in the supply chain provides a powerful incentive for violent behavior and provides the financial wherewithal to support the extensive criminal syndicates and lower level gangs which feed off the trade.

So to repeat: America doesn't need Mexican Walls, more ICE agents or additional hobnailed boots in the DEA (Drug Enforcement Agency) to stop the needless scourges of illegal drug crime. Just decriminalize all drugs and let the equivalent of Phillip Morris and the teamsters union truck drivers handle their sales and distribution.

After all, the often brutal violence that does occur along the US-Mexico border is most definitely not perpetrated by desperate parents willing to kill in order to find work on the US side of the border to support their families.

Instead, it's the result of drug syndicate warfare over territory and trade, and the heavy-handed — often militarized — effort of the DEA, Border Patrol and local law enforcement to accomplish the impossible. That is, interdict and extinguish the ultra-lucrative commerce in illicit drugs, which their futile efforts at restricting supply, ironically, make even more insanely remunerative.

Moreover, notwithstanding the illegal drug trade noise in the data, the immigrant crime story still doesn't wash. The fact is, at the very time that the inflow of immigrants has surged, violent crime rates in the US have fallen dramatically.

Thus, during the 28-year interval between 1960 and 1988, total immigration was just *12.3 million* or about 440,000 persons per year. After that, immigration rates surged by 2.3X. The inflow averaged 1.01 million per year during 1989-2016 and totaled *28.5 million* over the period.

Accordingly, the foreign born share of the US population climbed sharply after 1990, rising from a near historic low of *6.0%* back toward the long-term historic norm at *13.0%*.

At the same time, however, the rate of violent crime in the US fell from 750 per 100,000 residents in 1991 to 380 in 2012 or by nearly *50%;* and has more or less plateaued since then on a nationwide basis (despite flare-ups in a few aberrant cities like Baltimore and Chicago).

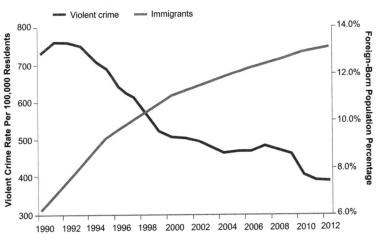

Immigrants and Violent Crime Rate

Source: National Survey on Drug Use and Health

Nor is the above especially surprising when the absolute source of US crime incidence is broken out. To wit, US citizens account for **90% to 98%** of all major crime categories, save for drug trafficking and the self-evident role of illegal immigrants in bringing illegal drugs across the border.

Equally notable is the fact that the estimated **11 million** illegal immigrants committed a slightly smaller share of these crimes (other than drug trafficking) than their **3.5%** share of the U.S. population. And the same is true of the **14 million** immigrants who have legal status.

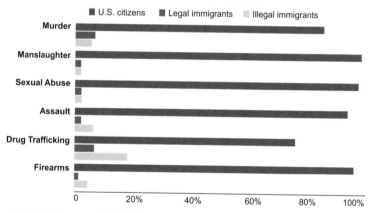

Citizens Vastly Outnumber Immigrants on Most Violent Crimes

Note: Data is based on 71,003 defendants sentenced under the Sentencing Reform Act between Oct. 2014 and Sept. 2015. SRA only collects information on cases sentenced under their guidelines. Crimes outside these guidelines are not included.

Source: United States Sentencing Commission

In this context, it should be noted that there were 44.7 million foreign-born residents in the US in 2015, of which 20 million were naturalized citizens and are reflected in the green bars below. There were also 11 million undocumented persons (light pink bars) and about 14 million non-citizens who had temporary or permanent legal status (dark red bars).

Needless to say, the chart below blows the illegal immigrant crime wave thesis to smithereens and then some. The Trumpite/

GOP Border Wars brigade is simply promulgating a Big Lie for one not very concealed purpose.

To wit, the hard-core Trumpite/GOP has seen that immigrants vote disproportionately for Democrats, and have accordingly misappropriated the machinery of state to help them win elections by conducting Border Wars. Self-evidently, the illicit purpose of these actions has been to keep unwanted voters out of America and to propagate fear and xenophobic reactions among the citizenry.

There are few more egregious assaults on the Constitution than this in all of American history.

America's True History: Melting Pot Of Immigrants

So at the end of the day, the immigrant crime story is a complete red herring. Instead, the underlying motivation is a faulty zero-sum economic theory, rank political opportunism by the GOP and the rise of a nativist chauvinism that glorifies a mythical American "nation" that never really existed.

Unlike most other more homogenous nation-states on the planet, in fact, America was never rooted in a tribe, folk, people or nationality. To the contrary, it was a vast melting pot of diverse ethnicities and nationalities bound together by the ideas of personal liberty, constitutional democracy and free market opportunity and prosperity, not the kind of chauvinistic nationalism propagated by today's fear-mongering GOP anti-immigrant wing.

Indeed, the latter impulse has become so militant and vehement that it tends to obfuscate the stupid economics and the threadbare nationalism on which the GOP's anti-immigrant campaign has been based.

For instance, the heated rhetoric about undocumented immigrants being some kind of egregious class of law-breakers is unwarranted and irrational. Aside from the special case of the government induced illegal drug business, the only legal infraction committed by the overwhelming share of the 11 million undocumenteds is the misdemeanor of crossing the US border without a visa, green card or other legal authorization.

Yet this "crime" is essentially victimless, thoroughly un-American and capable of being eliminated by the stroke of a simple statute. Namely, a law authorizing the issuance of guest worker papers at the border to any worker and his family members who want to come to the US to take a job.

As we have seen, in fact, if you decriminalize drugs and legalize work by foreigners, virtually the entirety of immigrant crime would disappear. That is, the drug trade originated felonies against persons and property would vanish and the misdemeanors for not having the requisite papers (or felonies owing to entering the US "illegally" more than once) would never happen.

Needless to say, America's greatest period of growth and prosperity from 1870 to 1914 was built on exactly that principle. The only documents work-seeking immigrants needed was to

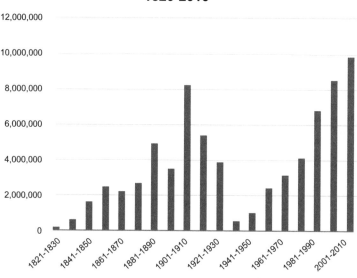

Immigration into the United States, 1820-2010

sign-in at Ellis Island.

There were, in fact, no passports to enter the US until May 1918, and even that was the result of the anti-German hysteria elicited by Woodrow Wilson's phony patriotism and crusade to make the world safe for his foggy brand of "democracy."

Thus, in 1870 the population of the US was just *39 million*. During the next 44 years more than *25 million* immigrants entered the country — a figure which represented nearly two-thirds of the 1870 population!

Yet notwithstanding a half dozen short-lived recessions or "panics" during that interval, real GDP growth averaged **3.8%** per year for more than four decades running. That level of continuous growth had not been achieved before, nor has it since.

During 1907, for example, 1.3 million immigrants entered the US, representing more than **1.5%** of the existing US population (85 million).

Overall, during the first decade of the 20th century nearly nine million immigrants were admitted to the US. That amounted to about *12%* of the US population of 76 million in 1900. By contrast, a century later the 10.4 million immigrants arriving during 2000-2010 represented just *3.7%* of the 282 million population in the year 2000.

Obviously, that contrast thoroughly debunks the current hysterical claims that America is being over-run with immigrants. During 2016, for instance, the immigrant inflow of 1.2 million amounted to just *0.4%* of the nation's 325 million population.

Likewise, immigrants during the pre-1914 golden age of economic growth and rising middle class prosperity represented a far larger share of the work force. Without them, the booming industrial belt from Pittsburg through Youngstown, Cleveland, Toledo, Detroit, Gary, Chicago, Milwaukee, Rockford, the Quad cities of Iowa and St. Louis simply would have never happened.

As is evident in the chart below, the foreign born population peaked at just under *15%* of the total US population during 1890 to 1914, and then began a long descent. This interim decline was triggered initially by the interruption of global commerce and labor mobility during WWI and then the restrictive immigration act of 1924. The latter established immigration quotas based on national origin for Europeans, but did not restrict immigrations from the western hemisphere, including the Donald's sh*thole countries of present renown.

Immigrant Share of U.S. Population Nears Historic High

Percent of U.S. population that is foreign born

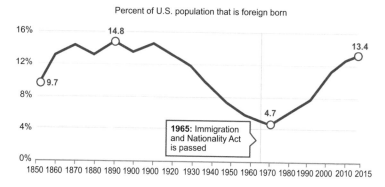

Source: U.S. Census Bureau, "Historical Census Statistics on the Foreign-Born Population of the United States: 1850-2000" and Pew Research Center tabulations of 2010 and 2015 American Community Survey (IPUMS).

So while total immigration was cut by *70%* from the pre-1914 peak levels, it still exceeded 4 million during the economic boom of the 1920s. What caused the annual inflow to collapse to barely 40,000 persons per year during the 1930s was the Great Depression. Foreigners stopped coming when there was no work or economic opportunity — even when the new quotas would have permitted far larger numbers.

Indeed, the historic lesson that immigrants came to America overwhelmingly for jobs and opportunity couldn't be more obvious. Not surprisingly, therefore, when prosperity returned in the mid-1950s, annual inflows rebounded to the **300,000** per year level as permitted by the national origin quotas. The latter amounted to an annual limit equal to 2% of the 1890 level of foreign-born persons in the US from each European country, which favored northern European nationals, and also excluded Asians entirely.

At length, however, the national origin system became unworkable, unfair and increasingly obsolete — so it was abolished in 1965.

But its replacement was hardly any better since it was not governed by economics and work-seeking. Instead, 6% of the total quota was reserved for refugees — with the balance allocated to family reunification (74%), professionals, scientists and artists (10%) and workers in short supply (10%) to be later defined by bureaucrats and business lobbyists. Subsequently, the Refugee Act of 1980 detached refugee admissions from the overall quota system and set up comprehensive procedures for handling refugees.

Stated differently, the economically based, work-driven, quota-free system that prevailed prior to 1914, and which had worked so brilliantly to fuel America's industrial might, was replaced by a politically driven system. The latter shifted the determinants of the flow and composition of immigration from the free market to the legislative and bureaucratic arenas of the state, and to the vast networks of influence peddling and lobbying which drive their action.

Not surprisingly, this evolution has increasingly turned immigration into a matter of pure partisanship — with the Dems now looking for a route to electoral dominance through an immigration fueled increase in the non-white population, while the GOP fights a nativist rearguard action to preserve the electoral dominance of its Red State coalitions.

Still, the dramatic rebound in the foreign born share of the US population since the 1965 Act became law was overwhelmingly driven by economics and work-seeking — the agricultural industries, hotel and restaurant sectors, lawn and home care, domestic service and countless more lower-skilled sectors are testament to that truth; and notwithstanding Washington's endless politically-inspired battles over the machinery of immigration control.

But with the native-born working age population set to shrink by more than 8 million over the next two decades (2015-2035), all time for the nativist chauvinism being propagated by the GOP's anti-immigration caucus has finally expired.

The GOP's policy is now so out of step with economic realities that it has become a source of serious economic harm. Yet as we have seen, the argument made in behalf of prohibiting willing immigrants from committing acts of voluntary commerce (i.e. taking jobs at the offer price) is groundless and stupid.

In fact, it is the same old restrictionist argument that has long been the stock in trade of the unions. When your author first came to Washington in the early 1970s, for instance, he was visited by a lobbyist from the building trades union. The latter was carrying a sack of cash which he offered to help with our boss' next election campaign.

Needless to say, the union man was thrown out of the office forthwith — along with his argument that "foreigners" and scabs were threatening union pay scales.

Actually, they were, and for good reason. Union monopolies were actually contributing to an inflationary cost spiral and a consequent reduction in real output and wealth. For the construction sector to prosper and the economy to grow, the market needed to clear wage rates at competitive levels.

Back then Republican understood what amounts to nothing more than the free market doing god's work. Today they are so focused on manipulating the immigration rules for electoral advantage that they have forgotten entirely these crucial principles.

Therefore, debunking the modern day building trades arguments of the GOP immigrant-thumpers is crucial, as we explain below. Owing to the economic and fiscal facts of life, a dramatic pivot back to pre-1914 work- and economics-driven immigration policy could not come too soon

Why Trump's Anti-Immigrant Folly Is Fiscally Fatal

The starting point for understanding the economic threat posed by the current Trumpian Border Wars is the impending fiscal calamity, which is most dramatically embodied in the massive social insurance system. At the present time, the actuarial deficit of Social Security/Medicare (OASDHI) is in the range of *$55 trillion* on a NPV basis, and even in the world of big numbers that's downright daunting.

Accordingly, we have long felt — and not entirely facetiously — that the only way to avoid fiscal catastrophe is to annex Mexico. In a very real sense, though, the GOP's anti-immigrant program amounts to its mirror opposite — a Mexico/Central America de-annexation policy.

The fact is, the average age of Mexico's 128 millions citizens is just 26 years, meaning that there are lots of potential *Tax Mules* south of the border to bailout America's rapidly aging wave of *Baby Boomers*. And as we showed in Part 2, there is truly no way to describe the latter except to call it a demographic tsunami: The 54 million Americans 65 and older today will become 80 million by 2035 and eventually 105 million.

So not withstanding the literal impracticality (and obvious inappropriateness) of annexing Mexico, it is crucial to understand the labor force demographics, immigration assumptions and the fiscal Ponzi embedded in the social insurance system (Medicare and Social Security). That's because these fundamental realities expose the utter folly of the GOP's virtual war on immigrants and pales into insignificance the current Washington contretemps about Dreamers, funding the Donald's Mexican Wall and putative caravans of "invaders."

What the facts actually show, of course, is that America needs to be *importing* immigrant workers, not **deporting** them. There is simply no conceivable level of tax increases or benefit cuts that can cope with the prospective doubling of the beneficiary rolls and tripling of real costs per beneficiary that we outlined in Part 1.

At least not in the context of what America's politicians and public believe to be a sacrosanct inter-generational transfer payment system. Yet one which, as we have seen, is fatally flawed because it incorporates virtually 100% of annual labor productivity into an endlessly rising level of real benefits over time.

We are referring here to the issue of "wage-indexing" versus "price-indexing" of each worker's earnings history, and the self-evident fact that the long-run cost of the system is being massively swollen by wage-indexing.

Even then, however, there is a second not so hidden feature of the "social insurance" system that throws the whole fiscal equation into a cocked-hat. Namely, the fact that the nation's vaunted "social insurance" system has nothing whatsoever to do with insurance.

There is no investment committee ala Met Life putting the payroll tax receipts to work in stocks, bonds, real estate, alternate asset classes, etc. Instead, there are dozens of Congressional *spending committees* allocating every single dime of payroll taxes to the current good works and boongoogles of the Federal government, and as fast as those payroll tax receipts flow into the US Treasury.

So the whole multi-trillion per year system is pay-as-you-go, not insurance.

During the first 70 years of the system, of course, the payroll tax did generate more cash inflow each year than the outgo for benefits and administrative costs. But those surpluses were not invested; they were spent on aircraft carriers, education grants, farm subsidies, civil service salaries and anything else financed by the general fund. Accordingly, the *$2.9 trillion* of purported cumulative surpluses and assets of the OASDHI system are really nothing more than accounting confetti.

Since 2009 it's gotten far worse. The system is now running a considerable cash deficit — $62 billion in 2016 alone — and is already insolvent, save for the phony book-keeping exercise under which that the $2.9 trillion pile of accounting confetti is being drawn down to cover the shortfall and is earnings interest, too!.

So forget the trust fund accounting hocus pocus and got straight to the lick log. To wit, the so-called social insurance system is built on the assumption of a *permanent and robustly expanding labor force*, world without end.

That's the only way that pay-as-you go taxes on $50,000 of wages in 2020 could square with benefits based on those same earnings that under the current law would be roughly (wage) indexed up to $242,000 by 2060.

In other words, the so-called social insurance programs are on a giant fiscal treadmill. When you propose to pay benefits to our hypothetical worker at retirement in say 2068 (at age 68) based on cumulative labor productivity through 2060 versus the taxes paid on much lower actual wages (pre-indexed) decades earlier, which were completely spent the day they come into the door at the US treasury, the implication isn't hard to figure.

Namely, you will need tens of millions of new workers by 2068 to fund the huge inter-temporal gap. That's just another way of saying, of course, that Social Security/Medicare as now structured is the greatest Ponzi scheme ever invented.

As explained earlier, your author didn't discover this daunting math last week. Indeed, as a young GOP staffer on Capitol Hill in 1972 when Nixon loudly signed into law wage indexing on the eve of his election landslide that year, we even wrote a memo about the mathematical unsustainability of wage-indexing over the long-haul.

Yet given that the working age labor force (25-64) grew by nearly 21 million during the 1975-1985 decade (or peak of the baby boom labor force entry), the Ponzi seemed well enough supplied with new tax mules. Indeed, no politicians — GOP or Dem — operating on a two-year election cycle got very excited about a 75 year demographic cycle that went all pear-shaped at the far end.

By the early 1980s, of course, the crashing US birth rate suggested trouble ahead, which is one of the reasons we championed a package of social security reforms in the Reagan White House. These crucial reforms would have curtailed early retirement and replaced wage-indexing with price-indexing, among numerous other cost-savings changes.

To be sure, even that didn't solve the inherent actuarial fraud of social insurance, but it did sharply reduce the long-run cost of the system, thereby making a start on the emerging demographic/fiscal bust.

Meanwhile, the demographics were beginning to take on a wholly new contour. During the 1985-1995 decade, for example, the prime-age labor force grew by *20 million* again, but only *15 million* of these new tax mules were from native born families — meaning that immigration accounted for the other 5 million.

And during the 1995-2005 decade the trend became undeniable. There were again 20 million new tax mules but only *10.6 million* new native born workers; the rest were immigrants.

At that stage of the game, however, the GOP's anti-immigrant caucus was still in its relative infancy. So there was no evident breach in the Ponzi: 20 million new taxpayers were being drafted into service each decade — even if a rapidly rising (and ignored) share were immigrants.

The GOP's Great 1981 Welfare State Cop-Out

Needless to say, you can't have it both ways. That is, you can't shut-off the supply of new Tax Mules by clamping down on immigration while also taking the cowardly way out politically on the social insurance monster.

However, that is precisely what the GOP has done over the last four decades.

The GOP's cowardly default on reforming the giant middle class entitlements of the US Welfare State happened way back in 1981; and after that seminal whiff, it was essentially all over except the shouting.

We are referring to the devastating rebuke by the Congressional GOP of an effort by the Reagan White House in the spring of 1981 to address the structural fiscal defects at the heart of the social insurance system. To this end, your author helped formulate a plan to eliminate the utterly unaffordable "early retirement" (at age 62) feature of the system and to replace the fiscal doom-loop of wage-indexing with a far less costly and more honest mechanism called "price-indexing" of lifetime wages.

The latter essentially said that workers lifetime wage records would be made whole for cumulative inflation, but not the pure windfall element that derives from also indexing actually wages for future earnings gains above and beyond inflation.

Since early retirement and wage-indexing were (and remain) the leading drivers of Welfare State expansion and the long-run fiscal collapse of social insurance, the 1981 reform plan had fiscal math and political honesty on its side, but, alas, not the votes.

In fact, these crucial reforms never saw the light of day outside of the White House and were effectively killed in the legislative cradle within days of the unveiling. That is, in May 1981 without the benefit of even a days of hearings or policy review of any kind, the GOP Senate leadership passed a resolution denouncing these reforms by a vote of 96 for, 0 against and 4 gone fishing.

The festering new problem that has emerged since 1981, however, is that the US economy has stopped producing breadwinner jobs, which generate lifetime earnings that mostly fall in the low replacement rate brackets of *32%* and **15%**, thereby giving the system some fiscal wiggle room

As we indicated in chapter 8, in fact, the 74.1 million Breadwinner jobs reported by the BLS in September 2018 was essentially the same number as the 72.7 million reported during the month Bill Clinton was packing his bags to vacate the White House nearly 18 years ago.

By contrast, since the turn of the century there has been a healthy growth in what we call the Part-Time Economy — jobs where workers clock only about 26 hours per week at $14 per hour. Here the job count is up by *19%*, but, of course, these are only two-fifth jobs in an income sense because average annualized pay is just $20,000 compared to $50,000 or more for Breadwinner jobs.

So as we also indicated in chapter 8, the faltering US economic growth and jobs trend means that the weighted average wage replacement rate under social security is steadily rising. This means, in turn, that the system is hurtling toward insolvency all the faster.

To be sure, even low, part-time wages are better than no wages at all. Still, the giant skunk in the woodpile remains. To wit, during the decade between 2005 and 2015, the prime age labor force grew by only 13.3 million versus 20 million per decade after 1970, meaning that the Ponzi is now visibly fading.

Moreover, only 4.8 million of those new workers were from native-born households. For the first time, in fact, upwards of 64% of the growth in the US labor pool during that period consisted of immigrants or workers born into families of immigrants.

Stated differently, during the 1980s when the GOP was coping out on social insurance reform but still relatively rational about immigration, nearly 20 million new native-born Tax Mules joined the work force.

By contrast, now that the GOP has gone over to the Trumpian dark side on immigration and long ago threw-in the towel on Welfare State retrenchment, it is in the ignominious position of standing four-square for fiscal disaster.

GOP-Triggered Disaster On The Dark Side

Moreover, on a go-forward basis the GOP's fiscal faithlessness only gets worse. It is now plain as day that the social insurance Ponzi is already totally dependent upon immigrant labor for survival. That's because what's baked into the cake about the *native-born work* force is that the very concept of "growth" is over and done — and as far as the demographer's eye can see.

As shown in the second graph below, during the decade between 2015 and 2025 the native born prime age work force will *shrink by 4.3 million*. The only thing keeping the total work force above the flat line is the projected growth of immigrant workers!

Even then, with the 9.2 million gain over the decade in immigrant workers, the net gain for the total labor force will be just 4.9 million of prime-age workers.

So the Ponzi scheme is now unequivocally heading for the rocks. Compared to the workforce gain of 21 million during the decade after wage-indexing was adopted in 1972, we are now down to just *4.9* million gain in the current decade and roughly the same number during the 2025-2035 decade — all of whom are accounted for by immigrants and then some.

In that context, we are quite confident that the GOP anti-immigrant caucus has never looked at the graphs above. To wit, without immigrant workers the prime working age population

Immigrants and Their U.S.-Born Children Expected to Drive Growth in U.S. Working-Age Population

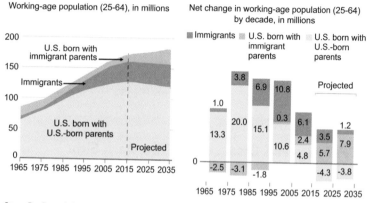

Source: Pew Research Center estimates for 1965-2015 base on adjusted census data; Pew Research Center projections for 2015-2015. Note: Numbers for 2015 onward are projections.

of *173 million* in 2015 would shrink to just *166 million* by 2035.

That is to say, you need upwards of 20 million new workers per decade in order to sustain the Ponzi, and there is only one place to get them — from foreign lands. Today's Republican clowns would apparently prefer to blow the system sky-high rather than recognize this cardinal reality.

The fact is, native-born Americans haven't been making enough babies and future workers for a long time. The native-born fertility rate is currently just 1.7 per child bearing female, meaning that the native born work force is unequivocally on the downside of the slope.

As shown below, the number of babies from native-born mothers in 2014 was 10% below where it was back in 1970 — right before Washington so blithely incorporated wage-indexing and other costly benefit enhancements into the system.

Even if Washington were now to suddenly adopt a giant baby subsidy program to increase family size, it wouldn't materially impact the labor force demographics until 2050 or beyond. And by then, the system will have already crashed.

In sum, the Trump/GOP anti-immigrant campaign

amounts to inadvertently administering last rites to the nation's social insurance Ponzi, which is listing badly already based on total demographics. If we use a generous projection of immigrant worker growth the labor force is still hitting the flat-line in the decades ahead — even as the inherent social insurance Ponzi requires an endless rise from the lower left to the upper right on the work force charts.

Births to Immigrant Moms Tripled Since 1970

Annual number of U.S. births, by mother's nativity (millions)

U.S. Born

3.46   3.25   3.10

Foreign Born

1.08   0.90

0.27

1970   1980   1990   2000   2007 2010 2014

Source: Pew Research Center analysis of National Center for Health Statistics data. "Births outside of marriage decline for immigrant woman"

Indeed, there is only one way at this late date in the actuarial drama to avoid a crash landing. That is, a national policy of obtaining already-made babies (working age immigrants) to goose the size of the prospective work force dramatically during the next thirty years as the baby-boom ages out and the baby-bust shrinks the native-born work force.

In that context, for instance, the very thought of deporting the Dreamers is ludicrous. Each one of these 800,000 persons represents potential life-time payroll taxes of upwards of *$300,000*. And even if those new tax mules do not ultimately pay for themselves — since few do under Social Security/Medicare combined — they would dramatically ease the fiscal crunch during 2020-2050 when the baby-boom benefit cost hits its maximum.

As we have indicated, the only rational immigration policy is one that focuses on **importing**, not *deporting*, working age persons. And that could be accomplished in a heart-beat by adopting a guest-worker program with a long-term path to citizenship based on cumulative tax contributions over several decades.

Unfortunately, the GOP immigrant thumpers have created an utterly false narrative over the years about immigrant based crime and economic harm to domestic workers. And for that reason is can be well and truly said that the GOP's big lies and risible misdirection about the so-called border problem — hoary myths that the Donald's rank demoguery and bile about rapists, murders, criminals and drugs has only made all the more insidious — will prove to be the proximate trigger for the nation's rendezvous with fiscal and economic calamity during the decades ahead..

Indeed, the already dire outlook for the social insurance system shown in the chart below actually assumes the contribution of 18 million new immigrant Tax Mules over the

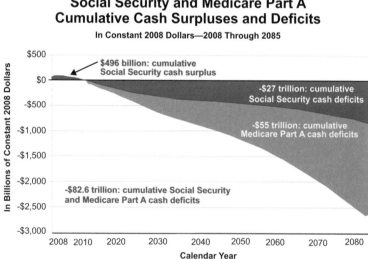

Social Security and Medicare Part A Cumulative Cash Surpluses and Deficits
In Constant 2008 Dollars—2008 Through 2085

Source: Social Security Trustee's Report—March 2008 (Intermediate Projections)

20-years between 2015 and 2035.

So if Washington were to put the GOP's irrationally restrictionist immigration policies in place, there would be only one possibly outcome: A crisis that is already barreling down the road for the 2030s would be turned into a calamity in the 2020s.

CHAPTER 31

The Donald's Paris Climate Accord Haymaker — A Glorious Blow Against Statism

Who would have thunk it? The most statist GOP President of modern times — and he's got considerable company — delivered one of the greatest blows to statism ever when he deep-sixed the Paris Climate Accord.

We have welcomed the Donald all along as the Great Disrupter, but his June 2017 Rose Garden haymaker to the political class' climate change catechism was above and beyond the call of duty. At least on that particular day it was vintage Trump — no double-talking mainstream speech-crafter slipped in even a hint of equivocation. Not a single olive branch of accommodation was offered to the ruling elites anywhere on the planet.

To be sure, the whole thing was done in the name of a pugnacious "America First" narrative. It was delivered by the forceful but unprincipled occupant of the Oval Office who has appointed himself America's jobs czar. In that capacity, Trump opposes the Paris Accord mainly because of its threat to jobs rather than the even more crucial matter that it amounts to a statist crusade to control the totality of economic life based on dubious science.

So Trump's junking the Paris Accord is not the same thing at all as a policy of liberating the free market to generate jobs, economic value and true prosperity — or even to leave the people at liberty to fish, hunt, hike, drink and be merry if they wish. In fact, we are reasonably sure that if the Paris Accord was likely to create American jobs, the Donald would be all for it.

Still, Trump's motivation was a whole lot better than that of the legions of government apparatchiks, liberals, environmental scolds, regulators, globalists, crony capitalists, lobbyists, media megaphones, etc. who were cringing and harrumphing at every word of his magnificent Rose Garden rebuke.

After all, exiting the Paris Accord had nothing much to do with genuine environmental protection. Nor was it even really about American jobs for that matter.

Those kinds of policy wonk debates — about parts per million of C02 and the relative number of coal-miner versus solar panel installer jobs — are what the ruling elites thrive upon.

But what they can't abide is a fundamental assault on the foundations of their statist ideologies. And Trump's courageous head of state diatribe from the Rose Garden — which was long-winded and repetitive enough to make Fidel Castro's ghost envious — was exactly that.

It was a frontal rejection of the kind of ritualized policy narrative that is concocted over and again by the political class and the permanent nomenklatura of the modern state — professors, think tankers, lobbyists, career apparatchiks, officialdom — in order to gather and exercise state power.

To again paraphrase Randolph Bourne, inventing purported failings of capitalism — such as a propensity to burn too much hydrocarbon — is the health of the state. Indeed, fabrication of false problems and threats that purportedly can only be solved by heavy-handed state intervention has become the modus operandi of a political class that has usurped near complete control of modern democracy.

So doing, however, the ruling elites have gotten used to such unimpeded success that they have become sloppy, superficial, careless and dishonest.

The Risible Myth Of Climate Equipoise

That is to say, the global warming narrative is the most risible manifestation yet of this leap into self-righteous disregard for evidence, logic and plausibility. For when you step back from the shrill, sanctimonious narrative that passes for the global warming catechism, the ridiculousness of its central claim that industrial society is destroying the climatic equipoise of the planet is self-evident.

For crying out loud, there never has been equipoise!

What there's been is 4 billion years of wildly oscillating and often violent geologic evolution and climate disequilibrium — owing to manifold natural causes ranging from plate tectonics, to asteroid bombardments, to the multi-hundred million years succession of Ice Ages and the warming intervals in between.

Even the simple textbook extracts from the History Channel cited below remind us that what may or may not have been happening to the global temperature since it allegedly began rising again around 1980 amounts to a white noise rounding error in the grand scheme of things.

In fact, scientists have recorded five significant ice ages throughout the Earth's history. There have naturally been extended periods of global warming in-between, and it goes without saying that we are now in the latest of them:

- *the Huronian (2.4-2.1 billion years ago),*
- *Cryogenian (850-635 million years ago),*
- *Andean-Saharan (460-430 mya),*
- *Karoo (360-260 mya) and the*
- *Quaternary (2.6 mya-present).....*

From the last of these periods, numerous major glaciations have occurred over the past one million years. The largest of these peaked 650,000 years ago and lasted for 50,000 years.

The most recent of these cycles is known simply as the "Ice Age." It experienced peak glacial conditions some 20,000 years back before giving way to the modern far warmer and wetter climate of the interglacial Holocene epoch.

Needless to say, even during the most recent 20,000 year cycle, the oscillations in climate conditions dramatically exceeded anything being measured on current yardsticks of climate change.

For instance, at the peak the current Ice Age, the ice grew to more than 12,000 feet thick as sheets spread across Canada, Scandinavia, Russia and South America.

Consequently, sea levels feel by more than 400 feet, while global temperatures dipped around 10 degrees Fahrenheit on average and up to 40 degrees in some areas. Moreover, climate-driven topographies shifted dramatically: The climate of today's northern latitudes migrated to the region of the Gulf Coast, which was dotted with the pine forests and prairie grasses found today in Canada.

Among these causes of sweeping climate change are the ones that most reasonably attentive school boys can even remember from their textbook diagrams. That is, the images of the earth's orbit elongating and then rounding over approximate 100,000 year intervals (eccentricity) with its obvious implications for temperature at the elliptical extremes; and also the facts that the earth's rotation wobbles (precession) and that the tilt of its axis changes over time (obliquity) in something like 40,000 year cycles.

To be sure, the scientific debates still rage as to which of these three monumental planetary forces drive climate cycles and the precise mechanics, durations and climatic oscillations of the periodic Ice Ages; and also as to how these solar-focussed forces are complimented by other large natural climate drivers such as plate tectonics.

Still, when the relatively tiny contribution of carbon emissions from the 400 million cars or so on the planet's surface today is compared to the gigantic planetary forces referenced above, we'll go with the wonders of the natural universe.

Thus, as the History Channel tutorial further observes about the evolution of modern climate cycles study,

The second important figure in the development of these studies was Serbian mathematician Milutin Milankovitch. Seeking to chart the Earth's temperature from the past 600,000 years, Milankovitch carefully calculated how orbital variations such as eccentricity, precession and axial tilt affected solar radiation levels, publishing his work in the 1941 book Canon of Insolation and the Ice Age Problem. Milankovitch's findings were corroborated when technological improvements in the 1960s allowed for the analyzation of deep sea ice cores and plankton shells, which helped pinpoint periods of glaciation.

Along with solar radiation levels, it is believed that global warming and cooling is connected to plate tectonic activity. The shifting of the Earth's plates creates large-scale changes to continental masses, which impacts ocean and atmospheric currents, and triggers volcanic activity that releases carbon dioxide into the air.

This much reasonably educated people have known all along. But now that the Donald has shattered the mold, perhaps the ragged case of the global warming fear-mongers can presently be taken apart limb for limb, as it deserves.

If debunking global warming orthodoxy becomes contagious, in fact, perhaps even greater secrets will be revealed.

To wit, much of today's statist orthodoxy about other interventionist causes — such as the alleged need for monetary central planning at the Fed, progressive taxation and income redistribution or even Pax Americana — are mainly self-serving inventions, concoctions and lies. They are designed to keep the foot of the state firmly on the neck of free markets, free citizens and all the associated accoutrements of liberty.

In any event, anyone with a working knowledge of geology, archeology and human history undoubtedly suspected the following but here it is.

Climate In Historical Context — We're Now In A Spell of Cooler Amid A Trend Of Warmer

To wit, we are probably sitting at one of the *cooler spells in the last 10,000 years*. To be sure, the latter period comprises a mere spec of time in the planet's natural history, but the important point is that after the peak of the last ice age +/- 20,000 years ago, it generally got considerably warmer for the next 10,000 years.

And that was especially true at the poles: Antarctica warmed about 20 degrees Fahrenheit between about 20,000 and 10,000 years ago, while the average temperature worldwide rose about 7 degrees Fahrenheit. It is not surprising that temperature variations are far greater at the poles, but what needs be noted is that the 7 degrees Fahrenheit rise after the last glacial peak is far more than the 3-5 degrees Fahrenheit temperature increases being projected by the alarmist for the year 2100.

Even more crucially, during the last 10,000 years it has been generally getting cooler again — on the irregular basis depicted by the green arc in the chart below. And at the periodic warming peaks — most recently the Minoan, Roman and Medieval Warmings — average temperatures were considerably higher than today.

As is evident from the chart, there have also been intervals in which average temperatures spiked sharply lower. Mini ice ages, as it were. And those documented colder spells — from ice core samples, ocean sediment readings and other scientific techniques — are extremely important backdrops for the current global warming hysteria.

Undoubtedly what is happening at present, in fact, is that the planet has been modestly rebounding from one of the most recent — and most severe — of these colder spell anomalies, which have occurred within the context of the warmer trends of the Holocene.

This last of these cold spells is known as the Little Ice Age

(LIA) or Maunder Minimum. It bottomed around 1600 to 1750 when it got much colder than almost anytime in the last 10,000 years — a fact which was evident at the time in the form of shorter growing seasons and the icing-over of rivers in Europe that had previously been clear year around.

Quite evidently, of course, the Maunder Minimum's coldish bottom, as depicted from these Greenland ice core measures, opened up a lot of room for an upward trending regression to the Holocene Era's general warming norm.

Greenland GISP2 Ice Core - Last 10,000 Years Interglacial Temperature

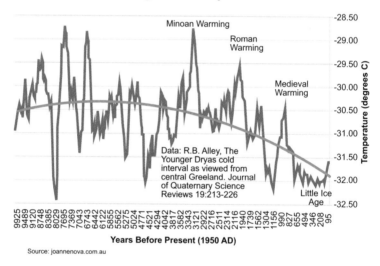

Source: joannenova.com.au

Moreover, the above graph is not merely some kind of "climate deniers" trick based on disputed or anomalous conditions in Greenland. In fact, the above chart is often dismissed by the global warmers as a mere "regional aberration" to be ignored — given its obvious inconsistency with the approved global warming catechism.

Then again, there's this. To wit, evidence of the Medieval and earlier warming periods and the subsequent Little Ice Age taken from soil carbon measurements on the *Great Plains*. Quite naturally, global temperatures have been rising since the Maunder Minimum bottom shown below, and not owing to fossil fuels, either.

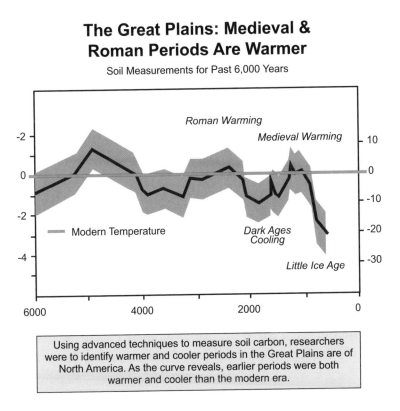

The Great Plains: Medieval & Roman Periods Are Warmer

Soil Measurements for Past 6,000 Years

Using advanced techniques to measure soil carbon, researchers were to identify warmer and cooler periods in the Great Plains are of North America. As the curve reveals, earlier periods were both warmer and cooler than the modern era.

And if the Great Plains are too close to Greenland — just 3,000 miles — to escape the "regional" epithet, there is always this evidence taken from the southern hemisphere and the deep ocean waters of the Indo-Pacific Warm pool.

There, too, the Roman and Medieval warmings are more than evident, as is the Little Ice Age temperature plunge. And along with those pre-industrial climate cyclings from cold to warm to cold and back, the present temperature rebound is

The Roman & Medieval Periods:
Unprecedented Warming
Indo-Pacific Modern Warming Only Lukewarm

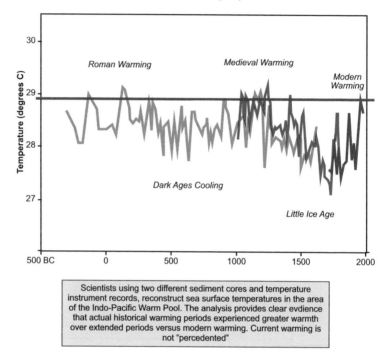

Scientists using two different sediment cores and temperature instrument records, reconstruct sea surface temperatures in the area of the Indo-Pacific Warm Pool. The analysis provides clear evdience that actual historical warming periods experienced greater warmth over extended periods versus modern warming. Current warming is not "percedented"

absolutely nothing out of the plant's ordinary climate oscillation.

Even readings taken from South African caves point to the same story. It was not the global auto fleet or coal-fired power plants at work during the 3,000 year span shown below when temperatures equaled or exceeded present levels.

Indeed, when the Hellenic and Roman cultures were first flowering, it was fortunately warmer than now and fossil fuel combustion had absolutely nothing to do with it.

Given this evidence, we are inclined to say, stop right there!

The ballyhooed threat that global temperatures will soar if Al Gore and his anti-carbon Gestapo do not get their way is about as context-free and historically ignorant as it gets.

Nevertheless, this typical squib from the *Wall Street*

South African Cave Temperature Records
Roman & Medieval Warming Significantly Higher Than Modern Temperatures

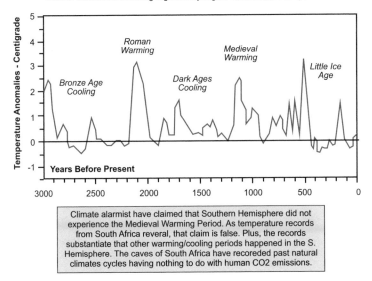

Climate alarmist have claimed that Southern Hemisphere did not experience the Medieval Warming Period. As temperature records from South Africa reveral, that claim is false. Plus, the records substantiate that other warming/cooling periods happened in the S. Hemisphere. The caves of South Africa have recoreded past natural climates cycles having nothing to do with human CO2 emissions.

Journal's coverage of the Trump announcement shows not the slightest recognition that the purported planet saving temperature reduction from the Paris Accord is nothing special at all. It's happened over and again during geologic time — even multiple times during the most recent interglacial cycle.

The agreement aims to keep average global temperatures from rising more than 2 degrees Celsius, or ***3.6 degrees*** Fahrenheit, above ***preindustrial levels***.

Then again, it might be wondered exactly which "preindustrial levels" are being referred to — those of the Medieval Warming around 1100 AD or the Maunder Minimum circa 1730?

So let us repair further to the textbooks to drive this crucial point home with respect to the most recent geologic era — the period during which modern human settlements and societies also arose.

Warming of Earth and glacial retreat began about 14,000

years ago (12,000 BC). The warming was shortly interrupted by a sudden cooling at about 10,000 - 8500 BC known as the Younger-Dryas. The warming resumed by 8500 BC. The younger-dryas event is significant because it shows that even during an otherwise tranquil period (the current interglacial), rapid climate shifts can still occur.

By 5000 to 3000 BC average global temperatures reached their maximum level during the Holocene and were 1 to 2 degrees Celsius warmer than they are today. Climatologists call this period either the Climatic Optimum or the Holocene Optimum.

During the climatic optimum many of the Earth's great ancient civilizations began and flourished. In Africa, the Nile River had three times its present volume, indicating a much larger tropical region. 6,000 years ago the Sahara was far more fertile than today and supported large herds of animals, as evidenced by the Tassili N'Ajjer frescoes of Algeria (right).

From 3000 to 2000 BC a cooling trend occurred. This cooling caused large drops in sea level and the emergence of many islands (Bahamas) and coastal areas that are still above sea level today.

A short warming trend took place from 2000 to 1500 BC, followed once again by colder conditions. Colder temperatures from 1500 - 750 BC caused renewed ice growth in continental glaciers and alpine glaciers, and a sea level drop of between 2 to 3 meters below present day levels.

The period from 750 BC - 800 AD saw warming up to 150 BC. Temperatures, however, did not get as warm as the Climatic Optimum. During the time of Roman Empire (150 BC - 300 AD) a cooling began that lasted until about 900 AD, although Global average temperature remained relatively warm until about 600 AD.

From 600-900 AD (the "Dark Ages"), global average temperatures were significantly colder than today. At its height, the cooling caused the Nile River (829 AD) and the Black Sea (800-801 AD) to freeze.

The period 1100 - 1300 AD has been called either the Little

Climatic Optimum or the Medieval Warm Period. It represents the warmest climate since the Climatic Optimum.

During this period, the Vikings established settlements on Greenland and Iceland. The snow line in the Rocky Mountains was about 370 meters above current levels.

A period of cool and more extreme weather followed the Little Climatic Optimum. There are records of floods, great droughts and extreme seasonal climate fluctuations up to the 1400s. Horrendous floods devastated China in 1332 (reported to have killed several million people).

A great drought in the American southwest occurred between 1276 and 1299. During this period occurred the abandonment of settlements in the Southwest United States, including those in Chaco Canyon and Mesa Verde. Tree ring analysis has identified a period of "no" rain between 1276 and 1299 in these areas.

The cold winters of the little Ice Age were recorded in Dutch and Flemish paintings such as Hunters in the Snow by Pieter Bruegel (c. 1525-69)

From 1550 to 1850 AD global temperatures were at their coldest since the beginning of the Holocene. Scientists call this period the Little Ice Age.

During the period 1580 to 1600, the western United States experienced one of its longest and most severe droughts in the last 500 years. Cold weather in Iceland from 1753 and 1759 caused 25% of the population to die from crop failure and famine. Newspapers in New England were calling 1816 the year without a summer.

During the Medieval warm period (1100-1300 AD), global average temperatures were only 1°C (or less) warmer than in 1900, but in Europe the Vikings established a colony on Greenland (where) farming was productive (and has not been possible again since that time). Grape vines were grown in England and wheat was grown in Norway (64° North latitude) — also not possible at present.

Remnants of Greenland farming village during medieval warmings

At end of period, the Viking colony was lost to sea ice expansion, and the remaining settlers' last winter turned out to be one of rampant cannibalism as archeologists have documented with respect to the remains of the settlement pictured below.

Canals freeze In Holland during little ice age

Needless to say, as gory as the cannibalism might have been, it does prove that the Vikings were not color-blind when they named today's pure white glacier, Greenland.

Long before the industrial era, Greenland was so warm, wet and fertile, that major colonization occurred after 980AD in conjunction with the Medieval Warming period. At its peak it included upwards of 10,000 settlers, extensive farming, numerous catholic churches and a parliament that eventually voted for union with Norway.

By contrast, during the Little Ice Age (1550-1850 AD), which wiped out the Greenland settlements, the global average temperatures became substantially colder.

In Europe, glaciers came down the mountains, thereby covering houses and villages in the Swiss Alps, while canals in Holland froze for three months straight — a rare occurrence before or after. Agricultural productivity also dropped significantly, even becoming impossible in parts of northern Europe.

The Hockey Stick Hoax And Today's Piltdown Mann

This brings us to the climatic Piltdown Mann — named for one Michael Mann, newly minted PhD in 1998 who became the IPCC's (International Panel on Climate Change) lead investigator and advocate for what famously became the "hockey stick" proof of global warming.

The latter, of course, was the blatant fraud embedded in the image that Al Gore made famous in his propagandistic tour de force called "An Inconvenient Truth" in 2006. Suffice to say that the purpose of the hockey stick was to wipe out all of the evidence summarized above.

That is, in lieu of the planet's long-term and recent severe climate oscillations, the IPCC posited an entirely opposite thesis. Namely, that for the pre-industrial millennium before 1900, *global temperatures were nearly flat as a board*.

Accordingly, only when the industrial age got a head of steam and reached full force after 1950 did today's warming temperatures first appear, or so it was alleged. The suggestion, of course, was that an uncontrolled temperature breakout to the upside was well underway and that a planetary disaster was just around the corner.

The only problem is that Mann's graph was as phony as the Piltdown Man that was confected in England in 1912 and conveniently "discovered" by an amateur anthropologist who claimed it was the missing link in human evolution. At length, it was shown that the fossil was a forgery; it consisted of a modern human cranium and an orangutan jaw with filed-down teeth.

In this case, professor Mann and his accomplices at the IPCC doctored the evidence, used misleading data from Southwestern US tree rings in lieu of abundant alternative data showing the contrary, and jiggered their computer models to generate pre-conceived results.

That is, the models were *goal-seeked* by Mann and his associates to prove the manmade warming thesis. In essence, it was accomplished by simply pasting modern temperature records showing steady increases on top of a pre-industrial baseline that never happened.

The phony pre-industrial baseline is depicted by the yellow area in the graph for the period 1400-1900. The hockey stick like eruption of the yellow space after 1900, of course, allegedly depicts the man-made temperature rise since the onset of the hydrocarbon age.

By contrast, the corrected version is in blue. In this version

Hockey Stick Unmasked

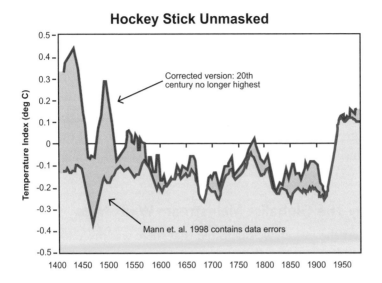

Corrected version: 20th century no longer highest

Mann et. al. 1998 contains data errors

— which comports with the history of climate oscillations cited above — there is no hockey stick because the shaft never happened; it was ***invented*** by computer model manipulations,

12,000 Year Climate Framework

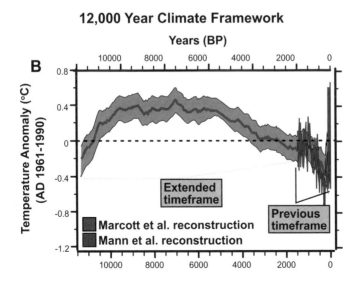

not extracted from the abundant scientific data bases on which the Mann study was allegedly based.

More importantly, when the 600 year time frame in the above graph is put in a longer 12,000 year historical framework, per the graph below, the whole hockey stick disappears entirely. Long before the iron age (1200 to 700 BC) or even the rise of the great River Civilizations (3000 BC), which first made use of extensive man-made combustion, temperatures were often well higher than today.

Why The Globalist Mainstream Went Nuts

At the outset, we suggested that there was more to the Donald's haymaker than a mere challenge to the Paris Accord or even the possibility that the essential hoax behind it will now become more thoroughly exposed.

In fact, the Paris Accord is an ideological totem worshipped by mainstream statists so fanatically that their initial reaction to the Donald's haymaker was more than telling. Said the insufferable Fareed Zakaria on CNN within hours of the exit announcement:

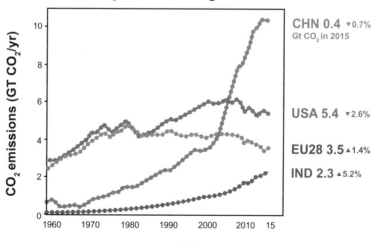

The Real Hockey Stick: Soaring CO2 In The Red Ponzi

"This means America has given up leadership of the free world."

We are inclined to ask for a map of the "free" versus "unfree" parts of the current global array of nation-states, but for now let's just settle for the abandonment of "leadership" part of Zakaria's charge.

When we consider the calamitous ruin — broken states, destroyed cities, lifeless economies, millions of destitute, homeless refugees — that blanket the territories from the Hindu Kush through the entire middle east to the suburbs of Tripoli, we are inclined to ask as to what demented form of liberal group-think would possibly call that "leadership"?

Indeed, it puts you in mind of the Hindu ascetic and leader of India's liberation from the British Empire, Mahatma Gandhi, who was asked what he thought of western civilization after his victorious struggle had ended in 1947. He famously replied, "It would be a good idea."

It would also be a "good idea" to stop talking about Imperial Washington's destructive "leadership" of the free world. At least that discussion the Donald got started in the Rose Garden, too.

As to the feigned ignominy of acceding leadership of the world to China, we will wait for the Red Ponzi's impending demise to resolve the matter. In any event, it would appear that when it comes to "leadership" in the race to maximize CO_2 emissions, China has already won hands-down.

The Donald got that one right, too.

CHAPTER 32

Leviathan, Gun Control And The Baleful Legacy Of The Second Amendment

There have been several horrific school shootings in recent years, including the one in Santa Fe, Texas in May 2018, and, predictably, they unleashed a torrent of purple prose regarding what Washington should do about it. All of these proffered solutions, of course, involved increased Federal intervention — from more gun control to more mental health funding to more school safety funding and much more.

We beg to disagree. Profoundly.

As horrible as these incidents are, there is flat-out nothing that Washington can or should do about them....except to keep its cotton-picking hands off the matter entirely.

That's in part because gun control won't work in a gun-obsessed nation where there are already more civilian guns in circulation (380 million) than people (327 million); and also because Washington is way too broke to fund more education and mental health programs, which should be a local responsibility anyway.

The truth is, there are *13,500* school districts in America with boards elected by the local citizenry and which are funded primarily by heavy property taxes levied on the same. It is their job to assess the operations of these schools and the threats of gun violence that may arise from either within the student body or from outsiders who may enter the schools.

If after careful investigation and review of the pertinent

facts, the threat of gun violence is deemed to be real and palpable — and we'd bet in thousands of school districts it would not be — then there is a ready solution as unpalatable as it may seem.

How To Make Schools Safe — Screen Them At The Door

To wit, don't arm the teachers or pick a losing fight with the NRA. Instead, just keep everyone in the building — students, faculty and visitors alike — **_disarmed_** by sharply limiting the number of entrances to the schools and requiring rigorous airport-style screening at the doors, where any and all guns could be confiscated. After all, bringing a gun into a school is an inherently dangerous anti-social act.

The demented shooter at Santa Fe, for instance, with his black trench coat, pistol and shotgun could never have gotten through the metal detector and likely wouldn't have tried; and the same is true for the shooters at Great Mills, Parkland and the preponderant share of incidents before.

Moreover, if more in-school counseling, mental health support and trained security guards are deemed needed or constructive, then let school districts make the case and assess their own taxpayers: For crying out loud, it's the safety of their own children which is at issue.

In a larger sense, however, the school shooter contretemps is a dramatic case of why the abject failure of Federalism has enabled the rise and dominance of the Washington Leviathan that is bankrupting the nation and causing democratic governance to descend into PAC-dominated racketeering.

That is to say, eliminating gun violence in schools is no more a job for Washington pols and bureaucrats than is treating with bullying, reading scores or socially-transmitted diseases.

What the misplaced guns-in-schools debate actually does is permit big-spending Democrats to distract the voters with sermons about the evils of guns (which are mostly true by our lights).

The GOP's Second Amendment Cop-Out

At the same time, it allows hypocritical and weak-spinned Republicans to duck the all the tough issues. That is, spending discipline, fiscal rectitude, containment of the surveillance and spying machinery of the $75 billion Intelligence Community and control of the military-industrial complex.

Instead, they gum noisily about defense of the Second Amendment, and think they are doing god's work for the conservative cause.

Indeed, the phony and inappropriate school shooting debate in Washington provides a striking window on why Leviathan goes untamed and virtually unchallenged.

In the first place, Washington already has a massively greater problem with guns and violence. It's called a *$750 billion* annual national security budget and imperial foreign policy that kills scores — sometimes hundreds — of innocent people practically every day.

Yet the Empire doesn't get challenged because the natural opposition — the Dems — has now pledged allegiance to the Deep State in order to re-litigate the last election.

At the same time, the GOP has been taken over by a gang of factions which care not at all about the alleged conservative party's core mission. That is, combatting the natural growth and insolvency of Leviathan on the playing field of modern democratic politics.

So owing to the dysfunction of governance, the American people will be saddled with a doubling of the public debt to *$40 trillion* within the decade.

This debt-bloated Leviathan, in turn, will eventually crush capitalist prosperity under the dual burdens of massive economic waste from military and domestic pork barrels and rampant welfare entitlements, on the one hand, and the soon to be soaring carry cost of the national debt, on the other.

And that get's us to the topic at hand: Namely that there is virtually zero political force in present day American democracy to stop the Leviathan State because the GOP — the once and former party of the old time religion of fiscal rectitude — has been hijacked by zealots whose priorities have nothing to do with keeping the State small and solvent.

We are referring, of course, to the neocons, the anti-abortion and anti-gay social conservatives, the MAGA protectionists and border control xenophobes and most especially the Second Amendment worshippers and fanatics.

Needless to say, there is virtually nothing in the agenda of these groups which has anything to do with advancing the cause of liberty, true homeland security, capitalist prosperity or minimalist, solvent government.

They simply lead the GOP into the briar patch of extraneous matters, thereby leaving the Dems, the Deep State and the permanent governing class of the Imperial City (such as 55-year public sector lifers like Mitch McConnell) in charge of Leviathan by default.

Ironically, the relentless right-wing crusade for the Second Amendment is not actually about the defense of liberty or public safety as its proponents proclaim. Nor is there any real individual right to bear arms for the purpose of hunting, target shooting or even self-defense under the Constitution.

The Second Amendment Was Not Designed To Protect Duck Hunters

The fact is, the second amendment was a device to keep the newly formed Federal government in Washington from disarming the state militias. Period.

Stated differently, the Second Amendment was designed to be a bulwark of Federalism and limited central government — a cause that the overwhelming share of beltway-domesticated Republican staffers and office-holders abandoned decades ago.

As we discuss are greater length below, the gun lobby has ripped the second amendment from its historical moorings and invented out of wholecloth an individual right to bear arms for purposes unrelated to revolutionary era militias.

But as former Chief Justice Warren Burger observed as recently as 1991, the idea of an *individual right to bear arms* is — *"one of the greatest pieces of fraud — I repeat the word 'fraud' — on the American public by special-interest groups that I have ever seen in my lifetime."*

Nevertheless, let us be clear from the outset. We vehemently oppose Big Government and Nanny State regulation including most gun control statutes. But we also have no use for guns, find hunting distasteful and wish that James Madison had never dreamed up the Second Amendment while politicking for the Constitution.

The so-called right to bear arms is truly a vestigial relic of the 18th century and has precious little to do with personal liberty or public security in the 21st century.

At the same time, we seriously doubt whether any more Federal gun controls are possible or would reduce gun crimes against innocent citizens in a nation where the aforementioned 380 million guns — 40% of the world's non-military total — are already in circulation.

That's especially the case because of this humongous total about 37% are hand-guns (140 million) and another 28% are shotguns (105 million), neither of which even the most vociferous gun control proponents have proposed to ban.

Indeed, as it happened, the Santa Fe shooter carried out his deadly caper with a pistol and shotgun. No assault rifle or bump stock was needed to kill 10 innocent victims in a relative flash of time.

Moreover, of the 135 million rifles in circulation, less than 5 million are automatic assault weapons of the AR-15 type, while another modest portion of semi-automatics could be made even more deadly than they already are via accessories and retrofits like bump stocks.

And that leads to the elephant in the room: Namely, the horse of plausible gun control has long been out the barn door in America owing to the massive inventory of weapons in circulation. There current market value is well over *$100 billion*, and that number would soar in the event of a draconian clamp-down on the sale of new guns.

Stated differently, unless the existing huge inventory is confiscated or taking off the streets with massive bounty payments, gun control is simply a will-o-wisp that will drive up the value of the current stock.

To be sure, a confiscation style war on guns would never pass through the legislative halls manned by the NRA and their allies in a million years. But even if it did, the result would be a colossal failure — a war on drugs 2.0, which would magnify gun related violence by orders of magnitude and make underground criminals plying such contraband either filthy rich or dead.

In any event, with virtually zero support for confiscation, the gun control debate in Congress is a pointless waste of legislative time. The only thing it accomplishes is to fuel the conservative anti-gun control crusade.

Yet the latter is truly misbegotten; it amounts to a monumental waste of political energies and resources against the wrong target.

The Federal Leviathan State — The Real Threat To Individual Liberty

The real threat emanating from our Federal Leviathan is not the non-existent boogeyman of gun confiscation or abridgement of the dubious right to bear arms. What is running unchecked like never before is Imperial Washington's penchant for taxing, spending, borrowing, regulating, meddling, money printing, and foreign intervention and military adventurism.

It's almost as if the Left has baited conservatives into a diversionary political battle over guns — -the better to leave Leviathan unhindered in its unwarranted, unjust and unproductive intrusions upon the economic and social life of the American people.

In that respect, rather than falling for a grand but pointless battle over guns, true conservatives would be far better advised to attack the source of gun violence where it might actually make a huge difference.

To wit, the better course of action would be to dramatically shrink the scale of the criminal enterprise by wholesale decriminalization of drugs — all of them. So doing, Washington would at once rollback the state from an area that is none of its business, while transferring the drug distribution business from the violent operations of El Chapo to the civil operations of say, Phillip Morris.

Indeed, seconding the drug trade to the non-violent salesmen, deliverymen, warehousemen, and business managers of the tobacco companies would eliminate more crimes and gun violence than any conceivable scheme of background checks, registration and firearms regulation.

The truth is, there are about *10,000* gun based homicides in the US per year, and one recent study by Narco News estimated that up to 10% were directly due to drug trade based killings. But that's not the half of it.

The giant global network for illegal drug trafficking is like any other state enabled monopoly. The artificial scarcity created by drug prohibition creates monumental windfall revenues that enable the El Chapo's of the world and their vast networks of distribution to recruit, train, fund and reward the largest private armies of killers and criminals that the world have ever seen.

In many lower income communities especially, the ranks

of the drug distribution pyramid amount to an open air crime school. Likewise, domestic prisons populated with up to **500,000** mostly small time distributors or users amount to graduate schools for the same.

In short, the NRA slogan that it's people not guns which kill surely needs amendment. What really kills is bloviating legislators and Congressmen who keep passing drug prohibition laws which prodigiously fund the heart of the organized crime enterprise in the United States.

Yes, the US Constitution — -as battered and impaired as it is — -is still the bulwark of our liberties and the ultimate restraint on the aggrandizing impulses of the modern state. But the constitution and its 27 amendments contain **7,591** words, and all of them are not created equal.

Where The Second Amendment Really Came From — An Archaic 1780s Debate About How To Control The Military

In fact, the following **27 words** are among the very least important and do not rank even close to the First, Fourth, Fifth and Tenth Amendments in the hierarchy of liberty's safeguards:

A well regulated militia being necessary to the security of a free state, the right of the people to keep and bear arms shall not be infringed.

A lot has transpired in the 227 years since these words were ratified and duly certified by Secretary of State Thomas Jefferson in 1791 — — among them the rise of hunting for sport and the public's fear of criminal intrusion on their person and property.

But the second amendment has no more bearing on these contemporary matters than it does on the right to fly a kite.

The tip-off is the governing clause and predicate which makes clear that the amendment is all about assurance of a "well regulated militia." But that involved an archaic 1780's argument between Federalists and anti-Federalists that has nothing to do with the contemporary notions of an individual's right to own firearms for the purpose of self-protection, hunting or target shooting.

To make a long story short, the Articles of Confederation had put defense of the nation in the hands of the state militias. By contrast, the new constitution shifted the power to raise a standing military and arm the state militias to the Federal government (Article I, Section 8).

Needless to say, that shift caused grave apprehension among anti-Federalist purists about militarily enforced Federal tyranny. So Madison's deft Second Amendment compromise was designed to reassure anti-Federalists that the state militias could not be disarmed by an aggrandizing central government.

Indeed, it cannot be emphasized enough that the whole debate was about how to organize the government's instruments of military violence as between citizen-based militias controlled at the State level and standing armies and militias controlled at the Federal level.

Thus, the Articles of Confederation had placed this obligation primarily on the former:

......every State shall always keep up a well-regulated and disciplined militia, sufficiently armed and accoutered, and shall provide and constantly have ready for use, in public stores, a due number of field pieces and tents, and a proper quantity of arms, ammunition and camp equipage.

By contrast, Section 8 of the Constitution not only authorized the Federal government to raise a standing army and navy, but also empowered it to call up the state militias in order to execute the laws of the union, repel invasions and to even suppress domestic insurrections.

Furthermore, it shifted control of the militias to the Federal government and granted to Congress the powers of....

.... organizing, arming, and disciplining, the Militia, and for governing such Part of them as may be employed in the Service

of the United States, reserving to the States respectively, the Appointment of the Officers, and the Authority of training the Militia according to the discipline prescribed by Congress.

In that context, the anti-Federalists harkened back to King James II, the last Catholic King of England who attempted to disarm the protestant militias in the 1680s, and to British and Loyalist efforts to disarm the colonial Patriot militia armories in the early phases of the American Revolution.

Against that kind of tyranny, Noah Webster, among many others, explained the reason for the Second Amendment in a nutshell:

Before a standing army can rule the people must be disarmed; as they are in almost every kingdom in Europe. The supreme power in America cannot enforce unjust laws by the sword; because the whole body of the people are armed, and constitute a force superior to any band of regular troops that can be, on any pretence, raised in the United States.

Moreover, the founders' pre-occupation with preserving the role of citizen based state militias could have not been made more strikingly evident than in a key legislative enactment by Congress less than one year after the Second Amendment was ratified.

This law provided for the "National Defence" by establishing a "Uniform Militia" throughout the United States, and mandating universal enrollment in the state militias.

The very words of it tell you that it had nothing to do with Ducks Unlimited or the NRA's soporific propaganda about the Second Amendment:

Each and every free able-bodied white male citizen of the respective States, resident therein, who is or shall be of age of eighteen years, and under the age of forty-five years (except as is herein after excepted) shall severally and respectively be enrolled in the militia...[and] every citizen so enrolled and notified, shall, within six months thereafter, provide himself with a good musket or firelock, a sufficient bayonet and belt, two spare flints, and a knapsack, a pouch with a box therein to contain not less than twenty-four cartridges, suited to the bore of his musket or firelock, each cartridge to contain a proper quantity of powder and ball....... and shall appear, so armed, accoutred and provided, when called out to exercise, or into service, except, that when called out on company days to exercise only, he may appear without a knapsack.

Folks, a musket, bayonet, two spare flints and a knapsack have nothing to do with either national defense or individual liberty in this day and age. For better or worse, the era of the citizen militia is over and done; and the fact that we even waste public funds on the state based national guards is nothing more than a tribute to nostalgia and pork barrel politics.

So the Second Amendment belongs in a museum along with the muskets and knapsacks of the ancient state militias.

No one in the right mind can argue that in the face of the modern state's insuperable monopoly on high tech military violence that an armed citizen insurrection would lead to anything more than a proliferation of government massacres like those at Ruby Ridge and Waco Texas. Ballot boxes, not bullets, are the only present day recourse against a tyrannical government.

Needless to say, the true history and purpose of the Second Amendment as passed down by the framers did not stop a 5/4 Supreme Court majority from embracing just the opposite in Justice Scalia's rambling, incoherent exercise in Constitution writing from wholecloth in the 2008 *Heller* decision.

Against Scalia's verbose ruminations, Justice Stevens cut to the chase for the minority:

".....the "right to keep and bear arms" protects only a right to possess and use firearms in connection with service in a state-organized militia. Had the Framers wished to expand the meaning of the phrase "bear arms" to encompass civilian possession and use, they could have done so by the addition of phrases such as "for the defense of themselves."

And that gets to another salient issue — — the domestic policing function. Needless to say, the Constitution was not written by anarchists, even if the vast majority of the Founders were imbued with a republican distrust of state power.

Accordingly, they contemplated that the powers reserved to the states included the protection of their citizens' lives and property by means of criminal statutes and their enforcement by duly constituted officers of the law and courts. Indeed, that is at the very core of the appropriate functions of the state; and along with the common defense against invasion, it is the valid basis for levying taxes.

Law Enforcement Is The Proper Function Of Gendarmes Of The State, Not Armed Civilians

Nowhere in the constitutional debates or the subsequent practice of the American Republic was there a vigilante do-it-yourself notion of law enforcement or idea that the first line of defense against criminal assault was armed civilians.

Even in the frontier west, people banded together to hire a marshall who was sworn to uphold the laws of the state and to whom the function of protecting citizen lives and property from criminal intrusion was delegated.

Yes, contemporary America is plagued with an inordinate amount of crime against persons and property, but the idea that a gun in every closet is therefore warranted and an indispensable element of public safety and security is wholly specious; it is a product of contemporary NRA and gun lobby propaganda, not historical precedent or even practical assessment.

To be sure, there is no reason for the state to tell Michelle Obama's lonely farm wife in the boondocks of Iowa that she can't have a gun for self-protection. Nor for that matter should it deny a Park Avenue lady who lunches the freedom to have a pistol in her dresser drawer — — or the liberty to fly a kite or smoke a joint, either.

But that's private liberty and much to be treasured. It's not law enforcement, however, or a meaningful element in improving public safety. For that we need to liberate the cops.

That is to say, clear the criminal code of victimless crimes and social regulation. Enable the police forces and courts to focus their time and resources exclusively on prevention and punishment of crimes against the persons and property of citizens by third parties who violate the law.

The fact is, law enforcement today is drastically overburdened and distracted by the pursuit of innumerable victimless crimes including the classic trio of drugs, prostitution and gambling.

Without the absolute stupidity of the nation's 45-year war on drugs, for example, the DEA would not even exist, El Chapo would have been chopping chickens in La Tuna, and "Breaking Bad" wouldn't have lasted even one season.

Likewise, the massive enterprise of enforcing gambling laws and other anti-vice statutes and the underworld of crime it spawns actually gets more preposterous by the day. Practically every few months we have a significant share of the population and media hyperventilating about a billion dollar Powerball jackpot where the odds are 380 million to one.

So why in the world does a nation of gamblers persist in prosecuting illegal gambling?

Again, clear the statutes, eliminate the gambling underworld of violence and free the cops to pursue real criminals.

Finally, we get to the truth that there is an arguable police function with respect to guns, but it's scope is far smaller than the gun control advocates would have us believe. The fact is, there is not an epidemic of gun violence in America that is any business of the Central State or that can be fixed by an appropriate exercise of the inherent police powers of the states and localities.

Indeed, the actual gun deaths problem is one of *suicide*, not *homicide*, anyway. There were 33,000 gun deaths during 2013 in the US, but *21,175* of them were suicides, and another 1,000 or so were due to accidental discharges or other undetermined reasons.

But if people choose to kill themselves or to be careless, that is none of the state's business — -nor could regulation of one means — firearms — by which such tragedies are accomplished make any difference.

After all, you would need to regulate rope and strychnine, too. The statistics show that each year 7,000 people take their lives by poisoning and another 11,000 by "suffocation" aka, hanging.

In fact, it would appear that in a typical year there are more suicides by hanging than there are homicides by guns. And that comparison is even more telling when you consider that some considerable share of the 10,000 or so annual gun-homicides stem from activities such as drug distribution, gambling and prostitution that would not involve any murders at all had they not been driven into the criminal underground by the proscriptions and prohibitions of the state.

Still, there is one angle on gun control that fully merits exercising the domestic police powers of the state. First, the states or localities ought to enact a stiff automatic surcharge on the ordinary sentence of anyone convicted of using a gun in the commission of a crime against the person or property of another citizen. Deterrence is a legitimate and necessary component of the law enforcement function.

Secondly, the states should enact strict liability laws on retailers. Accordingly, knowingly or carelessly selling a gun to any person who has been adjudicated as mentally ill or is undergoing active psychiatric treatment would give rise to large compensation claims by victims or their families.

Even then, you wouldn't need a Federal bureaucracy to enforce the law. Gun sellers would pay private services for the background checks in much they same manner as they do private credit bureaus in order to protect themselves from liability and potential financial ruin.

To be sure, freedom of commerce is the essence of capitalist prosperity and is to be protected at all hazards. But you are not free to emit poisons into the waters or air, either deliberately or by "accident." Nor should you be free to sell guns by accident to the next whacko who decides to attack the innocent public at an elementary school, mall or movie house.

At the end of the say, however, the most important goal of all is to keep every single Washington official, lobbyist and hanger-on out of the equation entirely. The national debate over gun control is so misdirected and metastasized that nothing good can come of a single additional word from Washington on the topic.

On this matter, the great American jurist, Louis Brandeis, should be given the last word.

He was profoundly correct when he said that the states were meant to be "laboratories of democracy", and most especially in the matter of criminal law and the domestic policing function. And surely it is not beyond their capacity to use such powers to keep guns out of the hands of psychotics or to lock away criminals who turn firearms on innocent citizens.

Obviously, such a sensible path is way too much to be hoped for.

On the one hand, the political Left has thrown in the towel on the Warfare State and foreign military adventurism. So when it comes to the scourge of killing and violence, it has effectively retreated to its feckless campaign against guns to rally the troops and raise the political loot.

On the other hand, the so-called conservative party continues to take the bait on gun control and thereby defaults on its real job in democratic politics — which is to challenge and roll-back the prosperity, solvency and liberty crushing depredations of the modern Leviathan State.

Indeed, what a baleful irony!

An archaic and vestigial feature of the Constitution, which was designed to forestall the rise of Leviathan in a different time and place, has been transformed by modern day right wing politicians into the helpmate of the 21st century Leviathan that actually reigns, largely unchecked, on the banks of the Potomac.